AMERICAN HUNTING RIFLES

AMERICAN HUNTING RIFLES

Their Application in the Field for Practical Shooting, with Notes on Handguns and Shotguns

Craig Boddington

Safari Press

P.O Box 3095, Long Beach, CA 90803-0095, USA

Boddington, Craig

Safari Press Inc.

Second edition

1995, Long Beach, California.

ISBN 1-57157-223-6

Library of Congress Catalog Card Number: 94-067700

10 9 8 7 6 5 4

Readers wishing to receive the Safari Press catalog, featuring many fine books on big-game hunting, wingshooting, and sporting firearms, should write to Safari Press Inc., P.O. Box 3095, Long Beach, CA 90803, USA.
Tel: (714) 894-9080 or visit our Web site at www.safaripress.com.

CONTENTS

Part III: Guns For Game

Part IV: Appendices

Author's Introduction

The North American continent spans every imaginable climatic condition and habitat, from the steamy jungles of the Yucatan to the permanently frozen tundras of Canada's northern islands. In between are deserts, forests, mountains, plains, and swamps. The game that inhabit these diverse regions are also varied. They are a rich legacy with which American hunters are uniquely blessed. Our continent does not have the great diversity of wildlife that Africa offers, nor that of Asia, but in numbers of big-game species, it easily ranks third among the continents.

In terms of hunting opportunities, though, North America has no equal. It almost didn't turn out that way, however. The eastern part of what is now the United States and Canada was generally heavily forested when Europeans first touched land. Climax woodlands create a relatively sterile environment for wildlife, so game populations were spotty in the beginning. Agriculture quickly created the edge habitats in which many of our game species thrive, but a couple of centuries of unlimited subsistence hunting nearly finished the game in the eastern part of the continent.

As westward expansion began, early explorers found much of the west to be a great reservoir of wildlife. While its diversity never matched that of Africa, in the years before the Civil War, the plentitude of wildlife probably surpassed even the Serengeti. The figure of sixty million is often given for bison in the 1850s. The numbers of pronghorn, elk, mule deer, and mountain sheep are unknown, but undoubtedly each existed in the millions as well. Some species, particularly the pronghorn, may well have exceeded the bison numerically.

Predators never matched the populations of their prey, but before the massive westward expansion, grizzly bears, cougars, and wolves roamed the west in numbers that stagger the imagination.

This didn't last long. Within a quarter-century of human excess, an ecosystem many thousands of years in the making was completely undone. By the early 1880s, the bison were nearly gone. By 1900, nearly every large mammal within what is now the continental United States was in serious trouble. Canada, with vast wilderness regions and a much smaller human population, was more fortunate. Mexico, too, had a more localized human population and vast unoccupied areas. She would have her problems with wildlife, and still does, but in 1900, Mexico's game situation was far better than it was in most of the United States.

American hunters are fortunate that Theodore Roosevelt came along. A dedicated hunter himself, he undoubtedly participated in the excesses of his day, but he realized that American wildlife was on a river of no return. Along with other sportsmen, he led the way in conserving our wildlife.

In America during the twentieth century, wildlife has had a chance for a comeback. While bison will never reach their former numbers, some species that benefit from human agriculture now exist in greater numbers than ever before. Over twenty million white-tailed deer now exist. They are the most plentiful large mammal on earth next to man. Along with the deer, almost all North American big-game species now exist in healthy populations that are big enough to hunt. Regrettably, a few subspecies have been lost altogether, including Merriam and eastern elk, California grizzly, and the Audubon bighorn.

Traditionally, American hunters counted twenty-seven varieties of North American big game. These were white-tailed, Coues, black-tailed, and mule deer; barren-ground, mountain, Quebec-Labrador, and woodland caribou; Canada, Alaskan-Yukon, and Shiras moose; desert, bighorn, Stone, and Dall sheep; mountain goat; pronghorn; elk; black, grizzly, Alaskan brown, and polar bear; mountain lion; muskox; bison; walrus; and jaguar.

Most hunters add Sitka black-tailed, Central Canada barren-ground caribou, and Roosevelt elk to the list of twenty-seven traditional animals. Many would also add desert mule deer and tule elk, while most unaccountably ignore the unique little brocket deer of southern Mexico. At this writing, it seems unlikely that jaguar will ever again be hunted, almost certainly not in North America. Although walruses are plentiful, the politics of hunting them seems insurmountable.

My focus in this book is on firearms and cartridges for hunting North American big game. As a hunter considering a list of game, recognize that almost any list includes significant subspecies hunted under very similar conditions. For instance, whether you feel there are four or five different caribou, sensible selection of hardware varies little among them. Much the same can be said for moose.

On the other hand, our whitetail category lumps together a couple dozen subspecies hunted under amazingly diverse conditions. There might be just one whitetail, but there is certainly more than one type of whitetail hunting and more than one prescription for hunting whitetail.

Nor is my list yet complete. One must also consider small big game (or big small game), such as javelina. The wolf, whether it is big game or not, is still a great prize. Predators, such as coyote, lynx, and bobcat are hunted as big game. There is also a wonderful diversity of introduced species, many of which are free-ranging in various parts of the country, such as the wild boar, Axis deer, and others.

In this book, I have made no effort to define or redefine what constitutes big game on the North American continent. What you choose to hunt is up to you, which is a legacy of our freedom. I have tried to analyze American hunting strictly from the standpoint of sensible choices of center fire rifles, handguns, and shotguns that are appropriate for the conditions you may encounter.

The choice of a firearm is ultimately a personal decision. There are no absolutes. Within sensible parameters, whatever works for you is indeed a good choice. I have attempted to keep my discussions within those parameters, which are based on my own experiences. I doubt that there will be universal agreement, so if you happen not to agree with me, take notes. If we share a campfire someday, we'll have plenty to talk about.

Craig Boddington
Lakewood, Colorado

Foreword

I've been an avid (but severely critical) reader and collector of hunting, shooting, and firearms literature for well over half a century, and three decades of my professional life have been largely devoted to the editing of books and articles in this field. For several years, I had the responsibility of accepting or rejecting sporting-book manuscripts for a well-known publisher—not always a pleasant duty. Since then, I've served several publishers in an advisory capacity. I've become rather selective about taking on editing assignments (because that's not always a pleasant job, either), but I jumped at the chance to edit this new book by Craig Boddington. About six years ago I had edited his magnificent book, *Safari Rifles*, and I expected no less an accomplishment. In the foreword of *Safari Rifles*, I had called Craig's work astonishing. This new book is similarly astonishing—and at least as great an accomplishment. It is, in fact, unique.

Editing anything by Craig Boddington is exceptionally easy because he's not only an excellent, superlatively knowledgeable writer but also a highly skilled editor himself. For many years he has edited a fine and authoritative magazine, *Petersen's Hunting*; hence, it's hardly surprising that I (or any editor) will seldom find so much as a typographical error in the manuscript of a Boddington chapter. And that's about all some editors try to do, which is why many books in this genre fail to deliver what they promise, or seem to promise. Actually, the first thing an editor *should* do is to give a new manuscript a quick first reading, making notes and then judging whether the thing fulfills the implied promise of fresh and genuinely worthwhile material. Comparisons with other books help. In this instance, comparisons were obvious and easy.

My personal library contains (among many other volumes in this general field) the following works specifically pertaining to—though not always discussing in detail—rifles and cartridges for North American game: Elmer Keith's *Big Game Hunting* (1948); Clyde Ormond's *Hunting in the Northwest* (1948); Grancel Fitz's *North American Head Hunting* (1957); Jack O'Connor's *Complete Book of Shooting* (1965) and *The Art of Hunting Big Game in North America* (1967); Warren Page's *The Accurate Rifle* (1973); Byron Dalrymple's *North American Big Game Hunting* (1974); Jim Carmichel's *The Modern Rifle* (1975) and *Book of the Rifle* (1985); Tom Brakefield's *Hunting Big-Game Trophies* (1976); and Bob Hagel's *Hunting North America's Big Game* (1986).

Some of these books furnish much more information about marksmanship, hunting, rifle technology, or some other related topic than about the selection of suitable rifles and cartridges, but they all offer preferences or recommendations, directly or indirectly. I've included "Lefty" Page's work on accurate rifles because, although it focuses sharply on target shooting, it also deals at least briefly with hunting rifles, cartridges, and scopes. I haven't bothered to include a great many other books that are limited to deer, or mountain hunting, or small game, or varmints and predators, or a single species such as elk or black bear or whatever. I suppose I should add that, in addition to these, I'm familiar with older, informative but long outdated writings by Askins, Whelen, Hatcher, and others. I've read (and in some cases edited) many of the writings of O'Connor, Page, Keith, Ormond, Hagel, Dalrymple, Carmichel, Larry Koller, Andy Russell, Jim Zumbo, John Wootters, Wayne van Zwoll, and quite a few more. Having thus qualified myself to make comparisons, I will now venture a forthright verdict: None of their works–not one–compares with this book.

What Craig has done is unprecedented. His *Safari Rifles* supplanted and eclipsed everything that had preceded it in more than half a century–H.C. Maydon's *Big Game Shooting in Africa*, John Taylor's *African Rifles and Cartridges*, and James Mellon's *African Hunter*. This new book does for American hunting rifles and cartridges what *Safari Rifles* did for African rifles and cartridges. In fact, it does more–it supplants and eclipses everything that has *ever* preceded it.

No one would deny that O'Connor, Keith, and Page richly deserved the reverence that was accorded them, but all three were somewhat limited in their perspective by personal axes they had (or liked) to grind. Keith and O'Connor in particular were further victimized by their absurd feud and the need they felt to defend pet calibers, loads, bullets, and even actions for too wide a variety of game and against all logic (which is to say, against each other). Moreover–what the hell, I've been guilty of heresy before and surely will be again!–they were also quite limited in their experience, at least by comparison with Craig Boddington.

For the moment, let's just focus on American game. Craig has killed more black bears, mountain grizzlies, and Alaskan brown bears than any of them. Ditto for pronghorn. Ditto for at least some varieties of deer. O'Connor took more sheep, but neither O'Connor nor the others topped Craig's experience with mountain goat, elk, moose, or caribou. And here's a fact that may be even more to the point: Keith, O'Connor, and Page tended to use one or two types of rifle and a very small array of cartridges on a wide variety of game. By sharp contrast, Craig Boddington has used all the *appropriate* cartridges, loads, and bullets (including some that hadn't been developed when his predecessors hunted) on all types of American game, and he's also used every type of rifle action appropriate to a given game species or class of game. All told, he's taken more North American trophies than any of them, perhaps more than all three combined. And he's done so in every conceivable kind of North American terrain and habitat, under all conditions–again and again.

Now what about African experience? Does that count, too, in an American context? If you've been there, you know it does. American sportsmen who have made safaris (especially those with a keen interest in the performance of rifles, cartridges, and bullets) are fond of comparing or contrasting African game with the game of this continent. In many instances, that makes very good sense. With a given load, for example, is a deer-sized African antelope easier or harder to anchor than a mule deer? Are the two likely to be shot at the same sort of range, and will the same cartridge and bullet, loaded to the same velocity and energy, be equally effective on both? Or how about a warthog in comparison with a wild boar? Or a Cape buffalo in comparison with a bison? What can African game teach us–and have our writers given us reliable information about this?

Shooting writers have often stated that African game tends to be tougher to anchor and kill than American game. With exceptions conscientiously noted, Craig Boddington disproves that generalization–and in doing so, he makes this book all the more valuable as a practical reference, while also making it more fascinating, giving us "a really good read," as reviewers are fond of saying. But can we trust the proofs he offers, his judgments about African versus American hunting? He has made more than thirty African safaris–more than Keith, O'Connor, and Page put together, more than any American shooting writer. A number of those safaris were extensive, and he has taken almost every variety of African game, including many notable trophies collected under the most demanding conditions. Experience counts. Unrivaled experience on *both* continents is a large part of this book's unequaled value as a truly comprehensive and absolutely trustworthy trove of information for every hunter.

Almost incredible thoroughness–inclusiveness–is another large part of its value. If you haven't already scanned the table of contents, take a few minutes to do so. Those forty-two chapters and two appendices cover it all, in detail and with an authority that cannot be challenged. Craig even covers rifled-barrel and rifled-choke shotguns, since they're used as rifles and are equally effective at appropriate ranges on appropriate game. He also covers handguns for hunting, since the distinction between sidearms and rifles has been blurred (for the uses he cites) by modern developments in cartridges, handgun design and construction, and handgun scopes. The vast bulk of the material does, however, deal with rifles and rifle cartridges, just as the title of this book implies. In doing so, it's thoroughness, wealth of information, and *reliability* are (here's that inescapable word again!) unprecedented.

That, of course, would be quite enough to make any hunter a Boddington fan, but there's more. Firearms and hunting are so rich in colorful, often surprising tradition that it's a disappointment to me (and to many others, I'm sure) when a book on rifles fails to acknowledge the past. I happen to have a keen interest in firearms history; I've done considerable research in this field and, as many of you know, I've written as well as edited works on firearms history.

I therefore took special delight in Chapter 19–on American rifles from 1865 to 1940–plus the historical details and insights interwoven wherever appropriate in many other chapters. An understanding of the past helps us immeasurably to understand the direction of firearms developments right up to the present. And in this realm, too, Craig has encyclopedic, totally trustworthy knowledge which he shares in a deceptively casual, conversational manner that made me keep turning pages and forget to look for typographical errors. (I had better state parenthetically that I, too, am conscientious, and I read those pages again carefully.)

In this book, Craig's writing reveals two more virtues that I must mention before signing off and letting you get to the meat of the volume. First, he's just plain exciting to read. When he inserts an anecdote about a personal experience, he does so because it illustrates a legitimate point, and he does it better–more vividly–than most writers or campfire yarn-spinners. I've never had the good fortune to hunt with Craig, though I've known him for years, but there are passages in these pages that made me feel I was right there with him–there for the stalk, there for the shot. Those passages will make you feel the same way. This is a magnificent reference work, but by no means a typically dry one. The reading that's ahead for you will not only be enriching but fun. The second virtue I haven't yet mentioned is an honesty that is downright courageous for a writer, and this honesty deserves a separate (last, I promise) paragraph.

In devastating contrast to at least a couple of the excellent writers I've cited, Craig truly hates to alibi. He comes right out and tells you when he's made a mistake, whether it was taking a wrong rifle to Alaska and seeing fine walnut ruined or missing when he should have hit (he's an outstanding marksman, by the way) or choosing a less than ideal rifle and/or load for a given kind of game or a given set of hunting conditions. No hunter or rifleman is immune to error, and we all hope we learn from our mistakes. After a lifetime of experience, Craig seldom makes mistakes, but he enjoys sharing those he has made in the past because he has learned from them–and we can learn from them, too. But of course we'll learn immeasurably more from his sharing of knowledge that can prevent mistakes. Between these covers is an enormous trove of that knowledge, never until now available to American hunters.

Robert Elman

CAUTION!

This book contains data on handloading and firearms that reflect the particular experiences of the author. The author used specific firearms, ammunition, and reloading equipment under conditions not necessarily reported in the book. Under NO circumstances should the reader try to copy the loads mentioned in this book. The handloading of ammunition and the discharging of a firearm should never be attempted without the supervision of an adult experienced in both handloading and firearms. The publisher or author cannot accept responsibility for the firearms and handloading data in this book.

Dedication

To Mom and Dad–Jeanne and Bud Boddington of Kansas City, Kansas–who urged me to find a way to make a living doing something I enjoyed . . . and always believed that I could.

Part I

Cartridges for North American Hunting

Chapter 1

.22 Centerfires: Big-Game Cartridges?

This is a book I've wanted to write for a long time. I expect that the farther I get into it, the more fun the writing will be, and I hope the reading of it will be equally enjoyable. I also expect that some of the chapters will be fully accepted by most readers, while some may stir up a bit of controversy. That's okay, but I sure hate to start this volume in the middle of one of the most heated controversies surrounding American hunting rifles and cartridges: Are the .22 centerfires suitable for big-game hunting?

Still, every book must have a starting point, and it seems most sensible to start at the bottom and work our way up. In this regard, though in relatively few others, I will follow the general format of my earlier work, *Safari Rifles*. Immediately, however, we will see a significant and fundamental difference between African and American game–and the hunting of same. As I mentioned in the Introduction, Africa has a much greater number of diverse game species than North America–and many of those different species are often found in the same area. On a given day, the African hunter might encounter a wide range of antelope for which a very light caliber would be truly ideal: smaller gazelles, duikers, dik-diks, steenbok, oribi, and many more–all under 60 pounds on the hoof. Of course, much larger animals might be encountered as well–but it isn't unusual to have more than one hunting rifle available, one carried by the hunter and another by a tracker. That's not the case here in America. We tend to have one rifle available, and with few exceptions we're hunting one specific animal. We expect that one rifle to handle any and all shooting situations that might be encountered. Can a .22 do that?

First off, let's take as a given that the .22s *will* take game. With very careful shot placement at close range–read that to mean brain shots–even a .22 rimfire is capable of dropping large animals. However, the .22 rimfire, including the fairly potent .22 WMR, or .22 Magnum, is not legal for big game in any jurisdiction in the U.S. or Canada, so we'll leave the rimfires out of this discussion. Instead, we're talking about .22 centerfires, ranging from the .22 Hornet–a 45-grain bullet at 2,690 feet per second (fps) yielding 723 foot/pounds (ft/lbs) of energy–up to the .220 Swift, which delivers 3,600 fps and 1,727 ft/lbs with a 60-grain bullet. There are several factory cartridges within this range, plus numerous wildcats–a very few of which exceed the .220 Swift in velocity and energy. All will take very large animals with carefully placed head or neck shots, and most are at least deer-capable with well-chosen body shots. The real question is whether they make sensible choices.

The consensus of conventional wisdom is that they do not, and this is borne out by the fact that .22 calibers are illegal for all big game in most jurisdictions, and illegal for big game larger than deer in every state or province that holds larger game. However, .22 centerfires are quite legal for deer in numerous areas, and quite a few hunters swear by them. Are they nuts, or do they know something the rest of us should learn?

Throughout the history of smokeless powder, there are countless examples of asking tiny bullets to do big work–often with stunning success. One of the very first .22 centerfires was the .22 Savage Hi-Power, introduced in the Savage Model 99 in 1912. It fired a long, stable 70-grain bullet at a very fast (for the day) 2,790 fps, yielding 1,228 ft/lbs. Varmint hunting as we know it was unheard of then; the .22 Savage HP was conceived as a big-game cartridge! Controversy immediately surrounded it; some hunters loved it and others hated it. Some early gun writers touted it as a new kind of death ray while others berated it. As might be imagined, with poor shot placement it didn't work–and in those pre-scope days, shot placement at longer ranges could not be as exact as it is today. It lacked the energy for really large game, but with proper shot placement it was extremely effective on deer. Those who loved it used it far beyond its capabilities. Karamojo Bell wrote of shooting buffalo (in the ear, thank goodness!) with the .22 Savage, and there's a wonderful photo of an early China missionary with two huge tigers taken with it. But eventually the tales of wounded game won out, and the .22 Savage languished.

For many years, the diminutive .222 Remington was the arm of choice among the Inuits of northern Canada. Accurate and with compact, inexpensive ammunition, it suited them so well that they used it not only for head-shooting seals, but also to hunt caribou and polar bear. On recent trips to the high Arctic, I've seen more and more Inuits toting 7mm Magnums–but many still cling to their beloved .222's.

Let's take a look at where the .22's properly fit in. There's big game, and then there's *big* game. With apologies to the very courageous .222-toting Inuits, no .22 is suitable for hunting game larger than deer. Brain shots aren't always possible or practical, and the energy just isn't there for reliable body shots. Colonel Townsend Whelen theorized many years ago that 1,000 ft/lbs of energy *at the target* was needed for clean kills on deer-sized game.

Bullet weight and shot placement both make a difference, but in the last 75 years nobody has come up with a better general rule of thumb. Whelen's theory goes on to demand 2,000 ft/lbs for elk-sized game, and I'd say that's right on as well. Most of the .22 centerfires, except for the .22 Hornet and .218 Bee, make the 1,000 ft/lb threshold–but none come close to 2,000 even at the muzzle.

So, in theory, the hotter .22 centerfires have what it takes to be deer cartridges. Indeed they are, under the right conditions–but there are deer and then there are deer. There's a huge difference between the average Texas or southeastern whitetail weighing 130 to 150 pounds and a huge northern monster that can top 300 pounds. Likewise, there's an equally big difference between a nice eatin'-size forkhorn mulie and a high-country giant. Even among the smaller whitetail subspecies of the South, bucks well in excess of 200 pounds are occasionally encountered.

I don't think even the hottest .22 centerfires are suitable for the largest deer, and for a couple of reasons. First, the energy and penetration are getting sketchy on anything except the most perfect shot placement. And second, big bucks are survivors by nature. They are the least likely to offer that perfect shot placement–and they're also the most likely to start off a bout of buck fever that further inhibits pinpoint shot placement! In other words, the .22s are extremely poor choices for serious trophy-buck hunters. Trophy hunters simply must use a cartridge that ensures adequate penetration and plenty of energy with any reasonable shot.

On the other hand, where legal, the hotter .22 centerfires make extremely effective tools for small and mid-sized deer–given cool hands and straight shooting. Actually, so long as ranges are close to moderate and only good shot presentations are taken, the .22 centerfires have a lot going for them. These little calibers are usually chambered to extremely accurate rifles, and because of their almost nonexistent recoil they're extremely easy to shoot well. I don't particularly like, or generally recommend, head and neck shots–just the slightest error and horrible but not immediately fatal wounds can occur. However, nothing is easier to use in making such shots than an accurate, well-scoped .22 centerfire–and they're consistently deadly. Body shots, too, are dramatically effective on smaller deer–provided great care is taken with shot placement.

I've shot quite a few deer–mostly does and smallish bucks–with both the .223 Remington and the .22-250. Obviously, a head or neck shot will achieve instantaneous results, but on body shots both calibers have produced some of the most spectacular one-shot takedowns I've ever seen. There's a good reason for this. Until very recently, almost all .22-caliber bullets have been produced with varmints in mind. They have thin jackets for very rapid expansion, designed to literally explode on impact with small varmints such as prairie dogs and woodchucks. On larger animals, the bullet performance is much the same. A shoulder shot invites disaster; the bullet is not designed to penetrate and often won't. But a behind-the-shoulder shot into the lung area will generally penetrate well enough to vaporize in the lungs, causing much more damage and shock than larger-caliber bullets actually designed for the job. The results of a behind-the-shoulder broadside shot on deer of modest size simply must be seen to be believed!

If such calibers are to be used on deer, bullet selection becomes critical. Today there are better choices than ever for the high-velocity .22 centerfires, but even the best bullets can't help the Hornet and Bee too much. Although I've seen them used, and used well, I can't condone the use of the .22 Hornet and .218 Bee on deer. The best use for those two calibers is for sniping wild turkeys in areas where rifles are legal.

In the ballistically similar .222 Remington, .222 Remington Magnum, and .223 Remington, I'd avoid the lighter bullets and stick with 55-grain slugs at a minimum. For handloaders, and even in factory loads, there's a better choice for the .223, .22-250, and .220 Swift. That's the relatively new 60-grain bullet.

In all honesty, I don't recommend any .22 centerfire for deer hunting. Yes, they can work, and I've made them work and seen them work enough to know that. But the only cases where they really make sense is in very patient, very expert hands for culling does or harvesting a meat buck. If you insist on using them, the more heavily-constructed 60-grain bullets are absolutely the way to go. On deer, they do not allow you to take quartering shots or shots through heavy bone with impunity–but they are constructed heavily enough to give you much better penetration than you can hope for with the lighter bullets built for varmints.

For handloaders, there's a super 60-grain .223 Trophy Bonded Bearclaw bullet, essentially a scaled down big-game bullet that will give all the edge you can possibly achieve if you must hunt deer with a .22. Several other companies also offer component bullets in 60 grains and heavier, and there are 60-grain factory loads in .223, .22-250, and .220 Swift.

Although deer hunting probably constitutes at least 80 percent of all the big-game hunting in North America, deer hunting isn't the only hunting there is. It may be the outer limit of hunting uses for the .22's, but it certainly isn't the only use. In America, we're a little short on big game smaller than our smaller white-tailed deer. Europeans love the .22 centerfires for roe deer topping out at 60 pounds. They don't have a lot of "varmints" as we know them, but roebuck are their most common game animals, so the .222 is one of their most common "big-game" rifles! As I mentioned, .22s are also ideal for an amazing array of African antelope. But except for small deer, we're limited.

An obvious choice for the hotter .22s–especially the .22-250 and .220 Swift–would be pronghorn hunting. These animals are a bit smaller than most deer, generally about 100 to 110 pounds, and the flat-shooting abilities would be nice. Unfortunately, even the hottest of the .22s is a poor choice for long-range shooting at big game. Both the .22-250 and the .220 Swift drop below 1,000 ft/lbs of energy around the 200-yard mark, even with the 60-grain bullet. Although pronghorns are smaller than deer, they are fairly hardy and simply must be well-hit in the vitals. Whether for deer or antelope, if any of the .22s are used, shots should be held to around 200 yards–and that can be very limiting with pronghorns.

The only other native big game smaller than our smallest deer is javelina. These fierce-looking but generally harmless creatures weigh about 40 pounds, and the .22 centerfires are just perfect for them.

Then there are the non-native species. Full-sized animals like axis and sika deer should probably be approached with traditional deer calibers, but the hotter .22 centerfires are ideal for 60-pound Indian blackbuck, usually shot at fairly long range. They're quite adequate, too, for wild goats and mouflon sheep, which usually weigh much less than 150 pounds.

I used a Kimber .223 with 60-grain Trophy Bonded Bearclaws on an Iranian red sheep I shot in the Texas Hill Country a couple of years ago. These little sheep were spooky as heck, and we had worked our tails off to get a shot. Toward dark of the second day, we crawled into a herd feeding at the junction of two *senderos*. We picked out the largest ram, and I rose up behind a low bush to take the shot. I put the crosshairs as carefully as I could behind the shoulder of the chosen ram, but when the rifle went off sheep exploded in all directions–mine among them.

Dark was coming quickly, and I instantly wished I'd selected a more potent rifle. I needn't have worried. My ram made it into the brushline, but just barely. He'd gone less than 50 yards, and that little bullet had gone through his heart, broken the off-shoulder, and exited, showing good expansion but no blowup.

Although the focus of this book is on big game, it would be unfair to the .22s to not mention their primary intended use: varmint hunting. This is where the .22 centerfires really shine, both for hunting pests such as woodchucks, prairie dogs, and other rodents, and for hunting the furbearers–coyotes, foxes, and bobcats. For the former use, the cartridge chosen pretty much depends on the conditions. The .22 Hornet can't be stretched much beyond 150 yards, so it's well-suited to the roving hunter who likes to hunt varmints to practice stalking skills. The .222 and .223 are super performers out to 200 yards or so, while the .22-250 and .220 Swift are for those who like to reach out a long way–and those two cartridges also buck wind much better than the slower numbers.

In predator hunting, the little Hornet and Bee are useful only for the close-cover caller or for the bobcat hunter with hounds. The faster .22s are all extremely effective, perhaps too much so. Predator hunters who want to harvest fur often use full-metal-jacketed bullets to avoid pelt damage, even though coyotes can be extremely tough. A better choice, especially for coyotes, might be one of the 60-grain "big-game" bullets, which should pass through without the explosive expansion of a varmint bullet–but will certainly do more damage than an FMJ.

Except for javelina and a few odds and ends, I can't regard the .22 centerfires–even the hottest among them–as serious rifles for North

American big game. I don't question that they can perform wonders in the right hands. A skilled hunter and expert shot can certainly do well with them, but they're even more limited than that. Not only must the hunter be patient enough to wait for the right shot *and* a cool enough marksman to place the little bullet precisely. He should also be somewhat limited in his hunting goals–much more interested in venison than in harvesting a big buck. With that in mind, let's turn to what most hunters consider a sensible starting point for big-game cartridges.

Chapter 2

6mm–Everyone's "Minimum"

It was a clear, sunny day on the Wyoming prairie, and I was a chunky almost-teenager who wanted desperately to be a big-game hunter. I'd practiced endlessly, first with a single-shot .22 rimfire, then with a repeater, and finally with my brand-new big-game rifle. I'd read and reread O'Connor and Page until I could recite song and verse, and probably had more gun and hunting knowledge crammed into my skull than most hunters thrice my age. I knew I possessed the hunting and stalking skills of Davy Crockett and Daniel Boone, and paper targets had shown that I was a marksman without peer. But so far the day hadn't gone exactly according to plan.

Those pronghorns were not only spooky–they were *fast*. Worse, I couldn't control my shaking hands and fluttering heartbeat. In short, I'd missed a whole bunch of them, and now late afternoon was upon us. Lester Wright, owner of the ranch that would one day become Wright, Wyoming, led me down a shallow draw, peeked over the lip at a spot he'd chosen, and helped me get into position. The buck stood apart from his does, about 200 yards away, golden and snow-white with the afternoon sun glinting off his horns and black facial markings. This time–for the first time–I did it right. With wonder, boyish excitement, and not a little touch of sadness, I could walk up on my very first big-game animal.

The rifle was, of course, a .243 Winchester–and I wonder how many thousands of youngsters before and since have shared their first hunting experience with that wonderful little 6mm?

Remington's .244 and Winchester's .243 were parallel developments that arrived on the scene in 1955. They were the first modern American hunting cartridges in the 6mm, or .24-caliber, bullet diameter, but the bore size was far from new. Back in 1895, the 6mm Lee Navy was adopted for a short time by the Navy and Marine Corps, and both the cartridge and its straight-pull Lee bolt-action rifle saw some use in military and civilian markets. Overseas, a number of 6mm sporting cartridges were developed in the first quarter of this century, including the potent .240 Belted Rimless Nitro Express, a fairly long, belted cartridge that just happens to have almost identical ballistics to the much more compact .243 Winchester. But somehow the caliber languished until the mid-1950s.

Although the .244 Remington and .243 Winchester came along at the same time, the two companies had totally different visions for their cartridges. Remington viewed the .244 as a wind-bucking long-range wonder for the growing sport of varminting, so they gave their rifle barrels a relatively slow-for-caliber one-in-12-inch twist to best stabilize light bullets that could be driven fast. As a result, accuracy become very sketchy with bullets over 90 grains.

Winchester apparently saw their brainchild as a dual-purpose cartridge–a varmint rifle with 80-grain bullets and a deer/pronghorn rifle with 100-grain bullets. They gave their barrels a one-in-10-inch twist to stabilize both weights. The rest is history; the .243 was an overnight success, and remains so to this day. The .244, although a bit faster due to its larger case capacity, almost died. Years later, Remington corrected their error by renaming the cartridge 6mm Remington, changing the twist to one-in-nine, and adding a 100-grain factory loading. Although it's a very fine cartridge–perhaps technically better than the .243–the 6mm Remington has never recovered from its slow start; its sales still languish far behind the .243.

In 1968, Roy Weatherby introduced the .240 Weatherby Magnum, a true short magnum with its own unique case dimensions. This rounded out our modern trio of 6mm hunting cartridges, and each is a superb cartridge. So good, in fact, that I think the bore size has come to be considerably overrated for big-game hunting!

There's absolutely no question that the 6mm is, to most hunters, the sensible minimum for big game. This is reflected by the majority of hunting regulations stipulating either .23 or .24 caliber as the legal minimum for use on big game. Most hunters would agree that the 6mms are deer and pronghorn cartridges and are not elk cartridges. The misconception, to me, is that they are regarded as superb long-range choices *and* as ideal beginners' rifles. I think they are neither.

Bullet choice is fairly clear with all of our 6mms. There are a few component bullets in the 90- to 95-grain range, but the common weights are 80 and 100 grains, with a scattering of bullets over 100 grains. The lighter bullets are varmint bullets and the heavier bullets are game bullets. With a 100-grain loading, the .243 Winchester offers around 2,960 fps at the muzzle, with just under 2,000 foot/pounds of energy. With its greater case capacity, the 6mm Remington starts a 100-grain bullet at 3,100 fps and yields just over 2,100 foot/pounds. The .240 Weatherby is a real velocity star, starting a 100-grain slug at almost 3,400 fps and offering more than 2,500 foot/pounds. Those are all very good figures for so light a bullet, and all hold their velocity and downrange energy very well.

However, these figures aren't giant killers from the start, and by the time the 300-yard line is reached, energy is dropping very quickly. All three do reach that distance with over 1,000 foot/pounds of remaining energy, so all three are at least in theory 300-yard deer rifles. The .240 Weatherby has almost 1,500 foot/pounds at 300 yards with a 100-grain bullet, and carries 1,000 foot/pounds to a bit past 400 yards. So, in theory, you might say that the .240 Weatherby is good for at least that distance.

The problem is that bullet expansion will begin to decrease somewhat as range increases and velocity diminishes, and although the cartridges all carry significant bullet energy a long way out, the bullets are light and their wound channels are narrow. For pronghorn and smallish deer, I have no problem considering the .243 and 6mm sensible 300-yard cartridges, nor any problem adding 100 yards for the .240 Weatherby. Those are certainly long distances; 300 yards is a decent long shot for anyone, and 400 yards is beyond most hunters' capabilities. However, those are truly the maximum big-game ranges for the cartridges, and all three are becoming marginal at those ranges. I can't consider them true long-range performers.

Provided ranges are kept sensible, all three are very fine choices for pronghorn. All three are also sound cartridges for much deer hunting, from Texas and Southeastern whitetails to blacktails and Coues deer–again provided their users are willing to accept range limitations. I don't think they're the best choices for our largest deer, whether big-bodied Northern or Midwestern whitetails or Rocky Mountain mulies. For darned sure, based on caliber, bullet weight, and energy, I think they're all done before you get to game larger than deer!

The business about the 6mm as a beginner's rifle takes some explaining. These cartridges, especially the .243 and 6mm, have a lot going for them. The recoil is mild, yet the punch is significant. The dual-purpose aspect is also a plus; novice shooters can use their 6mms for varminting and gain invaluable field experience–not to mention intimate familiarity with their rifles. The problem arises in this: The 6mms are marginal for big game, especially if big deer or anything bigger than deer is hunted. Precise shot placement is required, and discretion must be used in taking shots. Both requirements are asking a lot of beginning hunters.

Obviously, it depends on the country. In areas where the deer are on the small side and very long shots are unlikely, the .243 or 6mm is a very fine choice for beginners. They remain good choices in open country, provided the shooter is carefully schooled on what shots to accept and what shots to pass. Certainly I was very pleased with my little .243 as a first big-game rifle, and I was able to use it for woodchucks, jackrabbits, and prairie dogs as well. However, it should not be chosen as a first rifle that might be used under all conditions. Actually, I tend to view the 6mms as rifles for serious experts–hunters who enjoy the mild recoil and, given good shot placement, deadly efficiency of these little bullets. Such hunters must accept and live within the limitations of their choice, possessing the patience to pass long shots or marginal presentations. Given those qualities, the 6mms are marvelous cartridges and, like so many thousands of hunters, I enjoy using them very much. Let's take a closer look at our three modern 6mms.

.243 Winchester: Introduced in 1955, the .243 Winchester was an overnight success and remains extremely popular today. It's essentially the .308 Winchester case necked down, so its short 2.045-inch case can fit into true short-action rifles. Winchester brought it out in their Model 70 bolt-action, but it was also offered in their Model 88 lever-action and Model 100 autoloader. Other lever-actions, including the Savage Model 99 and Browning BLR, have added to the .243's popularity.

My own favorite .243 was–and still is–a Ruger No. 1 single-shot. When I was a kid, I traded a Browning shotgun (bad trade, but gun nuts like me rarely make sensible ones–if you want a gun, you just have to have it!) for the new Ruger single-shot. I lost it in a burglary in 1981–then recovered it from a pawn shop five years later. I still have it, and it remains a favorite for stalking pronghorns and smallish deer. Actually, though, I acquired it for exactly the purpose Winchester had in mind. I was doing quite a lot of prairie-dog shooting on the windy Kansas prairies then–not steady shooting over big towns, but the kind of shooting where you'd get a half-dozen shots, then have to move a bit. The sporter-barreled Ruger was just the ticket for that, and I figured it would be just as perfect for pronghorns and smaller deer. Indeed it was!

Traditional loadings for the .243 are an 80-grain varmint bullet and a 100-grain big-game bullet. Today there are lighter, faster 60- and 75-grain varmint loads, plus Remington's 105-grain Extended Range factory load. Handloaders have a wider selection, but those are essentially the weight parameters. Factory loads quote the 100-grain bullet at 2,960 feet per second, and handloads can't beat that by much, if at all.

My favorite hunting bullet in the .243 was, for many years, a now-discontinued 95-grain Nosler Partition. With it I shot a great many pronghorns and quite a few Texas whitetails, and I never found it wanting. It was with that rifle and bullet that I shot my best-ever pronghorn, at least so far.

I'd spotted him the day before opening day, and I knew I could recognize the way his horns hooked sharply backward if I saw him again. I left him undisturbed, so it was no great surprise that he was in the same general area early the next morning. He was tending his does in some rolling sage hills, ideal stalking country. Mostly belly-crawling, I followed him over one hill and then another, closing the distance all the while. When I peeked over the crest of the fifth or sixth hill, he was just topping the next rise. I straightened into a prone position, wrapped the sling around my arm, and shot him with one very careful shot at about 150 yards. *That* was an ideal situation for a .243–not attempting to reach out over vast distances, but using cover to close in.

It was ideal, too, for whitetails in the Texas Hill Country, where ranges are generally fairly short, and equally perfect for a lot of Coues-deer and black-tailed-deer hunting. As I said, I have never found the .243 wanting–but I've never used it for serious mule-deer hunting, nor for big-bodied Northern whitetails, nor for larger game such as elk. Many others have, and with good presentation and excellent shot placement at moderate range the little cartridge can perform such tasks. But not for me–I've never been disappointed in the .243, and I don't want to stretch it to the point where it lets me down!

6mm Remington: As stated, the 6mm Remington first saw light as the .244 Remington, initially conceived as a varmint cartridge rather than a big-game or dual-purpose round. That was a big mistake, and even though the cartridge was later reintroduced as the 6mm Remington and its rifles given a twist that would stabilize both light and heavy bullets, it has never caught up to the .243 in popularity. Ballistically, the cartridges are very similar. However, the 6mm Remington is based on the longer 7mm Mauser case necked down, so with a case length of 2.233 inches it has significantly greater case capacity than the .243. In factory loads, the 6mm is only 140 feet per second faster with the 100-grain bullet. Handloads can increase the edge only slightly. A hundred feet per second isn't much, but it's something–especially with light, small-caliber bullets. Therefore, it's fair to say that, all things considered, the 6mm Remington is a better cartridge than the .243. Well, at least insofar as performance goes.

The problem is that the 6mm Remington isn't enough better that it can do things the .243 should not be asked to do. And since it's a great deal less popular than the .243, factory loads are very limited and very hard to find. The 6mm Remington is also too long for short bolt-actions and cannot be chambered in lever-actions like the Savage 99. It's strictly a proposition for a standard-length bolt-action or a single-shot. However, if you happen to be a handloader and you're considering acquiring a light rifle along these lines, take a hard look at the 6mm Remington before you bow to popular opinion and choose a .243!

.240 Weatherby Magnum: Roy Weatherby, Sr.'s last cartridge, introduced in 1968 (his son, Ed Weatherby, brought out the .416 Weatherby), is a unique little cartridge. Although it is a belted magnum with Weatherby's distinctive "double-Venturi" shoulder, it is not based on an existing belted case. Rather, it's essentially a .30-06 case necked down with a belt added. The .240 Weatherby Magnum wins the 6mm velocity race hands down. It starts a 100-grain bullet at nearly 3,400 feet per second, yielding 2,560 foot/pounds at the muzzle and over 1,200 foot/pounds at 400 yards. If a case could be made for long-range shooting with a 6mm cartridge, this is the one to do it with!

With its very light, small-caliber bullet, I don't think even the great velocity of the .240 makes it suitable for game larger than small deer. It *is* extremely flat-shooting; sighted three inches high at 100 yards, it drops only 8½ inches at 400 yards. With a trajectory like that, hunters who like it and are familiar with it would make a case for its use on smallish mountain game like desert sheep and Dall sheep, but nothing can convince me that you can base an elk cartridge around a 100-grain 6mm projectile at any velocity.

Except for custom rifles, the .240 Weatherby Magnum has never been chambered in any rifle other than the Mark V Weatherby, and of course the factory ammo is available only in the Weatherby brand. Undoubtedly, these limitations have sharply limited the popularity of this hot little number. To give it proper credit, it's a fine open-country cartridge for pronghorns and small deer. However, stress that "open-country" caveat; 100-grain 6mm bullets are designed to perform at .243 and 6mm Remington velocities, so at .240 Weatherby velocities those same bullets can be extremely destructive at shorter ranges. This is a pronghorn rifle for the guy who likes to reach out, or who hunts open sagebrush flats where stalking to moderate ranges is difficult.

All three of our current 6mm cartridges are very fine hunting rounds, and all three perform very fine service–especially in skilled hands and with their real limitations kept in mind. There are good reasons why the 6mms are regarded as a sensible minimum for big game by so many hunters–and equally good reasons why they should be restricted to use on our smaller varieties of big game.

Chapter 3

Quarter-Bores: Light Recoil and Lots of Reach!

The .25-caliber is almost entirely an American proposition, and our fondness for it goes back to the very beginning of smokeless powder—maybe even a bit farther back. The mild little .25-20, propelling an 86-grain bullet at a bit under 1,500 feet per second, was a popular chambering for Winchester's slick little '92, and Marlin brought it back recently in their Model 1894. It would be easy to dismiss the .25-20 as a hunting cartridge, but it was used—and used well—by a whole lot of folks who never saw a ballistics chart. My old friend and colleague, the late Dave Hetzler, loved to tell that he shot his first deer in the hills above Los Angeles with a .25-20. And I used an ancient Colt Lightning slide-action in .25-20 on my first cougar hunt 20-odd years ago. I won't dismiss it lightly, but we'll pass by after saying that it's just right for javelina and coyotes called in close—and not much more.

A far more serious cartridge was the .25-35, an early chambering for the Winchester Model 94 and many other turn-of-the-century rifles. Firing a 117-grain bullet at 2,230 feet per second, it was actually slower than the .30-30. Due to the necessity of shooting flat-point bullets in the tubular-magazine rifles in which it was most commonly chambered, it wasn't flatter-shooting, either, but it had a significant following for many years. Jack O'Connor's desert-sheep guide, the famed desert rat Charlie Ren, swore by his .25-35—and so did many who used it. The .25-20 was a bit too powerful for small game and underpowered for big game. The .25-35 had plenty of power for deer-sized game, but it lacked reach. Other than bore diameter, neither has anything at all in common with our quartet of modern .25-caliber hunting cartridges formed by the .250 Savage, .257 Roberts, .25-06, and .257 Weatherby Magnum.

These four cartridges, listed in ascending order of potency, are all fast, flat, and effective hunting cartridges. All are well-suited to pronghorn and smallish deer. Some, if not all, bridge the gap into larger deer, plus sheep and goats. And just maybe, with the right bullets, the most powerful of these could be considered for elk. While it might be relatively easy to consider our three 6mm cartridges as a group, with the .25s each one deserves careful separate discussion.

.250 Savage: This fine little cartridge was the brainchild of firearms genius Charles Newton. Introduced in 1915, it was originally termed the .250-3000 because, with its initial 87-grain loading, it was the first commercial cartridge to break the 3,000-feet-per-second barrier. It was introduced in the Savage Model 99 lever-action, and in that package it was truly a hunter's delight. Its use spawned some of the liveliest velocity-versus-bullet-weight debate ever seen in the American sporting press, much more heated than the war of words between Elmer Keith and Jack O'Connor ever became.

As might be expected, early users of the .250-3000 found it killed like lightning on deer-sized game, given good shot placement. Others claimed it was a great wounder. Both were exactly right. For one thing, the 87-grain .25-caliber bullet has very modest sectional density. It isn't going to penetrate all that well. For another, 1915-vintage bullet technology wasn't quite up to 3,000-fps speed. That little 87-grain pill almost certainly acted like a bomb–and with ideal shot placement probably dropped game like a bomb. With shoulder shots on larger game, it probably didn't work so well.

Bullet technology has improved a great deal–and so has American hunters' understanding of ballistics. Today we would generally agree that 87-grain .25-caliber bullets are varmint bullets, or for very small big game at best. In fact, the 87-grain loading that made the .250 Savage famous is no longer offered in factory ammunition. Handloaders, of course, can choose from the full range of .25-caliber bullets, but the "standard" .250 Savage factory load is a 100-grain bullet at 2,820 feet per second. That immediately begs a direct comparison with the .243. And that direct comparison is almost certainly what happened to the .250's popularity, for on the surface the .250 Savage doesn't come off that well. It's slower, and thus carries less energy at the muzzle. A 100-grain .25-caliber bullet has a lower ballistic coefficient than a 100-grain 6mm bullet; thus it will shed its velocity a bit more quickly. The .243 is equally suited to all action types.

The only cogent argument that can be made for the .250 Savage is its larger frontal area, and although I believe strongly in the effect of frontal area–or wound diameter–on game, I'm hard-pressed to argue that a huge difference exists between the .243 and .257 calibers. Handloaders, of course, can increase bullet weight significantly; hunting bullets up to 122 grains are readily available in .257-inch diameter. The .250 Savage lacks the case capacity to push heavier bullets to dizzying speeds, but those long, stable .25-caliber heavyweights do offer superb penetration.

In granddad's day a fair number of hunters swore by the .250-3000–with 87-grain bullets–for game up to elk and moose. Today, undoubtedly, 100-grain bullets from a .250 Savage still account for a fair number of elk annually. But so do 100-grain .243 bullets. If I had to use a .250 Savage on game larger than deer, I'd prefer to handload 115- or 117-grain bullets as fast as I could push them–but, even so, I can't call the .250 Savage a suitable elk rifle. Nor can I say that it has more reach than a .243. If anything, a bit less.

Perhaps it was for good reason that the 6mm cartridges stole the .250's thunder. Yet it remains a very fine cartridge, effective and with a huge amount of nostalgic appeal. A classic Savage 99 in .250 Savage just begs to be taken into the whitetail woods. And in a bolt-action, with the ability to soup up the loads a bit by seating the bullets well forward, it's the equal of any .243 and a good deal more. I had a lovely .250 Savage on a Mexican Mauser action once, and while I did relatively little North American hunting with it, I did take it to Africa one year. With 115-grain bullets pushed as fast as I could push them, it was pure lightning on impala and reedbuck and such. Undoubtedly, a .243 would have done just as well–but no .243 has the charisma of the old .250-3000. In recent years, some numbers of bolt-actions have been built around it, including Weatherby's slick little limited-edition whitetail rifle based on their Varmintmaster action. It should be no surprise that they were sold out almost immediately!

.257 Roberts: Until fairly recently, the .250 Savage and the lever-action Savage 99 were virtually inseparable. With their two-piece stocks and nonadjustable triggers, few lever-actions have the accuracy to be considered sound choices for varmint rifles. Thus, the .250 Savage was rarely considered a dual-purpose varmint and big-game round. Perhaps surprisingly, that's just what the .257 Roberts was touted as. Wildcatted some years earlier by gun writer Ned H. Roberts, it was introduced in factory form by Remington in 1934, and was fairly popular until the introduction of the .243 and .244.

Created by necking down the 7x57 Mauser case, the .257 Roberts has the case capacity to push heavy bullets at effective velocities and light bullets at very impressive speeds–especially with carefully worked up handloads in modern actions. Today there are several factory "+P" loads available, driving a 100-grain bullet at 3,000 feet per second and a 117- or 120-grain bullet at 2,780 fps. The former load immediately invites comparison with a .243 or, better, a 6mm Remington which shares the same 7x57 parent case. And, as is the case with the .250 Savage, the .257 Roberts doesn't do well in the comparison. But with, say, the Federal Premium 120-grain Nosler Partition +P load, the .257 Roberts still carries more than 1,000 foot/pounds of energy at the 400-yard line. Now you have more bullet weight, more energy, *and* more frontal diameter than the .243 or 6mm can muster.

Back in the 1950s, +P loadings–and high-performance ammo like Federal Premium, Winchester Supreme, and Remington Extended Range–were decades away. The .257 Roberts was never viewed as a giant killer. Rather, it was a fine deer and antelope rifle that also doubled as a good varmint gun. Both the .243 and 6mm were considered almost as good for deer and antelope, and better for varmints–and they almost killed the .257 Roberts. Only now is it starting to experience a significant comeback. But that should come as no surprise to those who have loved it all along.

Jack O'Connor, best known as a .270 man, loved the light-recoiling .257 Roberts and shot several of his many sheep with the cartridge. Bob Milek, possibly the most universally loved gun writer of all time, was also one of very few who had the nerve to admit he didn't like recoil. Milek was a .25-caliber man, and his loyalties were divided between the .257 Roberts and .25-06. Both were among his top choices for mule deer, and he took a number of elk with each.

Now, Bob Milek lived in elk country. If he didn't get the shot he wanted, he could come back next week. He was also a superb marksman, cool under pressure, and he believed in head and neck shots. In his hands, the .257 Roberts with a heavy bullet was, indeed, plenty of gun for elk. It isn't plenty of gun for me, nor for most hunters. But it is certainly a capable and adequate cartridge for deer and sheep—and for those purposes, a far more suitable cartridge than even the hottest of the 6mms. It is not, however, without limits. Although it carries the minimal 1,000 foot/pounds of energy to 400 yards, it falls below 1,500 foot/pounds at just 200 yards. I'd consider it a long-range cartridge for pronghorn and small deer, but for big mulie bucks and Northern whitetails, I'd take a step up to the next .25.

.25-06: More than any major manufacturer, Remington has a long history of taking popular wildcat cartridges and turning them into even more popular factory cartridges. Among such success stories are the .22-250 Remington, .257 Roberts, .280 Remington, and .35 Whelen—but among these "legitimized" wildcats it's likely that only the .22-250 has enjoyed more popularity than the .25-06. Developed by A.O. Niedner in 1920, it's a case that's easily made by necking down .30-06 brass. As a wildcat, it was offered my many custom gunsmiths and used by many gun cranks until Remington finally brought out the factory version in 1969.

It has the same advantages as all the .25s: light recoil and a fine selection of long, stable, heavy-for-caliber hunting bullets. But in the larger .30-06 case, the .25-06 can deliver superb velocity and outstanding downrange performance with those same bullets. Like the .250 Savage and .257 Roberts, the .25-06 can be considered a dual-purpose varmint and big-game cartridge; it can propel bullets of 87 grains and less at serious varmint velocities of 3,500 feet per second and more. There are even a few heavy-barreled varmint rifles so chambered, probably in recognition of the .25 caliber's wind-bucking ability when compared to centerfire .22s. However, recoil is a cumulative thing. Although mild in the spectrum of hunting cartridges, the recoil of a .25-06 is more than most varminters want for extended shooting sessions. I suspect that few hunters consider the .25-06 a dual-purpose cartridge, and even fewer consider it a pure varmint cartridge. Rather, its primary utility is as a hunting cartridge—and it's a dandy.

With 100-grain bullets at 3,230 feet per second, it's just right for pronghorns and our smaller deer—blacktails, Coues deer, and Texas whitetails. That bullet weight offers 2,300 foot/pounds of energy at the muzzle and doesn't drop below 1,000 until just before the 400-yard line. For larger deer and sheep, take your pick of several fine factory loads and component bullets from 117 to 122 grains. In factory form or handloaded, these bullets can deliver around 1,500 foot/pounds at 300 yards and well over 1,000 at 400 yards. At least in theory, that gives the .25-06 a good 300 yards of sensible effective range on the largest deer–and plenty of range for anything smaller. No, it isn't a huge step more powerful than the Roberts–but a big enough step to make a difference.

Accurate and easily built into light rifles, the .25-06 is often seen in sheep camps these days, and indeed it's well-suited to that purpose. Personally, I view it as one of the finest choices available for hunting mid-sized big game that often require long shots–pronghorn and Coues deer are prime examples, and the cartridge is unusually popular in South Texas, where tripod stands look down *senderos* that stretch into tomorrow. Hornady's 117-grain boat-tailed spire-point is a classic example of .25-06 trajectory: sighted 2½ inches high at 100 yards, it's dead-on at 250 and only 3½ inches low at 300 yards. That's a particularly good 100-yard sight-in, because it's much more common to overestimate range than to underestimate it. I don't mind sighting in 2½ or so inches high, but I get nervous if I have to sight in three or more inches high at 100 yards to get 300 yards of effective range without holdover. That means you can be as much as four or even five inches high at the midrange trajectory. And if you overestimate the range and hold slightly high on the shoulder as a result, it's awfully easy to shoot over a small-bodied deer. I've done it enough to know! The maximum trajectory height for that Hornady load, with that sight-in, is slightly under three inches–and you *still* have a good 300 yards of shooting with a dead-center hold. Now that's flat!

As mentioned earlier, Bob Milek was a great fan of the .25-06, and he and his sons shot many elk with the cartridge. Most were head and neck shots. I don't like those shots much (nor consider myself a good enough and cool enough marksman to rely on them), but an accurate, flat-shooting, light-kicking .25-06 is a fine tool for the head-and-neck specialist. Too, folks like the Mileks live in elk country. Local hunters rarely worry about trophy bulls, concentrating instead on a clean shot on a nice-eating cow or young bull. That gives more strength to the choice of a small caliber, since there are generally many freezer elk on the mountain for every trophy bull, and it's easier to wait for an ideal shot presentation. Hunters who live in elk country can come back next weekend. Trophy hunters from afar cannot.

In terms of energy, the .25-06 falls below 2,000 foot/pounds at about 100 yards. According to the theory that suggests 2,000 foot/pounds at the target for elk–a theory I subscribe to–the .25-06 is thus elk-capable only at very short range. That's not really true for the very careful and patient hunter who picks his shots and can place them. Such a hunter can work wonders with a .25-06, and with much smaller cartridges as well. But for me, and for the average hunter (whoever that may be!), I consider the .25-06 woefully inadequate for elk hunting.

I think it's fine for almost any sheep hunting on this continent, and I wouldn't hesitate to use it on caribou. Although bigger-bodied than most deer, caribou are not especially tough. They're also almost universally hunted in very open country, where flat-shooters like the .25-06 shine, and where reasonable shot presentation can usually be obtained.

I have owned only one .25-06, a wonderfully light, thin-barreled, synthetic-stocked job built by Randy Brooks of Barnes Bullets. I then made it heavier than necessary with a big 4-12X scope. I've had little occasion to use it so far, but my intentions are for it to be the ultimate pronghorn and Coues-deer rifle. I've used it on blacktails, and I'd use it on sheep. I doubt that I'd ever use it on caribou, but I might. I almost certainly will use it down South Texas *senderos.* But I will never carry it when I have an elk tag in my pocket, nor will I use it to hunt big mule deer or big-bodied Northern whitetails.

Nothing in North America is as difficult to obtain as a good mule deer today. My .25-06–or yours–would be perfect for about 85 percent of the shots that occur in mule-deer country. But a good mule deer is a great enough prize that I want a rifle capable of handling *all* the shots that might occur–far, near, stationary, running, broadside, quartering away, whatever. The .25-06 has the range but not the punch for an animal that could push 400 pounds and might be standing at the wrong angle.

Exactly the same can be said about Northern whitetails. There's a huge difference between a Southern or Texas whitetail topping out at 180 pounds (and that's *big*) and an Alberta or Saskatchewan or Montana buck topping 300 pounds and running across a wheat field at 250 yards. I've hunted that country enough to know that one opportunity in a week of hunting is a whole bunch, and the rifle must be capable of handling any reasonable shot presented.

If you insist on using the .25-06 for animals for which it is marginally capable–big deer, bighorn sheep, caribou, and elk–choose your bullets with care. Fortunately, very fine choices are available in both component and factory-load form. In factory loads, I'm tremendously impressed by Remington's Extended Range line. Their 122-grain ER load is the ultimate downrange performer, and the bullets work extremely well. There are, of course, no flies on the Federal Premium 120-grain Nosler load. You can do as well with component bullets, but not much better. Few custom or semi-custom bulletmakers have bothered with calibers below 7mm. One such is Trophy Bonded, a company that offers their marvelous Bearclaw in .257-caliber. I'd look to bullets like these if you ask your .25-06 to tackle game much above 200 pounds. Me, I'll consider my .25-06 just right for pin-point shooting at game between 100 and 150 pounds!

.257 Weatherby Magnum: The .257 Weatherby Magnum is the king of the quarter-bore tribe, no doubt about it. Perhaps surprisingly, this is one of Roy Weatherby's earlier developments; he started playing with it in 1944 and introduced it in 1948. It's the smallest of the Weatherby Magnums based on the .300 Holland & Holland case; in the .257, the basic .300 case is shortened to 2.545 inches, and of course necked to .257 with Weatherby's distinctive shoulder. Legend has it that the .257 was Roy Weatherby's personal favorite among all of his cartridges, and it's no legend. He told me so himself on several occasions. Now, Roy Weatherby was one of the finest men this industry has ever seen. I first met him when I was about 12 years old, and even then he had plenty of time for a kid who loved guns. Mr. Weatherby–I never called him Roy, though he asked everyone to–always had time for anyone who wanted to talk about guns. For more than 40 years, he was a presence at every N.R.A. convention, every big hunters' show, every major shooting event–and he never wavered from his belief in the supremacy of bullet velocity. I dislike funerals very much, and certainly don't plan to attend mine, but it was a great honor as well as a great sadness to be present when Roy Weatherby was laid to rest. He believed in his products, and I believed him when he told about that quartering-away Cape buffalo that he dropped with his .257 Weatherby Magnum.

But as much as I loved and respected the man, I cannot accept his .257 as a buffalo cartridge. It *is* the ultimate in velocity, at least in the .25-caliber world, and with few peers throughout the great spectrum of sporting cartridges. With the light .25-caliber bullets, you can come perilously close to the 4,000-fps threshold. With hunting bullets, you can beat the pants off the great .25-06. With the Weatherby, a 100-grain bullet tops 3,500 fps, and a 120-grain bullet approaches 3,300. Folks, that's a 10 percent gain over the .25-06. In the velocity world, even five percent is significant.

With a good spitzer bullet of 120 grains or so, the .257 Weatherby Magnum carries as much as 1,500 foot/pounds to the 400-yard line. Sighted about 2½ inches high at 100 yards, it's only 10 inches low at 400 yards. If there's anything out there that shoots flatter and can be shot from the shoulder, I simply don't know what it is.

There are drawbacks. First and foremost, the .257 Weatherby simply must have a 26-inch barrel. Technically, a 28-inch barrel would be better. It's a whole bunch overbore capacity, but that means nothing provided you have a long enough tube to burn the powder and wring out the velocity.

A more serious problem, and a very real one, is erratic bullet performance. The .257 Weatherby is not a close-range cartridge; the bullets available for it were designed for .257 Roberts and just perhaps .25-06 velocities, but never for Weatherby velocities. Bullet blow-up at closer ranges is common. Farther out, where speeds have slowed to .25-06 or .257 Roberts velocities, the .257 Weatherby performs well.

Opinions often diverge on the .257. My longtime boss at *HUNTING* Magazine, Ken Elliott, has used his .257 Weatherby from California to the Kalahari. He maintains that it drops game like lightning bolts, and he swears by it. *His* boss, Robert E. Petersen, tells about several deer that got up again and had to be tracked after being hit with Pete's .257 Weatherby lightning bolt.

Hunters who swear by it–and there are many–tend to agree with Ken Elliott that it's an unusually devastating and deadly cartridge. I've seen it work that way enough to have tremendous respect for the round. One day, though, Finn Aagaard and I worked in quite close on a band of mouflon sheep on his place at Llano, Texas. It wasn't an ideal test for the .257, but it was the only shot we'd been able to get. So I shot the largest ram in the chest at about 40 yards. At full velocity on so small an animal, the .257 should have turned him inside out. Instead, he went off with the herd, and we couldn't be certain I'd even hit him. I had, and he didn't go far–but there was no visible sign of a hit. So much for lightning bolts!

That odd experience aside, I've used the cartridge some with very good results. My opinion is that it's everything the .25-06 is, plus 10 percent more–insofar as range is concerned. It's suited to the most open of country, but is not well-suited to close-in shooting, nor does its added velocity and energy take it significantly farther up into the realm of larger game than the .25-06. There simply is no quantum leap in energy, especially at longer ranges; a 120-grain .25-caliber bullet is still what it is, no matter how fast you push it. Provided the fans of this caliber understand that, all four of our current .25-caliber cartridges will serve them well.

Chapter 4

6.5mm–Europe's Forgotten Favorite

It's funny how regional preferences develop for certain calibers. The 7mm or .284 is more or less universally accepted, while the only slightly smaller .270 (.277 bullet diameter) is pretty much an American proposition. The .25s, too, are almost exclusively American in both manufacture and application. Take a very small step up in bullet diameter and you have the 6.5mm or .264 caliber. This caliber, offered in a big assortment of case dimensions and cartridge designations, has been a mainstay of European hunters for generations.

Around the turn of the century, even the staid British sportsmen often turned away from their big Nitro Express cartridges in favor of the light, handy 6.5x53R Mannlicher-Steyr and 6.5x54 Mannlicher-Schoenauer. The former cartridge was called the .256 Mannlicher by the Brits, following their often confusing habit of naming cartridges by *land* rather than *groove* diameter, but by our terms it's a 6.5mm or .264 caliber, not a .25. Cartridges like these were unimpressive by today's standards, firing 160-grain bullets at about 2,300 feet per second.

In those days, though, that was pretty impressive velocity–especially for hunters who grew up with black-powder cartridges. More importantly, those incredibly long, stable, heavy-for-caliber 6.5mms were among the first jacketed hunting bullets available. In game, they remained on course and penetrated like nothing their users had ever seen–and they were used on classes of game that, according to our current thinking, would be suicidal to tackle with a 6.5. On this continent, visiting sportsmen used the little 6.5s for elk, moose, and the biggest of bears. In Africa, early hunters like C.H. Stigand and W.D.M. Bell sang the praises of the 6.5 for game up to and including elephant!

The 6.5x53R has long been obsolete and the 6.5x54 barely hangs on, but as a bore diameter the 6.5 remains exceedingly popular in Europe. Starting with the 6.5x53R introduced in 1892, there have been something like 15 different European 6.5mm cartridges. Many were military, some were civilian, and a few of the most popular (like our .30-06 and .308) started as military cartridges and bridged the gap into commercial popularity.

The majority of these cartridges are ballistically similar to the 6.5x55 Swedish, arguably the most popular 6.5mm cartridge in the world. Current Norma loadings offer a 139-grain bullet at 2,850 feet per second and a 156-grain bullet at 2,650 fps. It is with this cartridge and these nominal ballistics that thousands of Finnish and Swedish hunters take their moose annually. Admittedly, European moose are a bit smaller than our larger varieties of moose–similar to Shiras and eastern Canada moose in body size. Also, European moose are very much managed for quantity rather than quality. Most of the harvest is cows and yearlings, with very few mature bulls in the mix. Even so, a moose is a moose, and it's still larger than our wapiti and much larger than any deer. Swedes never seem to find the 6.5x55 wanting, so it's worth casual discussion as to why this little cartridge seems so effective.

Although there are a couple of very fast 6.5s, obviously the 6.5x55 and its kin aren't velocity stars–adequate, but not spectacular. The caliber is just as obviously fairly small. The success, almost certainly, lies in the fact that 6.5mm hunting bullets of 140 to 160 grains are increasingly heavy for caliber, with high sectional densities that give them superb penetrating qualities–and that's just as true today as it was when the old-timers took on elephants with cartridges of this ilk.

Given the popularity of the 6.5mm, it's a bit surprising that the Europeans have made just a few attempts to increase 6.5mm velocity with a larger case. A 6.5x61 Mauser was introduced in the 1930s that pushed a 139-grain bullet over 2,900 feet per second and a 157-grain bullet at about 2,750. That one never made it past World War II, but its big brother, the 6.5x68 Schuler, was and is fairly popular.

The 6.5x68 was introduced by RWS just before World War II. Created by necking down 8x68S brass, it's a rimless cartridge ballistically very similar to our .264 Winchester Magnum. It's a fine cartridge, but is almost never seen in America. The standard European hunting load is a 123-grain bullet at 3,450 feet per second, a real screamer that shoots very flat. It is most popular in Germany and Austria, where it is relied upon for long-range shooting at chamois and also for red stag.

Against this backdrop of extreme popularity in Europe, it remains a mystery why the 6.5mm has done so poorly in America–despite several attempts. Although military-surplus rifles in 6.5 Japanese, 6.5x52 Carcano, 6.5x54 Mannlicher-Schoenauer, and all the other 6.5mm military chamberings are occasionally seen, of the numerous foreign 6.5s only the 6.5x55 Swedish has achieved any popularity here–and our domestic 6.5s haven't fared much better.

The first American 6.5 appeared clear back in 1913. It was Charles Newton's .256 Newton (following the British convention of naming it after land diameter), produced in factory form by the Western Cartridge Company. The .256 was a necked down .30-06 case with a long neck and fairly sharp shoulder and, like all Newton cartridges, it was a red-hot number for its day. The factory load pushed a 129-grain bullet at 2,760 feet per second–that in 1913, when .30-06 velocities were far below their current levels. With modern powders, much higher velocities are practical, so the .256 Newton and other case dimensions of 6.5-06 wildcats are still occasionally built by custom makers and wildcatters. But the .256 Newton enjoyed very limited popularity and lasted only a few years in factory form.

It was fully 45 years before another American 6.5mm was introduced in the form of the .264 Winchester Magnum. The .264 started out with a bang, but was soon eclipsed by the ballistically similar but more versatile 7mm Remington Magnum. The next–and, at least so far, last–introduction of an American 6.5mm was Remington's 1966-vintage 6.5mm Remington Magnum. Remington's 6.5 Magnum is a very short (2.170-inch) belted case created by necking down the .350 Remington Magnum. It was designed to fit into the very short Model 600-series action. That rifle's 18½-inch barrel sharply curtailed the cartridge's genuine accuracy potential–and it was further limited by the short action length, which limited usable bullet weight to 120 grains.

I still have my 1967 edition of the *Hornady Handbook of Cartridge Reloading*. The text portion preceding the data for the then-new 6.5mm Remington Magnum says, in part:

"The 18½-inch barrel of the Model 600 does not make full use of the velocity potential of the cartridge. Our testing, done with an F.N. Mauser custom 6.5mm with 24-inch barrel, develops up to 25 percent more velocity than is possible with the 18½-inch version. Less powerful than the .264 Winchester Magnum and less versatile than the .270 Winchester, the belted case and easy to handle factory carbine appear to have sales appeal."

Hmmm. I wonder if the Hornady folks wish they could erase that last line? Although there was much initial hoopla, the 6.5mm Remington Magnum never achieved significant popularity, and no factory rifles are currently so chambered. It is actually a pretty good little cartridge. With its original 18½-inch barrel, velocities much over 2,850 fps with a 120-grain bullet were almost impossible, but with a 24-inch tube velocities over 3,200 fps are easy to reach. Given an action that will handle longer bullets and a full-length barrel, velocities approaching 3,000 fps are possible with handloaded 140-grain bullets. Given those figures, the 6.5mm Remington Magnum is very similar to the .270 Winchester. In carbine form, though, both velocities and bullet weights are limited. For short-action, short-barreled carbines, there are more efficient choices, especially the 7mm-08 Remington.

The 6.5mm Remington Magnum was one of the last iterations of the "Magnum Craze" of the late 1950s and 1960s, when it appears that the major manufacturers thought any cartridge with a belt and the world "Magnum" as a tagline would sell. The 6.5mm Remington Magnum was and is a pretty good little cartridge–but even with its Magnum moniker it didn't sell well. Factory ammunition with the 120-grain bullet is still available, and probably will be for some time, but it seems very unlikely that 6.5mm Remington Magnum will be one of those rare cartridges to experience a rebirth.

One that has is the 6.5x55. It and the .264 Winchester Magnum are, to my thinking, the only 6.5mm cartridges popular enough on this continent to warrant detailed discussion.

6.5x55 Swedish: In the year these lines are written, 1994, the 6.5x55 is fully 100 years old. It wasn't the first of the smokeless 6.5mm loads–both the Italian 6.5mm Carcano and the 6.5x53R Mannlicher-Steyr, among others, preceded it. Nor is it the best of the small-cased European 6.5s. To my mind, that title should go to the 6.5x57 Mauser, obviously based on the 7x57 Mauser case necked down. But you can't always figure why a given cartridge wins a popularity race, and without a doubt the 6.5x55 won it hands down. Numerous surplus Swedish Mausers in the Models 94, 96, and 38 have been seen in this country, and the cartridge was also chambered in Norway's 1894 and 1912 Krag-Jorgensen rifles. The European military loadings were a 139-grain spitzer at 2,625 fps and a 156-grain roundnose at 2,395 fps. Current factory loads and a wide variety of published handloads beat the heck out of those figures, but great caution must be taken in selecting loads for older military rifles–especially as regards the relatively weak Krag action. For this reason, many loading manuals stop at about 2,500 fps for 140-grain bullets, although both case capacity and modern actions will handle much more.

Norma has long imported factory 6.5x55 loads into this country, but American factory ammo in 6.5x55 is a relatively new thing. El Dorado (PMC) offers a 139-grain spitzer soft-point at 2,850 fps and a 144-grain FMJ at 2,650 fps. Federal offers a Premium loading with a 140-grain Nosler Partition at 2,850 fps. And, brand new in 1994, Remington has a 140-grain Pointed Soft Point Core-Lokt load at a very conservative 2,550 fps. The Remington load is suited for older military actions, and should make an extremely effective whitetail load at modest ranges. The Federal, PMC, and current Norma loadings are much hotter, and should be used only in current rifles in good condition.

The American 6.5x55 factory loadings obviously reflect a resurgence of interest in the cartridge, and also a growing availability of new factory rifles so chambered. The Winchester Model 70 is available in 6.5x55, as is the Ruger M77. In 1994, the Remington Model 700 Limited Edition Classic is the 6.5x55–a sure sign that the cartridge will be added to standard M700 chamberings in years to come.

Even with the hottest of current loadings, the 6.5x55 is not dramatic in ballistic terms. The aerodynamics of a 140-grain 6.5mm spitzer are very good, so it carries velocity and energy downrange quite well–but it doesn't have a great deal of either velocity or energy to start with. The 140-grain Federal Premium loading has 2,525 foot/pounds of energy at the muzzle and carries 1,855 foot/pounds at 200 yards. At 400 yards, it still has 1,330 foot/pounds. That's real staying power, but even so–despite the success the Scandinavians have with it on their moose–the cartridge must be considered very marginal for elk, and not suitable for ranges past 200 yards.

It looks pretty good for deer, however. For pronghorn and smaller deer, it carries enough energy just as far as anyone has any business shooting. On larger deer, it should be fine out to 250 or 300 yards, and of course it would be just fine for sheep and mountain goat.

I will admit that I have never hunted with a 6.5x55. It's one of those cartridges I have long admired, and one of these days I'm going to spend some serious time with it. Like the Swedes, those who have it love it–and its fans are likely to use it on a wide range of game.

Although I can claim very limited experience with the cartridge, I don't personally see it as an extremely versatile round. For my money, its light, small-caliber bullets at moderate velocity preclude its use on elk-sized game. For the same reasons I don't recommend the hot .25s, I wouldn't use it for the largest deer. On the other hand, it's a marvelously efficient, light-recoiling cartridge that shoots fairly flat and will offer uniformly fabulous bullet performance.

I'd consider it a fine choice for almost any deer hunting in the country, except specialized quests for huge white-tailed or mule deer. It would be just fine for pronghorns, and it wouldn't be a bad choice for most sheep hunting. While I plan to get a 6.5x55 one of these days and, like most folks who have one, I'll probably fall in love with it, this is a cartridge not exclusively for veteran hunters. Its light recoil and efficiency make it a super choice for beginning hunters, especially youngsters or ladies. As a beginner's cartridge it beats the heck out of any 6mm or .24-caliber cartridge, and compares very well with the 7mm-08 Remington. In fact, the only advantage the 7mm-08 might have is that it can be chambered in short bolt-actions and lever-actions like the Savage, while the 6.5x55 needs a standard-length action that will accommodate at least a 7x57. But whether for beginner or expert, the 6.5x55 is a marvelous hunting cartridge that should not be underrated.

.264 Winchester Magnum: Winchester's quartet of short magnum cartridges based on the .458 Winchester Magnum case began with the .458 in 1956 and eventually included the .338 Winchester Magnum, .300 Winchester Magnum, and .264. Both the .338 and .264 were introduced in 1958, in the Model 70 Alaskan and Model 70 Westerner, respectively. The Westerner was a 26-inch-barreled rifle, and initial factory figures quoted a 100-grain bullet at 3,700 feet per second and a 140-grain bullet at 3,200 fps. Those were innocent pre-chronograph days for most of us. It's possible, with carefully worked-up handloads, to approach those original factory ballistics. But the original factory loads didn't do quite what they were said to do–and with a barrel shorter than 26 inches, those velocities are not even possible.

The .264 received a tremendous amount of press and was an important part of a massive advertising campaign from Winchester. It was initially extremely popular, and seemed well on its way to being one of the great long-range cartridges. In 1962, Remington introduced the 7mm Remington Magnum. It took off a bit more slowly than the .264, but gained ground steadily. By 1967, that same Hornady manual quoted earlier stated: "The Remington development seems destined for even greater popularity than its rival 6.5mm magnum, though the two cartridges are quite similar in size, power, and performance." Although the 7mm Remington gained ground slowly, by the early 1970s the .264 was languishing and the 7mm has never looked back.

Even though original .264 ballistics were a bit exaggerated, it was and is an unusually fine long-range cartridge. A total believer in all the hype, I got a .264 back in 1965. Mine was a 24-inch-barreled Model 700 Remington, so for darned sure I wasn't getting what I thought I was getting. Even so, I had a wonderfully flat-shooting and efficient open-country cartridge–and I used it with perfect satisfaction on a wide variety of Western game.

After a few years, Winchester dropped its 26-inch barrel in favor of a 24-inch tube. In time, the 100-grain loading was dropped altogether and the published ballistics of the 140-grain load were modified to reflect the genuine ballistics with a 24-inch barrel. As quoted today, a 140-grain bullet leaves the muzzle at 3,030 fps, yielding 2,854 foot/pounds. Like all 140-grain 6.5mm loads, it holds that velocity extremely well; at 400 yards, remaining velocity is 2,114 fps for nearly 1,400 foot/pounds. That ain't too bad, but it isn't any better than what the .270 Winchester can offer with a good aerodynamic 130-grain bullet. With heavy bullets, the 7mm Remington Magnum offers a great deal more energy, but as a long-range performer, one of the great arguments against the .264 is just that–it isn't any better than a .270, unless a 26-inch barrel is used. However, if you happen to have an original Westerner with a 26-inch barrel, don't throw it away. And if you're in the market for a brand-new open-country rifle, don't overlook a brand-new Model 70 .264, in either the post-1964 action or the new Classic reintroduced pre-'64 action. In 1994, they brought back the 26-inch barrel, and that's pretty interesting news to the few surviving .264 fans like me.

Supposing you could get that 140-grain bullet to 3,200 feet per second–and you can with a 26-inch barrel–then you've increased to 3,177 foot/pounds at the muzzle–and over 1,700 at 400 yards. No .270 load can come close, nor can any shoot as flat.

When I was a kid, my favorite .264 load was not the 140-grain bullet but a 129-grain Hornady Spire Point, which invites even more direct comparison with a .270. In my 24-inch barrel, I wasn't getting the velocity I thought I was getting. But I still had some of those handloads long after my original .264 was stolen, and I had the chance to chronograph them in a 26-inch-barrel Westerner. They were perhaps a bit hot, but I got well over 3,300 feet per second. Now, that load started with 3,114 foot/pounds, and it still has almost 1,500 foot/pounds at 400 yards. A boattailed .270 comes close, but only close.

As I said, I like the .264. It requires a longer barrel and thus a heavier rifle, so it isn't really better than the .270 for mountain hunting. Nor, for game heavier than sheep and deer, is it the equal of the 7mm magnums–7mm bullets from 160 grains on up beat it hands down. But it remains a superb choice for pronghorns, open-country deer, and mountain game. With 140-grain bullets, it is also my personal minimum for elk-sized game. I doubt that it will ever make a comeback, but with 26-inch barrels again available after so many years, I suspect it will at least remain in the lineup of available cartridges.

Chapter 5

.270–Jack O'Connor's Caliber

I simply can't imagine an American hunter who doesn't have a soft spot for the .270. At .277, it's a purely American bullet diameter, with just two different case dimensions: .270 Winchester and .270 Weatherby Magnum. Both are fine hunting cartridges, and each has a long and proud tradition. The Winchester cartridge, of course, dates back to 1925, when it was first introduced in Winchester's Model 54 bolt-action, forerunner of the Model 70. Less well known is the fact that the .270 Weatherby Magnum, developed in 1943, was Roy E. Weatherby's *first* cartridge development to be commercially produced.

It is perhaps a great credit to the .270 that so much controversy surrounds it. Jack O'Connor, then a young English professor at the University of Arizona, grabbed onto the cartridge almost immediately after its introduction and used it–not exclusively, but extensively–for the rest of his life. Elmer Keith–Montana cowboy, guide, and gun writer–was without a doubt one of the more knowledgeable firearms authorities this country ever produced. He grew up with big lever-actions and a smattering of old Sharps and Springfield single-shots. He believed in heavy bullets at moderate velocity, and he didn't believe in the .270.

There is much more to their 50-year feud in the sporting press than just slow, heavy bullets versus fast, light ones. Jack O'Connor, too, was an extremely knowledgeable gun hand–but he came to gun writing as a polished journalist, not only a professor but also a writer who had published a couple of pretty good novels. As a young staffer at *Guns & Ammo*, I had the privilege of editing a number of Elmer Keith's raw manuscripts. I mean no discredit to Elmer's memory when I say that raw is a mild word. Elmer Keith knew his onions, and even into his eighties he was a magnificent shot with rifle, shotgun, and handgun. But he had very little education, and his manuscripts as they left his typewriter were an editor's nightmare. O'Connor's manuscripts were as polished and smooth as you might expect from an English professor's hand. O'Connor could have been a successful writer in any genre or venue he chose, but he chose to write about guns and hunting and was extremely successful at it.

Elmer Keith was successful at it, too, and his success is a great credit to his knowledge and his tenacity. I suspect, however, that Elmer Keith always resented the fact that he never held a top position with one of the larger American magazines. For many decades, there were no "specialty" gun or hunting magazines. There were only what guys in my business call the Big Three, formed by *Outdoor Life*, *Sports Afield*, and *Field & Stream*. The most prestigious positions among hunting and shooting writers were that of Shooting Editor for these magazines. For many years, those positions were held by Warren Page at *Field & Stream*, Pete Brown at *Sports Afield*, and Jack O'Connor at *Outdoor Life*. I'm only speculating, but I think it likely that the keith-O'Connor feud was fueled by the fact that O'Connor held one of these titles and Keith never did. Then too, O'Connor eventually moved from this native Arizona right into Elmer Keith's backyard in Salmon, Idaho. I suspect that didn't sit well, either.

In his later years, Elmer Keith found a home in Robert E. Petersen's fledgling *Guns & Ammo* Magazine. Fifteen years later, after retirement from *Outdoor Life*, Jack O'Connor became the figurehead for Petersen's new venture, *Petersen's HUNTING* magazine. Now the feud could be waged in two magazine published by the same company—and any good editor knows that controversy is good for magazine sales.

The .270 was very much at the heart of this controversy, for it had become Jack O'Connor's talisman—the ideal cartridge for Mr. Sheep Hunter. And it epitomized not only Jack O'Connor, but the ballistic concept that Elmer Keith loathed: light bullets at high velocity. Elmer wrote, among many other things, that the .270 was a "damned adequate coyote cartridge." And O'Connor often wrote of shooting elk, moose, and even the occasional grizzly with the cartridge. Both were taking extreme views of what is really a very fine and very versatile hunting cartridge.

I had a fine .270 Winchester back in the 1970s, and I used it to hunt quite a wide variety of game: white-tailed and mule deer, black bear, pronghorn, wild hogs, and a couple of varieties of non-native big game such as Axis deer and ibex. I witnessed a catastrophic bullet failure with a 150-grain soft-point from my rifle, which seemingly failed to penetrate the shoulder of a mid-sized black bear. The rifle was later stolen, and that event with the bear worked on my mind enough that it was some years before I chose the .270 again. To characterize any cartridge based on the anomaly of one bullet failure is, of course, a gross disservice to the cartridge. Bullet failures are rare, but they can and do happen—and generally it should be the bullet that's suspected first, not the rifle that fired it. But it's common to blame the cartridge, and I did.

There's probably another reason why I shied away from the .270 for so long. When I acquired my first .270, I wasn't a writer yet, nor had I really dared dream of becoming one. I was a kid who'd been raised on Jack O'Connor's writings, and above all I wanted to hunt a variety of big game in far-off, exciting places. It was natural for me to acquire a .270, as did so many thousands of hunters who had grown up with Jack O'Connor. But by the time that .270 was stolen, I was a beginning writer, and I wanted to write about the rifles I used as well as the places I took them. What fledgling writer would have the temerity to write about Jack O'Connor's cartridge?

When that lovely custom-stocked .270 went away, I made a semi-conscious decision to switch to the .30-06.

In recent years, I have returned to the .270 more and more frequently. It has accounted for several white-tailed and mule deer for me, more pronghorns, and mountain goat. I have also used it for game such as hartebeest and impala in Africa; Himalayan tahr and chamois in New Zealand; red stag, roebuck, and Alpine ibex in Europe. That anomaly of a bullet failure so many years ago has not been repeated, and I have not found the cartridge wanting. Perhaps oddly, when I started writing this book I had not carried the .270 on a sheep hunt. The book is now written, and as I'm doing the final editing I can say that I have; just two weeks ago I used a .270 to take a wonderful bighorn ram. Perhaps not so oddly, I have not carried the .270 on an elk hunt–and I don't expect to.

Despite Elmer Keith's exaggeration, the .270 is much more than a "damned adequate coyote rifle." In both Winchester and Weatherby persuasion, it's one of our very best cartridges for mountain hunting for North American sheep and goats and for almost all deer hunting on this continent. Although a touch bigger than truly required, it's outstanding for pronghorn hunting, and darn near ideal for caribou. Along the way, with good bullets, it will do the job on black bear. Likewise, it's certainly elk-capable and undoubtedly accounts for hundreds of elk annually.

It's this last that gets us into trouble with the .270. Nobody questions its efficiency for deer/sheep/goat/pronghorn hunting. The real controversy is whether the .270 is an elk rifle or not, and opinions on this subject are so heated that it's a wonder more campfire discussions don't turn into fistfights.

I can't solve this argument. Folks who love the .270 are going to use it for elk–and they'll probably do just fine with it. Other folks will say it isn't enough gun. I say it's enough gun–but just barely, and for that reason I doubt if I'll use it for elk. The .270 is an accurate, light-recoiling, easy-to-shoot cartridge. It lends itself to the good bullet placement that is essential for elk no matter what cartridge is chosen–but is especially critical if marginal cartridges are chosen. Its heavier 150-grain bullets penetrate well, and there are a number of outstanding controlled-expansion .270 hunting bullets that can and will penetrate into the vitals on any broadside or slightly quartering shot on elk-sized game. It offers little margin for error, it is unlikely to provide complete through-and-through penetration, and the elk hunter who chooses the .270 simply must pick his shots with care and keep his range reasonable.

I think the .270 is marginal for elk, but it's on the right side of the margin. Provided its users understand its capabilities and limitations, it will get the job done. Elk are incredibly strong and very tough. Pound for pound, they are as hardy as anything we have in North America except our big bears. Elk blow holes in the myth that African game is tougher than American game!

I would feel more comfortable hunting the much larger but not nearly so hardy moose with a .270–and in fact I have hunted moose with a .270. But I have never hunted elk with a .270, and I don't plan to. Now, if I was on a mule-deer hunt and had an elk tag in my pocket just in case, and if a big bull presented himself and my rifle was a .270, I wouldn't hesitate. But it's not a cartridge I'd choose.

I would choose it for mountain hunting, as so many hunters have, and likewise for the gamut of deer hunting across North America. The only caveat is that I would not choose it for hunting the largest Northern whitetails, for the same reason I'd avoid the .25s and 6.5s: one shot is all you're likely to get, and you simply must be prepared to take it, whether it's ideal or not.

Our two .270 cartridges share the same bullets, but they're a long way from being identical. Let's look at each in more detail.

.270 Winchester: Thanks in no small part to the early praise Jack O'Connor gave the cartridge, the .270 Winchester was a howling success almost from the start. Available bullet weights and factory velocities changed very little for the first 60 years of this cartridge's history. Traditional bullet choices are a fairly useless 100-grain varmint loading at 3,430 feet per second muzzle velocity; a 130-grain bullet at 3,060 fps; and a 150-grain bullet at 2,850 fps. These bullet weights are offered by every major manufacturer in a great variety of bullet styles and designs. For the non-handloader, the .270 offers this great proliferation of superb factory loads, and also this: From the very start, .270 ammunition has been loaded to the top of the cartridge's performance. Unlike a great many fine cartridges, very little can be gained in velocity by handloading the .270.

While the 130- and 150-grain loads are traditional, in recent years a couple more weights have become available over the counter. Several companies now offer 140-grain factory loads with a muzzle velocity of about 2,960 feet per second, and Remington has a new 135-grain Extended Range load at 3,000 fps. In component bullets, handloaders have these weights to choose from, and can go up to 170 grains.

Jack O'Connor was a great fan of the 130-grain bullet. It starts fast, shoots flat, and out at 400 yards still has 1,200 foot/pounds of energy. For sheep and deer and such, it's indeed a fine choice. As a kid, I always preferred the 150-grain load–like Elmer Keith, I'm a believer in bullet weight! The 150-grain bullet is available in both round-nose and spitzer form, and of course the round-nose can't compare in downrange ballistics–but makes a good choice for black bear and such. With a spitzer bullet, the 150-grain bullet starts out slower but, due to its better ballistic coefficient, it holds velocity better. With aerodynamic bullets, it can offer as much as 1,500 foot/pounds at the 400-yard line.

These days, in my return to the .270, I've become a great fan of the 140-grain bullet. It starts out just a bit slower, true, but the 140s are built to go the distance, and indeed they do. All the factory-loaded 140s offer more than 1,400 foot/pounds at 400 yards. I don't plan to shoot quite that far, so perhaps more significant is that they retain over 2,000 foot/pounds at 200 yards and about 1,750 at 300 yards. Sighted 2½ inches high at 100 yards, the 140-grain load is dead-on at about 250 yards and just 3½ inches low at 300 yards. Drop at 400 yards is about 15½ inches. That's plenty flat for anyone's hunting needs!

A couple of years ago, I took a .270 Dakota and Remington's then-new 140-grain Extended Range factory loads to Scotland and then on to Austria, with red stag the game in both places. Now, the red stag is hard to characterize in North American terms. Biologically it's the same species as our elk, so it's a hardy, heavy-boned creature. But it's *much* smaller in the body, especially the Scottish variety. I'd suggest that Scottish stag are about the same size as caribou, while a big Austrian stag is at best the size of young bull elk.

Anyway, I shot three stags at ranges from a bit over 100 yards to a bit under 300 yards. All three were one-shot kills. Two Scottish stags, the closest shot and the longest shot, went less than 20 yard after the shot. The Austrian stag, by a margin the largest of the three animals, dropped in his tracks at about 250 yards. All three bullets penetrated fully and exited. To say that I was tremendously impressed with this load is a gross understatement, and I'll plan to use it a great deal more in the future.

Last fall, I went pronghorn hunting with Dwight Van Brunt of Burris scopes and *Outdoor Life*'s Joe Healey. Dwight had arranged to arm us with Remington .270s, of course mounted with Burris scopes, and shooting Remington's newest 135-grain Extended Range load. This one starts at 3,000 feet per second and 2,697 foot-pounds of energy, and also retains over 1,400 foot/pounds at 400 yards. I shot my pronghorn at quite a long distance, something a bit over 300 yards. Even at that range, bullet expansion was quite explosive, and among the three of us that proved consistent.

So, from the same company it appears you have both approaches to bullet performance within their "upgraded" line of Extended Range ammo: Great penetration and controlled expansion in the 140-grain load; and rapid expansion and tremendous shock in the 135-grain load. Neither approach is wrong, though it depends a bit on what kind of game you're hunting.

For me, I'll probably stick with 140-grain loads for most of my future hunting with the .270, though I might drop down to 130 or that 135 for pronghorn and small deer. If I felt the desire to take a .270 after elk (I doubt that I would, but you never know!), I'd choose a tough 150-grain load like a Nosler Partition spitzer. For black bear, I'd probably go with a round-nose 150-grainer, or I'd handload a 160- or 170-grain bullet. Like so many thousands of .270 users over the past 70 years, chances are I'd continue to be extremely happy with the cartridge.

.270 Weatherby Magnum: This initial Weatherby belted magnum is, like all of the Weatherby Magnums except the .224, .240, and the .378/.416/.460 trio of big boomers, based on the .300 Holland & Holland case. For the .270 Weatherby Magnum, Roy shortened the case to 2.545 inches, just a tad longer than the .270 Winchester's 2.540 case length. Of course, the fatter case and sharper shoulder give the Weatherby version much greater case capacity for significantly improved velocity.

Although you hear little about it, the .270 Weatherby is actually fairly popular among the Weatherby lineup–and to my mind it's a superb cartridge. Velocity improvement over the .270 Winchester is significant: a 130-grain bullet at 3,375 feet per second; and a 150-grain bullet at 3,245 fps. The former delivers up to 1,700 foot/pounds at 400 yards, depending on bullet aerodynamics; the latter can deliver over 2,000! By my own criteria, that of delivering 2,000 foot/pounds at the target, I simply cannot say that the .270 Weatherby Magnum with 150-grain bullet isn't an elk cartridge. I can say that I wouldn't choose it for elk, simply because I want more bullet weight and more frontal area, regardless of energy figures–but, as we've seen, the .270 Winchester will do the job on elk, and the .270 Weatherby will do it much more!

More significant, really, is the flat-shooting capability of this cartridge. Sight the 130-grain bullet three inches high at 100 yards, and it's dead-on at 300 yards and only 8½ inches low at 400 yards. The path of a spitzer 150-grain bullet is almost identical, due to its improved ballistic coefficient. Given the extreme velocity increase over the .270 Winchester (for which all .277 bullets are designed), bullet performance is generally more consistent with the heavier 150-grain slug, so that is definitely my choice with the .270 Weatherby Magnum.

I have used the cartridge some amount in both Africa and North America. Without a doubt, it's one of the best long-range cartridges available in the world. For sheep, goats, pronghorns, and deer in open country–and for hunting African antelope in short-grass savanna or desert country–it's awfully hard to beat. I have not personally felt that it hits game noticeably harder than the .270 Winchester–but the .270 Winchester is no slouch in that department, so seeing visual improvement is asking a lot. However, it is significantly flatter-shooting and does carry a good deal more energy at longer ranges.

This cartridge is Ed Weatherby's personal favorite due to its ranging abilities and light recoil. Ed is also one of the finest natural rifle shots I've ever seen. Some years ago in Colorado, we made a deer drive, and toward the end of the drive a nice buck came barreling along a sagebrush ridge about 250 yards opposite from where Ed was standing. Without hesitation, he dropped to a sitting position, brought his rifle up, swung with the deer, and fired–in much less time than it takes to read this sentence describing the action. Just as instantly the deer rolled headlong and lay still, absolutely pole-axed by one of the prettiest shots I have ever seen in my life. I only wish I'd made it–but I doubt that I've ever been capable of a performance like that!

A few years ago, I took a .270 Weatherby Fibermark on a Stone sheep and mountain-goat hunt in northern B.C. We never got a shot at a ram, which certainly wasn't the rifle's fault, but I did take a very nice goat. It wasn't a difficult shot, nor a long shot. After a very long and very scary stalk in precipitous country, we came in 100 yards above the goat and shot him when he stood from his bed. That wasn't much of a test of the .270 Weatherby's capabilities–but few animals can stand as much punishment as mountain goats, and I was very impressed at the way that 150-grain Nosler anchored the billy.

The only fly in the ointment with the .270 Weatherby Magnum–and it isn't really a drawback in the open country this cartridge is best-suited to–is that, like the .264 Winchester Magnum, it really deserves a 26-inch barrel to wring full velocity out of the cartridge, while the .270 Winchester is just fine with a tube as short as 22 inches.

Hunters who love the .270–in either persuasion–will continue to use it with great satisfaction for game up to elk and beyond. I won't; I see the .277-caliber as superb in the plains and mountains for game up to 350 pounds or so, and those are the uses I have for the cartridge. But I'll certainly not sell it short. It was great when Jack O'Connor first adopted it in 1925–and it remains just as useful and just as effective today.

Chapter 6
The Non-Belted Sevens

It's impossible to say why one caliber has become more popular than another, or why one caliber has done better in some places than others. The 6.5mm never made it in America. The .270 never made it big in Europe. Neither, in a big way, did the .30-caliber, 7.62 in metric terms. The 8mm, caliber .323, was and is extremely popular in Europe, but has been a flop on this side of the pond.

If bigger is better, then the .277 is better than the .264–and the .308 better than either. If the 6.5s strength is long bullets with high sectional density, then make longer, heavier bullets for the .277–but neither the constants nor the variables change from one side of the ocean to the other. And there's no way for rational folks to figure it other than to accept that some bore diameters have more appeal in some locales than others.

A big part of it is tradition. In Europe, the 8mm goes back to 1886; the 6.5mm back to 1892. In those years–and in years between them and subsequent to them–both bore diameters were adopted in military rifles by major powers. In America, the .30-caliber goes back to 1892, when the U.S. Army adopted the .30-40 Krag. It stands to reason that both the 6.5mm and the 8mm should be popular in Europe, and they are. It also stands to reason that the .30-caliber should be popular in America.

On the surface, it's a bit puzzling that the 7mm, bore diameter .284, should be as popular as it is in both Europe *and* the New World. After all, the 7mm has the same long tradition in Europe. The 7x57 Mauser was introduced in 1892. It saw service against the British in the Boer War, where it convinced a generation of British troopers that it was superior to their .303. In the same year of1898, it saw service against the Americans in Cuba, where it likewise convinced American troops of its superiority over the .30-40 Krag and .45-70 Springfields that many units were still armed with.

Although the 7x57 saw extensive use in World War I and performed admirably, if less prolifically, in World War II, perhaps it's those early turn-of-the-century encounters that gave the caliber its world-wide fame for all time. Along with the other early military smokeless cartridges, the 7x57 quickly found its way into civilian hands, and hunters found it performed as well in the game fields as on the battlefields. The British soon adopted it as their own, renaming it the .275 Rigby but changing neither load nor dimension.

The 7x57 rapidly achieved limited popularity in America. After World War I, both the Remington Model 30 and Winchester Model 54 were so chambered, as were other rifles of the day. American ammunition was loaded as well, although by 1940 the 7x57 had lost much ground to the .270 and seemed to be dying away.

In Great Britain and Europe the, 7x57 achieved lasting popularity–and spawned a great many fine cartridges using the same bullet diameter. Before 1920, the English alone created such 7mm cartridges as the .275 Belted Rimless Magnum Nitro Express, or .275 H&H; the 7mm Rigby Magnum; the .280 Rimless; and the .280 Flanged Nitro Express. In Europe, there were fewer 7mm cartridges, but there were some very good ones, including the 7x64 Brenneke and its rimmed counterpart, the 7x65R. Then there was the Canadian .280 Ross.

Both the .280 Ross and the .275 H&H achieved some popularity in America, but nothing like the popularity of the 7x57. The 7x57's strong suit was long, heavy bullets at moderate velocity. The bullets penetrated well and performed marvelously, giving the 7x57 a reputation on game that far exceeded its paper ballistics. The .280 Ross and .275 H&H offered extremely impressive paper ballistics, pushing light bullets very fast for the day. But bullet technology hadn't yet caught up with the velocity. The .280 Ross, particularly, gained the unfortunate reputation of getting numerous African hunters killed or maimed by lions. Both cartridges died away in America, while the 7x57 hung on. But, perhaps surprisingly, it did not spawn a great number of 7mm offspring until well after World War II.

The first modern American 7mm cartridge was Roy Weatherby's 1944-vintage 7mm Weatherby Magnum. Next was the 7x61 Sharpe & Hart in 1953–and then the parade began. Since then we've seen the .280 Remington, the 7mm Remington Magnum, the .284 Winchester, the 7mm-08 Remington, the 7-30 Waters, and a host of 7mm wildcats.

The 7mm bullet diameter has been the darling of many of America's top gun gurus for decades. Warren Page, P.O. Ackley, and even Elmer Keith wildcatted hot belted 7mms, and were at least partly responsible for the creation of the great 7mm Remington Magnum. Other great writers and hunters saw in the 7mm a bore diameter that didn't need belted cases and ultra-high velocities. Jack O'Connor himself was a great fan of the 7x57. His wife, Eleanor, a great hunter in her own right, used little else. Jim Carmichel was a great early fan of the .280 Remington–and remains so to this day. Ken Waters even figured the 7mm could give new life to the old '94 Winchester, and the 7-30 Waters was the result.

The hallmark of the 7mm is a pleasing combination of bullet weight and sectional density that creates efficiency on game that is hard to excel. This applies to standard and magnum cartridges alike. In terms of velocity alone, it's sometimes hard to say where the magnum sevens start and the non-magnums end. Efficiency is such that only a tiny gap exists between the largest unbelted and the smallest belted 7mms. But for purposes of this discussion, we'll draw the line and confine ourselves to the non-belted 7mms, with the magnum versions to come in the next chapter.

In factory cartridges, these non-magnums are the 7-30 Waters, 7mm Bench Rest Remington, 7x57 Mauser, 7mm-08 Remington, .284 Winchester, .280 Remington, and 7x64 Brenneke. The 7-30 Waters and 7mm B.R. are special-purpose cartridges, actually better suited to single-shot handguns than rifles. The rest are all fine hunting cartridges, period. They differ in the ranges at which they should be used, and in their ability to maintain velocity with the heaviest 7mm bullets. But none of them are cartridges to sneeze at. Nor are they more limited than the magnum sevens in the game they're suitable for–they're just a bit more restricted in their suitable *ranges*. Each one of these non-magnum sevens, including the mild 7-30 Waters and 7mm BR, is a fine hunting cartridge in its own right and deserves further discussion.

7-30 Waters: Following several years of wildcatting development by Ken Waters, U.S. Repeating Arms Company introduced the 7-30 Waters in their Model 1894 Winchester in 1983. Firing a 120-grain bullet at 2,700 feet per second (from the 24-inch-barrel version of the '94), it does indeed shoot significantly flatter than the .30-30 cartridge most traditional for the '94. It was not particularly popular, however, and U.S.R.A.C. has dropped the 7-30 from the Model 94 lineup.

At short range, it performs well on whitetails, but it loses too much energy long before it loses effective range. Sighted 2.6 inches high at 100 yards, it's dead-on at 200 yards and 12 inches low at 300 yards. The problem is that it's already below 1,000 foot/pounds at 200 yards, and has only 685 foot/pounds remaining at 300 yards. Even with the best loads, the .30-30 isn't much better–but nobody ever said the .30-30 was even a 200-yard cartridge!

The 7-30 might well have become just a footnote to 7mm history were it not for the handgun hunters. Thompson/Center started offering 7-30 Waters barrels for the Contender shortly after the cartridge was introduced, and it has become a popular deer cartridge among handgunners. In a handgun, it has the decided advantage of spitzer bullets, whereas in the '94 lever-action flat-points or very blunt round-nose slugs are required. Velocity is lower with the T/C's 14-inch barrel, of course; a 120-grain bullet can be pushed about 2,450 feet per second and a 140-grain bullet about 2,250 feet per second. The former load, even with spitzer bullets, runs out of steam almost as quickly as the 120-grain flat-nose from a rifle, but it does carry a bit over 1,000 foot/pounds to 200 yards. A 140-grain spitzer, even at the relatively slow 2,250 fps muzzle velocity, also carries 1,000 foot/pounds beyond 200 yards.

Outdoor writer Larry Weishuhn, a dedicated handgunner and T/C Contender fan, swears by his 7-30 Waters for white-tailed deer. By using fairly frangible bullets that will open at the lower velocities, he has had nonslip success with the cartridge, even on big-bodied Northern whitetails. But in rifles, the 7-30 Waters is badly underpowered for the ranges it's capable of, and should be considered pretty much a dead issue.

7mm Bench Rest Remington: The 7mm B.R. is based on a shortened .308 Winchester case specially made with a small-rifle primer pocket. For many years, it was strictly a handloading proposition, but was becoming an extremely popular chambering for the XP-100 and similar single-shot specialty pistols. As its name implies, the 7mm B.R.'s strong suit is accuracy–and its short (1.520-inch) case is extremely efficient in the 14- and 15-inch barrels of these handguns. It's actually part of a family of Bench Rest wildcats that include the .22 and 6mm B.R. Remingtons. As the caliber goes down, making the cases becomes ever more difficult. Actually, starting with .308x1 ½-inch cases, even making the 7 B.R. cases isn't easy. Largely at the urging of dedicated handgunners like Bob Milek and Dave Hetzler, Remington eventually offered factory brass. The next step was loaded ammunition, which is now available with a 140-grain soft-point bullet.

The 7mm B.R. retains its inherent accuracy, whether in a rifle or a pistol. Remington's 40XB target rifle has been so chambered, and in a rifle its velocity should be about 2,550 fps with a 140-grain bullet. In other words, it's a super-accurate cartridge that runs out of energy before it runs out of range.

In a handgun, where range is already somewhat limited, it's a real star. Attainable velocities are about the same as for the 7-30 Waters, but the inherent accuracy of the 7mm B.R., mated to a bolt-action pistol with a good scope, makes it an ideal choice for long-range handgunning. With a 140-grain bullet started at 2,550 fps, it carries 1,000 foot/pounds all the way to 250 yards–which is a very sensible limit for handgunning deer-sized game.

The cartridge was a favorite with both Bob Milek and Dave Hetzler for pronghorn and deer, and Remington's long-time public-relations director, Dick Dietz, has also used it extensively, not only for deer and antelope at longer ranges but also for wild hogs at fairly close range. I've used it, too, and rate it one of the best handgun cartridges for use in open country. Unlike some of the full-size cartridges also available in handguns, it offers downrange efficiency at a very affordable cost in recoil.

7X57 Mauser: The good old 7mm Mauser is one of the world's great hunting cartridges. Although its popularity has stayed pretty constant in Europe, it went through a bad time in this country from about World War II until fairly recently. Its ballistics aren't flashy, and there was a time when Americans worshipped velocity above all else. Today it seems that the magnum craze is pretty much over and there's a resurgence of interest in mild-recoiling, efficient cartridges that just plain get the job done without a lot of fuss. Evidence of this trend can be seen in the increasing number of American-made 7x57 rifles, now including the big three of Remington, Ruger, and Winchester.

It can also be seen in modern factory loadings for the 7x57. Like the 6.5x55, traditional factory loadings have been pretty anemic, loaded mild on purpose for use in older actions. These loads aren't all that bad, by the way. The load that made the 7x57's reputation was a 175-grain soft-point at 2,440 feet per second. That long, heavy bullet at moderate velocity penetrates exceptionally well. Provided ranges are short, this remains a super choice for larger game. But for general use there are better choices today.

More or less standard is a 140-grain bullet at about 2,660 feet per second. The only factory load that currently exceeds that is Hornady's 139-grain boattailed spire-point at 2,700 fps. Energy is around 2,200 foot/pounds at the muzzle, not overly impressive. But that's where the aerodynamics of the 7mm take over. At 400 yards, every single 7x57 140-grain spitzer factory load still carries over 1,000 foot/pounds. That's impressive!

Unfortunately, in spite of such figures, current 7x57 factory loads remain quite mild for the sake of safe use in older rifles. The only fairly stiff factory load is Norma's 154-grain soft-point at 2,690 feet per second. It's a dandy, offering over 1,500 foot/pounds at 300 yards and nearly 1,300 at 400 yards–and it gives a taste of what handloaders can do with the 7x57, given a good rifle.

Most reloading manuals show no trouble taking a 140-grain bullet to 2,800 feet per second, and some show as high as 2,900. With a 150-grain bullet, 2,800 is no problem, but that's about where you start to run out of case capacity. It's more difficult to get a 160-grain bullet over 2,650 fps, and even harder to get a 175-grain bullet over 2,550 fps. Still, these reflect very significant increases over factory velocities and, regrettably, dictate that the 7x57 is at its best in the hands of shooters who handload.

Whether in factory or handload form, though, it's a wonderfully efficient little cartridge, and one of my personal favorites. With a 139- or 140-grain bullet, it's just right for small to mid-sized deer, all right for sheep, and plenty flat-shooting enough for pronghorn. With 150-grain bullets pushed fast, it's better for sheep and adequate for any deer hunting, provided ranges are kept within 250 yards, 300 at the most. With 160-grain bullets, it becomes an elk cartridge, again keeping ranges reasonable. And with a 175-grain bullet at close range, it's a fine black-bear cartridge and will do for any moose that walks. In truth, it's that bullet in solid form that has done in many an elephant; and in soft-point form, it has done the job on lion, tiger, and Kodiak bear. It will do the same today–but would not be my choice for such game.

I'll let Karamojo Bell shoot his elephants with the 7x57. For *my* purposes, the 7x57 is one of the best whitetail cartridges you can find, suitable for any whitetail hunting except those Northern giants I keep harping about. I'd use it on darn near any sheep hunt, provided I could load the ammo myself, and I'd use it for mule deer and even elk in country where I could keep the range modest.

The director of the National Rifle Association's Whittington Center in New Mexico, Mike Ballew, is an old buddy of mine. He used to manage a place in northern California that was stiff with wild hogs. I have plenty of respect for wild hogs, and so does Mike. He should; he guided hunters to several thousand of them. Now, Mike is one of those rare guys who will admit that he doesn't like recoil. For his black-tailed deer on the ranch, he was always a fan of the .243 and .257 Roberts. But when he went hog hunting, whether for himself or to back up his clients, he got out a big gun. A big gun to him was a 7x57, and he never felt he needed more on even the largest hogs.

I've used the 7x57 on quite a few hogs, and it's extremely impressive. I remember one pig that I shot with a 150-grain Hirtenberger bullet, one of the largest pigs I've ever seen. He was in a deep ravine, and I crawled up to the edge and looked almost straight down at him. That little 7x57 drove him into the ground; he rolled down the steep ravine from sheer gravity, but never moved a muscle after the shot.

Until now, my shooting with 7x57s–and there's been quite a lot of it–has been with test guns; I'd never owned one, although I always planned to. Finally, I now have a wonderful 7x57 of my very own that Pennsylvania gunsmith Mark Bansner put together for me. It sports a fiberglass stock and is a real tackdriver. I envisioned it as a go-anywhere workhorse of a deer rifle and perhaps a sheep rifle. It arrived too late last fall for me to baptize it properly, so this spring I'm going to use it on a Montana black bear with one of those slow, unstoppable 175-grain slugs. I expect it will work as well for me as it did back in 1892!

7mm-08 Remington: Created by necking down the .308 Winchester case, the 7mm-08 was introduced in 1980 and is thus one of our newer hunting cartridges. Ballistically, it's very similar to the 7x57, but it has the distinct advantage of fitting into a short bolt-action or a lever-action like the standard-length BLR or Savage 99. It also has the advantage of factory ammo that is loaded very close to the cartridge's potential. Factory 140-grain ammo moves out at 2,800 feet per second or better, and Remington's new 154-grain ammo has a muzzle velocity of 2,715 fps.

If you're a handloader, you can beat the 7mm-08 with the 7x57; you've got more case capacity to work with. If you aren't a handloader, the nod must go to the 7mm-08. Of course, if you're exceptionally weight-conscious and want to build a rifle as light as possible, there's also no decision: go with the 7mm-08.

Like the 7x57, it's a wonderful little cartridge that has gained popularity with blinding speed. No, it won't do anything the 7x57 won't do. And vice versa, although with handloads the greater case capacity of the 7x57 dictates that it does a bit better with bullets of 160 grains or better.

The first time I was impressed with the 7mm-08 was on a pig hunt with Nosler's Chub Eastman. I'm not sure I'd actually *seen* a 7mm-08 before that! He plopped himself down and shot a very big boar with a 140-grain Nosler Ballistic Tip, one of the first shots at game fired with that then-experimental bullet. I was all set to back him up, but I was wasting my time. That little bullet went through the gristle plate, broke the on-shoulder, ruined the lungs, broke the off-shoulder, and then *exited* through the gristle plate on the other side. Since then I've often recommended the 7mm-08 as a fine choice for beginners. In fact, there may not be a better choice.

The 7mm-08 is one of the standard chamberings for Remington's XP-100 handgun. It's not a bad choice, although the case is really too big to be efficient in a handgun. However, it doesn't have the wrist-numbing recoil of a full-size .308, and provides both accuracy and reach. I shot a pronghorn last fall with an XP in 7mm-08, and had no trouble at all doing so. But then, with that cartridge, I didn't expect to have any trouble!

.284 Winchester: The .284 is a classic example of a cartridge designed to fit into a rifle action, rather than the other way 'round. It has a short, fat case with a sharp shoulder and a rebated rim, meaning the rim is smaller in diameter than the case body. Introduced in 1963, the cartridge was designed to offer .280 Remington performance in the Model 88 lever-action and Model 100 autoloader. This it does, as well it should. Although the rim is .30-06-size, the case body is almost as big as a belted magnum. Originally, it was offered with a very fast 125-grain load and a 150-grain load. The lighter bullet has long since gone away, leaving only the 150-grain load in factory form. Muzzle velocity is 2,860 feet per second, an insignificant 30 feet per second behind the 150-grain factory load for the .280. If the .284 has a limitation, it's the rifles it was designed to fit into. That 150-grain load is the limit for the .284. Or, better put, the 150-grain .284 is all that will fit into a Model 88 or Model 100 Winchester. Or, for that matter, into a Savage 99, which was also so chambered for a short time. Maximum overall length is 2.8 inches, which means heavier bullets can't be seated far enough out and begin to eat into powder capacity.

No production rifles are currently chambered for the .284. A few semi-custom and custom makers have latched onto the cartridge for use in short-action bolt guns, among them Mel Forbes' Ultra Light Arms. The theory is that, with a bit more overall length available, the cartridge can be loaded to exceed .280 Remington ballistics yet still fit into a short bolt-action. This is true—but the .280 can also be hopped up by seating bullets farther out, and for that matter its case can be improved, as many wildcatters have done.

With bullets up to 150 grains, there's no real distinction between the .280 and the .284. With heavier bullets, the .280 wins, unless the rifle is slightly out of the ordinary. Of course, saying a cartridge is almost identical to the .280 is no faint praise. The .284 is an excellent and under-rated cartridge—and in Model 88 or Savage 99 guise, quite possibly makes the most versatile lever-actions ever produced.

7x64 Brenneke: This popular European cartridge is ballistically identical to the .280 Remington (actually vice versa, since the 7x64 came first!). It has a slightly smaller head diameter than the .30-06 family, so the two cartridges are not interchangeable in any way, but loading data for the .280 is good for the 7x64. A superb cartridge in every way, it is almost never seen in the U.S., due to the proliferation of our own 7mm cartridges. Surprisingly, though, Remington offered not one but two 7x64 factory loads in 1994, the first time this cartridge has been loaded in America. Remington's ballistics for this load are 2,950 feet per second for a 140-grain pointed soft-point and 2,650 fps for a 175-grain Core-Lokt. Federal also now has a factory loading, a 160-grain Nosler Partition bullet at 2,650 fps.

.280 Remington: In the realm of non-belted 7mm's–and just possibly among *all* 7mm cartridges–this is saving the best for last. Utilizing the case capacity of the .30-06, the .280 offers far more velocity than the 7x57 is capable of, and it can handle heavier bullets than either the smaller-cased 7mms or the .270 Winchester. It cannot beat .30-06 velocities with like bullet weights, but 165-grain 7mm bullets will offer far better sectional density than 165-grain .30-caliber bullets, likewise 150s and so forth. The .280 Remington is one of the best general-purpose hunting cartridges in the world.

Oddly, although introduced clear back in 1957, the .280 is just now starting to receive the recognition and popularity it always deserved. The .280 was first introduced in Remington's Model 740 semiautomatic, then the 760 slide-action, and seemingly as an afterthought it was finally chambered in Remington's bolt-actions–originally the 721 series, and then the Model 700. Original factory loadings were mild, probably to ensure flawless functioning in the semiauto. Handloaders figured out right away what the cartridge was capable of, and wildcatters already knew; various forms of 7mm-06 wildcats had been popular for years. But the general public did not embrace the .280. I doubt that it was in danger of being dropped, but it was also in no danger of reaching stardom.

In 1979, Remington tried a name change. After all, it had worked for the .244/6mm, so why not for the .280? Factory loads were beefed up a bit and the cartridge was renamed the 7mm Express Remington. Well, eventually it was. A little-known piece of firearms trivia is that, although Remington had absolutely determined to change the name, there was some disagreement over what to change it to. A whole run of barrels got stamped "7mm-06" before "7mm Express Remington" was settled on. A very few rifles stamped "7mm-06," and even a couple of cartridges with that headstamp, made it out the door and may be encountered as genuine collector's oddities.

The new moniker sounded great, and the publicity that surrounded the change is perhaps responsible for the .280 finally getting on the map. But in the long run, the fancy new name didn't work. There was too much confusion between 7mm Express and 7mm Magnum, and in 1981–with a great deal less fanfare–the 7mm Express Remington became the .280 once again.

If a proliferation of factory rifles and an ever-increasing selection of factory loads are any indication, the .280 has finally made it. Chances are it will never catch up with either the .270 or the .30-06 in popularity, but it has certainly become one of America's more accepted hunting cartridges. Of course, it's been the favorite of serious rifle cranks for many years. As mentioned earlier, *Outdoor Life's* Jim Carmichel has touted the cartridge for years, and almost certainly can claim some responsibility for its ultimate acceptance. Former Kenya professional hunter Finn Aagaard swears by it as well. Both men use it on game up to and including elk with no reservations whatever.

Factory loads run from 120 grains to 165 grains, but of course the cartridge can handle the full gamut of 7mm bullets–and has the case capacity to obtain acceptable velocities out of even the heavy 175-grain bullets. To my mind, the most useful bullet weights in this cartridge range from 140 to 165 grains. For small deer and pronghorn, the 140-grain load gives all the reach you need; factory velocities run from 3,000 to 3,050 feet per second, depending on the brand. For larger deer and sheep, a 150-grain load at almost 2,900 fps is a good choice. And for caribou and larger game, a 160- or 165-grain load at a bit over 2,800 fps makes a good choice.

As a handloader, I tend not to be too much of an experimenter. I load for a number of rifles, so I like to find one or two loads that work extremely well and stick with them. In my .280, I pretty much settled on a near-maximum charge of Hodgdon 4350 and 160-grain bullets. For lighter game, I use a Sierra boattail; for heavier game, a Nosler Partition. My load is a bit faster than the factory load, around 2,900 fps. It carries 2,000 foot/pounds beyond 300 yards, and the long, aerodynamic 160-grain bullet shoots extremely flat. Sighted just two inches high at 100 yards, it requires no holdover at 300 yards.

Although I would not hesitate to, I have not used the .280 for elk. I have used it for a wide variety of deer hunting, and it's one of my favorites for backpacking for sheep and other mountain game. The belted 7mms give a slight velocity edge, and thus a bit more reach without holdover–but not as much as you might think. In factory loads, the 7mm Remington Magnum is only some 150 feet per second faster, and handloading doesn't really open the gap. A gain of 150 fps is not insignificant, but achieving it requires a longer barrel, generally a somewhat heavier rifle, and a whole bunch more powder. The belted 7mms are very good, but they are not necessarily more useful or more versatile than the .280–and certainly they are not as efficient. For many years, only handloaders could realize the full potential of the .280. Today there are a number of very fine factory loads, including some with outstanding hunting bullets.

If there's a disadvantage to the .280, it's simply that it requires a full-length action and cannot be built into so light a rifle as the 7mm-08 or .284. Nor does it have the charismatic appeal of the 7x57. But each of our non-belted sevens is a fine hunting cartridge in its own right, and undoubtedly that's why each continues to find a market among American hunters.

Chapter 7

The Magnum Sevens–Was Warren Page Right?

As we have seen, a .284-inch bullet diameter is both a useful and versatile caliber to build hunting rifles around. Sectional density is pretty good on light bullets that can be driven fast–and truly outstanding on heavy bullets in the 160- to 175-grain weight. If mild cartridges like the 7x57 and 7mm-08 Remington are good, then faster numbers like the .280 must be even better. And if that's true, then true high-velocity 7mms that can push the heaviest bullets at speeds approaching (or exceeding) 3,000 feet per second must rank among the ultimate in hunting cartridges.

Warren Page, longtime Shooting Editor of *Field & Stream*, certainly thought so. He was a lifetime proponent of fast 7mms for all but the heaviest game, and he had the credentials to know what he was talking about. Perhaps best known as a rifle technician through works such as his classic *The Accurate Rifle*, Page was a much more experienced hunter than he is often given credit for. Although he was not as experienced a sheep hunter as O'Connor (who is?), he had extensive experience hunting bears and antlered game in North America, and was much more experienced in African hunting than O'Connor or any other writer of his generation. He felt that long, heavy-for-caliber 7mm bullets pushed at higher velocities than the 7x57 was capable of were the ultimate both for long-range work and for obtaining deep penetration on virtually any thin-skinned game.

Page wasn't entirely wrong, nor were his ideas altogether new. As mentioned in the previous chapter, there have been high-velocity 7mm cartridges since the early years of this century. As a cartridge, there's absolutely nothing wrong with the .275 H&H–especially with modern powders and bullets. Likewise the unbelted .280 Ross. Throughout late '40s and '50s, many prominent hunters and writers clamored for a commercial 7mm cartridge with lots of powder capacity. Page's was the loudest voice, but hardly the only one. Why there seems to have been almost no interest in reviving the .275 H&H or the Ross I simply can't say.

Nor do I understand why the first–and still the fastest–of the American 7mms was all but ignored. Roy Weatherby's 7mm Weatherby Magnum is not a new development. It saw the light of day in 1944, and thus was one of the first of the Weatherby Magnums. Like the .270 Weatherby Magnum, it's based on a shortened and blown-out .300 H&H case. In fact, except for being very slightly longer and possessing Weatherby's distinctive shoulder, it's very similar to the much later and much more popular 7mm Remington Magnum. Certainly it will do everything both the Remington and the numerous wildcats that led up to the Remington will do.

For reasons unknown to me, Weatherby's cartridges were considered "hands off" by the major manufacturers until very recently. Remington rarely hesitated to chamber rifles for a Winchester cartridge, such as the .270 Winchester; and Winchester rarely hesitated to chamber rifles to a Remington introduction, like the 7mm Remington Magnum. But the larger manufacturers steered clear of Weatherby's cartridges, similar to Great Britain's "proprietary" system whereby .350 Rigby rifles were made only by Rigby, while .425 Westley Richards rifles were made only by Westley Richards. Some cartridges, like the .375 H&H, were released to the gun trade and made by everyone–but only with approval of the originator. Almost certainly, Roy Weatherby preferred to have a monopoly on his rifles and ammunition for them; it was part of the mystique he created. Only recently have other companies begun making rifles and ammunition for Weatherby cartridges. That's probably unfortunate, certainly for the other manufacturers since they had to spend research-and-development dollars covering ground Weatherby had covered long before.

Quite possibly, it was unfortunate for Weatherby, too, but that's an open question–would Weatherby have sold more or fewer rifles over the years if his cartridges were better known and more available? No one can say for sure.

It can be said, for sure, that since 1944 a perfectly viable and very effective American 7mm magnum has existed–but gun cranks kept clamoring for one, as if the Weatherby didn't exist. In 1953 they got another in the form of the 7x61 Sharpe & Hart. This is a most unusual belted magnum in that it has a slightly smaller rim and body diameter than the .300 H&H case that spawned almost all of its kin. It's also a good deal shorter, having a case length of 2.394 inches whereas most of our "short" belted magnums have cases around 2.5 inches (the 7mm Weatherby Magnum's case is 2.545, while Remington's version is 2.500). Not by coincidence, about the maximum case a .30-06-length action can handle is just over 2.5 inches. Developed by handloading authorities Phil Sharpe and Richard F. Hart in the years following World War II, the 7x61 was available in factory rifles only from the Danish firm of Schultz & Larsen; and Norma loaded the only factory ammunition. It achieved some popularity in the years before the 7mm Remington came along. Quite a number of custom 7x61 rifles were made, and a great many more rifles were rebarreled or rechambered to handle it.

It's an efficient little cartridge, lagging just a bit behind the Remington and Weatherby in potential velocity. Chances are it would have had quite a future had the 7mm Remington Magnum not been introduced. But it was, in 1962. Despite the presence of both the Weatherby and the Sharpe & Hart, not to mention the long-forgotten Holland & Holland and Ross cartridges, the 7mm Remington Magnum was touted as the answer for all who had prayed for a fast 7mm cartridge.

It took off very quickly and has never looked back, becoming a world-standard hunting cartridge in a relatively short time. In the process of becoming so popular, it literally blew several good cartridges into a very obscure corner if not off the market. The 7x61 almost vanished, and the 7mm Weatherby Magnum survived, of course, but has remained one of the lesser-known of the Weatherby Magnums.

Ballistically, all three of these 7mm cartridges are very similar; all send bullets up to 154 grains well over 3,000 feet per second, and the slowest of them can reach 2,900 fps even with 175-grain bullets. We'll briefly discuss the advantages and disadvantages of each, but first let's investigate what a hot 7mm magnum is all about.

First off, I have no patience with bullets under 150 grains, regardless of which of these cartridges you prefer. The beauty of the 7mm is its bullet weight for caliber, the sectional density and, with good aerodynamics, the high ballistic coefficient that enables long, stable 7mm bullets to retain their velocity and energy over the long haul. And, perhaps more importantly, to provide deep, straight-line penetration on game.

All of the 7mm cartridges shoot bullets that do these things. The difference with the belted 7mms is that they have enough powder capacity to drive the heaviest 7mm bullets at very impressive velocities. Yes, you can push a 139- or 140-grain bullet at sizzling speed. But these shorter bullets shed velocity and energy at a much greater rate than longer, heavier bullets–and under no circumstances will they penetrate as well or perform as consistently on game. The light bullets make much sense in the 7x57 and 7mm-08 because they can flatten the trajectory curve of these mild cartridges. But they make no sense with a magnum 7mm.

I'm personally a fan of the 160- to 165-grain bullets in the 7mm magnums. True, the ultimate bullet for larger game is the 175-grain bullet. And bullets of 150 to 154 grains make a lot of sense for long-range work on deer and sheep. It probably depends on how you view the 7mm magnums.

Without a doubt, the 7mm Remington Magnum is one of the most popular elk rifles in America. If that's your game, or if you use the caliber at its outer limits for moose and big bears, then the 175-grain slug is a sensible choice. I would use it on elk, and with a good bullet I wouldn't hesitate to use it on grizzly or moose. But none of these things is my primary use for the hot 7mms.

I don't see them as giant killers, but rather as extremely versatile general-purpose hunting rifles. Big mule deer, perfect. Mountain hunting, just right. Caribou, ideal. whitetail hunting where the deer are big and the ranges can be long, no problem. As you've no doubt picked up on, I'm a big fan of plenty adequate calibers for hunting big Northern whitetails. On two Alberta hunts and several in Montana, the 7mm Remington Magnum has been my choice. I've also used the cartridge on game as small as Coues deer and as big as moose, and I've taken it to Africa and

Here's the epitome of a modern hunting rig—a bolt-action with muzzle brake (in this case a Browning BOSS) and a high-power variable (Leupold's 4.5-14X). The author admits, grudgingly, that the high-power variables are indeed handy in very open country.

When shooting rifle cartridges in shorter-barreled handguns, bullet selection is a bit different. These 7mm bullets between 115 and 154 grains have worked well in the 7mm Bench Rest; heavier bullets may fail to open.

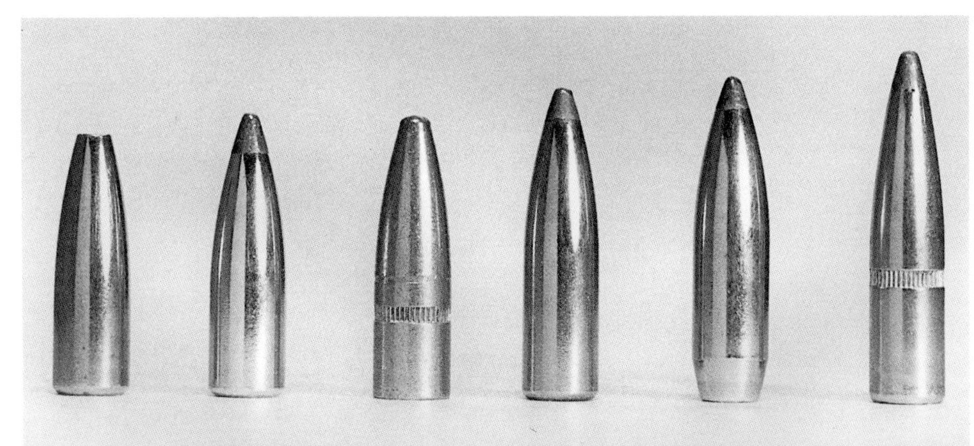

In terms of record-book quality, this Sitka blacktail is the author's best deer trophy. The shot was about 375 yards, and the author could not have done it with the .35 Whelen he carried. A hunting partner loaned him a well-zeroed .300 Winchester Magnum, and it saved the day.

The author's .280 Remington with a good Montana pronghorn. Always a fine choice, the .280 was enhanced by a fast handload with 150-grain Nosler Ballistic Tip and a Harris bipod to help steady the shot.

After 21 years of applying, the author banked his long-dreamed-of Montana sheep tag on a Dakota Model 76 in .270 Winchester, an extremely traditional choice that worked just as well now as it has worked for nearly 70 years.

This caribou was one of three animals shot during an Alaska mixed-bag hunt. The .300 Weatherby used to kill this caribou has more power than needed for this animal, but is just right for a grizzly. (SP Photo Library)

North America has little native game ideally suited to the .22 centerfires. The blackbuck antelope, introduced from India, is a perfect example of game that something like a .22-250 would be absolutely perfect for.

In areas where rifles are legal for turkey hunting, a .22 Hornet is ideal. This tom was shot with a .22-250, which is much too destructive for body shots but accurate enough to make head and neck shots practical.

This is the kind of country where the .264 shines. It's not really the powerhouse it was touted to be, but with good handloads it is one of the flattest-shooting cartridges around.

A .22 Hornet was used to drop this South Carolina whitetail in his tracks. It was legal, and the hunter knew exactly what he was doing. Of course it can be done–but only by patient hunters willing to pick their shots and place them precisely.

The .340 Weatherby Magnum was used to take this mountain grizzly. The range was very long for this kind of animal, something over 200 yards--but the .340 takes the guesswork out of that kind of shooting.

A Ruger No. 1 in .243 has been one of the author's favorite rifles for pronghorn and small deer since the late 1970s. It is not a long-range rig, but makes a superb stalking rifle.

All deer are not created equal. There's a big difference between an adequate cartridge for the average 2½-year-old "eatin," buck and a fully mature trophy buck; the 6mms and lighter .25s are fine for the former but marginal for the latter.

Where decoys are safe to use or where the ground allows close stalking, cartridges like the .243 are outstanding for pronghorn, but in open country where shots beyond 200 or 250 yards are likely, something with a bit more downrange energy is desirable.

The author used a .257 Weatherby Magnum on this mouflon, taken from a free-ranging Texas herd. The cartridge should have been devastating on so small an animal, but was just adequate. Such anomalies occur, which is why conclusions shouldn't be drawn from limited field experience.

Outdoor writer Gary Sitton took this fine Texas whitetail with a Dakota single-shot .25-06. The .25-06 is especially popular in Texas, as well it should be. Few cartridges shoot flatter for those long *senderos*, and the power range is ideal for mid-sized Texas bucks.

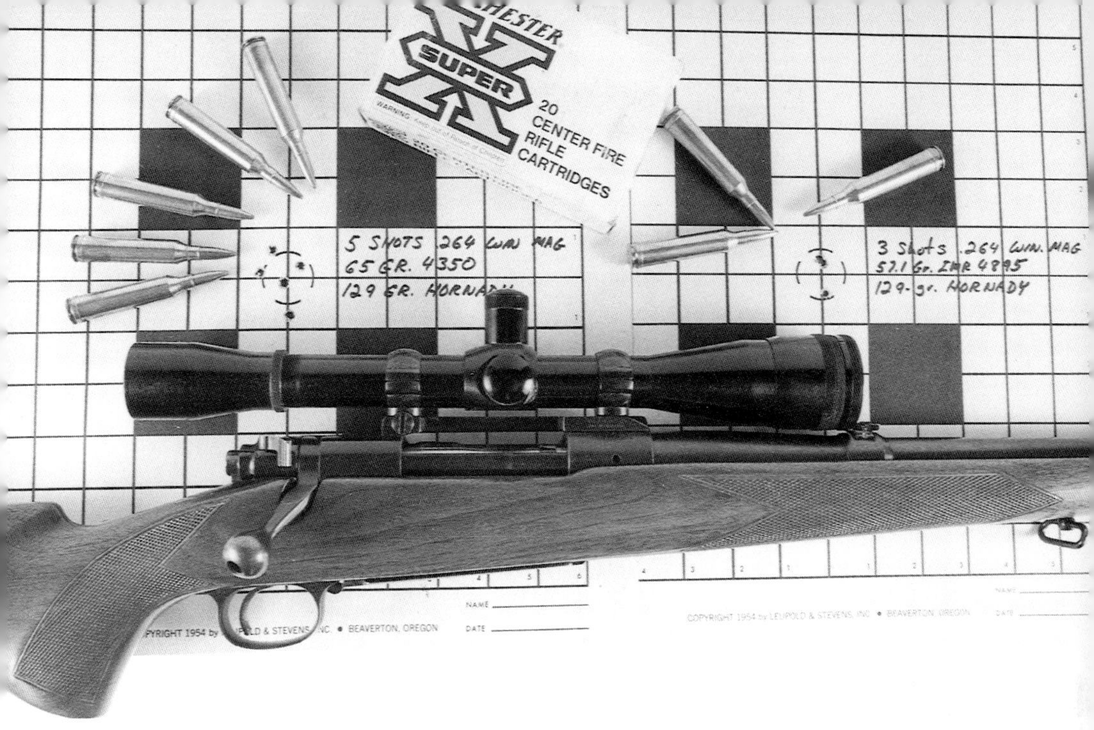

The Model 70 Westerner with 26-inch barrel was the original .264 Winchester Magnum. It created quite a stir and was becoming very popular until the 7mm Remington Magnum blew it off the market. It's a surprisingly accurate cartridge and remains a wonderful open-country choice.

The author's .25-06 is based on a Ruger M77 Mark II action. With good bullets like the Barnes X or Remington's 122-grain Extended Range factory loads, it's an ideal pronghorn rig, and just as ideal for blacktails, Coues deer, and all but the largest varieties of whitetail.

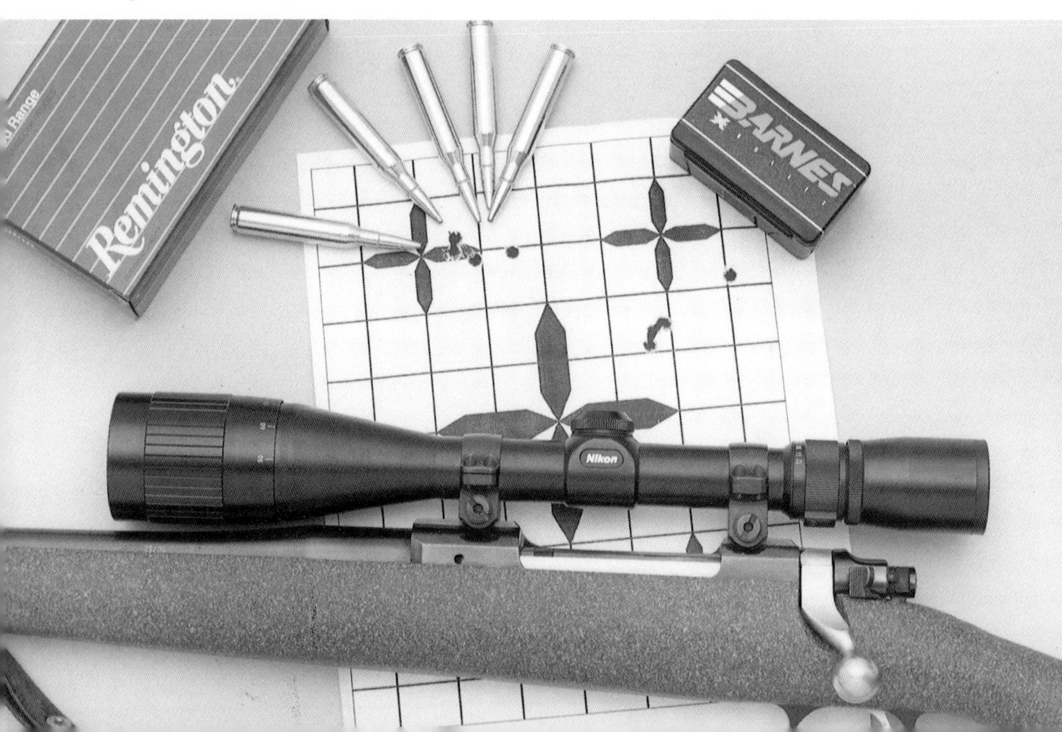

Remington's Model 7400 is the best-selling semiauto hunting rifle in America. It's accurate, reliable, and available in chamberings for a variety of fine hunting cartridges.

Winchester's John Falk used a Model 100 in .308 on this California wild hog. The Model 100 semiauto, now discontinued, was a companion to the Model 88 lever-action.

Left to right: .243 Winchester, 6mm Remington, .250 Savage, .257 Roberts, .25-06. These are the cartridges most people consider dual-purpose varmint and big-game rounds. The 6mms are better choices for varmints and the .25s better choices for big game, but all do, indeed, bridge that gap effectively.

Arizona guide Butch Saunders with a superb Coues deer. Normally a .270 Winchester is not needed for a 100 lb. buck like this one; however, the terrain is rough and the shots are often long in Coues-deer country. A little extra gun makes sense under these circumstances. (SP Photo Library)

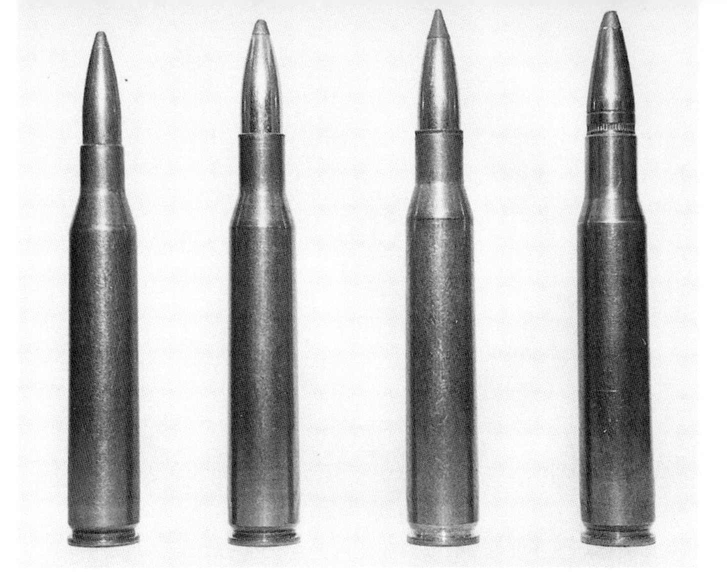

Left to right: .25-06 Remington, .270 Winchester, .280 Remington, .30-06. All of these cartridges based on the .30-06 case are versatile and flat-shooting, and all have their following. In both ballistics and performance, the .270, .280, and .30-06 are surprisingly similar.

The Russian bear is essentially identical to his cousin, the Alaskan brown bear. This is a particularly large specimen, taken with a .340 Weatherby Magnum firing 250-grain Nosler Partition bullets.

The author had his scoped .338 Winchester Magnum when he had a chance at this beautiful Alberta cinnamon bear. Good thing, too, since the range was 250 yards and no chance to get closer.

The family of factory cartridges based on the .308 Winchester case consists of, left to right: .358 Winchester, .308 Winchester, 7mm-08 Remington, .243 Winchester. Although the .358 has lagged in popularity lately, all four of these cartridges are stellar performers.

A 7mm Remington Magnum with 160-grain Nosler Partitions was used on this Quebec caribou. In open, windy country, the 7mm really shines.

This record-class Alaskan bull was taken with the then-new .416 Remington Magnum. It worked, but the truth is that moose are hard to impress. Shot placement with good bullets is much more important than sheer power.

A pet 7mm magnum was used for this Arizona pronghorn. Although that level of power is not required, there are lots of good reasons why the 7mm Remington Magnum has become the most popular belted cartridge in the world, and one of our most popular centerfires.

The .270 Winchester, shown next to a bighorn-sheep track, is the quintessential mountain-hunting cartridge—made so by Jack O'Connor's fine writing as much as its own considerable merit.

The .270 is just as perfect for pronghorn and deer as it is for mountain game. This skillet-size pronghorn was taken with one shot at 250 yards–easy pickings for a .270.

Left to right: .243 Winchester, 6mm Remington, .240 Weatherby Magnum, .257 Roberts, .25-06, .257 Weatherby Magnum, .264 Winchester Magnum, .270 Winchester, .270 Weatherby Magnum, .280 Remington. These flat-shooting cartridges all offer fine performance with light to moderate recoil. Those from the .25-06 upward are ideal all-round deer, pronghorn, and sheep cartridges–but all are on the light side for elk.

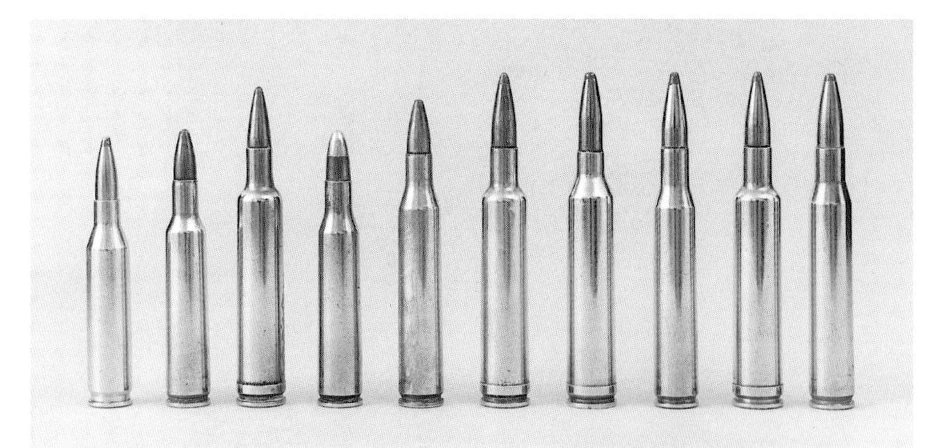

This Remington Model 700 in .280 has long been one of the author's favorite all-round rifles. In truth, for most hunting purposes a 7mm-08 or 7x57 would be equally suitable.

The author glassing for sheep in Montana's bighorn country. The rifle is a Dakota Model 76 .270--a classic mountain rifle in a classic caliber.

The author's .280 with 160-grain Nosler Partitions accounted for his best-ever mule deer, taken in Sonora.

The versatility of the .338 shouldn't be overlooked. Adrian Flores used a 200-grain Nosler Ballistic Tip loaded very fast to take his first pronghorn.

A custom-stocked Remington M700 in 7mm Remington Magnum was the choice on a Quebec caribou hunt. The 7mm magnum is a fine candidate for almost any North American hunt—but especially in open, windy country.

A Steyr-Mannlicher 7x57 accounted for this New Mexico pronghorn. The 7x57 requires handloads to realize its potential, but with good loads it's flat-shooting, efficient, and has very light recoil.

A lever action in .30-30 caliber is an ideal rifle for pumas. It is light to carry, and typically the shots on this game are very close, so a laser-like trajectory is not needed. The blunt-nosed .30 bullet transmits a great deal of energy making for instantaneous kills. (SP Photo Library)

The author's David Miller custom 7mm magnum took this exceptional California blacktail. That level of power is not needed for small deer, but there are few places where the 7mm Remington Magnum is out of place.

Left to right: .25-06, .257 Weatherby Magnum, .264 Winchester Magnum, .270 Winchester, .270 Weatherby Magnum, .280 Remington, 7mm Remington Magnum, 7mm Weatherby Magnum. These are among the best choices available for true open-country hunting, be it for pronghorn, caribou, or plains deer.

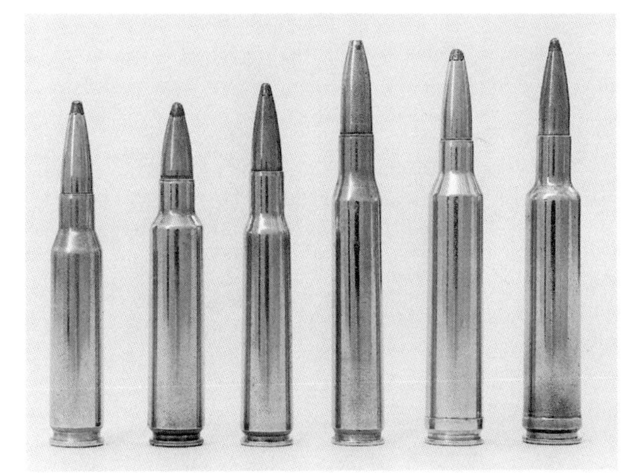

Left to right: 7mm-08 Remington, .284 Winchester, 7x57 Mauser, .280 Remington, 7mm Remington Magnum, 7mm Weatherby Magnum. All six of these 7mm cartridges are efficient, versatile deer hunting cartridges. The latter three will also kill elk under most circumstances.

Left to right: .35 Remington, .358 Winchester, .356 Winchester, .348 Winchester, .444 Marlin, .45-70, .35 Whelen, .308 Winchester, .30-06, 7mm Remington Magnum. Here's a gamut of outstanding black-bear/wild-boar cartridges. The four at right are ideal for stalking situations, while the rest are perfect for bait or hound hunting.

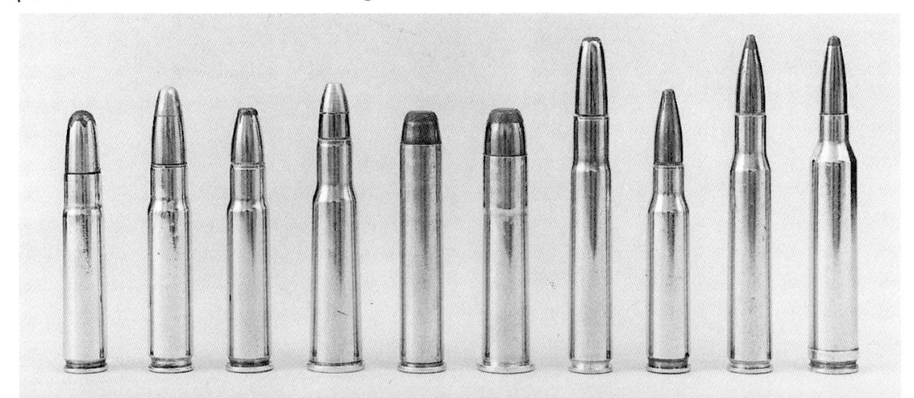

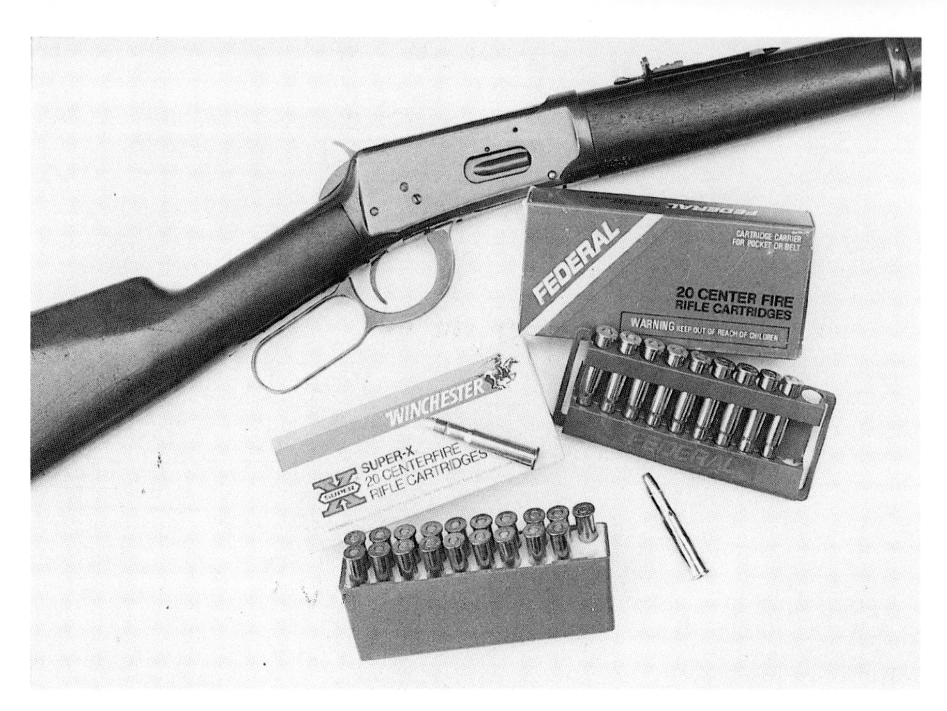

The great old .30-30 Winchester cartridge and equally great Winchester Model 94 remain amazingly popular after 100 years of production. And with good reason: The cartridge is effective, and the rifles so chambered are a pleasure to carry and shoot.

The author's current and best-ever .30-06 is a Model 700 from Remington's custom shop. It is still hard to imagine a better all-round North American rig than a good .30-06.

A short-barreled Model 94 Trapper .30-30 did a fine job on this lovely Texas whitetail–just as it's been doing on whitetails all over the country since 1895.

This Browning Stainless Stalker A-Bolt .30-06 printed groups like this right out of the box with factory ammo. The .30-06 may not be our most accurate cartridge–but it's sure no slouch!

Although, like everyone else of his generation, the author owned a 1903 Springfield in his youth, this Ruger M77, shown with Boddington's first Coues deer, was the first .30-06 he hunted with. It made him a true believer in the '06.

The .300 Winchester Magnum is said to be less accurate than many cartridges, and technically that's true. But hunting accuracy is another story. A good .300 Winchester Magnum will deliver all the accuracy any hunter needs.

You hardly need a .300 Weatherby for a Texas whitetail. However, excessive meat damage isn't a certainty. This buck was taken with a Speer Mag-Tip designed for high velocity. It did its work just fine and created no undue damage in the process.

This California blacktail was shot in open country with a .270 Winchester with a fiberglass stock. Given the large amount of rain in Northern California, a fiberglass stock is very practical for this type of hunting. (SP Photo Library)

The author's father (right) has never hunted with anything other than his custom-stocked Model 70 Featherweight in .308. He's taken not only pronghorn, but deer, bear, and moose with it. Like many who use it, he swears by the little .308.

A repeating version of the XP-100 pistol is now available. One of its chamberings is the ancient .35 Remington, which has received a new lease on life as a handgun cartridge.

In Alaskan bear country there's a great deal of comfort to be had in a .375. Although the .338 has made inroads, the .375 remains the arm of choice for most Alaskan brown-bear hunters.

Left to right: .250 Savage, .257 Roberts, .25-06, .257 Weatherby Magnum. This quartet represents our modern quarter-bore cartridges. All are useful and effective hunting cartridges.

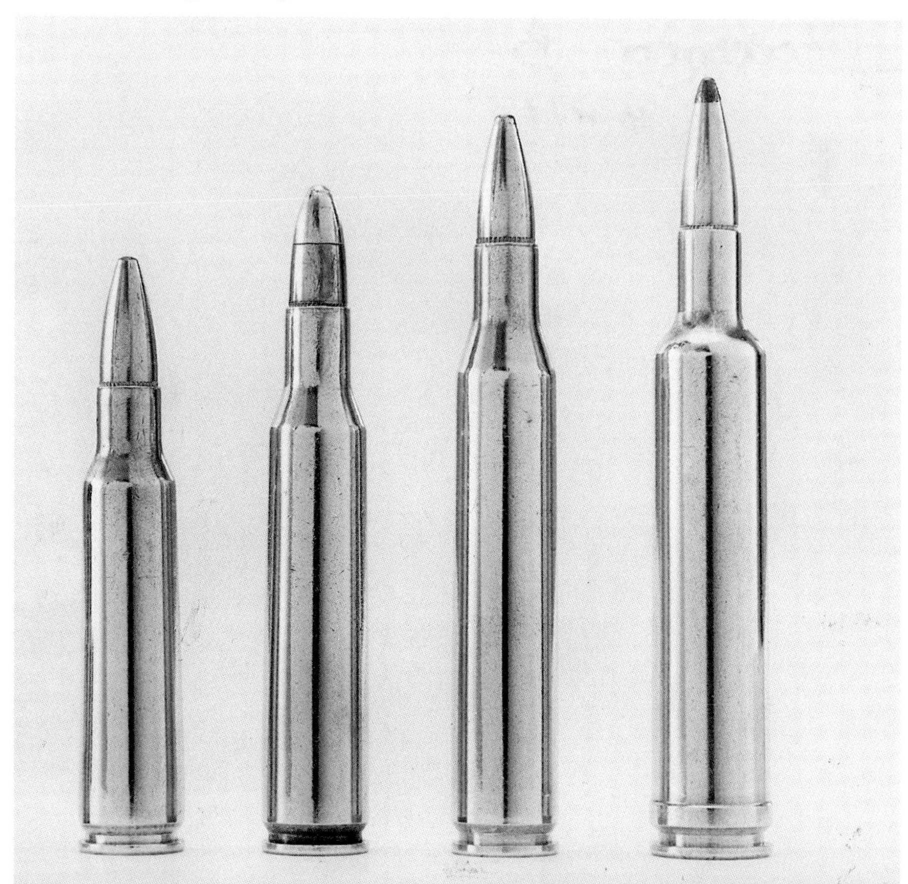

Left to right: .356 Winchester, .358 Winchester, .348 Winchester, .444 Marlin, .45-70. Here are some of the more powerful rounds offered in lever-actions today. All are quite capable of handling any elk or moose, and will serve for big bears in a pinch.

Left to right: .35 Remington, .358 Winchester, .350 Remington Magnum, .358 Norma Magnum, .35 Whelen. The entire family of .35-caliber cartridges is a capable, dependable bunch–but this bore diameter has never really caught the public's eye.

Grizzlies are never to be underestimated. This Alaskan specimen was shot with a .300 Weatherby using 180-grain bullets. A rifle of this caliber is an ideal set up for hunting in Alaska where animals as diverse in body weight as sheep and moose can be encountered. (SP Photo Library)

The instant acceptance and volume of sales were a real surprise to Remington when they chambered their slide-action to .35 Whelen. The Whelen gives real authority to a pump gun, and has remained a good seller in certain parts of the country.

A bonus to the .35 Whelen seems to be its inherent accuracy. This rifle was one of the prototypes, and was one of the most accurate out-of-the-box rifles the author has ever seen. Head-shooting grouse for the pot was no problem at all!

The .375 H&H is a big gun, but for most hunters its recoil is quite manageable. Adequate gun weight, which this Sako Safari Grade surely has, helps a great deal.

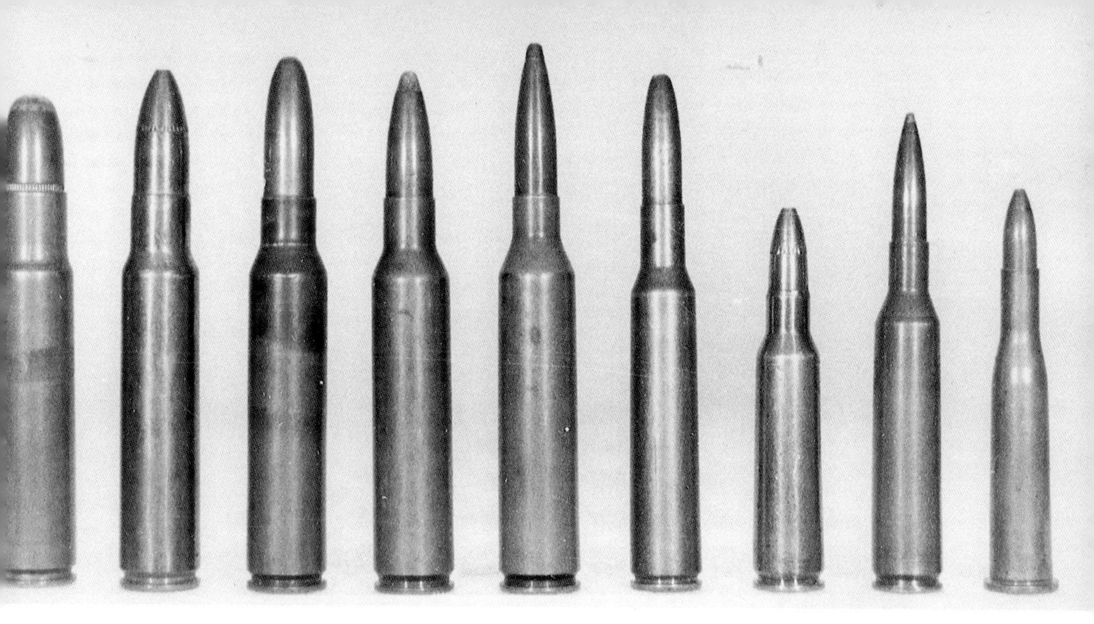

Charles Newton was a prolific inventor of very fine cartridges, mostly ahead of their time. Only the .250 Savage survives today. Left to right: .40 Newton, .35 Newton, .33 Newton, .30 Newton, .280 Newton, .256 Newton, .250 Savage, .22 Newton, .22 Savage Hi-Power.

Shown are three .338 bullets, all 200-grainers. The sectional density is identical, since that figure is weight in relation to diameter. Ballistic coefficiencts differ significantly, however, since BC takes into account shape and resulting aerodynamics.

This Brown Precision .375 is a bear hunter's dream–light, powerful, and impervious to the elements.

Joe Bishop took this beautiful brown bear with a .416 Remington Magnum. If there's a place for the over-.40 cartridges in North America, it's surely for use on our biggest bears.

used it on a wide array of plains game. I have used lighter bullets and heavier bullets, but the vast majority of the 100-plus big-game animals I've taken with the 7mm magnum have been with 160-, 162-, or 165-grain bullets. They shoot a bit flatter than 175-grain bullets, and have never failed to penetrate extremely well.

Now, I don't think the 7mm magnums are perfect. In fact, although I've used the 7mm Remington Magnum a tremendous amount, the cartridge actually isn't one of my personal favorites. In truth, it's not all that much faster than handloads for the .280 Remington, given bullets not heavier than 160 grains. To gain its velocity advantage, it needs a longer barrel and thus a heavier rifle, and of course the ammo is heavier and bulkier. The best rifle I own–and probably ever will own–is a David Miller 7mm Remington Magnum. It's a gorgeous rifle, not only exceptionally accurate, but unusually dependable as well. It hasn't shifted zero so much as half an inch since I got it six years ago.

As fine a rifle as it is, I've often said that the only thing wrong with it is that it's chambered to 7mm Remington Magnum. For hunting mountain game, I'd like the rifle better if it were chambered to .280. It would shoot just as flat, give or take fractions of inches, and it would have a higher magazine capacity and would use lighter, less bulky ammunition. For larger game, whether elk or the gamut of larger African antelope, I'd like the rifle better if it were chambered to .30-06. A 160- or 175-grain 7mm bullet is extremely effective, no doubt about it. But for game much larger than deer, I have more confidence in a 180- or 200-grain .30-caliber bullet. The 7mm magnums do shoot flatter–but at any but the longest ranges, the difference between a 175-grain from a 7mm Remington Magnum and a 180-grain spitzer from an '06 is pretty negligible.

Having gotten that off my chest, I should say that the hot 7mms are versatile, useful, and extremely deadly hunting cartridges. Like most of us, the one that I have in-depth experience with is the 7mm Remington Magnum. It has treated me very well over the years, and although I have a slight personal preference for unbelted cartridges in this general power range, I have no hesitation recommending–or using–the 7mm magnums for virtually the entire spectrum of North American hunting. Let's take a closer look at the three currently available 7mm magnums.

7x61 Sharpe & Hart: I believe the Danish firm of Schultz & Larsen, and perhaps a very few other European makers, still chamber rifles in this caliber. Norma still offers a 154-grain factory load at a very fast 3,060 feet per second. Although the 7x61 has become an "also-ran" to the 7mm Remington Magnum, it remains a very fine cartridge. Although it has slightly less powder capacity, current handloading manuals rate it the equal of the Remington number, bullet for bullet. That means that 160-grain bullets can be driven to 3,000 fps with relative ease, and 175-grain bullets can be pushed to 2,900 fps. With the greater availability of both the

Remington and Weatherby magnums there is no real reason to seek out a 7x61–but if you see one on a used-gun rack, there's also no reason to shy away from it.

7mm Remington Magnum: In terms of reloading-die sales and ammunition sales, Remington's "Big Seven" is not only the most popular 7mm cartridge in America; it's also the most popular belted magnum–probably in the world. It is a wonderfully effective cartridge and deserves both its popularity and its reputation. It propels those long, stable 7mm bullets at impressive velocities, thus delivering both flat trajectory and very high retained energy. It is also one of our most misunderstood cartridges.

You see, as effective as it is, the 7mm Remington Magnum is not a death ray. With carefully selected aerodynamic bullets of 160 grains and heavier, it can indeed carry 2,000 foot/pounds of energy to 300 yards, and in some cases almost to 400 yards. But it is not a 500-yard elk rifle. (Nor is anything else!) It does indeed, offer more than 3,000 foot/pounds at the muzzle–but it is not a charge-stopper for brown bear (or anything else!). It is extremely flat-shooting–but it does not shoot a great deal flatter than a .30-06, given similar bullet aerodynamics.

Here's an example. Federal's 160-grain Nosler Partition load for the 7mm Remington Magnum features a well-shaped spitzer at an impressive muzzle velocity of 2,950 feet per second. Sighted to be dead-on at 250 yards, it will be a bit less than four inches low at 300 yards and a bit more than 16 inches low at 400 yards. That ain't bad. Remington's Pointed Soft Point Core-Lokt 165-grain .30-06 load features another well-shaped spitzer, this one starting at 2,800 fps. Sighted to be dead on at the same 250 yards, this 165-grain '06 load will be about 4½ inches low at 300 yards and a bit over 20 inches low at 400 yards.

Sure, there's a difference. And the difference is enough to make the 7mm Remington Magnum a better choice if you know the range is going to be long–after all, at anything much past 200 yards most of us need all the help we can get. The point is that the difference isn't all that significant–and really isn't enough of a difference to cause a miss on deer-sized game. The .30-06 isn't a 500-yard elk rifle, either, not by any stretch. Nor is it a charge-stopper for brown bear. But if I had to choose between a 175-grain 7mm and a 180-grain .30-caliber, I'd go for frontal area. Better, I'd use a 220-grain .30-caliber, which no 7mm bullet can match.

None of this is said to knock the 7mm Remington Magnum, only to put it in proper perspective as a very fine game cartridge but not a giant killer nor the ultimate in long-range performance.

I have used it, and used it well, on a great many occasions. As I said, my favorite bullet weights run from 160 to 165 grains. This range seems to me to wring the utmost in downrange performance from the cartridge, yet the weight is adequate for almost anything that should reasonably be hunted with a 7mm.

For many years, my favorite load was a maximum charge of Hodgdon H870, a ball powder that meters beautifully and has delivered both very fine velocity and unbelievable accuracy from all of my 7mm magnums. A drawback to this load is that the H870 powder burns fairly dirty; a thorough cleaning is required after a dozen or so shots if accuracy is to be maintained.

Because of this, I have generally switched to Hercules RL-22. The accuracy is almost as good and the velocity even better. My chronograph tells me I get a bit over 3,050 feet per second with a 160-grain load. I can sight in to be dead on at 250 yards, and I'm good to nearly 350 yards without worrying unduly about holdover.

For deer-sized game I generally use a 160-grain Sierra boattail. It's accurate, it opens nicely, and I have a huge amount of faith in it. It was with that bullet, from my Miller rifle, that I shot my best-ever white-tailed buck. He had been horning a mesquite way down a Texas *sendero* for quite some time, and although I could have stalked closer I felt I was rapidly running out of time. Just one step and he could be in impenetrable brush, and it was very late in the morning. So I crawled up into a mesquite and, ignoring the thorns, grabbed a handful of twigs together to help support the fore-end. There was still a great deal of movement, with the rifle swinging wildly from one end of the deer to the other. He looked a long way out, too. Finally I got it steady enough, and I squeezed off with the horizontal crosswire showing just a bit of daylight above the backline.

He was a good 375 yards, the way I paced it–but not quite as far as I'd thought. I could well have overshot him, but I didn't. The Sierra boattail broke his spine at the shoulders and kept on going. Up close, it probably wouldn't have exited, but it's a bullet that I've had very good luck with over the years and I certainly did on that day.

For larger game, or for black bear or big mule deer, I'm more likely to choose a 160-grain Nosler Partition. I've had this bullet exit the ham of a quartering-on caribou that was shot in the front shoulder. And I've also had it penetrate fully from the other end. Now, I don't recommend a "Texas heart shot." It's a chancy shot, and before you even attempt it you should have (1) no other option and (2) a very good bullet from a pretty stout caliber. The last time I had to make such a shot was on a very fine, very big-bodied mule deer. He was in a clearing, but the rut was on and he was too covered up by does for a shot to be possible. They were all heading into some thick oak brush, and when the buck finally cleared he was stern-end to and still going away. I waited until he was almost in cover, hoping he would shift enough to offer at least some flank if not some shoulder. He never did, so I shot him from behind just before he entered the cover. He dropped in his tracks, and that Nosler Partition is still going for all I know.

As I've made plain, the 7mm Remington Magnum, at least philosophically, is not my favorite caliber. But two of the 7mm Remington Magnum rifles I've owned have been among my favorites, so I've used this cartridge a great deal: on pronghorn, mountain goat, Dall sheep, black bear, mule deer, white-tailed deer, Coues deer, black-tailed deer, and a variety of African and European game. With it I've made some of my longest shots, some of my best shots (and a couple of disastrous misses), and the shots that dropped some of my most prized trophies. It's an exceptionally versatile cartridge, and one of very few that can be considered a true all-round choice for anything save very large and very dangerous beasts.

7mm Weatherby Magnum: Everything that can be said for the 7mm Remington goes for the 7mm Weatherby–plus just a bit more. There is relatively little difference in case capacity between the two cartridges, so the Weatherby version is only very slightly faster. Its advantage, if there is one, is that Weatherby rifles traditionally sport 26-inch barrels, and this wrings out a bit more velocity. Weatherby ammunition, as loaded by Norma, is also generally a bit hotter than American factory loads.

Since the Weatherby already existed, there really has never been great justification for the creation of the 7mm Remington Magnum. But it was created, and is available in a bewildering array of fine factory loads. That being the case, there is really no reason to choose the 7mm Weatherby over the Remington–even though the Weatherby is theoretically a slightly better cartridge. Factory figures for the 160-grain 7mm Weatherby Magnum load suggest 3,200 feet per second with a 160-grain load and 3,070 with a 175-grain load. With a 26-inch barrel, Weatherby factory loads will come pretty close to these impressive figures, but duplicating them with currently published data is very difficult.

It's perhaps unfortunate that the Remington version became the world standard instead of the Weatherby, but there is very little noticeable performance difference between the two. Shooters who like the Weatherby Mark V rifle may choose the Weatherby version with perfect confidence, knowing they have one of the flattest-shooting factory cartridges available. Shooters who choose the Remington version instead, however, need not hang their heads in shame!

Chapter 8

The Un-Magnum .30s—America's Favorites

The military cartridge of any nation is very likely to become one of the most popular sporting rounds for that country's hunters. We've seen that in Sweden, where the 6.5x55 still reigns. In Spain—among many other countries—the 7mm is the most popular. In Germany, an 8x57 is encountered with unusual frequency. To an even greater degree, American hunters often choose a .30-caliber, bullet diameter .308. The .30-06 is one good reason for this. After all, it was America's service cartridge for more than 50 years, two world wars, and countless military interventions.

The .30-06 is not the only reason, however. It is just one of four .30-caliber American military cartridges that, collectively, have been in use for more than a century. First was the .30-40 Krag, or .30 U.S. Army. It saw the most limited use as a military cartridge, only from 1892 to 1903. But it brought the American military from black powder to smokeless, and it has had a much longer life as a sporting cartridge. Most recent is the .308 Winchester or 7.62mm NATO, adopted in 1954. In 1964, the M-14 rifle chambered to 7.62 began being phased out in favor of the much lighter 5.56mm M16, but the 7.62mm remains in use today as our light machine-gun cartridge and the chambering for our M24 sniper rifle. From World War II until the early 1960s, there was also the little M1 Carbine, originally conceived as a more combat-efficient replacement for a handgun—but issued in millions to officers, communicators, drivers, and whoever could get their hands on one. Its cartridge was, of course, the .30 Carbine—also caliber .308.

Unlike many popular calibers the world over, the all-American .30 had yet another boost to its lasting popularity. Shortly after the U.S. Army adopted the .30-40 Krag, Winchester introduced what would become its most popular lever-action, and one of the most popular sporting rifles of all time. This was the Model 1894 Winchester, still in production today after more than 100 years and many millions of guns. The original 1894 chamberings for the '94 were two older black-powder cartridges, the .32-40 and .38-55. But in 1895 Winchester unveiled what would become one of the most popular sporting cartridges of all time: the .30 Winchester Centerfire (WCF), or .30-30 Winchester.

By today's standards, the .30-30 seems a mild-mannered little round. But in the 1890s its original 160-grain bullet, at nearly 2,000 feet per second, was fast, flat, and offered unprecedented penetration. In the '94 it also offered those qualities in a compact, lightweight package. To get similar energy and penetration, hunters of the day were accustomed to carrying much heavier '76 and '86 Winchesters or big single-shots–and carrying big black-powder cartridges three times the bulk of the little .30-30.

Between the Model 94 and later Marlin .30-30 lever-actions, the .30-40 Krag, and America's beloved Springfield in .30-06, the stage was set. For a century now, the .308 bullet diameter has been an American standard, and this is unlikely to change. Generations of American hunters have started with–and often stayed with–.30s.

I'm certainly no exception. My Dad was a bird hunter, which made a lot of sense in our home state of Kansas. Deer were considered extinct in the state from the 1920s until after World War II, and our first modern season wasn't held until 1965. Pheasant and quail were abundant, and that's what Kansans hunted. Sportsmen who ventured to Colorado to hunt mule deer and elk were local heroes, and I knew few hunters who journeyed farther afield than that. I came to centerfire rifles early, at about the age of 11. But Dad got there at the same time because of my interest. His first centerfire rifle was, predictably, a Winchester Model 94 in .30-30. Mine was equally predictable: a surplus Springfield 1903 in .30-06. I think it cost all of $40 or a bit less.

Supplies of surplus Springfields ran out many years ago, and even Garands, much less suited to conversion to hunting rifles, command high prices today. I suspect huge numbers of beginning American hunters will continue to start with inexpensive .30-30 lever-actions, but the days of inexpensive converted Springfield bolt-actions are almost over. Even so, I seriously doubt if the caliber will fall from grace among American hunters during my lifetime!

Although overly simplistic, it's relatively easy to divide the .30-caliber cartridges into three groups: mild, relatively short-range cartridges, effective for close-cover deer and such; general-purpose .30 calibers that offer a bit more velocity and energy and thus cover a broader range of hunting needs; and large-cased .30s that offer the ultimate, for the caliber, in velocity and energy. We'll cover the last group–the magnum .30's–in the next chapter.

The classic cartridge among the first group is the .30-30 Winchester, but also included should be the 7.62x39 Russian and obsolete cartridges like the .303 Savage and .30 Remington. The second group probably starts with the .30-40 Krag and includes cartridges such as the .300 Savage and .307 Winchester as you work your way up to the .308 Winchester and .30-06. Although the M1 Carbine is a fun gun to shoot and perhaps has some utility for javelina and coyotes, the .30 Carbine's 110-grain bullet at under 2,000 feet per second is no deer cartridge and we won't discuss it further.

.30-30 Winchester and Kin: The .30-30 is so called after the custom of naming black-powder cartridges by the caliber and then the charge of powder. The .45-70, for example, used a .45-caliber bullet propelled by 70 grains of black powder. The .30-30's original loading used 30 grains of then-new smokeless powder–and in its day it was a red-hot performer. While it's the cartridge that has gone the distance, it had several kissing cousins at the turn of the century. Almost following the British proprietary system, both Savage and Remington followed Winchester's example with slightly different cartridges possessing almost identical ballistics. The .303 Savage, conceived as a potential military cartridge in 1895, was introduced commercially in the brand-new Savage 99 in 1899. It was loaded with somewhat heavier bullets than the .30-30–190 grains was the initial loading, later followed by a 180-grain bullet–but it is ballistically identical to the .30-30 and very similar in appearance. Remington's version, the .30 Remington, is essentially a rimless .30-30, introduced in 1906 for Remington's Model 8 semiautomatic. It was also chambered in the 1912-vintage Model 14 slide-action and later in the Model 30 bolt-action. It is also ballistically identical to the .30-30.

There are enough .303 Savage and .30 Remington rifles out there that ammunition is still loaded, but neither cartridge has had the lasting popularity of the .30-30. While the .30-30's initial loading used a 160-grain bullet, for many years the standard loading has been a 150-grain bullet at 2,390 feet per second, yielding 1,903 foot/pounds; and a 170-grain bullet delivering 2,200 fps and 1,827 foot/pounds. More recently, Remington offers a 55-grain sabot "Accelerator" .30-30 load, and Federal also offers a 125-grain hollow-point load. I don't honestly see much attraction in varmint hunting with the .30-30, so the traditional 150- and 170-grain slugs are far and away the most useful.

By today's standards, the .30-30 is slow, has fairly unimpressive energy figures, and has a trajectory like a rainbow. Regardless of bullet weight, it's a short-range cartridge. Energy figures fall below 1,000 foot/pounds before you reach 200 yards, and the trajectory is such that making hits at that distance becomes somewhat uncertain. That said, the .30-30 remains popular for two reasons: First, it's chambered in light, handy, dependable rifles that have huge amounts of charismatic appeal. Second, it *works*.

Guys in my business, me included, tend to get all wrapped up in pinpoint accuracy, impressive ballistics, and flat trajectories. The .30-30 has none of those things–but within 150 yards or so it's a remarkably effective cartridge on game and should not be underrated. It's effectiveness, in my view, comes from several factors. Among them is the simple fact that it's plenty of gun. Its energy figures, though hardly flashy, are well within what most authorities consider perfectly adequate for deer-sized game. Within 100 yards–the distance most game is taken with this caliber–it will offer up to 1,500 foot/pounds of energy, which is more than enough.

Perhaps more significant is that there's more to bullet performance on game than paper ballistics always show. Bullets for the .30-30 have a couple of advantages. For one thing, they're fairly heavy. On stout game like wild hogs and black bear, I'll take a 150- or 170-grain .30-caliber bullet over a

100-grain 6mm or 120-grain .25-caliber any day of the week, regardless of which shows the most energy on paper. The very nature of a .30-30 bullet is also important. Since most .30-30 rifles have tubular magazines, only extremely blunt round-nose bullets or, better, flat-points, are suitable. Blunt-nosed bullets, especially true flat-points, transfer energy much more abruptly than most spitzer bullets, which generally penetrate to some degree before expansion begins. This last is almost impossible to measure, and thus is subjective speculation on my part–but I think it's a partial explanation of why the .30-30 seems to hit very hard on game despite unimpressive energy and velocity.

The last consideration is that .30-30 bullets have, for a century now, been designed to expand and penetrate at .30-30 velocities. Although a .30-30 sheds velocity quickly, there isn't all that much difference between muzzle velocity and 100-yard velocity. The most popular 150-grain load starts at 2,390 and at 100 yards is still going over 2,000 feet per second. A higher-velocity cartridge intended for use at long range might lose 1,000 feet per second or more between the time it leaves the muzzle and the time it arrives at the animal 350 or 400 yards downrange. It's a whole lot easier to make a bullet perform with a 350- to 400-feet-per-second window than within a 1,000-feet-per-second window!

I grew up hunting in open country, so have done relatively little deer hunting with the .30-30, even though I had access to one as a kid. I have done a fair amount of hog hunting and some black-bear hunting with the cartridge–enough to know that it shouldn't be taken lightly.

Unless heavy bone is struck, the .30-30 is not generally a dramatic sudden-death killer. On deer-sized game, the higher velocity of the 150-grain bullet tends to impart a bit more shock, but even so one should expect deer hit in the heart/lung area to exhibit little reaction to receiving the bullet. I've historically been more a fan of the 170-grain bullet, on the theory that since there isn't much velocity anyway you might as well have the added penetration of the heavier bullet. With that load I've shot quite a number of wild hogs, and while I can't recall ever flattening a pig with a .30-30–except with head and spine shots–I can't recall one going very far, either.

More recently, though, I've been rethinking my preference for the heavier bullet. A little while back, I shot a very fine whitetail with my short-barreled '94 Trapper, at about 90 yards with a 170-grain bullet. The deer showed no reaction other than to run into the brush, but I heard the distinct slap of the bullet striking home and, since I was shooting down from an elevated stand, I saw the bullet hit the ground at an angle that confirmed I had hit the deer and shot right through him.

My hold had been just behind the shoulder for a lung shot, and I felt certain the bullet had hit the right place. But there was no blood at all, and the ground was too hard for any tracks save the deep gouge where the buck had jumped. I could have lost that deer, but with assistance from John

Wootters' wife, Jeannie, we finally found him–stone dead in thick brush not 50 yards from where he'd been shot.

That experience has not made me question the effectiveness of the .30-30. After all, the shot went exactly where I'd wanted it to go, the bullet had penetrated completely, and the deer had dropped very quickly. But there had clearly been little bullet shock, and the exit hole showed almost no expansion. I'll stick with the 170-grain bullet for pigs and black bear, but in the future I think I'll do two things on any deer I might shoot with the .30-30. First, I think I'll go to the 150-grain bullet, and, second, rather than my customary behind-the-shoulder lung shot, I think I'll shoot for the shoulder and try to break some bone.

The .30-30 has accounted for millions of deer over the years, and it's as a short-range deer cartridge that it's most at home. It has also accounted for a great many elk, but to me that's pushing the cartridge's capabilities very hard–especially at any distance beyond point-blank range. It's also a bit underpowered for the largest of black bears, but for hound hunting or bear hunting over bait it will do the job–provided the shooter is very careful. A bear-guide friend of mine used to hunt down problem bears for a timber company in the Northwest. He and his hounds ran down literally hundreds of bears, and he typically used a .30-30. Until one fine day he failed to stop a smallish black bear. After several weeks in the hospital, he gave up his .30-30 in favor of a .350 Remington Magnum!

But with careful shooting at moderate range, the .30-30 continues to be the effective deer cartridge it has always been, no more and no less.

7.62x39 Russian: While most of the foreign military rifles lack the accuracy and the precision sights desired for hunting, there are a few pretty good semiautos in this chambering, not the least of which is Ruger's Mini Thirty. Designed for high-capacity military weapons, the short-cased 7.62x39 has often been compared to the .30-30 in power and field effectiveness. In terms of paper ballistics, this is true. The standard load is a 125-grain bullet at a bit over 2,300 feet per second, yielding around 1,500 foot/pounds of energy. That isn't quite what the .30-30 delivers, but the spitzer bullet holds its velocity better than a flat-point .30-30 bullet does. It won't quite deliver 1,000 foot/pounds at 200 yards, but it will come close. I have no problem suggesting that the cartridge would be effective on small deer at short range, but it is not the equal of the .30-30. One of the .30-30's strengths is its relatively heavy, blunt-nosed bullets. The 7.62x39 has bullets that are neither heavy nor blunt, and under no circumstances will it be as effective on game. But for casual shooting and very short-range work, the 7.62x39 can be considered a deer cartridge.

.30-40 Krag, .303 British, .300 Savage: Although radically different cartridges, these three can be considered ballistic cousins. The oldest, of course, is the .303 British. It is not technically a .30 caliber, since it fires a .311-inch bullet. But it served the forces of the British Empire well from

1887 to 1957, and remains a popular hunting cartridge wherever British influence has been felt. The most common factory loads today are a 150-grain bullet at 2,690 feet per second and a 180-grain bullet at 2,460 fps, but the bullet that made the cartridge's reputation on game was a 215-grain slug at just a bit over 2,000 fps. It isn't flashy, but the heavier .30-caliber bullets at these moderate velocities penetrate extremely well and give very consistent performance.

Relatively few American hunters have used the .303, but it remains extremely popular in Canada, where thousands of hunters take their moose with it annually and experience no difficulties. Provided ranges are kept moderate, the .303 will do its work just fine!

Like the .303, the .30-40 Krag is a rimmed cartridge that started life as a military round. Like the .303 British, it was quickly adapted to sporting rifles and rapidly gained a following among hunters. After the Springfield was adopted by the American military, surplus Krag-Jorgensen rifles became readily available, and Americans came to love this butter-smooth action.

In addition to the Krag bolt-action, the .30-40 was chambered in the Winchester high-wall single-shot, the Lee straight-pull bolt-action, Remington's rolling-block single-shot, and Winchester's Model 1895 lever-action. None of the repeaters, the Krag included, have particularly strong actions, so .30-40 ammunition has always been loaded to mild pressures and modest ballistics. The only surviving factory load is a 180-grain bullet at 2,430 feet per second, but an old standby was the long, stable 220-grain bullet at 2,200 fps. In either bullet weight, the .30-40 is a reliable game cartridge, just as good today as it was a century ago. The low velocity limits its range, but it's easily a 250-yard deer cartridge and, given its heavy bullets, is fully elk-capable so long as ranges are kept short.

The .300 Savage came along quite a bit later, in 1920. It's essentially the .250 Savage case necked up to .30 caliber, and the concept was to duplicate .30-06 performance in the short Savage 99 lever-action. Remembering that .30-06 loads in 1920 were much milder than they are today, it didn't fall far short of the mark! With modern powders, it isn't the equal of the .308 Winchester, let alone the .30-06. In fact, it isn't quite the equal of the .30-40 Krag with bullets of 180 grains. But it is a very fine cartridge that offers superb medium-range performance on deer at a very modest price in recoil. It has been chambered not only in the Savage 99, but in quite a few bolt-actions–including a recent limited run in the Remington Model 700 Limited Edition Classic.

With a 150-grain bullet at 2,630 feet per second, it's a fine deer rifle to 250 yards or so; and with a 180-grain bullet at 2,350 it, like the Krag, is quite suitable for short-range work on elk. Today, with so many fine cartridges available, there may seem to be little place for the old .300 Savage. I disagree. Whether in Savage 99 or bolt-action form, it makes a fine beginner's deer rifle. With .30-caliber bullet weight and frontal area, it's much more effective than 6mms or .25s, and has the light recoil that youngsters and ladies should start with. It should not be overlooked.

.308 and .307 Winchester: Okay, I'll admit it. I've never been a fan of the .308 Winchester and am unlikely to become one. I've often written that, bullet for bullet, it lags 100 feet per second behind the .30-06, more with bullets over 180 grains, and thus is inferior. That's true. However, its case is truly a model of efficiency. With a case length of 2.015 inches, it's almost a half-inch shorter than the '06, yet comes very close to .30-06 performance. Not only can it be put into a true short bolt-action; it can also be chambered in lever-actions like the Savage 99, Browning BLR, and the discontinued Winchester Model 88. For technical reasons that absolutely escape me, it's also a fact that the .308 Winchester is inherently a much more accurate cartridge than the .30-06.

As much as I hate to admit it, the .308 Winchester is indistinguishable from the .30-06 in the field, except at longer ranges or with the heaviest of .30-caliber bullets—and it can be built into a significantly lighter rifle.

Although commercially introduced in 1952 by Winchester, only in recent years has the .308 competed with the .30-06 in the diversity of factory loads available. Today there's a bewildering array of fine .308 loads. And while .30-06 velocities have remained static for many years, today's .308 factory loads have narrowed the gap considerably. The hottest current .30-06 factory loads are a 150-grain bullet at 2,910 feet per second; a 165-grain bullet at 2,800 fps; and a 178-grain bullet at 2,720 fps. Corresponding .308 Winchester loads push a 150-grain bullet at 2,820 fps; a 165-grain bullet at 2,700 fps; and a 178-grain bullet 2,620 fps. That 90- to 100-feet per second difference will rarely be seen in the field and will not be felt by game. The greatest difference, of course, is that careful handloading can increase .30-06 velocities by a fair margin, while factory .308 velocities can't be improved by much.

Still and all, the .308 is a fine hunting cartridge. For deer, either a 150-grain bullet or, better, a 165-grain bullet, will carry 1,000 foot/pounds to the 400-yard mark. For elk, an aerodynamic 180-grain bullet carries 2,000 foot/pounds beyond 200 yards. Yes, it's true that I much prefer the .30-06—but I must give the .308 its due, and its due is that it's a wonderful cartridge.

John Wootters is a longtime .308 fan, especially for his whitetail hunting. His short-barreled .308 Sako has become something of a legend, as well it should be. The fellow who taught me how to shoot a centerfire rifle and how to handload, Jack Pohl, was a longtime .308 fan. Sometime before I was born, Jack bought the Warsaw, Missouri, gunstock factory of E.C. Bishop & Son from Old Man Bishop. The same small town also holds the Reinhart Fajen gunstock company, and the two together give Warsaw reasonable claim to its title of "gunstock capital of the world." Jack was as much a benchrest competitor as a hunter, so it stands to reason that he loved the super-accurate .308. His pet rifle was a Winchester Model 70 Featherweight in .308, and he used it on many Wyoming elk hunts in the 1950s and early 1960s.

Jack left us for elk pastures elsewhere some time back. In his day, "party hunting" was more acceptable than it is today, so I hope he wouldn't mind my recounting in print his favorite elk story. It was late in the hunt and his entire party was in the process of getting skunked when Jack rode into an open alpine park that was full of elk. He grabbed his little .308 out of its saddle scabbard, jumped off his horse, and proceeded to drop five elk with five shots. And then, as you can imagine, the real work started!

When I became interested in rifle shooting, Dad called his old friend Jack Pohl, and he took me down to Warsaw several times so we could both be educated together. Never was there a better or more patient teacher than Jack Pohl. He schooled me–really both Dad and me–on the range, at the reloading bench, and on Ozark groundhogs. Dad had gotten me a .243, but at the conclusion of our education–just before the "final exam" that was to be a Wyoming pronghorn hunt–Jack "sold" Dad his pet .308 for a fraction of its worth.

That's still Dad's rifle today, and while he claims to be a terrible rifle shot, I've seen him do some wonderful things with his .308 and the 180-grain bullets that rifle loves. In Wyoming, I've seen him roll pronghorns running as only pronghorns can run. In British Columbia, he absolutely pole-axed a big bull moose with a single-shot. And in Montana a few years ago, he missed a wonderfully easy shot at a fine bedded mule deer–then flattened him with a head-on shot through the throat patch when he stood up. Honest, unless you're a dedicated handloader there isn't much to pick from between a .30-06 and a .308–much as I dislike admitting it!

The .307 is the newest of our factory .30 calibers. It was brought out in 1983 in Winchester's beefed-up version of the Model 94, the "Big Bore 94," along with the .356 Winchester. Marlin followed suit in their 336, but neither chambering proved popular and Marlin has dropped them both.

The idea was to offer .308 performance in a '94 action, and the .307 Winchester comes close to doing just that. The cartridge is actually a semi-rimmed version of the .308 that lags only slightly behind the .308 in velocity potential. The only factory ammunition still available is a 150-grain loading rated at 2,760 feet per second, but there was originally also a 180-grain load at 2,510. Unfortunately, these are theoretical velocities, clocked from a 24-inch barrel, while the rifles made for this caliber have a 20-inch barrel. Actual velocities are closer to 2,550 fps for the 150-grain bullet and 2,360 for a 180-grain bullet. The .307 is also unable to compare ballistically with the .308 because of the necessity to use velocity-shedding flat-point bullets in tubular-magazine rifles. Even so, the .307 is a vast improvement over the .30-30 Winchester and does extend the range of the Model 94 Winchester significantly.

.30-06 Springfield: I will not take back all the good things I have just said about the .308. The cartridge deserves such praise. But, given a choice, unless I wanted to use a lever-action or was bound and determined to build the lightest bolt-action I could, I'd take a .30-06 hands down.

While it was the 1903 Springfield that made the cartridge famous, our .30-06 is not the original 1903 cartridge. The original cartridge featured a 220-grain round-nose at 2,300 feet per second, but in 1906 the case neck was shortened .07-inch and the military load changed to a 150-grain spitzer at a then-impressive velocity of 2,700 fps. In 1926, the military load was changed again, to a 172-grain boattail spitzer at the same 2,700 fps, though the case remained the same that time.

As the military load evolved, so has sporting ammunition for the good old '06. Since it has been America's most popular sporting cartridge for at least 75 years, no other cartridge has seen the load development or factory-load proliferation of the .30-06. Today, a 150-grain factory load clocks 2,900 feet per second; a 165-grain bullet 2,800 fps; and a 180-grain bullet 2,700 fps. A 220-grain bullet reaches 2,410 feet per second, not too bad for such a heavy bullet! Factory loads are available in almost any bullet style imaginable, including a good selection of "premium" hunting bullets like the Trophy Bonded Bearclaw, Barnes "X", Nosler Partition, and many more.

Much handload development, too, has centered around the .30-06. While the difference between .308 and .30-06 factory loads isn't earth-shaking, handloading can make a difference. It's no trick at all to obtain increases of 100 feet per second in all bullet weights, including the 220-grain heavyweight. In fact, due to greater case capacity, it's in the heavy bullets that the .30-06 really begins to outstrip the .308. A very fine and reasonably flat-shooting elk and bear load can be had by pushing 200-grain bullets to 2,650 feet per second. And the 220-grain bullet can be hand-loaded to a solid 2,550 fps.

Although a 1903 Springfield was my first centerfire rifle, I never hunted with it. Oddly, I still own that rifle but to this day have never shot game with it. I "discovered" the .30-06 quite late in my hunting career, in 1977 when I took a Ruger Model 77 as the light rifle on my first African hunt. I had something like 14 straight one-shot kills with that rifle and hand-loaded 180-grain Noslers, and overnight I became a .30-06 fan. I still am, and I still have a soft spot for the 180-grain Nosler!

As we have seen, the 7mm magnum shoots a bit flatter, as do many cartridges of lighter caliber. But the .30-06 shoots plenty flat enough for all but the most open of country. It also packs plenty of punch when it gets there. For deer, I would have no qualms about using the most popular 150-grain loading. But a quick look at ballistics tables tells you that, even though the 165-grain bullet starts slower, its better aerodynamics catch up quickly. Without a doubt, the 165-grain bullet is a better long-range and better all-round choice.

For larger game, the 180-grain bullet is hard to beat. Whether in a factory load, or a handload at 2,800 feet per second, the 180-grain bullet is just plain effective–and I honestly believe that its greater weight, combined with greater frontal area, renders it much more deadly than any 7mm. Of course, you can go up to 200 grains, and a 200-grain load would be my choice for moose and just perhaps for the largest of black bear. I would probably not choose the .30-06 for brown bear, at least not on purpose. But if I had to, that's when I'd break out those long, unstoppable 220-grain bullets.

The .30-06 is the lightest caliber I have chosen for elk. Combined with a 180-grain bullet, it hasn't let me down and I doubt it ever would. With 165-grain bullets, I've used it with perfect satisfaction on pronghorns and a great many deer, including some fairly long shots. Actually, though, a 180-grain bullet pushed fast gives up very little to a 165-grain bullet, in much the same way that the 165-grain slug beats the 150-grain bullet. With bullets above 180 grains, velocity starts to fall off quickly–and, at .30-06 velocities, you get such wonderful bullet performance from a 180-grain bullet that you really don't need heavier weights except for very special uses.

More years ago than I care to recall, I rode up to the edge of a deep, juniper-choked canyon and two big mule-deer bucks jumped from their beds in the bottom. I bailed off my horse and lay down on a rocky outcropping, but there was no way to get a shot as the deer plowed through the thick brush. The distance was getting very long, but the deer would have to show themselves where the brush thinned on the opposite lip. I got as comfortable as I could and waited.

The lead buck slowed to a fast trot just before he topped out, and as he cleared the brush I led him a body length or so and held most of a body width high. Nothing happened at the shot; the buck just trotted on into the brush. Then the second buck appeared and he was even bigger. I led him just a bit more, kept the same height, and fired twice more. On the last shot I saw the buck hump just a bit. Then he, too trotted into the brush.

It took a while to cross the canyon, but when I got there and found the spot where the deer had disappeared I found not one but two very big and very dead mule deer, one shot through the lungs once, the other shot through the lungs twice.

Although I've shot a variety of African game up to about 800 pounds body weight with the .30-06, elk is the largest North American game I've hunted with the caliber. I think it's an ideal choice for almost all of our deer hunting, and of course runs the gamut of sheep, goat, caribou, black bear, and such. It's the minimum I would personally choose for elk and moose–but as you've gathered, I'm pretty conservative in my personal minimums. The .30-06 is plenty of gun for our largest antlered game, except only that it's a poor choice if you expect to do long shooting in high Alpine basins. On elk, ranges should be kept to a maximum of 300 yards–better yet, 250 yards.

As an all-round, do-anything North American rifle, the only restriction I would place on the .30-06 is for deliberate long-range shooting in very open country; and I'd consider it very marginal at best for hunting our largest bears. With these exceptions, the .30-06 is one of our most effective and most versatile hunting cartridges. That's why it remains so popular after so many years.

Chapter 9

Magnum .30s–The Versatility Kings

If a little's good, then a whole lot is better, right? Few people have ever questioned the .30-06's capabilities as a hunting cartridge, so it would have to be even a better deal if .30-06 velocities could be boosted significantly, wouldn't it? The large-cased .30-calibers, what we call magnum .30s, genuinely offer significantly improved velocities over what the .30-06 can deliver.

Now, "magnum" is just a marketing term that originated from the French word for an extra-large bottle of champagne. That's apt, because we tend to think of magnum cases as being extra large. We have also come to associate a magnum with a belted case. That's misleading. The shoulder on the belt does create a spot for positive headspacing, and it may theoretically strengthen the case in the belt area. But a belt in and of itself has nothing to do with velocity–witness the 6.5mm Remington Magnum, which has neither a large case nor improved velocities over non-belted 6.5s. While we may think of a big, belted case when we hear the word "magnum," what we're really thinking about is a cartridge that offers increased performance over "standard" cartridges in the same caliber. The .264 Winchester Magnum is certainly a magnum compared to the 6.5x55–but so is the unbelted European cartridge designated 6.5x68. One could even argue that the great 7mm Remington Magnum isn't really a magnum, since it actually gains very little over the .280 Remington.

But no one can argue that our .300 magnums, all four of them, are not magnums. The .300 H&H, .308 Norma, .300 Winchester, and .300 Weatherby Magnums all offer significant gains over .30-06 velocities. That does not, in all contexts, make them *better* cartridges–but it does give them more downrange energy, flatter trajectories, and greater reach.

The idea of a super-high-velocity .30-caliber cartridge is nothing new. If it were a test question, I suspect the majority of hunters the world over would give the credit for the first magnum .30 to Holland & Holland for introducing their "Super 30"–the .300 H&H Magnum–in 1925. They'd be wrong. The first red-hot .30 was an American development that preceded the H&H Super 30 by a dozen years. Charles Newton developed it for Fred Adolph in 1913 and initially called it the Adolph Express. Several years passed before both rifles and cartridges were produced, and in factory form it was called the .30 Newton. Newton rifles ceased production in the 1920s–before the .300 H&H ever saw the light of day–but factory ammo was loaded until just before World War II.

The .30 Newton is a rimless, unbelted cartridge with a greater diameter and thus greater powder capacity than the .30-06. It will not match current .300 magnum loadings, but its factory load of a 180-grain bullet at 2,860 feet per second beat the heck out of then-current .30-06 loadings. Yep, it was for sure a magnum.

The .300 H&H was first loaded by the Western Cartridge Company in 1925, the same year it was introduced in England. It didn't really catch on until it was used to win the 1935 Wimbledon 1,000-yard match. Then it caught on big time and remained very popular until the "short magnums" began to take over. In terms of lineage, the .300 Weatherby Magnum came next, in 1944. It uses the .300 H&H case significantly blown out, with greatly increased performance. The .308 Norma Magnum followed in 1960 and was gaining a following rapidly until Winchester introduced the .300 Winchester Magnum in 1963.

We'll look at each of these current .300 magnums separately, but in truth all are quite similar. Differences center around whether or not you handload and what barrel length and type of rifle you prefer, but all offer very significant improvement over .30-06 velocities. The question, then, is why doesn't everyone forget the .30-06 and go to a .300 magnum?

A simple answer is that not everyone *needs* .300 magnum performance! You see, you can't obtain that performance without cost. The price is primarily in recoil; depending on gun weight and bullet weight, a .30-06 can recoil from around 20 foot/pounds to almost 30 foot/pounds. Also depending on gun weight and bullet weight, a .300 Weatherby can recoil from a bit under 40 foot/pounds to over 50 foot/pounds. *Macho* stoicism aside, recoil approaching 50 foot/pounds is serious recoil indeed. Most hunters can learn to deal with recoil of that level, but why put up with it if you don't need it?

Of course, there are other costs. The .300 magnums need longer barrels to burn up all that powder. Barrels of 24 inches are minimal, and 26-inch barrels are much more efficient–especially for the Weatherby. Unless you're of small stature or you hunt in very thick country, I don't believe a 26-inch barrel makes a rifle unwieldy. But it does add gun weight, and of course you really want more gun weight to keep the recoil down. That means you have to carry that extra gun weight. There's also more muzzle blast, less magazine capacity, and the ammunition is heavier and more bulky. Magnum ammunition also costs more to buy over the counter and, for handloaders, generally has reduced case life and burns a lot more powder.

Those are the negatives. The positives are obvious: increased velocity, which translates both to flatter trajectory and increased downrange energies; and, because of the greater powder capacity, significantly increased performance with the heaviest of .30-caliber bullets.

Do you need these advantages, and are they worth the trade-off? For most hunters, the answer is no. If you take an aerodynamic 165-grain bullet loaded in a .30-06 at 2,800 fps muzzle velocity, you can sight-in to be about three inches high at 100 yards. You'll be dead-on at around 250 yards and only four inches low, or thereabouts, at 300 yards. For most of us, 300 yards is a very long shot, and for most of us that's actually starting to stretch our capabilities. At 300 yards, that bullet from a .30-06 will still have almost 1,800 foot/pounds. That isn't quite enough to be optimum for elk, but 300 yards is awful far to be shooting at an animal as big and tough as an elk. It's plenty enough for any deer, sheep, or goat that walks.

Now, let's take a .300 Weatherby with a 180-grain bullet, and let's push it to the maximum of 3,300 feet per second muzzle velocity. If you sight that same three inches high at 100 yards, you're going to be dead-on at 300 yards and only 81/2 inches low at 400 yards. You'll have over 2,800 foot/pounds of energy at 300 yards and about 2,400 foot/pounds at 400 yards. Wow! That's fast, flat, and really carries the energy.

If you're an extremely accomplished marksman *and* you hunt wide-open country where very long shots are likely, then it's obvious that a .300 magnum gives you a tremendous edge. But relatively few people have a need to shoot beyond 300 yards. Even if you do, you may not hunt game that requires a .300's long-range punch. Elk certainly do, as do moose. But most deer hunting does not, nor do sheep, goat, pronghorn, and such. Sure, a few extra foot/pounds are better than not having enough, but for most hunters recoil starts to get serious at about the .300 magnum level. There's no reason to put up with it unless you need it.

Then, too, for more than eight decades most .30-caliber bullets have been designed to perform at .30-06, velocities. With the .30-06 (and, for that matter, the .308 Winchester) you can be almost assured of obtaining consistently outstanding bullet performance. A great many .30-caliber bullets have not been designed to perform at velocities 400 to 500 feet per second faster, and many will not. With the .30-06 you can shoot 150-grain bullets on deer, 165-grain bullets for all-round use, and 180-grain bullets for heavy game, and be reasonably certain you will get the expansion and penetration the bullet was designed to offer. With the .300s, you need to use heavier and tougher bullets. Unless you're reasonably certain the ranges will be long (and thus the bullet will have slowed considerably before it reaches the game) sensible bullet weights for the .300s start at 180 grains. Spitzer .30s of 180 and 200 grains are wonderfully stable–but heavy bullets at high velocity mean more recoil yet.

This all may sound like I'm knocking the .300s. I'm certainly not. To the contrary, they are among the very finest general-purpose hunting cartridges in the world. But I'm not recommending that anyone trade in a .308 or .30-06–or, for that matter, a .270, .280, or 7mm Remington Magnum–for a .300 without giving it serious thought. With well-chosen bullets they can absolutely handle larger game than the lesser .30s are ideal for, and they can handle larger game a good deal farther away.

The .300s, for instance, would be a fine choice for combination elk/mule-deer hunting–especially in high Alpine country. They are also fine choices for serious quests for trophy mule deer and big Northern whitetails. In either case, the bucks can exceed 400 pounds–and you need the capability to take them where and when you see them.

In general, I would not choose a .300 magnum for most sheep hunting. However, a .300 makes a fine choice for hunting a combination such as sheep and moose or sheep and grizzly–plenty flat enough for the sheep and plenty powerful enough for the moose or bear.

The .300s are also excellent choices for African hunting, especially in savanna or desert regions. Over there, a single day's hunt might find you encountering anything from a 20-pound duiker to an 800-pound zebra or 1,500-pound eland. A .300 with 200-grain bullets becomes a much sounder choice than a .30-06.

Regardless of continent and size of game, there's also a case to be built for choosing a .300 to hunt almost any unfamiliar game in unfamiliar country. Distance is hard enough to judge in country you understand and with game you're intimately familiar with. Take country you haven't been in before, be it desert or mountain; and add in game you haven't hunted before and thus have no way to judge the size against the surroundings–and range estimation becomes very difficult. It makes sense to choose a cartridge that eliminates the need for guesswork at any reasonable shooting distance. The .300s will do this. They are not flatter than cartridges like the .25-06, .270 Weatherby, or the 7mm magnums–but they do hit harder with heavier bullets, and thus are more versatile.

Most of the Weatherby Award winners have been staunch proponents of the .300 magnums, and not out of deference to Roy Weatherby. These guys hunt the world, and are almost always hunting unfamiliar country for new and different species. With a .300 magnum, they have plenty of gun and rarely have to worry about range estimation. Their choice makes plenty of sense to them–and it might to you, just so long as you understand the price you'll pay in gun weight and recoil.

In terms of what the .300s are suitable for, on this continent there are no limits. A .300 magnum with 180- or 200-grain bullets is a fine elk rifle, and with 200-grain bullets is plenty of gun for mountain grizzly. A larger caliber might be a bit better, but a .300 with 200- or 220-grain bullets is not a poor choice for even the largest of Alaskan brown bears or polar bears. And of course it has the flat trajectory for any mountain game under any conditions. Understanding that our four .300s are ballistically very similar, let's briefly look at each.

.300 Holland & Holland Magnum: The grandfather of the .300's is, at least in terms of factory ammo, the weakest of the four. This is almost certainly due to the fact that many older guns are so chambered, and the factories are leaning toward the conservative side. The .300 H&H has fallen off significantly in popularity since the appearance of the .300 Winchester Magnum, and the only remaining factory load features 180-grain bullets. Muzzle velocity is 2,880 feet per second, hardly red-hot.

If you handload, you can beat this velocity considerably. If you don't handload, then I wouldn't recommend the .300 H&H. The factory ammo is good, and 2,880 feet per second still makes it a flat-shooter—but there's virtually no selection of bullet styles and types, and of course just the one bullet weight.

The .300 H&H uses a full-length case of 2.850 inches, based on a necked-down .375 H&H. It requires a magnum-length action, but even with top handloads delivers no better performance than can be had with a .300 Winchester Magnum, which fits into a .30-06-length action. The case is archaic in design, with a lot of body taper, a long, gently sloping shoulder, and a long neck. The design reduces powder capacity significantly and thus was ripe for the kind of improvement that Roy Weatherby achieved with his .300 Weatherby Magnum.

However, that gently tapering case does have one significant advantage, and that's unbelievably smooth, trouble-free feeding. Fans of the .300 H&H have known this for years, and that's one reason so many of them cling to their .300 H&Hs.

With good loads, it will do everything any of the other .300s will do, which is anything that needs doing on this continent.

.308 Norma Magnum: Introduced in 1960, the .308 Norma Magnum is a bit of an oddity. It was created by Norma in Sweden—but for the American market—and initially there were neither rifles nor loaded ammunition, only unprimed brass. It was pretty much blown off the market by the .300 Winchester Magnum's 1963 introduction, but a number of European rifles have been so chambered, and Norma still offers factory-loaded ammo.

The .308 Norma is almost identical to most versions of the .30-338 wildcat, differing only in that it has a slightly shorter case of 2.560 inches. In that regard, it is ballistically identical to (but *not* interchangeable with!) the .300 Winchester Magnum, differing in that the .300 Winchester Magnum has a slightly longer case of 2.620 inches and a neck that's considerably shorter by .040 inch. The .308 Norma and .30-.338 are popular with 1,000-yard match shooters, while the .300 Winchester Magnum is not. Serious benchresters consider the .300 Winchester Magnum's neck too short to properly hold the bullet; thus the .308 Norma has a reputation for greater accuracy.

In hunting terms, it's unlikely this is significant. What is significant is that the .308 Norma Magnum is available only in hard-to-find Norma ammunition, and, like the .300 H&H, only with a 180-grain bullet. As is the case with most Norma ammo, it is loaded pretty hot—muzzle velocity is a very fast 3,020 fps. Obviously, handloaders have the full range of bullet weights and options available, but due to the scarcity of factory ammo I would rate the .308 Norma as the least desirable of our four .300s.

.300 Winchester Magnum: Okay, so it's got a short neck and hasn't won a whole lot of 1,000-yard matches. In terms of popularity, this cartridge has won the .300 magnum race going away, and as the most popular .300 has the distinct advantage of a wide variety of easily obtainable factory loads. Like the .308 Norma, but unlike the H&H and the Weatherby, it has a compact case designed to fit into .30-06-length actions.

The .300 Winchester Magnum, introduced in 1963, is the last of Winchester's family of short magnums that began with the .458 in 1956 and also includes the .264 and .338 Winchester Magnums. Bullet weights in factory loads range from 150 to 220 grains, and include the widest selection of bullet types and designs. The cartridge's ballistics are pretty good out of the factory, but can be improved very slightly by handloading. And, as is always the case, handloading can tailor the ammunition to your rifle. But in terms of bullet selection, there's really no reason to handload for the .300 Winchester Magnum. Noslers, ultra-aerodynamic boat tails, "X"-bullets, Trophy Bonded Bearclaws, and more are all available over the counter.

Pretty much standard is a 180-grain bullet at 2,960 feet per second, yielding 3,500 foot/pounds at the muzzle, about 2,200 foot/pounds at 300 yards, and about 1,850 at 400 yards. Even better, in terms of long-range energy, are aerodynamic 190- and 200-grain loads. These start a bit slower, but because of higher ballistic coefficients they carry 2,000 foot/pounds well beyond 400 yards. My preference in the .300s has long been a 200-grain spitzer, and the ballistic charts quickly validate that choice.

For general use, especially on the larger game the .300 is best suited for, I'll stick with bullets from 180 to 200 grains. However, I learned a couple of valuable lessons in the last couple of years and they're worth sharing. I went on a Sitka blacktail hunt on Kodiak Island in '92, my first time on the island. I'd heard the stories about bears coming to a rifle shot like it was a dinner bell, and I'd heard about having to fight your way through heavy brush. So I had a mental picture of short-range shots and the potential for bear encounters. I chose a .35 Whelen with 225-grain bullets, and I couldn't have been more wrong.

Late in the season, the grass and brush are beaten down by wind and rain, and the slopes of Kodiak Island are wide open. I shot three bucks, and the closest was 300 yards. I was totally outclassed with my .35 Whelen. My hunting partner, Jake Jacobson, lives on Kodiak. He had wisely chosen a .300 Winchester Magnum and stoked it with handloaded 150-grain Nosler Ballistic Tips–a soft bullet for a .300, but Jake knew there would be no close shots on the good bucks we were looking for. I shot my first buck with the .35 and finally got him down–and after that I borrowed Jake's .300!

I shot one buck in his bed at about 350 yards, and my last and best buck at an honest 375 yards as he faced me. Now, that little 150-grain bullet started at 3,400 feet per second, and I have no doubt it would have been a bomb at close range. But at the ranges I shot those deer, it had slowed to somewhere around 2,200 feet per second and bullet performance was perfect.

He had the rifle sighted three inches high at 100 yards, which put it dead-on at 300 and just 10 inches low at 400. On the first buck, I held the crosshairs on the backline–overestimating the range slightly, as is common–and smashed the buck's spine. On the second buck, a Boone and Crockett deer that I had missed earlier in the day and wanted very badly, I held a bit to the right to account for a crosswind, and put the crosshairs just above the white throat patch as he faced me. The deer dropped so quickly that I had no idea whether I'd hit or missed.

That same year, in Spain, I used my outfitter's .300 Winchester Magnum Sako to shoot a very fine Spanish ibex. He also preferred 150-grain bullets, knowing the shot would almost certainly exceed 200 yards. It did; I shot my billy at about 250 yards. The .300 made it easy, and bullet performance was perfect.

I'm certainly not recommending lighter bullets for game bigger than deer, but I now realize they have a place–and I'll almost certainly use more of them in years to come. For larger game, though, the heavier bullets win hands down. They do kick more, but shoot very flat and offer the deep straight-line penetration that you really want.

.300 Weatherby Magnum: Although there are some faster wildcats, the .300 Weatherby is the over-the-counter .30-caliber velocity king. Developed by Roy Weatherby in 1944, his .300 is the most popular cartridge in the Weatherby lineup and has become a world standard all-round hunting cartridge. Weatherby ammunition, as loaded by Norma, is very hot, and ballistics are extremely impressive for all bullet weights. The lightest, 150-grain bullets start at 3,600 feet per second; 180s at 3,300; and 220s at 2,900. Given a 26-inch barrel, most lots of factory ammo come awfully close to these figures, but handloaders generally find it most difficult to match them and impossible to top them.

The .300 Weatherby is a big cartridge with a full-length (2.820-inch) case based on a blown-out .300 H&H. It requires a full-length action, and really needs a 26-inch barrel to burn all that powder. If you don't mind hauling around the bigger action, longer barrel, and bulkier ammunition, the .300 Weatherby is an unbelievably deadly and flat-shooting cartridge.

Because of the significant velocity increase over the .300 Winchester, I have no use for 150-grain bullets in this cartridge, even for fairly specialized purposes. You could perhaps use a very good 165-grain bullet like the "X" or Bearclaw, but useful bullets really start at 180 grains.

A number of years ago, I was looking for a big mule deer in the oak-brush canyons near Montrose, Colorado. I saw a big buck wander up through the brush on an opposite ridge, then bed on a little knoll right across from me. It was an impossible situation. I knew exactly where the buck was because I could see just his antlers. But I knew that if I tried to approach I'd be lost in the brush and couldn't possibly get to him quietly enough to get a shot. I found a nice, flat boulder that, with my daypack atop it, would rival a benchrest. And I waited. I knew the buck was pushing 500 yards real hard, and I knew that sooner or later he would stand up and give me the only shot I was likely to get. It was very cold and there was quite a lot of snow. I thought I'd freeze to death before that buck finally stood, but eventually he did.

I was shooting Weatherby factory ammo that day, a 180-grain Nosler that would be on at about 300 yards and two feet low at 500. At such long range, I'm no great shakes at judging distance, nor is anyone else without a rangefinder. I knew he was well past 450 yards, but beyond that I couldn't tell you. It was probably not a sensible shot, but I knew the rifle and load and it was a dead-calm morning. When he stood, I waited until he turned broadside, then held about a half-body width above his backline at the shoulder and fired.

The bullet caught him very low in the chest, and to date he's the second-largest mule deer I've ever taken. I was a bit off on the range; it was too up-and-down to pace, but given the bullet's drop he must have been about 525 yards. With a lesser cartridge, I would have hit low–but with a lesser cartridge, I probably wouldn't have attempted the shot!

Much more recently, I shot a very fine whitetail with a different Weatherby Mark V in .300. It wasn't much of a shot for such a cartridge–about 60 yards. The 180-grain bullet (this time a Speer Mag-Tip rather than a Nosler) absolutely flattened the buck, but passed through without undue damage. Yes, the .300s–all of them–will ruin a lot of meat. But not if you stick with tough, fairly heavy bullets that are designed to hold up at the .300s great velocity.

I'm a great fan of the 180-grain bullet for deer-sized game, but for larger game or for general use it's hard to beat a good 200-grain bullet in the .300 Weatherby. Regrettably, there isn't such a factory load at this writing, but there are plenty of good component bullets. Velocity is a bit lower–you can get 3,000 feet per second, but not much more. Even so, trajectory is exceptionally flat due to the improved ballistic coefficient. On several occasions, I've taken a .300 Weatherby with 200-grain bullets as my "light" rifle for African plains game, and I've found it ideal for the full range of plains game, several of which are much larger than elk.

All of the .300s, given sensible bullet selection, are fully adequate for every game species that walks the North American continent. But it must be accepted that the .300 Weatherby Magnum is by some margin the most powerful of all. It needs a heavy rifle with a long barrel, but it's a formidable cartridge in the hands of hunters who learn how to use it.

Chapter 10

.32–The Caliber That Didn't Make It

In caliber, the .32, or 8mm, is just a small step up from the .30–but the 7mm, caliber .284, is even a smaller step up from the .270. It's hard to explain in rational terms why neither .32s nor 8mms, whichever one chooses to call them, don't seem to have a chance among American hunters.

It certainly wasn't always that way. In the closing days of the black-powder era and the first two decades of smokeless powder, there were a great many .32s. In fact, Frank Barnes' excellent reference, *Cartridges of the World*, lists fully 10 obsolete American .32-caliber cartridges. Most of these are truly forgotten, but designations like .32-40, .32 Remington, and .32 Winchester Self-Loading may ring a few bells. By comparison, the same reference lists just four current American .32s–the .32-20, .32 Winchester Special, 8mm Mauser, and 8mm Remington Magnum. Some of these have had their day in the sun, but none are currently burning up the American marketplace.

The .32-20 is a fun little cartridge. It was chambered in several lever- and slide-action rifles, and even in a couple of bolt-actions. It was also chambered in several different revolvers. Although it's substantially more powerful than the .25-20, even with its hottest loads it does not approach 1,000 foot/pounds of muzzle energy and is not by any stretch a deer cartridge. Marlin recently revived it in the Model 1894 lever-action, and a whole new generation can learn what a fun old cartridge it really is. However, its hunting utility is limited to javelina, predators called in close, or bobcats and perhaps cougar hunted with hounds. And of course, the full gamut of small game and varmints within the 100-yard limits of the cartridge.

The .32 Winchester Special has always seemed a really strange duck to me. Introduced in 1895, it was offered as a chambering for Winchester's Model 1894 for many, many years. Factory literature used to suggest that it was more powerful than the .30-30, but in truth it is not. Or at least not enough to be worth talking about. It fires a 170-grain bullet at 2,280 feet per second, a shade faster than the .30-30's 170-grain bullet. However, its poorer sectional density makes it lose that velocity more quickly, so it's pretty much a toss-up. Frank Barnes provides a good explanation for Winchester's creation of another cartridge so similar to the .30-30. In *Cartridges of the World,* he states that it was created as a smokeless round that could be reloaded with black powder more satisfactorily than the .30-30. The .30-30 has a fairly fast twist of one turn in 12 inches, which would foul very quickly if loaded with black powder. The .32 has a one-in-16 twist and would be better suited to reloading with black powder.

If that's an explanation for the creation of the cartridge, I can find no explanation for why it lasted as long as it did. Except that, on the surface, it seems more powerful than the .30-30 and must have found favor with deep-woods hunters going after black bear or larger deer. It will certainly do everything the .30-30 will do, but nothing more.

The 8mm Mauser, or 8x57, is a world-standard hunting cartridge, and a darned good one. It shares the case of the 7x57, but necked up to accept a .323 bullet. Now, that bullet diameter is designated "S" or "JS." Until 1905, the 8x57 was loaded with a .318-inch bullet, so if you run across a very old European 8x57, make sure you know what you're dealing with!

8mm Mauser ammunition is offered by Winchester, Remington, and Federal, with a "standard" load of a 170-grain bullet at 2,360 feet per second. This is a very mild load suitable for older rifles, but is not indicative of what the 8mm Mauser is capable of. Norma offers two loadings that are a great deal more stout: A 165-grain bullet at 2,850 feet per second and a 196-grain bullet at 2,530 fps. Both loads, obviously, match very closely what a .30-06 delivers!

The 8mm Mauser was once fairly popular in America due to the many thousands of surplus military bolt-actions so chambered. Although supplies have pretty much dried up, many of these rifles are still in use so the cartridge is far from dead.

Although almost no American rifles have been so chambered, the 8x57 remains very popular in Europe, and well it should. As the Norma loadings show, it's very similar to the .30-06 both in ballistics and in effect on game. The lighter bullets have a poorer sectional density than .30-caliber bullets of similar weight, so they shed velocity more quickly and generally won't penetrate as well on game. However, the greater frontal area, at least in theory, means they will hit a bit harder and transfer energy more quickly. With good handloads or Norma ammo, at anything less than fairly long range the 8x57 should be considered as effective as the .30-06 or .308 Winchester. That means it's a fine hunting cartridge and will almost certainly continue to be popular in Europe–but it seems very unlikely that it will stage a comeback in America.

The only post-war American .32 is Remington's 8mm Remington Magnum, introduced in 1978. Based on the full-length .375 H&H case and using a 2.850-inch case, the 8mm Remington is a powerful, flat-shooting cartridge. Initially it received a great deal of favorable press from America's top gun writers, and was touted as an ideal long-range cartridge for elk and similar game. Indeed it is, and it should have become much more popular.

In actuality, this underrated cartridge has been a commercial failure, and just 16 years after its introduction it seems in danger of fading away altogether. I have long thought that its main problem was in the available bullets. The two factory loadings are a 185-grain Remington Core-Lokt at

3,080 feet per second and a 220-grain Core-Lokt at 2,830 feet per second. These are adequate velocities, but not what the great case capacity is capable of delivering. These are also very fine bullets that perform well on game—the 185 for deer-sized game and the 220 for elk and such.

Unfortunately, there aren't many other bullets on the market that are suitable for the caliber. Most 8mm bullets are designed for the 8x57, and what the 8mm Remington Magnum really needs is heavier bullets, up to 250 grains. There are a few, including a Barnes 250, but not enough of a selection to make the cartridge interesting to handloaders.

The funny thing is that most people who have used the 8mm Remington Magnum really like it. John Wootters was one of the first to take an elk with the cartridge, and he still has a fondness for it. I have used it on elk with the 220-grain factory load and on muskox with handloaded 200-grain Nosler Partitions. I can't say it's better than a .300 magnum with similar bullet weights, nor am I prepared to say that it's quite as deadly as a .338 Winchester or .340 Weatherby Magnum—but it is a wonderfully effective cartridge that carries the mail a long way.

It came into a marketplace that already had both .30- and .33-caliber magnums established, and perhaps it is simply too close to both without offering anything special that the others don't have. One could speculate endlessly as to why a given cartridge didn't make it commercially, but the fact is that it has not, and now seems unlikely to. Factory ammunition will certainly be available for a great many years to come, so if you have a hankering for an 8mm Remington Magnum, by all means go get one. It is a fine cartridge that will perform well on elk, moose, and grizzly.

It would certainly work on the largest bears, but for such work it really should have a heavier bullet. It's a reasonably good long-range cartridge, but it will not carry 2,000 foot/pounds to the 400-yard line. The hotter .300 magnums will, with the proper bullets. And so will the .338 Winchester Magnum with both 225- and 250-grain spitzers. Perhaps this is the reason why it languishes on the market—it's a good cartridge, but it doesn't quite match its competition. With the right bullets it could, but it also lacks the popularity to inspire the bulletmakers into the needed R&D.

Other than the 8x57, we have not mentioned any of a whole host of European 8mm cartridges. Most of these are ballistically similar to the 8x57—some a bit more powerful, some a bit less. Many are sporting versions of now-obsolete military cartridges, and as such many of them have some popularity in their countries of origin. Relatively few of these are seen in North America, and there seems little likelihood of a sudden interest in the 8mm over here.

One European 8mm worth mentioning briefly is the 8x68S or 8x68S Magnum. This is a big, unbelted case that delivers performance on a par with the 8mm Remington Magnum, perhaps a bit better. The 196-grain factory load has a muzzle velocity of 3,050 feet per second with energy of

4,045 foot/pounds. Its advantage is that the unbelted case allows greater magazine capacity, and its Brenneke-designed RWS bullets are superb. Europeans are likely to use the 8x68S as we would use the .338 Winchester Magnum or .375 H&H. They swear by it, as well they should–but if our own 8mm Remington Magnum didn't make it, it's unlikely that we'll see any great influx of 8x68S rifles and ammo over here.

So, without further speculation as to why the .32-caliber hasn't done better, let's turn to a bore diameter that is becoming more popular all the time!

Chapter 11

.33–The All-American Big Bore

The era of smokeless powder was well underway before the first .33-caliber cartridge appeared. It was 1902 when the .33 WCF appeared, the last and most common chambering of the great Model 1886 Winchester. After it was discontinued in 1936, two more decades passed before there was another American factory .33-caliber cartridge. This was, of course, the .338 Winchester Magnum. But there was a great deal of cartridge development between the .33 WCF in 1902 and the .338 Winchester Magnum in 1958.

The 7mm and 8mm had their origins in Europe, while the .30-caliber (.308-inch bullet diameter in America, .311-inch for the British .303) can be considered both English and American. The .33, likewise, is both a British and American diameter. The .338-inch .33 Winchester was the world's first factory .33-caliber, and continental Europe has, to date, never developed a cartridge with this bullet diameter. But following hard on the heels of the .33 WCF were several fine British cartridges with bullet diameters that were similar–though not exactly the same.

The first of these was the 1910-vintage .318 Westley Richards, also called .318 Rimless Nitro Express. This cartridge follows the oft-used but inconsistent British convention of naming cartridges by *land* rather than *groove* diameter. The .318 actually uses a .330-inch bullet, and thus is a true .33-caliber. It was an extremely popular cartridge in its day and has often been compared with the .30-06. With its 180-grain bullet at 2,700 feet per second, that's pretty much true, but the preferred hunting load for the .318 was a 250-grain bullet at 2,400 fps. That's obviously both a heavier bullet and much greater frontal area than the .30-06 offers. With that long, heavy bullet at modest velocity, the .318 is an extremely reliable killer on all soft-skinned game, and in days gone by was even recommended for use on lion, buffalo, and elephant.

Almost as popular as the .318 was the .333 Rimless Nitro Express, or .333 Jeffery. Introduced about 1911, this one had a bit more powder capacity than the .318 and was loaded to a bit higher velocity. The factory loadings were a 250-grain bullet at 2,500 feet per second and a 300-grain bullet at 2,200 fps. The bullet diameter is .333, and the cartridge was considered a perfectly adequate "medium" for African hunting–well suited to all plains game and, like the .318, used with some frequency on even the largest game. The .333 bullets were used for a number of wildcatting developments that eventually led to the .338 Winchester Magnum, including Elmer Keith's famed .333 OKH.

There was also a British .338, the .33 Belted Rimless Nitro Express, or .33 BSA. Although it's a belted cartridge, it has a relatively short case with somewhat limited powder capacity. Introduced in 1923, this one could have been extremely popular but for the inexplicably poor choice in bullets. The only factory load ever offered featured a 165-grain bullet at 3,000 feet per second–very fast for the day, but horribly lacking in sectional density and a dismal failure on anything but very light game.

Although none of the British .33s achieved a widespread following on our continent, the bullet diameter was the subject of years of wildcatting as numerous experimenters began searching for a fast, flat-shooting .33. Elmer Keith was one of the most outspoken proponents of a fast .33. In conjunction with Charles O'Neil and Don Hopkins, Keith developed the .333 OKH around 1945. Based on the .30-06 case necked up to accept .333-inch bullets, it's obviously very similar to the currently popular wildcat .338-06.

A couple of years later, the OKH team followed with the .334 OKH, this one a real hot number based on the .300 H&H case necked up and blown out. It's the legitimate forerunner of the .338 Winchester Magnum, and at least in part inspired the creation of that cartridge. However, with the full-length .300 H&H case capacity, it's actually more similar ballistically to the .340 Weatherby Magnum.

You'll note that these wildcats used the .333-inch Jeffery bullet diameter rather than the .338. Flat-pointed bullets in .338 were available for the .33 WCF, but were hardly suitable for high-velocity, high-performance cartridges. Bullets in .333-inch diameter were available, so most of the pre-1958 wildcats used that diameter. Sources for .330-inch bullets for the .318 Westley Richards have long been sparse. Bullets for the .333 have been somewhat more available, and can quite easily be swaged down. When I had a .318, Randy Brooks at Barnes Bullets swaged down .338-inch bullets in two steps, and they worked just fine–but obtaining large supplies of either .330- or .333-inch bullets is very difficult today.

When Winchester introduced their .338 Winchester Magnum in 1958, they pretty much standardized the .33 as a .338-inch bullet diameter. With a major cartridge introduction in that diameter from one of America's largest manufacturers, the bulletmakers had the needed impetus to develop component bullets for the .338. After a few years of furious R&D, there were fine component bullets available, ranging from 200 to 300 grains, and factory loads for the .338 spanned the same range. Velocity started to drop rapidly with the 300-grain heavyweight, and that factory load was eventually dropped due to lack of sales. Today, only specialty bulletmakers like Barnes offer a 300-grain .338-inch bullet. The "standard" range for component bullets and factory loads runs from 200 to 250 grains, with Speer's 275-grain round-nose being the heaviest .338 bullet commonly available.

The .338 Winchester is a superb cartridge, and its initial offering in the Winchester Model 70, then the most popular bolt-action rifle in the world, hardly hurt its acceptance. Roy Weatherby followed relatively quickly, in 1962, with his own .338-inch magnum. His, of course, is the .340 Weatherby Magnum. Using the full-length .300 H&H case blown out, Weatherby easily achieved very significant increases in velocity and energy with the .340.

To this day, the .338 Winchester Magnum and .340 Weatherby are the only factory .33s currently available. We'll discuss each in more detail, and we'll also cover the wildcat .338-06. Elsewhere in this volume, there will be a separate chapter on wildcats, but I think it's important to cover the .338-06 in this chapter for two reasons. First, it's an exceedingly popular wildcat cartridge today. Most major reloading manuals now provide loading data, and of course the proliferation of good .338 bullets and the simplicity of reboring or rebarreling a .30-06 makes it an unusually easy wildcat to pursue. Second, I honestly believe that the .338-06 will become a factory cartridge before these lines see the light of day. Before we get into detail on the cartridges themselves, though, let's look at where the .33s fit in the American hunting scene.

Winchester introduced the .338 in a version of the Model 70 called the "Alaskan." Clearly they saw their powerful new cartridge as a natural for the continent's largest bears and moose–and they weren't wrong. Sectional densities of our .338 bullets are quite high. The 250-grain, for instance, has a sectional density of .313. This is *higher* than the sectional density of even a 200-grain .30-caliber. It's also significantly higher than a 270-grain .375 bullet (sectional density .274) and slightly higher than even the 300-grain .375 (sectional density .305). The sectional density alone translates to improved penetrating qualities on game. All things being equal (velocity, bullet design, etc.), a 250-grain .338 bullet will outpenetrate any .375 bullet, and that's a fact. With equal aerodynamics, a .338 bullet will also have a higher ballistic coefficient, and *that* translates to increased retained velocity and energy at longer ranges.

Thus, as a caliber, the .338 has a lot going for it. It also has significantly increased frontal area over the .30s. The only problem the .33s have is that at higher velocities recoil becomes quite severe. A surprising number of hunters who use them do use them for everything; depending on the cartridge chosen, trajectory is plenty flat enough for any shooting anywhere. However, you don't really need a .33 cartridge for hunting deer, sheep, goat, caribou, and such. As an elk caliber, the .33 really comes into its own, and it becomes ideal when game such as moose and grizzly are the quarry. If we include the .338-06, then we have three current .33-caliber cartridges, and each is in its own distinct velocity and energy category. That makes it easier to look at each separately.

.338-06: Quite possibly the most popular wildcat at this writing, the .338-06 is really an update of the .333 OKH, using .338-inch bullets instead of .333. It's a very simple wildcat to make, created by necking .30-06 brass up to .33 caliber in one step, then fire-forming to achieve the more-or-less standard 17½ degree shoulder.

A great number of very knowledgeable people wax eloquent on the .338-06 these days, among them Nosler's Chub Eastman and gun writer and handloading authority Gary Sitton. Performance is actually quite similar to that of the .35 Whelen, but there's a much better selection of .338-inch bullets out there. Too, the .338-inch bullet diameter seems to wring almost maximum effectiveness out of the .30-06 case.

A 200- or 210-grain bullet can be pushed to around 2,700 feet per second with little difficulty. Due to differences in bearing surface and such, that velocity is very difficult to achieve with a 200-grain .30-caliber in a .30-06. With somewhat limited case capacity, 250-grain bullets are quite a bit slower. The Nosler manual suggests that it's tough to get much over 2,400 fps, while the Sierra manual lists a couple of loads that hit 2,550 fps.

Depending on your rifle, with any bullet weight the .338-06 will lag from as little as 150 to as much as 300 feet per second behind the .338 Winchester Magnum. Even at their extremes, these are not earthshaking differences. A .338 Winchester Magnum firing a 250-grain bullet at 2,700 feet per second has a bit over 4,000 foot/pounds of energy at the muzzle–and still offers some 2,200 foot/pounds at 400 yards. A .338-06 firing a 250-grain bullet at something over 2,400 feet per second won't carry a ton of energy to 400 yards, but it will carry it to 300 yards.

In essence, the .338-06 lags about 100 yards behind the .338 Winchester Magnum in energy. Inside of 300 yards, I suspect it would be difficult to tell the difference between the two in effect on game. The .338-06 will offer significantly reduced recoil, and of course it has the subtle advantage of increased magazine capacity and lighter, more compact ammunition.

It is not the long-range cartridge that the Winchester and Weatherby magnums are, nor does it offer the higher levels of energy that you might want on the biggest bears. But if you're looking for a powerful, effective elk rifle and shots beyond 250 yards or so are rare in your area, the .338-06 makes a sound choice. For these reasons, not to mention its unusual popularity as a wildcat, I think we'll see a factory version very soon.

I must admit to having no personal experience with the cartridge, although I certainly believe the glowing reports of those who have used it. I do have some experience with the .318 Westley Richards, and it's ballistically almost identical. At the somewhat reduced velocities–2,700 for a 200- or 210-grain bullet and 2,400 or so for a 250-grain bullet–I was consistently impressed with the uniformly superb bullet performance and deep penetration that I got from the .318. Chub Eastman, shooting his firm's 210-grain Nosler Partition, had superb results on moose with his .338-06. That doesn't surprise me much. But he also (lucky for him) got a one-shot kill on a record-book grizzly he surprised at 19 paces.

Since all .338 bullets on the market currently were designed for .338 Winchester Magnum and .340 Weatherby Magnum velocities, they're pretty tough bullets. When you drop velocities a bit to .338-06 level, they become tougher yet, and I theorize that the lighter bullets (like that 210-grain Nosler) that should expand violently at magnum velocities will become more controlled and offer greater penetration at .338-06 velocities. That means you can have your cake and eat it as well with the .338-06. With the lighter .338 bullets, you can have significantly reduced recoil, yet still have the highest velocities and flattest trajectories the cartridge is capable of–and *still* have good bullet performance on even the largest of game. But Chub didn't expect to have to shoot a big bear at spitting distance with that bullet in that cartridge. He was pleased with the outcome, as well he should have been, but for that kind of work I'd look to the other two .338 cartridges!

.338 Winchester Magnum: There's no doubt about the .338's acceptance and widespread popularity today. However, this cartridge has come on very slowly, and it really languished for the first decade or two of its existence.

Based on the .458 Winchester Magnum case necked down, it's a short magnum with a 2.500-inch case that fits perfectly into a .30-06-length action. The .338 is a truly powerful cartridge, and its slow acceptance may well have been caused by its reputation for stout recoil–it took a while for hunters to realize they really needed such a cartridge!

In fact, they do. We can talk about minimum calibers for elk, and we can talk about using heavier and/or specially constructed bullets to increase a cartridge's capabilities. But when we talk about the .338, we're talking about an *elk cartridge*. In factory loads, you can really take your pick between a 225-grain bullet at 2,780 feet per second or a 250-grain bullet at 2,660 fps. Either will carry 2,000 foot/pounds to 400 yards! Personally, I'd probably use the lighter, faster 225-grain bullet in open country but stick with the heavyweight 250-grainer in close cover.

Although it's big and brawny, the .338 is also versatile–provided the shooter can handle it. Factory loads or component bullets in 200 or 210 grains do shed velocity fairly quickly, but they can be pushed fast enough to make the .338 a very flat shooter over normal game ranges. For a "one rifle to do everything with," this is an impressive candidate; there really isn't anything the .338 can't do. Although needlessly powerful, it has the trajectory for pronghorn and mountain game–and with 250-grain bullets, is plenty of gun for our largest bears.

Jack Atcheson, Jr., the Butte, Montana, booking agent and bighorn-sheep guide, uses his battered .338 for *everything*. I have personally written that if I could have just one rifle for all North American hunting it would be the .338. I haven't changed my mind! Unlike Jack, though, I don't use it for everything. I haven't gone pronghorn hunting with a .338, nor have I carried one on a sheep mountain. I have used the .338 to hunt elk, moose, and grizzly. These animals are the natural habitat of the .338.

I have also used it for black bear and a fair amount of deer hunting, and of course I've shot some caribou and such along the way. Now, don't laugh. The average-sized black bear weighs about 200 pounds. That's one thing. A really big black bear can top 500, and that's a whole different animal. With a rifle like a .338, it doesn't really matter whether you get your chance at an average bear or the kind of bear you're hoping for. You're in good shape either way.

Deer hunting is much the same. You don't really need a .338 for any deer that walks, but it's comforting to have that margin of power for a difficult shot at a big-bodied, large-racked buck. My old friend Ed Nixon ranches in Montana's remote Swan Valley, home to some of the biggest and most difficult-to-hunt whitetails on the whole continent. Nixon traded in his .270 for a .338 some years ago and has never looked back. When I've hunted his country–heavy timber where few shots are long but none are easy–I've followed his lead and carried a .338 as well. And I've been happy I had it. It's also not a bad choice for really big mule deer anywhere. Like Atcheson says, "the .338 *numbs* them!"

Although I believe in big guns for the whitetails of Alberta and Saskatchewan, the .338 may not be the best choice there. Shooting can get extremely long sometimes, and although the .338 carries the mail beautifully for large game like elk, it is not remarkably flat-shooting. I have made some wonderfully long shots with the .338, but long shooting on smaller targets is not the cartridge's best suit.

But, man, does it work! Few cartridges that can be carried by hand will pound a moose or an elk like a .338, and with bullets from 200 to 225 grains it's unbelievably impressive on deer. The major cost, of course, is sheer recoil–and that's also impressive. A fairly heavy, wooden-stocked .338 will recoil from about 35 foot/pounds with light bullets to 40 plus with 250-grainers. My .338 is a lightweight, synthetic-stocked job. It starts in the low 40s with light bullets, and with 250-grain loads delivers a full 50 foot/pounds of recoil. My buddy Ed Nixon is a hard man, and he feels hunters must learn to accept recoil like that if they want to hunt tough game such as elk. I agree, but only to a point. People have different levels of recoil tolerance, and not everyone can stand up to .338 recoil. It's a great cartridge, but its bullets must be put in the right places. If you can't shoot a .338, then you must understand and accept that fact and learn to place bullets from a .30-06 or similar caliber with utmost precision. And if you're the least bit uncomfortable with a .338, don't even think about our last and most powerful .33!

.340 Weatherby Magnum: Roy Weatherby's .340 is everything the .338 is and a great deal more. Factory loads are rated at 3,260 feet per second for a 200-grain bullet, 3,250 for 210 grains, and 3,000 for 250-

grain bullets. This is one of the few sets of Weatherby factory figures that I have an issue with. Factory loads I have chronographed seem to come up about 100 fps short, and even then it's very difficult to concoct handloads to match.

But whether a 250-grain bullet goes 3,000 or the more realistic 2,900 fps, it's still a screamer. Add to the great sectional density the aerodynamics of a spitzer design, and you come up with ballistic coefficients that are out of this world. Sierra's 250-grain boattail has BC of .587 at close range and .619 at midrange velocities! The only hunting bullet on the scale that beats it is an exceptionally aerodynamic 175-grain 7mm bullet. Sight-in to be just 2½ inches high at 100 yards and you're dead-on at 250 yards and just 15 inches low at 400 yards. At the muzzle, you've got more than 4,500 foot/pounds of energy–and almost 3,000 at 400 yards. I'm not recommending 600-yard shooting at elk or anything else, but for comparison, the .340 Weatherby Magnum with a 250-grain spitzer still carries over a ton of energy at 600 yards. Almost nothing that a human being can fire from the shoulder will top that.

Recoil, unfortunately, is fierce. Depending on gun weight, it's going to recoil in mid-40s to the mid-50s. And it hits as fast as it does hard. I have a .340 that I'm very fond of, but I can't say it's pleasant to shoot. I can say it's a marvelously effective cartridge–in trajectory, it's sort of like a .270 or 7mm magnum, but in effect on game more like a .375.

For those who can handle it, it's one of the most effective long-range elk rigs going. I have not personally hunted elk with my .340, but I did shoot a Shiras moose at very long range with it, and I've used it on a couple of big bears as well as a wide range of African plains game.

One of the bears presented a classic situation for the .340 Weatherby Magnum. It was the last evening of the last day of the hunt, and we were stalking a grizzly well above timberline where cover was very limited. We had seen the bear literally miles away, feeding contentedly. We didn't realize until we got there that a very deep, sheer-sided gorge separated us from the bear. It was late enough in the day that we had no time left to regroup and go around, so we either had to pass the bear and end the hunt unsuccessfully or take the shot we had.

Size is hard to judge on bears, and judging cross-canyon distance is the hardest of all even if you know the exact size of your target. The shot wasn't all that long, but it could have been as little as 225 yards or as much as a bit over 300. I still have no idea exactly how far it was–but I was thankful for the .340 on that day.

The bear was facing us on a downhill slope, head down as he worried some particularly tasty succulent. I put the crosshairs on his hump, took a deep breath, and squeezed the trigger. The bullet hit almost exactly where I'd aimed, indicating the shot was right at 250 to 275 yards, and the bear was literally driven into the hillside. He rolled out of sight, and that made us extremely careful when we approached in the gathering dark—but he was dead before he started to roll. That 250-grain Nosler, by the way, broke his neck, penetrated into the chest cavity and wrecked everything there, and then exited just in front of the diaphragm.

Because of the great velocity, care must be taken with bullet selection for the .340. Although recoil is at its greatest, the 250-grain weight is the bullet of choice. If lighter bullets are selected, only very tough bullets like the Barnes "X" and Bearclaw should be considered. For me, the 250-grain bullet is the way to go. With a good 250-grainer in a .340, you're equipped to handle anything this continent has to offer—but it's a cartridge that takes serious practice to master!

Chapter 12

.35s–A Fine Selection of Also-Rans

I answer most of the "Questions and Answers" mail for *Petersen's HUNTING* magazine, and just today I got an interesting one. A reader from the big-timber country in Maine wrote to ask why nobody makes a combination gun in .358 Winchester/20 gauge. Since grouse and whitetail seasons coincided in his neighborhood, he figured such a firearm would be the ideal "meat gun" for him. He's probably right, but I'd have to rate him as one of the more optimistic folks I know. The .35-caliber hasn't fared quite as poorly as the .32 or 8mm, but it's extremely unlikely that anybody is going to design a whole new firearm around one!

There have been .35-caliber hunting cartridges since the very beginnings of smokeless powder. And unlike several bullet diameters we've discussed, the .35 was pretty universal. In Europe, the 9x56 Mannlicher-Schoenauer, 9x57 Mauser, and 9x63 all achieved some popularity, and the first two are still seen occasionally. In England, the first .35 was the .400-350 Nitro-Express, introduced by John Rigby in 1899. He followed with his .350 Rimless Magnum, or .350 Rigby, in 1908. Despite the fancy name and larger case, the .350 Rimless Magnum was only slightly more powerful than our .35 Whelen. The 9x63 is almost identical to the Whelen in both case size and ballistics. The rest, including the huge-cased .400-350 for double rifles, delivered ballistics on the order of the .358 Winchester.

In America, there were a few long-forgotten black-powder .35s–and several equally forgotten turn-of-the-century .35s. Among these were Winchester's mild .35 and, later, .351 Self-Loading cartridges for early semiautomatics. More useful for the hunter was Winchester's 1903-vintage .35 Winchester, chambered in the Model 1895 lever-action. Firing a 250-grain bullet at 2,195 feet per second, it wasn't a red-hot number but was considered extremely effective on fairly large game. It died with the '95.

Also long gone are two extremely powerful American .35s. The first was the .35 Newton, essentially the .30 Newton necked up to .35 caliber. Newton rifles and quite a few custom rifles were made in this chambering, and Western loaded ammo for it into the 1930s. It was a very powerful unbelted cartridge, a true magnum compared with other .35s. It offered a 250-grain bullet at 2,660 feet per second, and was rated quite adequate for game up to brown bear. The second was the .350 Griffin & Howe Magnum, developed by the New York gunsmithing firm of Griffin & Howe and also loaded by Western in the 1930s. It was based on the .375 H&H case necked down to .35, and was adopted by Holland & Holland as the .350

Holland & Holland Magnum. The factory load featured a 250-grain bullet at 2,700 feet per second, and that with 1930s powders.

With handloads, both the Newton and Griffin & Howe cartridges exceed the "modern" .358 Norma Magnum by some measure–but both are long forgotten today. The only early .35 still with us is the little .35 Remington, a mild, unassuming cartridge that simply refuses to die.

Today, including the .357 pistol cartridge which has been chambered in several rifles, we have fully eight .35-caliber cartridges still available in factory ammunition. Some are barely hanging on, while a couple have some regional popularity. But to date, none of them have become stars in the North American hunting marketplace. Why this should be is hard to figure–much more difficult than understanding why the .32s haven't made the big time. The .35 does reflect a significant step up in caliber from our "standard" .30s. As hunters who use them know, the heavier bullet weight combined with greatly increased frontal area makes the .35s wonderfully effective–devastating on deer and extremely deadly on black bear and even elk.

Perhaps we got too wrapped up in paper ballistics and velocities. Except for the .358 Norma Magnum, none of our .35s offer the high velocities and flat trajectories that American hunters seem to crave. Instead, they simply get their jobs done in a calm, efficient manner. We'll look at each separately.

.357 Magnum: This one we'll dispense with very quickly. A number of lever-action rifles, a couple of single-shots, and even the Savage Model 24 combo gun have been chambered in .357 Magnum. Although "street legal" for deer in numerous states, the .357 Magnum is not a deer cartridge. Velocities do increase significantly from longer rifle barrels, and it's no great trick to achieve the minimal 1,000 foot/pounds of muzzle energy. With some loads as much as 1,300 foot/pounds is possible. However, because of the poor sectional density of pistol bullets, velocities and energies drop very quickly. At best, the .357 should be considered a 50-yard gun for small deer–and much better suited to the same kinds of things the .25-20 and .32-20 are best for.

.35 Remington: Although hardly a hot number, the .35 Remington is a serious hunting cartridge. A rimless cartridge introduced in Remington's Model 8 semiauto, it has been offered in numerous rifles, including Remington slide-actions, semiautomatics, and bolt-actions, and was even briefly chambered in the Winchester Model 70. For many years now, Marlin's 336 remains the only rifle still chambered in .35 Remington, but the cartridge retains a reasonable following in the big timber of the Northeast and upper Midwest. On paper, it offers nothing over the .30-30 Winchester–factory loads include a 150-grain bullet at 2,300 feet per second for 1,762 foot/pounds and a 200-grain bullet at 2,080 fps for 1,921 foot/pounds. In practice, the greater frontal area–and especially the greater weight of the 200-grain bullet will indeed hit harder and offer significantly increased knockdown power at short range.

The .35 Remington is a very short-range cartridge, like the .30-30, but in close cover is probably a better choice for larger deer and black bear. However, I'd stay away from that 150-grain bullet, especially for bear. It has very poor sectional density and can't be expected to penetrate well.

The .35 Remington has now received a new lease on life as a handgun-hunting cartridge. Chambered in both Remington's XP-100 and Thompson/Center's Contender, its fairly small case capacity makes it quite efficient in the 14-inch pistol barrels—especially handloaded with faster powders. In a strong handgun, 180-grain bullets can be pushed to 2,100 feet per second and 200-grain bullets above 2,000 fps. In other words, with good handloads it's everything in a pistol that it ever was in a rifle!

Even with spitzer bullets, you can't make a long-range pistol out of the .35, but it does make a very fine choice for short-range deer hunting and for black bear and wild hogs and such. It was a great favorite of both Dave Hetzler and Bob Milek, and I've use a Thompson/Center .35 for quite a bit of wild-hog hunting. There's really no difference between shooting a hog with a .35 Remington from a rifle or a pistol—and that means it's an extremely effective handgun cartridge. It's hard to say whether Marlin will continue to offer the .35 in their lever-action, but whether they do or not, it's fairly certain that most of what future the .35 has left is in the long-barreled specialty pistols.

.348 Winchester: Introduced in 1936 in the Winchester Model 71 lever-action, the .348 is very much an oddity. It's the only cartridge ever produced with a .348-inch bullet diameter. The Winchester Model 71, the last iteration of John Browning's great Winchester Model 1886 action, is the only rifle ever chambered for the .348. And the Model 71 was never chambered in anything but the .348 Winchester. In spite of it being one rifle, one cartridge, and an oddball bullet diameter, the .348 is a legendary cartridge—and well it should be.

The '86 action, only slightly modified to the Model 71, is a big, beefy action, and it needs to be to house the .348 Winchester. The case is long for a lever-action, 2.255 inches, and has a rim diameter of .610-inch. With great action strength and plenty of case capacity, muzzle velocities are impressive—but because of the need to use flat-pointed bullets in the 71's tubular magazine, downrange velocities drop quickly.

Original loadings were a 150-grain bullet at 2,890 feet per second, a 200-grain loading at 2,530 fps, and a 250-grain loading at 2,350 fps. Although initially fast, the short 150-grain bullet shed velocity very quickly. It was the first .348 load to be dropped, and good riddance. Regrettably, the 250-grain load has also been dropped, and that's a shame. The 200-grain loading is a good one—but the velocity increase isn't enough to make up for the greater weight and sectional density of the 250-grain heavyweight.

Even the 200-grain load would undoubtedly have been dropped had Browning not recently produced a limited run of Model 71s. Let's hope they have given this grand old cartridge, if not a new lease on life, at least an extension.

For the last 15 years or so, I've made certain that I always have at least one Model 71 on hand. I've used the cartridge a great deal on wild hogs and some amount on black bear, and I even shot a bison with it. It's every bit as effective as its legend suggests. For deer and pigs, I have no trouble with the 200-grain factory load, but I much prefer the 250-grain bullet. The only source I'm aware of is Barnes Bullets, and their 250-grain flat-point has performed extremely well for me. With Hodgdon H380 powder or IMR 4064, it's no problem to reach 2,300 feet per second with the 250-grain bullet. That yields about 3,000 foot/pounds of energy, which is impressive enough. However, that kind of energy behind a 250-grain flat-pointed bullet really hits like a freight train. I've seen black bear literally picked up and thrown down by that bullet–and I get tremendous enjoyment out of using both the cartridge and that big, old lever-action.

.358 Winchester/.356 Winchester: The .358 is another unsung hero of a cartridge. It's a very compact little powerhouse, simply the .308 Winchester necked up to accept .358-inch bullets. Winchester introduced it in 1955 in both the Model 88 lever-action and Model 70 Featherweight rifles. Later, it was a popular chambering in the Savage Model 99, but today the only rifle available in .358 is Browning's slick little BLR.

Initial loadings were a 200-grain bullet at 2,530 feet per second and a 250-grain bullet at 2,250 fps. Unfortunately, just like the .348, the faster, lighter bullet outsold the heavier, more effective load. Only the 200-grain loading survives today.

Muzzle velocity with the 200-grain load is about the same as for the .348, but because the .358 was never offered in a tubular-magazine rifle, spitzer or at least semi-pointed bullets have been offered in factory loads and can be used by handloaders. This gives the .358 a very significant ballistic advantage over the .348 Winchester.

Thanks to the upsurge in popularity of the .35 Whelen, there are now a great many more .358 bullets to choose from than has been the case for many a year. I used to load 250-grain Speer bullets for my Savage 99, but the case capacity pretty much limits velocity. You can beat the original factory-load velocity of 2,250, but not by much. A better choice today would be one of the several very fine 225-grain spitzers. Nosler's reloading manual suggests that 2,500 feet per second can be reached with IMR4895. Such a load will exceed 3,000 foot/pounds of energy at the muzzle, and will carry 2,000 foot/pounds to 250 yards. That ain't bad for so small a case, and makes the .358 Winchester an extremely viable elk cartridge.

My own use for the cartridge, in both the Savage and Browning lever-actions, has been–as with the .348–mostly for black bear and wild hogs.

Like the .348, it's extremely effective–perhaps even more so because of better downrange ballistics. It's too bad this much underrated cartridge hasn't become more popular.

The .356 Winchester is essentially a semi-rimmed version of the .358, introduced in 1982 in a Winchester's beefed-up "Big Bore 94." The case has almost the same external dimensions, but thicker case walls for slightly less powder capacity. In a 24-inch barrel, the factory loads lag about 100 feet per second behind the .358, but in the 20-inch-barreled Model 94 you lose about another 100 fps. Unlike the .358, both 200- and 250-grain loads are still available. Flat-pointed bullets will reduce downrange ballistics considerably, but within 150 yards or so the .356 will be indistinguishable from the .358 in effect on game.

.350 Remington Magnum: The .348 retains its following, as does the .358. Fans are loyal but relatively few, and that is certainly the case with the .350 Remington Magnum. It came along after most of our popular short magnums, and enjoyed a brief run of magnum euphoria–then dropped off the face of the earth.

The .350 uses a very short, fat case with a length of 2.170 inches. Together with the 6.5mm Remington Magnum, it was designed to fit into the Remington Model 600 action. It did achieve greater popularity than the 6.5; after the Model 600 and later 660 carbines were discontinued, the .350 survived as a Model 700 chambering for a few years. A few other rifles have been so chambered, but currently no factory rifle is available for this cartridge.

The factory load has a 200-grain bullet at a very fast 2,710 feet per second. This is from a 24-inch barrel, and the more common 18- or 20-inch barrels will of course lose considerable velocity. Even so, it's an impressive little cartridge. Because of the 600's action length, heavier bullets must be seated so deeply that they begin to eat up powder space, but in longer actions, bullets up to 250 grains can be pushed to velocities significantly exceeding .35 Whelen speeds.

The .350 Remington proved to be a real handful in the very light Model 600 carbine, and it's entirely possible that its legendary recoil was its undoing on the marketplace. It's a very fine little cartridge that easily makes a medium-range elk rifle and a black-bear rifle without peer–but chances of its increasing in popularity seem very slim.

.35 Whelen: Remington's track record with cartridges developed by their R&D boys has been so-so. Their 7mm Remington Magnum has been a stunning success, as has their 7mm-08. Their .416 Remington Magnum has exceeded all expectations. But they blew it with the .244, had trouble getting the .280 off the ground, and had less than stunning success with their 6.5mm, .350, and 8mm Remington Magnums.

On the other hand, they have a marvelous track record of taking popular (or at least as popular as non-standard cartridges can be) wildcat cartridges and turning them into commercial successes. The .22-250 Remington, long a popular wildcat, is one example. Another is the .25-06 Remington. They hit the jackpot again with the .35 Whelen.

Largely at the urging of Remington's longtime public relations man, Dick Dietz, and their Custom Shop's Tim McCormick, Remington took what was considered a big chance by chambering their 1987 Model 700 Limited Edition Classic in .35 Whelen. At the same time, they brought out a 200-grain spitzer and 250-grain round-nose factory load, and at the last minute also decided to offer their Model 7600 slide-action in the "new" caliber.

The results are history. The .35 Whelen exceeded their wildest expectations in both bolt-action and slide-action form, and has since remained a fairly strong seller in Remington's line-up.

The cartridge is hardly new. Although named for the great gun writer Colonel Townsend Whelen, it was actually developed by Griffin & Howe's James Howe in 1922. Whelen had some input and did use the cartridge subsequently, but he should not be given more than partial credit for creating it. It has long been a fairly popular wildcat. It's a good option for reboring shot-out Springfield barrels, and also offers greater bullet weight and frontal area than the '06 at very respectable velocities, thus increasing killing power substantially. Colonel Whelen used the cartridge for moose and such, and was very pleased with it–as were numerous other hunters who used it for game up to brown bear and grizzly.

Remington's initial factory loads were a 200-grain spitzer at 2,675 feet per second and a 250-grain round-nose at 2,400 fps. Since then, they've added a 250-grain spitzer at the same velocity. All three are very good loads with good bullets, and accuracy in the several Remington .35 Whelens I've played with has been simply fabulous.

In the fall of 1987, I happened to have planned an Alaskan moose hunt, and Remington was good enough to get one of the first of their .35 Whelens and some 250-grain loads in my hands. Although the round-nose bullets lose their velocity quickly, there was certainly no adverse effect on accuracy. That particular rifle printed half-inch groups with boring regularity, and on the hunt my partner and I had a great time shooting the heads off grouse at sometimes amazing distances!

My chance for a moose came in heavy timber at about 60 yards. We spotted the bull from a ridgetop vantage point. He was chasing some cows and went into an island of thick spruce and didn't come out. After waiting a couple of hours, we concluded that he'd bedded for the day and we went in after him. We were lucky; we never saw him in his bed, but when he jumped up he stood facing us for several seconds. I put the 250-grain round-nose where neck joins shoulder, and at the report all I could see were four moose legs up in the air.

The .35 Whelen has a soft report and very mild recoil–it's a pussycat to shoot. But I've shot moose with the .338 Winchester Magnum, the .340

Weatherby, the .375 H&H, and the .416 Remington. I have *never* seen a moose go down like that big bull did from the little .35 Whelen. My hunting partner was a Colorado elk hunter who hunts thick oak brush. Up until then, he had used a .444 Marlin for elk and had been consistently pleased with it. He was so impressed that he promptly ordered a Model 7600 in .35 Whelen. *I* was so impressed that I immediately ordered a left-hand, synthetic-stocked Model 700 in .35 Whelen. We've both used them extensively since then!

The almost instant popularity of the .35 Whelen did wonders for bullet availability. There are now some excellent 225-grain bullets, which is a wonderful compromise weight. I use my .35 for bear, wild boar, and elk during bugling seasons, so I have little use for the 200-grain bullet even though it achieves enough velocity to make a good deer load. I like the 250-grain bullets a lot, but even with the best of handloads it's tough to get them much above 2,450 feet per second. That means your range becomes limited by trajectory. The 225-grain bullet is a good compromise load, and can be pushed to 2,550 or better with no difficulties.

Even so, the .35 Whelen is best thought of as a 250-yard cartridge. Beyond that, even though the energy is there, trajectory starts to get in the way of certain bullet placement. I have used the cartridge not only on moose, but also on elk, bear, deer, and wild hogs. Within 250 yards, it's absolutely devastating, in appearance every bit as effective as a .338 Winchester Magnum. And the recoil is significantly softer. Provided you don't have the need to reach out great distances, the cartridge is a real winner and should be with us for a long time.

.358 Norma Magnum: The big .358 Norma is the only truly high-velocity, high-performance .35 on the market today. It was introduced by Norma in 1959 and, like the .308 Norma, was originally available only in the form of brass and, later, loaded ammo, with no factory-made rifles so chambered. Schultz & Larsen made rifles for it, and the fairly new Danish firm of Varberger currently chambers for it. Norma ammunition is available, but can be a bit hard to come by. Undoubtedly, lack of readily available rifles *and* ammunition has severely limited this cartridge's popularity.

In the past, lack of bullets suited to the .358 Norma's velocity was undoubtedly a contributing factor as well, but the heavier bullets now designed for the .35 Whelen will generally perform well in the Norma. I've heard of quite a few custom rifles being made in this caliber lately, but I seriously doubt if it's going to give either the .338 or the .375 H&H a run for their money any time soon.

Popular or not, it is a fine and very powerful cartridge. A short magnum with a 2.519-inch case, factory loads deliver 2,800 feet per second with a 250-grain bullet. This gives it a muzzle energy of over 4,300 foot/pounds–about the same as the .375 H&H–and somewhat better ranging abilities. It makes a fine long-range elk cartridge and is easily powerful enough to tackle the biggest bears. It's in a tough bracket, however, having to compete with a cartridge as famous as the .375 H&H or as readily available as the .338 Winchester Magnum. Since its inception, it's been yet another .35-caliber "also-ran"–and chances are the .35 Whelen is the only cartridge in .35 caliber that has a significant future ahead of it.

Chapter 13

.375–Ultimate for North America?

As I write these lines, I'm en route to southeast Alaska to hunt Alaskan brown bear, one the greatest game animals on earth and arguably the most dangerous animal on the North American continent, possibly sharing that title only with the polar bear. In fact, the giant bears of Alaska must rate among the most fearsome beasts on this planet. The great cats are deadly, to be sure. I've faced lion charges, and nothing is as fast or as frightening. But a good-sized grizzly should outweigh a male African lion by two to one. And the salmon-fed bears of coastal Alaska and her offshore islands can outweigh a lion by as much as four to one.

The country, too, makes hunting the great coastal bears an interesting enterprise. There's little cover where polar bears are hunted. Save the odd ice ridge, the chances of surprising a bear at close range–or vice versa–are limited. Mountain grizzlies, too, are customarily spotted at long range and stalked. Brown bears are most often hunted in the thick alders along salmon streams or on hillsides covered with some of this continent's most dense brush. Long shots are extremely uncommon, and close encounters can be expected.

Much controversy surrounds how large an Alaskan brown bear can really be. Well-fed zoo specimens may get extremely heavy–and the largest specimens taken in the wild have never been weighed. I shot a very large brown bear back in 1981, and another good bear on Russia's Kamchatka Peninsula in 1992. The Alaskan bear was a fair amount bigger by squared hide, but the carcasses of each matched any Cape buffalo I've ever shot. Based on that, I would say that a legitimate fall weight for a very big bear could exceed 1,500 pounds. For sure, 1,000 to 1,200 pounds is well in the ballpark for a good-sized brownie.

The bear I shot back in '81 had a hide that, laid out flat and measured honestly with no stretching, squared an inch under 11 feet. The skull matched it as well. Stopping a bear like that is serious business, and while a lot of cartridges will do it, few are truly well-suited to the task. The medium magnums such as Remington's 8mm, Winchester's .338, and Weatherby's .340 will do the job. Certainly the various .416s will, and more than a few brown-bear guides choose to carry a .458 Winchester Magnum "just in case."

More or less standard for many decades, however, is the 1912-vintage .375 Holland & Holland Magnum. It was a .375 H&H that I chose back in 1981, and it's a .375 H&H that, even as I write these lines, is stored in the belly of the plane carrying me north. My choice of the .375 for this upcoming hunt is an obvious one, but it was not automatic. Using different rifles and cartridges in the field is always interesting, and while I have my favorites, I almost consider it a professional obligation to have some field experience with as wide an array of rifles and cartridges as possible. When I began planning this hunt more than a year ago, the .375 was a prime candidate for use–but not the only one.

I have a .358 Norma Magnum on order, and I had considered using it. Knowing I'd need time to work up loads and such, I established a cutoff date in my mind. The rifle didn't arrive by that date, so I eliminated it from consideration. I gave passing thought to a .338 or .340 Weatherby, more than passing thought to a .348 Winchester or .35 Whelen, and I even toyed with using my .416 Rigby. When it came time for final sighting-in, though, I settled on what is unquestionably the classic brown-bear cartridge: Holland & Holland's marvelous .375.

The .375 H&H was not the first cartridge to use that bullet diameter, nor has it been the last. It had a British forerunner in the .375 Velopex, a cartridge that used a short, belted case and delivered ho-hum ballistics. There was a much better cartridge on the Continent, the 9.5 Mannlicher-Schoenauer. Holland saw this 9.5 as creating stiff competition, and they set out to create a versatile medium-bore cartridge that would bring market share back to merry England. The result was the .375 H&H, a stunning success in 1912 and still a world-standard cartridge today.

Original loadings were a light, fast 235-grain bullet at about 2,900 feet per second, a 270-grain bullet at around 2,700, and a 300-grain bullet at 2,530 fps. Although fast and initially very flat-shooting, the short 235-grain bullet shed velocity very quickly, penetrated poorly, and was never very popular. It has long since been dropped, but the 270- and 300-grain loadings remain standard fare for the .375. Also available in factory form is a light-recoiling 250-grain load from Federal, delivering about 2,700 feet per second muzzle velocity.

There's a tremendous array of fine component bullets for the .375. Most center around the 270- and 300-grain weights, but there are also 235-grain bullets from Speer and Barnes, 240-grain bullets from Trophy Bonded, 250-grain Sierra bullets, 265-grain Nosler Partitions, 285-grain Speer Grand Slams, and 350-grain heavyweights from Barnes. For low-recoil practice loads, there are also 220-grain flat-points intended for the .375 Winchester. Over the years, I have used most of these bullets on game, and all have their uses.

It's interesting to speculate whether the .375 would have reached its worldwide popularity had it been retained by Holland as a proprietary cartridge. It was not; shortly after its introduction, it was released to the gun trade, and *everybody* made rifles for it. The first American loads were made by Western around 1926, but American rifles so chambered remained a custom proposition for quite some time. Using magnum

Mauser actions, Griffin & Howe probably made the most American .375s until 1937, when the cartridge was offered in Winchester's brand-new Model 70 bolt-action.

The .375 H&H was the first truly powerful cartridge chambered in an American rifle. Prior to that, domestic choices for big bear rifles—or for Africa-bound Americans—were very limited. Lever-actions in .348, .35, and .405 Winchester; bolt-actions in .30-06 rebored to .35 Whelen, plus the odd .35 Newton. That was about it. In the .375 H&H, Winchester offered not only an extremely powerful rifle, but one with reach as well. In power it was unrivaled until Winchester's .458 came along in 1956, and in power that reached out it was unrivaled until the same firm's .338 came along two years later. Today, some brown-bear guides choose a .458 while others choose a .338, both good choices. But the standard remains the .375 H&H, a choice that simply cannot be argued against.

The actual necessity for a .375 H&H—or any cartridge of similar or greater power—is quite limited in North America. Brown bear, polar bear, the largest of interior grizzlies, just perhaps bison, and you've said it all. However, unlike the shorter-ranged and much harder-kicking .416s and larger calibers, the .375 H&H is both shootable and versatile.

Its standard 270-grain bullets are not especially long on sectional density, but the velocity is high enough to give relatively flat trajectory over normal game ranges. Winchester's Power-Point is a semi-spitzer bullet that has been a standard .375 load for decades—and a good one. Zeroed two inches high at 100 yards, it's dead-on at 200 yards and just 10 inches low at 300 yards. Because of the relatively low sectional density and semi-spitzer design, it sheds velocity and energy quickly; at the muzzle, it offers more than 4,300 foot/pounds, but at 300 yards this has dropped to a bit more than 2,200. That's still more than plenty, especially since no one in his right mind shoots at big bears at 300 yards!

Better, to my thinking, is a 300-grain load—especially the more aerodynamic bullets like the Swift loaded in Remington's Safari line or the 300-grain Nosler Partition loaded in Federal Premium. Initial velocity is much slower, but the better ballistic coefficient gives the bullet about the same trajectory curve to 300 yards—and carries a great deal more energy to that distance and beyond. The 300-grain bullet, surprisingly, delivers over 2,900 foot/pounds at 300 yards, even though it starts out with a bit less energy than the lighter, faster 270-grain bullet.

My own love affair with the .375 began very early. Perhaps because I grew up at the height of the magnum craze, and perhaps because I started dreaming of African hunting at an early age, I was in my late teens when I got my first .375. Although I'm totally left-handed, I didn't yet know that left-handed bolt-actions existed. Like most lefties, I learned to shoot a bolt-action by reaching over the top. I could do it fast, too—and still can when I have to! That first .375 was on an FN magnum Mauser action, with a Hart barrel chambered by the great old Kansas City gunsmith Howard Baucher and stocked by Jack Pohl at Bishop's. It had a fairly heavy barrel and plenty of wood, so it handled like a dream even in tired hands and didn't kick badly.

With that rifle I explored literally all the purposes one could possibly have for a .375, and never found it wanting. In 1974, I shot my first grizzly with it, very probably the best shot I've ever made in my life. It was the last day of a spring hunt, a spring that was bringing a slow thaw to a record snowfall in the southern British Columbia mountains. The bears were just coming out, and we had to slog our way through drifts too deep for our horses so that we could glass the few open slides that might draw a bear. Finally, in late afternoon of the last day, we spotted a lone bear far up a mountainside. My guide, Ed Langlands, was stove up in the back and couldn't make the climb, but he trusted me enough to send me up alone–as if he could have stopped me. At about 300 yards, I was stopped by a clean expanse of white snow, with no trees sturdy enough for a rest.

Being very young, very foolish, and very confident, I took a shot that I would not take today. Offhand, wrapped into a tight sling, I held the crosshairs just above the bear's backline as it stopped broadside–and brought an avalanche of grizzly rolling my way. That was probably the second best shot of my life. The best was when I hit that rolling, bouncing bear yet again as it hurtled downslope to me–but the second shot wasn't necessary; the first Remington Core-Lokt 270-grain bullet had done its work.

Long before that episode with the grizzly, I had used my .375 for a wide variety of Western hunting–enough that I knew the rifle and cartridge pretty well, and my last-day desperation shot on that bear probably wasn't as desperate or uncertain as it sounds.

The grizzly was the first animal I hunted that really needed, or at least deserved, a .375's power. But in previous seasons I had taken elk, moose, caribou, and black bear with the rifle–not to mention sheep, goat, mule deer, and pronghorn! This last group shows what *can* be done with a .375, not necessarily what *should* be done. Given reasonable technique, almost anything can be stalked within easy .375 range! It was with that .375 that I shot my first elk, my first really good mule deer, my first wild sheep–and with which I made some of my most memorable shots. Not only that grizzly, but also a couple of running shots on pronghorn and deer.

The versatility of the .375 is what has made it so popular in Africa for so many years. Over there, you leave camp not knowing whether you'll encounter a 15-pound dik-dik, a 150-pound impala, or a 1,500-pound eland. The .375 has the accuracy, trajectory, and power for any of these encounters–and can also handle the elephant, buffalo, or lion you might run into. In North America, the .375 can indeed work wonders on white-tailed deer, mule deer, and even pronghorn and sheep–but you're rarely worried about running into an elephant, lion, or even a Kodiak bear while hunting such species. That the .375 will do the job is no issue, but there are plenty of flatter-shooting, lighter-recoiling calibers that will do an equally good job.

While deer and mountain game with a .375 may be stretching a point, there's absolutely nothing wrong with using a .375 for elk, moose, and black bear. In all cases, there might be calibers every bit as suitable–but there might not be anything much better!

Moose are not extremely tough animals, pound for pound–but they are as heavy as any eland or Cape buffalo, and that puts them in .375 country. Elk aren't nearly as large as moose, but pound for pound they're as tough as any animal that walks. Under certain conditions, a cartridge that shoots a bit flatter than the .375 might be desirable, but most elk hunting, too, is in .375 country.

The average black bear probably weighs 150 to 200 pounds and certainly doesn't require a .375. However, a really big black bear can top 500 pounds and is a whole different animal. By chance I've taken my two largest black bears, both genuine monsters, with a .375. Both were absolutely flattened with one shot and never moved again.

I would never suggest that you *need* a .375 H&H for black bear, elk, or moose. Or, for that matter, for bison or muskox. These animals do encompass the *potential* North American uses for this great caliber, while the only real *need* is for hunting the largest bears. Even for the latter, you may not need to rush out and buy a .375. But if you have one, don't hesitate to use it. Unlike lesser calibers that will simply get the job done, the .375 is extremely impressive on tough game like elk and big black bears.

While .375 factory loads are very good, the cartridge can be enhanced significantly by careful handloading. For lighter game, there are several good lightweights that offer significantly reduced recoil. For deer hunting and such, give some thought to Speer 235-grain bullets or Sierra 250-grain bullets. Speeds above 2,900 feet per second are easily achieved, and trajectories are quite flat in spite of the poor sectional density of these short bullets.

For elk hunting, lighter bullets are okay–but I'd go to premium hunting bullets designed to penetrate. In the lightweights, these would include Barnes "X" bullets in 235 and 250 grains, Trophy Bonded Bearclaws in 240-grain weight, and Nosler's new 265-grain Partition. The only elk I've shot recently with a .375 was a New Mexico bull I shot with a 240-grain Bearclaw. The bullet broke both shoulders and was lodged under the hide on the far side, picture-perfect and with well above 90 percent weight retention.

For serious work–read that to mean "big bears"–bullets between 270 and 300 grains are the normal choices. I started out a big fan of the 270-grain bullet, but in recent years have pretty much gravitated to the 300-

grain bullet. Several different powders will give a 300-grain bullet a muzzle velocity of 2,600 feet per second–nearly 100 fps better than the factory loads–and with decent bullet aerodynamics this makes the .375 surprisingly flat-shooting.

There are a myriad good component bullets available–and the wonderful thing is that, at .375 H&H velocities, there just aren't any bad .375 bullets. Hornady's 270- and 300-grain Interlock Spire Points are aerodynamically awesome and hold together well. Speer's 285-grain Grand Slam is superb, and one of my all-time favorites is Sierra's 300-grain boattail. Nosler's 300-grain Partition is back after a long absence, and is doing great. But so are "super-premium" bullets like the 300-grain Swift A-Frame, the Trophy Bonded Bearclaw, and the Barnes "X"-bullet.

In the .375 caliber, it's pretty clear where my loyalties lie, but in all fairness I must admit that the .375 H&H isn't the only .375-caliber cartridge. There are three others that rate at least brief discussion: the .375 Winchester and the .375 and .378 Weatherby Magnums. The first, the .375 Winchester, is a radical step down from .375 H&H performance. The other two are incremental increases up the power ladder–which may or may not be a good thing.

.375 Winchester: Introduced in 1978 in a beefed-up version of Winchester's timeless Model 94 dubbed the "94 Big Bore," the .375 Winchester is indeed a quantum leap upward from .30-30 Winchester performance. The straight-walled .375 Winchester case is very similar to the much older .38-55, a black-powder cartridge that was an original chambering for the Model 94. However, .375 Winchester brass is much stronger, and .38-55 rifles *will not* stand up to the pressures of the newer cartridge.

Caliber is .375, just like the .375 H&H. However, the only thing it shares with the .375 H&H is bullet diameter. Factory loads offer a 200-grain bullet at 2,200 feet per second and a 250-grain bullet at a very slow 1,900 fps, yielding 2,150 and 2,000 foot/pounds, respectively. The flat-pointed bullets shed velocity and energy very quickly; neither bullet weight carries 1,000 foot/pounds much beyond 200 yards. That probably doesn't matter, because this was intended to be a short-range cartridge capable of taking black bear, moose, and elk in heavy cover. This it is, and these things it will certainly do.

As can probably be seen, I'm not particularly impressed with this cartridge; I would prefer a .444 Marlin or .45-70 in a short-range, powerful lever-action–and the .348, 356, and .358 Winchester are all more versatile and offer more energy. However, the heavy, blunt-nosed slugs for the .375 Winchester deal a heavy blow. Paper ballistics show adequate energy levels, but the .375 Winchester's performance on game is much more than just adequate–provided ranges are kept very short. It's Winchester's answer to Marlin's .444 and .45-70, and for close-cover hunting of large game, it's a good answer.

The existence of the .375 Winchester has created several light flat-point .375 component bullets from 200 to 220 grains. These can be loaded in .375 H&H cases for low-recoil practice loads–but should not be expected to perform well on game at the much higher H&H velocities.

.375 Weatherby Magnum: The .375 Weatherby is just one of numerous "improved" versions of the .375 H&H created by taking the body taper out of the .375 H&H case and creating more powder capacity. P.O. Ackley's .375 Improved Ackley Magnum was probably one of the first improved .375s, and writer Jon Sundra's .375 JRS is one of the most recent. The .375 Weatherby is covered here because it was factory-available from Weatherby for a number of years and is now available again from A-Square.

Developed by Roy Weatherby in 1945, the .375 Weatherby was replaced in the Weatherby line by the much hotter .378 Weatherby in the mid-1950s. Personally, I wish they had stuck with the earlier version!

The .375 Weatherby offers a significant step up from the .375 in both velocity and energy. A-Square's factory loads, or carefully worked-up handloads, propel a 270-grain bullet at a bit over 2,900 feet per second and a 300-grain bullet to 2,800 fps. An aerodynamic 300-grain bullet at 2,800 fps yields well over 5,000 foot/pounds of muzzle energy–and still carries nearly 3,000 foot/pounds to 400 yards. Recoil is increased considerably over .375 H&H levels, but with adequate gun weight is not unbearable. Trajectory is flattened fairly significantly.

My uncle, Art Popham, used a .375 Improved extensively back in the 1950s and 1960s. With it he collected several habitat groups for the Kansas City Museum of Natural History, including Alaskan brown bear and bison. He always felt the extra velocity and energy were well worth the price in recoil–especially when he had to stop a lion charge in Tanganyika.

I have a .375 Weatherby from A-Square, and I agree completely. Especially with so many fine hunting bullets today that will stand up to the extra velocity and still perform, the .375 Weatherby is a most viable option. A-Square has both revived it and adopted it as a "proprietary" cartridge in their semi-custom rifle line, plus offering factory ammo in a variety of bullet styles. It's also well worth noting that *any* .375 H&H can be "improved" to .375 Weatherby through the application of a chamber reamer. Brass can be created by simply firing H&H ammunition to fire-form the brass, then reloading.

The increase in recoil is very significant; the .375 Weatherby is not for the faint of heart, nor is it a cartridge well-suited to a lightweight rifle. But whether in an older Weatherby factory rifle, a new rifle from A-Square, or a reamed-out .375, the boost in performance is noticeable.

.378 Weatherby Magnum: If the .375 Weatherby is good, then the .378 must be much better, right? I hope my friends at Weatherby will forgive me, but I find this one too much of a good thing. Developed by

Roy Weatherby in 1953, the .378 Weatherby Magnum was the most powerful cartridge available until its same case was used to create the .460 Weatherby Magnum.

Essentially a belted .416 Rigby case–nearly three inches long and with a belt diameter of .603 inch–the .378 Weatherby will fit in very few bolt-actions. Originally, Weatherby offered it in the big Schultz & Larsen action, but today crams it into their Mark V action–but with a big difference. Magazine capacity is just two for the .378/.416/.460 Weatherby family.

The velocity gain over the .375 Weatherby is about another 100 feet per second, putting a 300-grain bullet downrange at 2,900 fps or just a bit more. Obviously, this increases the energy and flattens the trajectory even more. Today, with ultra-tough .375 bullets like the Swift, "X", and Bear-claw, we have bullets that will hold together and perform at the high velocities. For an ultra-long-range elk or moose rifle, a strong case could be made for the .378 Weatherby.

Its problems for me are twofold. First, the recoil is far beyond what most shooters can tolerate and still be effective. Without doubt, the recoil is well beyond what *I* can tolerate. It not only hits hard, but because of the high velocity also hits very fast–in felt recoil, its actually worse than the .416 or .460 Weatherby Magnums. This is exacerbated by the relatively light weight of the .378 Mark V, the only production rifle so chambered. Some shooters are more or less impervious to recoil, and of course recoil can be tamed by gun weight and mechanical devices–muzzle brakes and such. But I have a personal problem with two-shot bolt-actions. I almost never carry a rifle with a round in the chamber, so for me a .378 is a two-shot rifle. I can't imagine needing more than two with a cartridge like this–but in spite of the higher energy and flatter trajectory, I'd just as soon stick with a .375 H&H or, at the most, an improved version of the H&H!

When I started this chapter, I wrote that I was en route to a brown bear hunt with a .375. Did I get him? No, not this time. I didn't quite see the bear I wanted, so I'll try again in the fall. But I sure felt comfortable slogging through dense alders with a .375. I think I'll stick with it for hunting our biggest bears!

Chapter 14

The Over-.40 Crowd

When the .375 H&H first appeared in U.S. production rifles in 1937, it was a *big* gun. Matched against Cape buffalo and elephant, the .375 really isn't very big. Adequate, yes, but hardly overpowering. We don't have a great many elephants in North America. Not a lot of rhino or Cape buffalo, either. On our side of the pond, the .375 remains a very big gun indeed, plenty big enough to get you out of any trouble this continent can dish up.

If the .375 H&H is a big gun, then anything bigger is a *really* big gun—and is clearly of extremely limited utility in North America. If we were talking about African hunting cartridges, we might divide up the .400's and .416s from the .450s, and the .450 to .475 group from the .500s and larger. In North America, anything over .40 is a very large caliber. We have big bears, and we have bison—but we don't hunt elephant in heavy cover. We have no reason to distinguish between calibers best suited to Cape buffalo and those that will stop an elephant's charge.

We do, however, have two clearcut classifications of calibers larger than .40-inch. First are the "brush-busters"—cartridges that, while large in caliber, are *not* in the elephant/buffalo class. These would include the .44 Magnum, .444 Marlin, and .45-70 Government. Short-ranged, but throwing heavy bullets with plenty of frontal area, cartridges like these are at their best hunting game such as black bear and wild boar in heavy cover. Then there are the powerhouses—our three factory .416s, the .458 Winchester Magnum, .460 Weatherby Magnum, and all the rest of the wildcat, British, and European big-bores. Such cartridges *are* elephant-capable, and clearly capable of handling brown bear, grizzly, and bison as well.

There's really no such thing as being overgunned, but there are limits of practicality. Under most circumstances in North America, there's little to be gained from hunting with an elephant gun. There are exceptions. Some number of brown-bear guides use .458 Winchester Magnums when playing tag with our biggest bears in the dense alders of coastal Alaska. Ron Hayes always relied on a .458 when hunting polar bear. A couple of old-time Alaskan guides even use double rifles. Harmon Helmerick has a beautiful Westley Richards .470, and I believe it's Joe Want who uses a double .500 on Kodiak Island. I would never question an expert's choice of armament—but under most circumstances in North America, the ability to reach out and stop an outbound bear at 200 yards is almost as important as the need to stop an inbound bear at 20 feet. The really big guns tend to be fairly short-ranged affairs, and thus have limited usefulness on this continent.

Now, if you like the big guns–and many do–there's certainly no reason not to use them. I've had a lot of fun hunting wild hogs with my double .470, and in close cover on any of our big game, where shots are almost certain to be 100 yards or less, there's no reason not to use the cannons if using them gives you pleasure. But unless your life's work includes stopping lots of big bears in heavy cover, don't expect me to tell you an elephant gun is needed over here!

On the other hand, there are uses for the "brush-busting" big-bores–and you could even make a case for the .416s and their ilk. Let's take a quick look at the big-bores that have realistic applications for North American hunting.

.44 Remington Magnum: This was the most powerful handgun cartridge in the world when introduced in 1955, and there have been semi-automatic and lever-action rifles so chambered for more than 30 years. The "standard" 240-grain pistol load, churning up something like 1,200 feet per second in a six-inch revolver, produces about 1,760 fps in a 20-inch carbine. Muzzle energy is about 1,650 foot/pounds, but due to the terrible sectional density of pistol bullets, velocity and energy drop very quickly. In rifles, you can play with heavier bullets and you can get a bit more velocity–but there's darn near nothing you can do to get a .44 Magnum to deliver 1,000 foot/pounds beyond 100 yards.

At best, then, this is a very short-range cartridge–short for rifles and even shorter in handguns. With hard-cast or soft-point bullets–preferably not hollow-points–the .44 Magnum is an adequate deer cartridge to 100 yards or so, and at very short range can do the job on black bear and wild boar. In either case, it makes a reasonable choice for hunting over hounds, but gives no reach whatever when other methods are used.

Handloading is essential to get any range out of the .44 Magnum, and equally essential if the cartridge is to be used on game larger than deer or smallish black bears. Component bullets up to 300 grains and beyond are available, and custom-loading firms such as Garrett offer hard-cast Keith-type bullets up to 330 grains. The increased sectional density improves performance–especially penetration–substantially. You can even get the .44 barely up into elk country, at very short range. But it's no dragonslayer, and must never be considered such. It *is* a very fine little cartridge–but even at its very best, it is not the equal of the .30-30 Winchester. Users of it, whether in rifle or pistol, simply must keep that in mind.

.444 Marlin: The most recent Marlin-designed cartridge, introduced in 1964, is at this writing 30 years old. The .444 Marlin is essentially a "super .44 Magnum," using the same .429-inch bullet but a much longer 2.225-inch case. The only rifle so chambered has been Marlin's 336 lever-action. Any bullet that can be used in a .44 Magnum pistol can be used in the .444 Marlin–provided it has a nose sufficiently flat to be safe in a tubular-magazine rifle.

Availability only in the one Marlin rifle has sharply limited the selection of factory loads. Remington has been the lone entry, and for many years the only choice was a 240-grain bullet at 2,350 feet per second, yielding 3,000 foot/pounds of energy. The figures are impressive, but unfortunately this is a pistol bullet and cannot be expected to be reliable at such enhanced velocities.

Some years ago, Remington responded to this concern with a factory load featuring the 265-grain Hornady bullet designed for the .444 Marlin. Unfortunately, the velocity wasn't as flashy and the load didn't sell well. It was dropped, and now we're back to just the 240-grain load.

From a sheer energy standpoint, the .444 Marlin has plenty of energy for any black bear that walks, plus elk and moose, at least to 100 yards. From a practicality standpoint, though, the .444 Marlin is much better for handloaders than for non-handloaders. To ensure penetration on larger game, it needs better, tougher bullets than the 240-grain pistol slug. For handloaders, there are such bullets–Hornady's 265-grain bullet, plus excellent Barnes bullets in 275 and 300 grains. The latter bullet can easily be loaded to 2,150 feet per second in a Marlin rifle, and it carries 2,000 foot/pounds well beyond 100 yards.

The .444 Marlin is truly a fine deep-woods cartridge, and with good bullets will flatten anything in its path up to and including grizzly and brown bear–but ranges simply must be kept very modest. The same is true with the next and perhaps greatest of the "brush-busting big-bores."

.45-70 Government: It seems truly strange–and equally wonderful–that this old warhorse is still with us. Adopted as the U.S. military cartridge in 1873, the .45-70 and its Trapdoor Springfield were standard issue for just 19 years, until the .30-40 Krag was adopted in 1892. Still, it was the .45-70 that Custer's troops carried at the Little Big Horn, that Crook's troops carried as they searched for Geronimo–and even the militia that accompanied Colonel Roosevelt up San Juan Hill in 1898 carried this grand old cartridge. I find it a wonderful piece of history that you can walk into a sporting-goods store today and buy a box of .45-70 cartridges–and even a greater miracle that this ancient cartridge is still useful in today's hunting world.

The original load was actually called .45-70-405, meaning a .45-caliber bullet, a charge of 70 grains of black powder, and a 405-grain bullet. Although current factory loads have used an equivalent charge of smokeless powder for many decades, this is still the "standard" .45-70 load, and as with all factory loads, pressures are kept very mild for safe use in the relatively weak Trapdoor Springfield action.

The 405-grain factory load has a muzzle velocity of 1,330 feet per second, for an energy of 1,570 foot/pounds. The equation for energy requires that velocity be squared, thus velocity plays an inordinately large part in determining foot/pounds of energy. Bullet weight figures in, but not exponentially like velocity. Frontal area figures in not at all. In some cases of low-velocity cartridges that use great, big bullets, conventional ballistics tables simply don't give a complete picture. This is absolutely the case with the .45-70; while its energy figure of 1,570 foot/pounds is adequate, it is effective far beyond its paper ballistics and has been for 120 years. That's why it's lasted so long!

It has a trajectory like a rainbow; sight it in two inches high at 50 yards and it will be dead-on at 100 yards. But it will be two feet low at 200 yards and almost seven feet low at 300 yards. It is not a long-range number. But even with the very weak factory load, that big 405-grain bullet will do its work at close range on anything that walks in North America.

Because there are a great many trapdoor Springfields still in use, the factories have been unwilling to improve pressure in loads. The only way to improve performance–or, at least, to increase velocity and flatten trajectory–without increasing pressure is to reduce bullet weight. The factories have done this with a selection of 300-grain loads, faster and flatter and, at least on paper, with higher energy figures. The standard 300-grain load has a muzzle velocity of 1,880 feet per second, with an energy of 2,355 foot/pounds. With this load, you can sight 2½ inches high at 100 yards to be dead-on at 150 yards. And then the rainbow begins. At 200 yards, you'll be down six inches, and then another two feet at 300 yards. Better, but certainly no real flat-shooter.

I simply can't imagine choosing a .45-70 as a deer cartridge; it just gets too hard to hit with much beyond 200 yards. But for wild hogs, black bear, and even elk and moose in very heavy cover, there's nothing wrong with the good old .45-70. I've used 300-grain loads for pigs and such, and would recommend them for deer and perhaps black bear. But if you're bound and determined to use the .45-70 for elk or moose and must use factory loads, forget flashy ballistics and go to that old, slow, heavy 405-grain bullet. And get plenty close!

Fortunately, factory loads aren't the only option. Over the years, a great many fine rifles have been chambered to .45-70. These include numerous single-shots, from the Remington Rolling Block and Winchester Hi-Wall to the Ruger No. 1. And lever-actions, from the Model 1886 Winchester to the current Model 1895 Marlin. The .45-70 case has a great deal of capacity–especially for smokeless powder. Most reloading manuals today offer three levels of loads for the .45-70. One level, of course, will produce safe loads in vintage rifles. The second level is for Marlin 1895 rifles. With the Marlin, you can reach 1,800 feet per second with a 400-grain bullet. That will yield some 3,000 foot/pounds–not only flattening the trajectory, but extending the effective range as well. The last level is for the ultra-strong Ruger No. 1 single-shot. With this action, 400-grain bullets can be pushed to almost 2,000 feet per second, lighter bullets much faster. Foot/pounds can be boosted above 4,000. In other words, this old Indian fighter can be brought into Cape buffalo capability with relative ease.

With heavier loads, the .45-70 can make a perfectly adequate brown-bear rifle in either lever-action or single-shot form–but you cannot turn it into a long-range rig, or even a medium-range rifle. At its best, it's a great black-bear and close-cover moose rifle–but most situations for elk and big bears are best served by a cartridge with a bit more reach if needed.

The .416s and Kin: Just six years ago, no high-performance factory cartridges were available spanning the gap between the .375 H&H and the .458 Winchester Magnum–but there were a whole bunch of more or less obsolete cartridges and wildcats trying to fill the hole. Among the "oldies" were the .404 Jeffery and .416 Rigby, both large-cased British cartridges dating back to about 1911. Both are good cartridges, but both require extra-large bolt-actions to accommodate their case size. Wildcat developments included American professional hunter George Hoffman's .416 Hoffman, based on the .375 H&H case blown out; the .416 Taylor, developed by gun writer Bob Chatfield-Taylor on the .338 Winchester Magnum case necked up; and the .425 Express, developed by Whit Collins and Cameron Hopkins, also based on the .338 case but using a .423-inch bullet (as does the .404 Jeffery).

Although I had no hand in developing any of the .416-class cartridges, I was kind of in the middle of things as interest heated up in the mid-1980s. I pretty much agreed with John Wootters that the .416 Taylor made the most sense; it would fit in a .30-06-length action and accomplished the goal of duplicating .416 Rigby ballistics–a 400-grain bullet at 2,400 feet per second. But the full-length .375 H&H case also made a lot of sense, and in about 1985 I acquired a .416 Hoffman built by Randy Brooks.

It was a super cartridge, easily achieving full .416 Rigby velocities. I used it on Cape buffalo and elephant with perfect satisfaction, and became a strong proponent of the .375-length .416.

The Hoffman could have made it into factory form. Certainly it strongly influenced Remington's .416–but it was not the exact model. Instead, Remington used their existing 8mm Remington Magnum when, with very little fanfare and almost no leaks, they introduced their .416 Remington Magnum in 1988.

I was invited on the inaugural hunt in October of that year, together with Bob Milek, Layne Simpson, Tom Fegely, Nick Sisley, and a few of Remington's folks. We just plain shot the heck out of big Alaskan moose on that hunt, with shots from very short range to beyond 200 yards. Without doubt, the .416 was exceptionally effective on moose, as it is on any large game on any continent. But you don't really need a .416 in North America.

And, honestly, if you don't need a .416 Remington, then you probably don't need a .416 Rigby or Weatherby Magnum, either. The old Rigby cartridge, of course, has been brought back by Federal in factory-ammo form. One of the most famous of the old British cartridges, its original Cordite load required a very large case that, with modest pressure, produced about 2,400 feet per second with a 410-grain bullet. With modern powders, you can do much better; I've got a .416 Rigby, and it's no trick to get it up to 2,600 feet per second with a 400-grain bullet. But the recoil starts getting severe.

The .416 Weatherby Magnum is essentially a .416 Rigby case with a belt on it. Factory ammo is very hot, pushing a 400-grain bullet at 2,700 feet per second. In 1989, Ed Weatherby and I took the new .416 Weatherby to Botswana, where we took several Cape buffalo with the cartridge. It was truly awesome–but is really overpowered for any North American game.

The thing about the .416s is that they're the largest cartridges that still offer relatively flat trajectory. Sighted to be dead-on at 200 yards, the .416 Remington or Rigby will drop about 10 inches at 300 yards, much like the .375 H&H. It isn't a long-range cartridge, but can carry the distance. Factory ballistics for the Rigby are identical, but of course hotter handloads shoot flatter, and the .416 Weatherby Magnum is extremely flat-shooting.

There is absolutely nothing wrong with choosing any of the .416s for hunting big bears. They're impressive on even the largest of game, and certainly give all the charge-stopping confidence anyone could need. My personal preference would be the .416 Rigby, since I have a fine rifle in that chambering. But the .416 Remington probably makes more sense due to its ability to be built into a much more compact rifle–especially now that Remington has a 350-grain Swift A-Frame factory load that should prove ideal for moose and elk. But unless you anticipate African hunting in the future, I would not purchase a .416 for North American hunting. And I certainly couldn't recommend anything any larger. If you have a big gun, by all means use it–but remember that you don't really need the power, and the lack of ranging abilities could rob you of an important shot someday!

Chapter 15

Wildcats and Proprietary Cartridges

So far in this volume, I've pretty much stayed with cartridges currently loaded by major American manufacturers. I think that's more than appropriate, since today's selection of factory cartridges is truly a broad array of calibers and case dimensions that pretty much cover any conceivable hunting need.

There are, however, two additional categories of cartridges that really deserve some discussion: wildcat cartridges and proprietary cartridges. We'll look at each in turn, but first these terms should be defined.

Wildcatting is a uniquely North American proposition, and is so because nowhere else in the world is handloading so widely practiced nor components so readily available. A wildcat cartridge is simply a nonstandard cartridge for which factory ammunition is not available. Some are one-of-a-kind cartridges that fulfill the designer's dream; others achieve some degree of popularity; and some are eventually picked up by major manufacturers.

Some wildcats are whimsical–even impractical–in design, while others are very practical cartridges designed to fill gaps in the line-up of current factory cartridges. Depending on how difficult it is to form the brass, loading wildcat cartridges can vary from a genuine nightmare to fairly straightforward reloading, but it's always an extra hassle since loaded ammunition–and generally ready-to-load brass–is not readily available. However, the simple act of *creating* a wildcat cartridge isn't all that difficult. Given a standard bullet diameter, about all that's required is a mechanical drawing so that a chamber reamer can be made. Then, among others, Huntington Die Specialties will custom-make reloading dies to specifications.

The best situation is a wildcat simple enough for existing cartridges to be fireformed in the new chamber. While dies can be made from mechanical drawings, the diemakers much prefer to have several fired cases to work with as well as dimensions. Both reamers and dies can be duplicated, just supposing your brainchild is so clever that all of your friends want one. Or you may wind up with the only one in existence–but it's all yours.

Proprietary cartridges were a British tradition, and to a lesser degree the convention was followed in continental Europe as well. The .416 Rigby, for instance, was a proprietary cartridge of John Rigby & Company. Only Rigby made the rifles–and although Kynoch loaded the ammunition, it was loaded for Rigby and, for many years, was available only through Rigby. Other examples include the .318 and .425 Westley Richards, the .500-465 Holland & Holland, and in Europe the 11.2x72 Schuler.

The idea is that the company that developed the cartridge made the only rifles for it–and also controlled distribution of the ammunition. While the system created a monopoly market among shooters who wanted that cartridge, it also sharply limited potential sales–and in some cases the very future–of the cartridge.

The system is hardly unheard of in America. To some extent, many cartridges in the black-powder era, including most of the Sharps cartridges, were proprietary. The most classic recent example, of course, has long been Roy Weatherby's line of Weatherby Magnums. Until very recently, except for custom rifles only Weatherby chambered for Weatherby cartridges–and only Weatherby marketed their Norma-produced ammunition. This is rapidly changing now, with several of the majors having picked up some of the most popular Weatherby cartridges in both rifles and loaded ammo.

Today, with several smaller manufacturers of both rifles and ammunition–and quite a few custom rifle and ammo firms–all doing brisk business, the lines between wildcats and proprietary cartridges are a bit muddy. A-Square, for instance, offers "store-bought" ammo for quite a number of cartridges that have been pure wildcats. A-Square also has its own line of proprietary cartridges, for which they make both rifles and ammunition. Dakota Arms, strictly a riflemaker, also has their own line of proprietary cartridges–not wildcats, since Dakota also offers loaded ammunition made to their specs first by A-Square and, more recently, by the new Superior ammo company. I would tend to call the .22 and 6mm PPC proprietary cartridges since, except for custom and semi-custom rifles, Sako has been the only source for both rifles and ammo. We'll look at some of the proprietaries later, but first let's take a look at some interesting wildcats.

Wildcatting Today: Although some wildcats have been developed for the sheer ego boost of having a cartridge named after oneself, the designers of most wildcat cartridges have endeavored to achieve either improved performance (in accuracy, velocity, or both) over factory cartridges or to fill a caliber niche left open by current factory cartridges–or, frequently, to improve performance in a shorter case.

The simplest and most common ways of creating wildcat cartridges are to neck an existing case up or down; and to increase powder capacity by removing body taper, changing shoulder angle, changing shoulder placement–or all of the above. A great many factory cartridges started as simple wildcats based on these principles, and many "pure" factory developments were also created in this fashion. In fact, as we have seen, a great many of our popular cartridges today started life as wildcats. These include the .22-250 Remington, .257 Roberts, .25-06 Remington, .35 Whelen, and more. Most of the Weatherby magnums were Roy Weatherby's wildcats–which he personally shepherded into accepted factory form.

Today's line-up of factory cartridges is so broad and diverse that it seems there is almost no room for wildcatting today. And yet the practice persists—and indeed there seems to be no end. "Improving" a cartridge—creating more powder capacity and thus more velocity—by removing body taper and changing the shoulder was and is an extremely popular pastime. Most of the Ackley cartridges, such as the .257 Ackley Improved, .30-30 Ackley Improved, .30-06 Ackley Improved, and at least several dozen others that the prolific P.O. Ackley experimented with, are simply existing cartridges blown out to increased chamber dimensions. With modern powders, some of these—the .30-06 Ackley Improved, for one—actually gain very little and are rarely seen today. Some, like the .257 Ackley Improved on the Roberts case, make pretty good headway and retain quite a following.

Sometimes wildcatting development has led to a slightly different factory cartridge that does, indeed, fill a niche—but in so doing negates any reason for the wildcat's continued existence. The *numerous* hot 7mm wildcats that led up to the 7mm Remington Magnum are good examples, as are Elmer Keith's .334 OKH and George Hoffman's .416 Hoffman. With factory-available .338 Winchester Magnums and .340 Weatherby Magnums, there's really no need for a .334 OKH today; and with .416 Remington Magnum, .416 Weatherby Magnum, and even the .416 Rigby available in factory form, the equally fine .416 Hoffman is suddenly obsolete.

Some good wildcats were created by circumstances that no longer exist. For instance, in the 1950s Harold Johnson of Cooper's Landing, Alaska, created the .450 Alaskan—a Model 71 Winchester rebored to .458, firing a necked-up .348 Winchester case. His theory was that no genuine American big-bore existed for stopping brown bears in their tracks. His .450 Alaskan did it—but the introduction of Winchester's .458 Magnum and the discontinuance of the Model 71 Winchester killed the justification for the cartridge and the availability of a rifle to put it in!

I must admit that I am not a wildcatter. I love to handload, but I don't like the extra hassle of fireforming, let alone the trimming, inside neck turning, and annealing that can also be required. I also like the extra insurance of being able to buy ammunition over the counter if I get short on time or, worse, get separated from my ammo on a trip. And I much prefer the safety and convenience of relying on printed loading data that has been pressure-tested, rather than jumping off into uncharted waters on my own.

There is also an insidious problem with many wildcats, and even some of the more obscure factory cartridges, especially those that have been around for some time. In the case of American factory cartridges, everyone knows what a .270 Winchester or a 7mm-08 Remington is. SAAMI—the Sporting Arms and Ammunition Manufacturers Institute—has a set of standard specifications, and all chambers and loaded cartridges can be expected to conform. With wildcats, there may be numerous different versions along the same theme. Shoulder angles, neck length, overall length, and almost any other dimension can vary slightly since there is no generally established or accepted norm. For instance, there are numerous versions of what we call the .30-338, one of which (but only one) is the .308 Norma Magnum. There were several versions of Harold Johnson's .450 Alaskan. The one I had was actually a .450-348 Ackley Improved!

I have a lovely Dumoulin .416 Rigby on a left-hand magnum Mauser action. I was thoroughly delighted when Federal decided to offer factory-loaded .416 Rigby ammo—but much less than pleased when I learned that Federal ammo won't chamber in my rifle. My Dumoulin, apparently made to outdated European specs, has a chamber just a few thousandths too short for the Federal loads! Few wildcats could be simpler than the .458 Lott, just the .375 H&H case blown out to accept a .458 bullet with a straight taper, no shoulder. And yet there are reamers for slightly different chamber lengths for the .458 Lott. With a wildcat, you simply must be absolutely certain you know what you're dealing with—and if a wildcat doesn't come with dies mated to its chamber, you could well be looking at making chamber casts and having custom dies made.

But despite the hassles, wildcatting remains surprising popular among American handloaders. Dimensions are commonly known for something like 300 different wildcat cartridges—and I wouldn't be surprised if there were at least twice that many if you included obsolete designs and one-of-a-kind wildcats. It would be impossible to try to cover all of them, or to cover many of them. But in spite of the superb array of factory cartridges, there are several wildcats that do indeed fill very useful purposes.

.22-Caliber: The .22 wildcats are legion, and for the average shooter they have relatively little to recommend them. Most varminters find the .220 Swift and .22-250 accurate enough and fast enough, but some wildcats can and do surpass them in one or the other category. Sometimes both. The .22 BR, based on Benchrest Remington brass necked down to .22 by an extremely painstaking process, makes an ideal and exceptionally accurate cartridge in the long-barreled specialty pistols. Jim Carmichel and Fred Huntington, two of America's most knowledgeable riflemen, collaborated on the .22 CHeetah, the full-length .308 BR necked down to .22. This cartridge beats the .220 Swift in velocity and is said to be more accurate than the .22-250.

6mm–.270: Forgive me, but I can find relatively few truly useful wildcats between calibers .243 and .277. The most fertile ground here has been in the development of handgun cartridges for use in Thompson/Center Contenders, Remington XP-100's, and other specialty pistols. Here, cartridges such as the 6mm Benchrest, 6mm Thompson/Center Ugalde (TCU), 6.5 JDJ, and a few others turn the single-shot pistol into an extremely efficient 200-yard pronghorn and deer pistol.

In rifle calibers, there are a number of "improved" versions in this caliber range that, in most cases, do improve velocity considerably, most notably the .257 Ackley Improved, which can increase .257 Roberts velocity by as much as 300 feet per second and thus treads very closely on the .25-06. Recently, too, there has been much wildcatting around the fat, rebated-rim .284 Winchester case–which has the case capacity to deliver stunning velocity from a short-action rifle. The 6mm-284 has been fairly popular, as has the 6.5-284.

The most popular 6.5mm wildcat, though, is the good old 6.5-06, simply the .30-06 case necked down to accept .264 bullets. It comes close to the factory-available .264 Winchester Magnum, but has the very real advantage of being unbelted, thus reducing ammo bulk and increasing magazine capacity.

In .277-caliber, one could play with the .308 Winchester or .284 Winchester cases to create a short-action .270–or one could go the other direction and use a full-length .300 H&H case for an ultra-velocity .270. All have been done, but I'm not sure I see the point.

7mm–.358: With our fabulous array of factory 7mm cartridges, there isn't much to be done in 7mm rifle cartridges. Or, with the 7mm Benchrest in factory form, in handgun cartridges, either. Worthy of note is the 7mm TCU, the .223 Remington case necked up to 7mm. It's a dandy little cartridge in the 14-inch Contender, producing up to about 2,100 feet per second with a 130-grain bullet.

Clear up at the other end of the 7mm spectrum is the 7mm Shooting Times Westerner (STW). Developed by Layne Simpson, it's a full-length magnum created by necking the 8mm Remington Magnum down to 7mm. It's truly a hot number, able to push 160-grain bullets above 3,300 feet per second and 175-grainers above 3,100 fps. Since these are significant increases over the 7mm Remington *and* Weatherby Magnums, there was much speculation that the 7mm STW would be picked up as a factory cartridge–but so far it hasn't happened. Now it appears that the 7mm STW is extremely hard on throats, so I don't give it a bright future.

In the middle, gunwriter Jon Sundra has done a fine job of pushing his 7mm JRS. The 7mm JRS is essentially an improved version of the .280, with the case blown out and a sharp shoulder moved forward for maximum case capacity. The JRS actually does in non-belted form at least 98 percent of what the 7mm Remington Magnum does, so it's truly a fine cartridge. I suspect both it and the 7mm STW suffer from the same PR problem, namely a surfeit of good 7mm cartridges already established in the market.

Likewise, there's little to be done with the .30 calibers. There are some fine .30-caliber handgun cartridges, like Steve Herrett and Bob Milek's .30 Herrett, based on a shortened, blown-out .30-30 case; and the .308x1.5" Barnes, based on shortened .308 brass.

At the upper end, there are also wildcats that boost .30-caliber velocities into the stratosphere. There have been .30-378s based on the .378 Weatherby case, but with any bore diameter you eventually get to diminishing returns. That's what overbore capacity really means—too small a hole to efficiently burn all the powder. The most recent "ultra-magnum" .30 is Art Alphin's .300 Petersen, named in honor of Robert E. Petersen (my boss!). The .300 Petersen is unbelted, with its own unique case and case-head diameter and massive 2.875-inch case. Technically, it's probably a proprietary cartridge, since Alphin's A-Square company will offer loaded ammo. But by any measure it's a hot number, propelling a 180-grain bullet to 3,500 feet per second! It's a super cartridge, but only time will tell whether it catches on.

The 8mm bore diameter is pretty dead, but there remains passing interest in the 8mm-06. It's a fine, flat-shooting cartridge, and rechambering 8x57 Mausers to this wildcat was once extremely commonplace, since shooters could then use abundant .30-06 brass rather than hard-to-find 8mm brass. It's a good cartridge, but has relatively little justification today.

In .338, there are numerous versions of "ultra-.33s" based on the .378 Weatherby case. One I heard about was the .338 Kubla Khan, and the very thought of its recoil probably causes the earth to shake. A very legitimate .338 wildcat would be based on the .308 Winchester case. It would not be dissimilar from the .358 Winchester, but would be just a touch faster and would enable one to take advantage of the many fine 200- and 210-grain .338-caliber bullets. That, of course, is one of the strengths of the .338-06 we discussed earlier. I still expect that one to make it into factory form.

In .358, there seems no justification whatever for further wildcatting efforts. In handguns, the wildcat .357 Herrett is hard to beat—but the factory .35 Remington is just as good. In rifles, from the .35 Remington to the .358 Norma Magnum just about any power niche desired seems to be filled. Of course, there are improved versions of almost everything—and the .35 Whelen Improved does indeed beat the standard version. But not enough to be worth the trouble as far as I'm concerned!

Big-Bore Wildcats: For North American hunting, anything from .375 up seems to me to be a big-bore. In the days before we had factory .416s, this was a fertile ground, but these days wildcatting the lower .40s seems a waste of time.

There *is* some interest in creating a short magnum .375, and it can be done quite easily by necking up .338 brass. Finn Aagaard has done some work in this area, and found that a .375-338 wildcat easily duplicated .375 H&H performance. Likewise, the .416 Taylor does indeed provide .416 Remington/Rigby performance in a .30-06-length action.

There are also numerous versions of full-length .375 cases necked up to accept .458, .465, and .475 bullets. All of these provide very similar ballistics, namely a 500-grain bullet at about 2,300 to 2,350 feet per second. There is little use for such powerhouses in North America, but they do provide a margin of power on elephant and buffalo that the short-cased .458 Winchester Magnum simply cannot offer.

Handguns, too, have seen a lot of big-bore wildcat development. Perhaps the most famous of these is the .375 JDJ. Based on the .444 Marlin case necked down to .375, the .375 JDJ in J.D. Jones' special SSK barrels for the Contender has become a standard for handgun hunters in search of the largest game. Yep, it's a real handful, pushing full-size .375 bullets over 2,000 feet per second!

Proprietary Cartridges: Over the years, there have been quite a few American proprietary cartridges that have lapsed into obscurity. For a trip down memory lane, can you recall the .401 Herter Powermag? It was a proprietary revolver and cartridge marketed in 1961, the heyday of Herter's, Inc.–the catalog folks from Waseca, Minnesota. Similar to the .41 Magnum, it was effectively destroyed by the .41's widespread introduction three years later.

Today, the creation of a full line of proprietary cartridges has become a vogue among semi-custom riflemakers. Semi-custom means, to me, limited production that offers a basic rifle with a wide variety of options–options that you wouldn't expect on a factory rifle but can obtain without the cost and time lag of a full-blown custom job.

Two such lines, as mentioned, are the Dakota Arms' Dakota cartridges and A-Square's A-Square Magnums. Both lines are quite sound, but approach things from different directions.

The Dakota line-up consists of 7mm, .300, .330, .375, .416, and .450 Dakota cartridges. All offer magnum performance, but in non-belted cartridges that simplify feeding and increase powder capacity while reducing magazine space required. The first five are based on the .404 Jeffery case, generally shortened, while the .450 is based on the .416 Rigby case necked up.

Velocities are not outrageous; all are more or less in line with their belted "standard" competitors (the .450 equates to the .458 Lott, the .416 to the .416 Remington, the .375 to the .375 H&H, the .330 to the .340 Weatherby, and so forth. They are very fine cartridges, and have an advantage over true wildcats in that Dakota can and will furnish loaded ammo, brass, dies, and reloading data.

A-Square specializes in big-bore rifles designed not to kick. They offer a wide variety of loaded ammo for obscure British and European numbers, popular wildcats, standard cartridges, and their own A-Square Magnums. Most of their A-Square proprietary cartridges are more powerful than needed for North America, but they do have some red-hot numbers.

Generally using the .460 Weatherby case (shortened, necked up, or necked down, as appropriate), A-Square cartridges include the .338 A-Square Magnum (250-grain bullet at 3,120 feet per second), .375 A-Square Magnum (300-grain bullet at 2,920 feet per second), and on up to the .500 A-Square (600-grain bullet at 2,470 fps)! A-Square also offers their own line of bullets–a fast-opening Lion Load; a controlled-expansion, bonded-core Dead Tough; and a homogenous-alloy Monolithic Solid. In factory loads, they generally also offer aerodynamic Sierra boattails in the lighter calibers.

A firm in Canada offers a line of Imperial Magnum proprietary cartridges–also based on the .404 Jeffery case. These look like very fine cartridges, but I haven't had first-hand opportunity to fool with them.

Whether wildcat or proprietary, few of these cartridges fill any real gaps in our standard factory lineup. But rest assured, even the hint of an opening and you'll find a wildcat out there somewhere. I can't say where this trend will go, but it's been an honored American tradition since the inception of smokeless powder and before. I hope it continues, since wildcatters have provided many of our finest hunting cartridges.

Chapter 16

Handgun Hunting Cartridges: The New Frontier

This book is about *rifles* and their cartridges for North American big-game hunting. It's not my intent to get sidetracked into lengthy discussions about related subjects, be they archery tackle, black powder, handguns, or even big-game shotguns. However, it's just as inappropriate to ignore these last two categories as it would be to spend undue time discussing them. Both are rapid growth areas for North American hunting–handgunning because a great many sportsmen are turning to the added challenge of handgun hunting; and shotguns because more and more suburban areas require shotguns for deer hunting every year. Both areas are also of great interest because their respective technologies are increasing by leaps and bounds.

As anyone who has followed my writing undoubtedly knows, I'm a rifle nut first and foremost. It might be surprising to learn that I also enjoy handgun hunting a great deal, and have done a fair amount of it off and on over the years. Back in the late '70s I even did some handgun hunting in Africa, long before it was fashionable to do so.

Now, for me handgun hunting is an enjoyable pastime but not a serious pursuit. Bob Milek (one of the greatest and most serious handgun hunters of our or any other generation) and I were always in surprising agreement on what made sense with handguns–and what didn't. Bob loved to hunt varmints with his long-range pistols (and short-range pistols, for that matter), and he loved to crawl through his Wyoming sagebrush after pronghorns and mule deer. He even took a few elk with a handgun, but unless conditions were ideal he felt that was getting shaky. He drew the line at some point before the category of the big bears, and never considered any of Africa's dangerous game appropriate quarry for a handgun. Realizing I'm stepping on a whole bunch of toes, I couldn't agree more.

Just a few years ago, handgun hunting meant a big revolver, and to me an open-sighted revolver remains the most enjoyable handgun-hunting tool. Revolvers, whether you prefer open sights or a low-powered scope, are short-range affairs. New cartridges and better bullets have made them more effective than ever, but have not materially increased their range. Wheelguns are best-suited to game taken at short range, such as black bear and wild hogs, plus deer and even elk and moose in very heavy cover.

The single-shot, long-barreled pistols are something else again. This is where most handgun cartridge and load development has gone in recent years, and today these single-shot pistols–Thompson/Center's Contender,

Remington's XP-100, and semi-custom pistols like the Wichita and Ultra Light Arms Model 20–are simply awesome. In truth, and almost certainly I'm stepping on toes again, when mounted with a good scope and chambered for a high-performance cartridge, these are much more like short rifles than conventional handguns.

There's something about the short, stiff barrels of these specialty pistols that promote unusual levels of accuracy. Numerous benchrest matches are being won–and new records set–with the likes of the XP-100 and Wichita. The problem, of course, is that the short barrels restrict velocity, so while the accuracy is there it's very difficult to get enough energy downrange past 200 to 250 yards. The other drawback–or restriction–to these pistols is that they simply must be fired from a steady rest. The fields of view and critical eye reliefs of handgun scopes make them almost impossible to shoot accurately without a rest. And for the same reasons, game almost must be stationary to ensure good shot placement. These limitations, of course, are part of the challenge of using such arms.

Hunting Cartridges for Revolvers: For many years, our field of handgun cartridges for hunting has been limited to the .357, .41, and .44 magnums. As stated earlier in this volume, the .357 is extremely limited as a hunting cartridge. I get the feeling that some folks believe handgun cartridges are subject to different laws of physics than rifle cartridges. To some small degree, frontal area and bullet performance can indeed make up for paper ballistics. But 1,000 foot/pounds is 1,000 foot/pounds, and I believe this is a sensible minimum for deer-sized game regardless of barrel length. The .357, though legal in many states, simply doesn't measure up. In fact, it doesn't measure up by a long way. The most potent .357 loads barely reach 600 foot/pounds, and I can't recommend that energy level for deer. The .357 does have hunting purposes, but they're limited to game such as varmints and javelina.

The .41 Remington Magnum is little better; even with hot 210-grain loads, it's hard to get 800 foot/pounds out of the .41. For hunting with a revolver, you really need to stick with the .44 Remington Magnum or its new big brother, the .454 Casull.

Even with the .44 Magnum, very few loads produce more than 1,000 foot/pounds–and none will hold that energy much beyond 50 yards. Standard "over-the-counter" 240-grain loads produce just under 1,000 foot/pounds at the muzzle. I've used loads of this type on wild hogs, and while they'll do the job, they are not particularly impressive. Better are handloads with heavier bullets, or ammo from semi-custom loaders like Garrett.

I've been playing with two different Garrett loads in my six-inch Model 29, a 310-grain hard-cast Keith-type bullet and a 330-grain truncated-cone hard-cast bullet. The former offers a full 1,320 feet per second and 1,200 foot/pounds at the muzzle; the latter reaches 1,280 fps and also achieves

1,200 foot/pounds. Recoil is fierce, but pressures seem to be fine in my revolver, and accuracy is superb. Neither load carries 1,000 foot/pounds to 100 yards, but both come close. Since I shoot open-sighted revolvers, 100-yard shooting is a moot point anyway.

For game larger than deer, the .454 Casull is a better choice. The big Casull revolver, made by Freedom Arms in Wyoming, is a truly fabulous piece of gear. Fitting and machining are outstanding, just like a Swiss watch–which helps it stand up to pressures generally considered beyond what revolvers can stand. The .454 is *not* an elephant pistol. It has its limits, but it's the most powerful over-the-counter revolver available. With 250-grain bullets, it offers 1,500 feet per second muzzle velocity for an energy of 1,249 foot/pounds. With the heavier 300-grain load, velocity is 1,400 feet per second for 1,306 foot/pounds. The heavier bullet delivers 1,083 foot/pounds at 50 yards, while the light bullet has 972 foot/pounds at that distance.

With judicious handloading and heavier bullets, these figures can be upped a bit, but it's still very difficult to get even the mighty Casull to carry 1,000 foot/pounds beyond 100 yards. It's an extremely effective pistol, but it is not a long-range affair. At close range, thanks to its big, heavy bullet, it could be considered adequate for elk-sized game and perhaps moose–but at the very best it's extremely marginal for brown bear and grizzly. At least in my opinion. However, it has been used on such game, and will be used again. If you must use a revolver to hunt such beasts, the .454 is certainly the odds-on choice.

Hunting Cartridges for Single-Shots: Even with the great single-shot pistols, it's extremely difficult to get high energy levels a long way down-range. There's only so much velocity to be wrung out of short barrels–and only so much any person's wrists can stand!

There are a great many fine wildcats for the specialty pistols, and also quite a few rifle cartridges that perform exceptionally well in handgun barrels. Very few of them offer the energy levels needed for elk-sized game at distances much past the muzzle, but there are a great many fine choices for hunting pronghorns and deer-sized game.

In the previous chapter, I discussed a few of the good wildcats, and some of the rifle cartridges that do well in handguns were mentioned previously as well. Among factory cartridges, there are some surprises. The .30-30, for instance, is a marvelous performer in the Contender–made even stronger by the ability to use spitzer bullets. In a 14-inch barrel, for instance, Sierra's 135-grain spitzer can be pushed to 2,300 feet per second. Such a load carries 1,000 foot/pounds to 200 yards–and shoots fairly flat while doing so!

The .250 Savage is another good option in the XP-100, and one of the best all-round handgun-hunting cartridges is easily the time-tested .35 Remington. The 7mm Benchrest, of course, was designed as primarily a handgun cartridge, and is a super choice for pronghorn and deer.

Both the full-length 7mm-08 Remington and .308 Winchester are also often chambered in bolt-action pistols. Both are real handfuls, but handloads with fairly fast powders can wring serious velocity out of both calibers. In the 7mm-08, 140-grain bullets can be loaded to 2,600 feet per second, the 130-grain bullet 100 fps faster. Similarly, in the .308 150-grain bullets can be pushed to 2,600 feet per second. That makes an elk load to at least 150 yards–but hold on real tight!

In most cases, I've always advocated heavy-for-caliber bullets. This is not necessarily the best course with handguns. Given the much lower velocities, it often makes sense to use lighter bullets to obtain better expansion. In the 6.5s, think about 100- and 120-grain bullets; in the 7mms, 140-grain bullets are a good choice. In the .30s, 125- to 150-grain bullets are pretty much the useable range. Several bulletmakers have supplied the growing number of handgun hunters with bullets designed specifically to perform at the lower velocities, and if available these are good slugs to go with. But under no circumstances choose the heaviest, toughest bullets you can find–they may well act just like solids, penetrating well but expanding not at all.

Wildcat and semi-custom cartridges are almost too numerous to count, let alone discuss. I've had real good luck with the 6mm Benchrest on javelina and such, and both the 6.5mm and 7mm TCU are extremely popular for deer hunting in the Contender. One of America's foremost handgunners, J.D. Jones, has developed quite an industry around handgun wildcats. I mentioned his .375 JDJ in the chapter on wildcats, and it's a dandy. But it's just the tip of the wildcat iceberg that Jones's SSK Industries produces. Using rimmed .225 Winchester and .444 Marlin cases as the base, SSK has a full line of Contender barrels, from the .226 JDJ to the .430 JDJ. The .375 is the most powerful, propelling a 300-grain .375 bullet to almost 2,000 feet per second for just under 2,500 foot/pounds of energy. Recoil is wicked, but for hunting large game with a handgun, one of J.D.'s "hand cannons" is hard to beat.

Years ago, I shot a mountain lion with one of J.D.'s .45-70 barrels for a Contender, and this has become a fairly common choice for hunting large game. Handloaded, you can actually beat factory loads; Sierra's manual suggests 1,950 feet per second can be reached with their 300-grain bullet in a 14-inch Contender! I'll be honest–I didn't care for the recoil.

More recently, I shot a nice pronghorn with an XP-100 in 7mm-08 Remington. The gun was manageable, but not particularly pleasant. I have great respect for what these pistols, at the upper end, can do. But I think I prefer not to push the upper end. I'll keep handgun hunting fun by plinking prairie dogs with my XP-100 in .223 and getting plenty close to big game with open-sighted revolvers. But to each his own!

Chapter 17

The Mysteries of Modern Hunting Bullets

We can talk endlessly about calibers and cartridges, but within reasonable energy parameters shot placement is far more critical than what the shot was made with. More important, too, is the bullet the shot is made with. You can talk ballistics endlessly, and it's good stuff for campfire arguments. But if the bullet doesn't get into the vitals and do its work, it can create a horrible wound but a lost animal. By the same token, a bullet that's too tough can pass through without transferring much energy, creating a fatal wound that may leave little blood and allow the animal enough time to escape—also a lost animal.

The most accurate bullets in a given rifle may not deliver the best performance on game. And the bullets that deliver the best performance on game may not be the most aerodynamic available.

Selection of hunting bullets is not a simple process. There's bullet weight to consider—and in some calibers there are many bullet weights to choose from. Then there's bullet shape—round-nose, spitzer, flat-point, boattail—and innumerable variations of each. And finally there's bullet design. Conventional soft-point, partition, bonded-core, hollow-point, Teflon-point, homogenous alloy, and more. What's it all about?

Fortunately, there are very few—if any—bad bullets on the market. Some choices may be better than others, but there are relatively few really poor choices in bullets. Especially if some common sense is used.

First let's look at some basic design features of bullets. Flat-points are just what their name implies, a flat meplat, or nose. Flat-points are essential for use in tubular magazines, since a sharp point—or even a roundnose—can cause the primer of the cartridge ahead of it to detonate under recoil. Flat-points are the worst, aerodynamically. They offer the most air resistance and thus shed velocity very quickly. On the surface, flat-points are very poor choices unless you simply have to use them. However, they do have one advantage: that flat point transfers energy very quickly, delivering an immediate blow that to some extent transcends paper ballistics. The flat-point bullet is, for example, one of the reasons behind the .30-30's century of success.

Round-nose bullets are also just that—a rounded nose. This bullet shape is more aerodynamic than a flat-point, but still sheds velocity fairly quickly. All things being equal, it will start to expand more quickly than a spitzer design—and under any circumstances will transfer energy a bit more quickly.

Spitzer bullets are sharp-pointed. They offer the least air resistance, and thus are the most aerodynamic. Not all spitzers are created equal. The curving portion of the bullet as it tapers to the point is called the ogive. The rapidity with which it tapers affects aerodynamics. A gently rounded ogive, called a tangent ogive, is less aerodynamic than a more rapid taper, called a secant ogive. And then there are boattails.

The boattail is a tapered bullet heel that reduces air friction by allowing a smoother flow around the base while the bullet is in flight. Boattails *are* more aerodynamic. They were initially adopted for military purposes because they significantly extended the effective range of tripod-mounted machine guns. There is a difference between laying down plunging fire at 1,300 meters against an enemy trenchline and trying to shoot a trophy ram at 350 yards. At normal game ranges, the boattails make a difference, but the flattening of trajectory is very slight.

As examples, let's look at three 180-grain .30-caliber bullets. We'll choose a 180-grain Hornady round-nose; a 180-grain Hornady Spire Point, an extremely aerodynamic flat-based bullet; and a Hornady 180-grain boattail Spire Point. We'll start each at 3,000 feet per second, and we'll sight each rifle in so that it's dead-on at 100 yards. At 300 yards, the round-nosed bullet has dropped 14.1 inches and has a retained velocity of 1,933 feet per second. The Spire Point will drop 11.3 inches at 300 yards, and will have a retained velocity of 2,363 fps. The boattail will drop 11.1 inches at 300 yards and will be traveling at 2,398 fps. You could play with these figures by using more or less aerodynamic spitzers and spitzer boattails—but the difference between a flat-based spitzer and a boattail amounts to fractions of inches until you get to very long range indeed. With these two Hornady Spire Points, for instance, the difference even at 500 yards is just two inches!

Mind you, I'm not against boattail bullets. Every little bit of trajectory edge you can get is worth having in some applications. However, there's another characteristic of boattails worth mentioning. Upon impact with game, the tapered heel of a boattail tends to make the core squirt out of the jacket. Jacket thickness helps, as do design features like Hornady's Interlock which binds the core into the jacket. But be advised that jacket and core separation—and reduction in penetration caused by the loss of bullet weight—is more likely with boattails than with flat-based bullets.

Two terms that are bandied about—in this volume as well as almost anything about shooting that's marginally technical—are *sectional density* and *ballistic coefficient.* Sectional density (SD) is a bullet's weight in relationship to its diameter, expressed as the ratio of a bullet's weight in pounds to the square of its diameter in inches. Sectional density is important to velocity retention in that longer, heavier-for-caliber bullets retain velocity better than shorter, lighter bullets. However, keep in mind that the figure given for a bullet's sectional density has nothing to do with its shape. Unless there are extreme differences, shape has more to do with velocity retention than sectional density. For instance, a spitzer 150-grain .30-caliber bullet will shoot flatter than a 180-grain round-nose.

Sectional density is important to the hunter, though. Sectional density, the ratio of weight to caliber, is extremely important to the bullet's ability to hold its course and penetrate. Bullet design makes a difference, but basic designs being equal, a heavier-for-caliber bullet will *always* penetrate better than a lighter bullet. The value in itself is not all that important except for comparing bullets of different calibers. For instance, you should know empirically that a 180-grain .30-caliber bullet has a higher sectional density than a 150-grain .30 caliber. It's only "nice to know" that *all* 180-grain .308-inch bullets have a sectional density of .271, while all 150-grain bullets in that caliber have a sectional density of .226.

Those numbers become more useful when comparing bullets of different calibers. We know, for instance, that a 180-grain .30-caliber bullet is relatively heavy for caliber, so a sectional density of .271 must be fairly high. A 175-grain 7mm bullet, however, takes a jump up to a sectional density of .310. All things, such as velocity and bullet design, being equal, a 175-grain 7mm bullet can be expected to penetrate better than a 180-grain .30-caliber. And that's generally true. The direct correlation between a 7mm bullet and the 180-grain .30 caliber bullet is the 154-grain 7mm bullet, with a sectional density of .273.

I mentioned earlier in this book that .338 bullets are very high in sectional density, and they are. The very light-for-caliber 200-grain .338 bullet has an SD of .250–not that bad. Bullets of 225 grains have an SD of .281, while 250-grain .338 bullets have a very high SD of .313. These figures are why a .338 will outpenetrate a .375, which has SDs of .274 for the 270-grain bullet and .305 for the 300-grain bullet.

Sectional density is a contributing factor to ballistic coefficient (BC). The ballistic coefficient, however, is a much more complex concept and much more difficult to determine mathematically. Also more difficult to understand.

In essence, the BC is an index of a projectile's ability to overcome resistance in flight. Also expressed in a three-digit decimal, BC is a direct indicator of flatness of trajectory and the ability to hold velocity and energy downrange. However, it's derived by computing the ratio of a bullet's weight to the product of the square of its diameter and its "form factor." That last is the problem for us laymen. The form factor, also called "coefficient of reduction," is a multiplier which relates the shape of the bullet in question to a "standard projectile" used to compute a given set of ballistic data.

Learning the ballistic coefficient of a bullet loaded in factory ammo can be a bit difficult, as this information is rarely printed. The bulletmakers' reloading manuals will give the BCs for their products, and they're useful for making comparisons. However, since the means for computing ballistics tables vary from one company to another, the "form factor" and thus BCs may not compare exactly from one company to another.

The Hornady reloading manual, for instance, provides one BC for Hornady bullets. The Sierra manual provides three–one computed at high velocity, one at intermediate, and one at low velocity. Chances are the different companies use different models, as can be seen in the widely differing values. For instance, Sierra's 180-grain .30-caliber round-nose has a high-velocity BC of .267. The very similar Hornady 180-grain round-nose has a BC of .241. It's pretty much a waste of time to try to compare these values and come up with anything meaningful.

You can use the BC to compare Hornady bullets with Hornady bullets and Sierra bullets with Sierra bullets, if your interest is finding the bullet that will best buck the wind and shoot the flattest. In the Sierra line, you can figure the 180-grain .30-caliber round-nose won't cut it. So how about the 180-grain Sierra boattail? That has a BC of .537, and you know for darn sure it will shoot flatter. But you can also use the figure to compare bullets of different calibers. Supposing the velocities were about the same, would you get a flatter trajectory with a 160-grain 7mm Sierra boattail? It has a BC of .563, so indeed you would. A 250-grain Sierra boattail .338 bullet has a higher BC yet, of .587, so it will shoot flatter yet. But to keep velocity the same you'll start to pay quite a price in recoil!

Ballistic coefficient is not something to get wrapped around the axle on. Any bullet with a BC above .500 is extremely streamlined and will shoot very flat. Anything below .400 will probably be a poor choice for long-range shooting. To simplify it further, any spitzer hunting bullet that's relatively heavy for caliber is going to be a good choice for shooting at longer ranges, provided you can get the velocity up to meaningful levels. For instance, an aerodynamic 200-grain .30-caliber bullet has an extremely high BC, nearly .600. At .300 magnum velocities, it will be the best long-range choice available. But you can't push bullets this heavy to meaningful velocities in the little .308 Winchester case, so you have to sacrifice BC and go to a shorter, lighter bullet to get the velocity up.

While sectional density does relate somewhat to bullet performance on game, ballistic coefficient really does not. Bullet performance depends on the right combination of penetration and expansion. These are not necessarily the same for all types of game, but on anything in the world except elephant, rhino, and possibly the biggest bovines, some expansion is desired to impart more shock and create a larger wound channel.

On thick-skinned, dangerous game, you must have penetration. Period. Expansion creates more resistance; thus, the more and faster expansion you get, the more limited penetration must be. Excluding elephant and such, there are two primary schools of thought regarding bullet performance on game. One group wants enough expansion to occur rapidly enough so that the bullet stops in the animal and expends all its energy. This train of thought reckons that any energy expending on the far side of the game is wasted. The other school wants some expansion, but prefers complete penetration–entrance wound and exit wound. Often stated as a reason is the desirability of entrance and exit for a better blood trail. I don't buy that, since ideal shot placement should preclude the need for a blood trail. However, I have always leaned toward complete penetration, at least on broadside shots. My reasoning is that, if a bullet will penetrate completely on a broadside shot, then I *know* it has the energy and penetrating abilities needed should I have to take a quartering-away shot that requires the bullet to pass through a lot of tissue en route to the vitals.

Now, make no mistake: A bullet that reaches the heart-lung area and expands violently in that area–or while passing through–will take an animal down much more quickly and dramatically than a bullet that expands more slowly, making a small wound channel and exiting. If you doubt this, shoot a broadside deer very carefully behind the shoulder with a 55-grain bullet from a .22-250. There will be no exit, and the effects will be immediate and dramatic. Unfortunately, you can't use that bullet or that caliber from anything but an ideal angle, which is why .22 centerfires are illegal for deer in so many states. And I don't like to use bullets that I can't rely on for whatever reasonable shot might present itself. I do like bullets to expand and do some damage, but I don't like too much of a good thing else the bullet can fail to penetrate on bad-angle shots or, worse, explode upon striking shoulder bones or even ribs and also fail to penetrate.

Expansion is enhanced–or controlled–by a variety of design features. Generally speaking, at one end of the spectrum you have full-metal-jacket, or solid bullets. Some match bullets, all military bullets, and bullets designed specifically to hunt thick-skinned game such as elephant and rhino, are designed not to expand at all. At the other end, you have hollow-point bullets, generally either match bullets or varmint bullets, that tend to expand explosively because of the cavity in the nose. This is not universal, though; some hunting bullets, like the homogenous-alloy Barnes "X" bullet, have a very small nose cavity to promote uniform expansion–and they work exceptionally well. There are also a great many "varmint" bullets that are not hollow-point but have thin jackets designed to expand like small bombs on hitting the slightest resistance.

Between these extremes are wide varieties of bullet designs, most of which work pretty well. Conventional soft-points are simply a lead core and a copper jacket, with a bit of lead exposed at the nose to initiate mushrooming. The degree of expansion of such bullets is controlled by thickness of jacket, amount of lead exposed, and the velocity at which the bullet strikes.

This last is the bulletmakers' greatest dilemma. A 180-grain bullet fired from a .30-06 might strike game at 2,700 feet per second, at the muzzle; or less than 2,000 feet per second at 400 yards. The same bullet fired from a .300 Weatherby Magnum, over the same ranges, must perform between 3,200 and 2,300 feet per second. It is impossible to build a bullet that works exactly the same at all velocities and all ranges, in all cartridges within a caliber—but today's bulletsmiths have come closer than ever.

There are numerous designs that do a pretty good job of controlling expansion. Nosler's famed Partition has a partition of jacket material between a front core and a rear core. The front core promotes expansion back to the partition, and indeed is often wiped at least partially away—but the rear core with the bulk of the bullet weight remains intact and penetrates. Trophy Bonded's Bearclaw bullet (like the older Bitterroot and several others) chemically bonds the core to the jacket so separation is physically impossible. Expansion is superb, but weight retention is awesome. Swift's A-Frame combines core-bonding with a partition. Speer's Grand Slam is a dual-core bullet with a harder alloy in the base and a softer nose core to promote expansion. The rear core is also folded into a swaged ring in the base. Hornady's Interlock, similarly, has the core locked into recesses in the jacket. Barnes's X-Bullet is a pure copper bullet with a slight nose cavity and an "X" indentation in the nose to start the characteristic petals peeling back.

Now, too much expansion control is not necessarily a good thing. I do prefer the controlled expansion designs for heavier game with thicker skin and heavier bones—*all* bears and wild pigs, and antlered or horned animals from, say 300 or 350 pounds on up. But for deer-sized game, sheep, mountain goats, and other game of similar size, expansion does not need to be controlled all that much. Conventional soft-points, conventional boattails, and bullets with devices to *promote* expansion are often fine choices for our smaller big-game animals. These last designs include bullets like Remington's Bronze Point, with a brass plug in the nose that drives back into the bullet on impact to initiate expansion; and Nosler's Ballistic Tip, with a similar Teflon plug. Such bullets do expand fairly quickly and, at higher velocities especially, may expand *too* quickly on larger game. But on deer-sized game, provided the caliber and weight are adequate, these bullets will do a fine job.

The ammunition makers almost across the board now offer lines of upgraded ammunition that feature "name" bullets. Federal's Premium line offers Nosler Partitions, Trophy Bonded Bearclaws, and Sierra boattails. Winchester has the Winchester Supreme Silvertips (for ranging abilities) and Fail Safe (for controlled expansion and penetration). Remington has the Extended Range bullets for improved aerodynamics and Safari (with Swift A-Frame) for penetration. El Dorado loads the X-Bullet. And so on. These are all very fine options for the hunter going on a special quest. However, I must say that there is *nothing* wrong with the "vanilla ice cream" bullets from the major manufacturers. Federal's Hi-Shok is an excellent conventional bullet, and I've had particularly good luck with both Remington Core-Lokt and Winchester Power Point bullets. In fact, these last are often my choice over one of the super-premium bullets.

As important as bullet design is adequate bullet weight for the job at hand. I'm a sectional-density freak. I admit it. I have no use for the lighter bullets within a given caliber. And if the bullet is heavy enough and designed for the velocity at which it is fired, it will do the job. In the milder 7mms, for instance, I might use 140- or 150-grain bullets; at the lower velocities, you can reduce bullet weight a bit. But in the .280 I stick with 160-grain bullets, and in the 7mm magnums I use bullets from 160 to 175 grains.

In the .270, I'm more likely to use 140- or 150-grain bullets than the ever-popular 130-grain load. In the .30-30, the 150-grain bullet is okay, and perhaps it's okay on deer in the .308. But I prefer the 165-grain bullet in the .308 and .30-06–and for anything heavier than deer, it's 180 grains or better. Nothing forgives poor shot placement. That's an absolute fact. But a little bit of extra bullet weight can forgive a bullet's design or manufacturing shortcomings.

An exception to this rule is that, within certain limits, the super-premium bullets can often be used in lighter weights, and thus at higher velocities, and still achieve the desired results. For instance, the Barnes X-Bullets, being all copper, are longer than lead-core bullets. And they will expand and penetrate with boring regularity. You can drop some bullet weight if you use them. Likewise Trophy Bonded's Bearclaw. With that bullet I'd use a 140-grain 7mm pill on fairly stout game. And while I wouldn't tackle a Cape buffalo or brown bear with it, I'd have no qualms about using their light-for-caliber 240-grain .375 bullet on elk and moose.

The premium bullets cost a great deal more, as much as $2 per bullet. If you insist on using calibers a bit on the light side for the game you're hunting, they're worth every cent. Likewise for that added confidence on dangerous game or for a long-range, long-awaited hunt. But we have very few–if any–"bad" bullets on the market today. If you choose bullets designed for the game you have in mind and keep away from the lightest bullets in any caliber, chances are you can't go wrong.

Chapter 18

Modern Shotgun Slugs

The concept of shooting single projectiles through a shotgun barrel is hardly new. In fact, it predates rifled arms by centuries. The forerunners of our shotgun slugs were the round balls fired through unrifled bores for generations, and our concept of "gauges" dates back to that era. The gauge is simply a means of expressing the number of round balls obtained from a pound of lead. Twelve gauge means 12 round balls to the pound, and just happens to mean a round ball of .729 caliber. In smoothbore days, the 12 bore, or 12 gauge, was a fairly common all-round hunting arm–and until fairly recently there was very little change.

The first major improvement over the round "pumpkin-ball" shotgun projectiles was the Foster slug–and for many years it was about all that was available. The Foster slug is a more or less conical, hollow-based projectile. The theory was that pressure from burning gases cause the base of the slug to upset, or expand, in the bore, thus creating a tighter fit to the barrel and greater accuracy. The next improvement was to cast the slug with shallow rifling grooves, which is the way virtually all Foster-type slugs are made today. The theory here was that air resistance would enable the "rifling" to impart a stabilizing spin to the slug. The actual effect of this rifling is questionable, and slug accuracy with an average shotgun is also very questionable.

The classic deer hunter's gun for a Foster-type slug is a fairly short-barreled, open-choked shotgun affixed with open sights or, better, a low-powered scope. The slug pretty much rattles down the open tube, but every shotgun is a law unto itself–no different from a hunting rifle, but the extremes are much greater. Different companies manufacture slugs to slightly different diameters, and there's no telling what might work best in a given shotgun. Some open-bored "slug guns" actually deliver very acceptable accuracy with one or another brand of Foster-type slugs. So do some shotguns with varying degrees of choke. Experimentation is the only way to determine what you can expect from your shotgun–and what slug will work best. One thing that is not in question is the devastating efficiency of the shotgun slug.

At muzzle velocities of around 1,600 feet per second, a one-ounce slug yields 2,500 foot/pounds of energy. A 1¼-ounce slug yields over 2,800 foot/pounds. That's a decent energy figure, and given the weight and diameter of the projectile, the blow it delivers is crushing–even out to 100 yards. However, with Foster-slug technology and a smoothbore barrel, there's often a lot of blue sky in figuring you have 100 yards of range. Fifty-yard groups of four inches are very, very good–and that probably means 10- to 12-inch groups at 100 yards. Given normal aiming errors, that's pushing things a bit!

I doubt that many hunters would choose a shotgun for deer if they could use a rifle instead. However, the shotgun is a short-range arm, and for generations it has been considered much safer to use in populated areas than a centerfire rifle. The white-tailed deer loves small woodlot and edge habitat, and thrives in small-farm areas and even in our suburbs. And as our suburbs have expanded, more and more areas have become and are becoming "shotgun only." These days, millions of deer hunters simply must use shotguns if they hunt deer with firearms other than muzzle-loaders–and as a result of this demand, slug technology has come many miles in the last few years.

Formerly one could choose between Foster-type slugs or buckshot. Buckshot may have a place in deer drives in very thick country or in following the Southern tradition of hunting deer over hounds. But buck-shot is a *very* short-range affair. My own tests with a variety of shotguns and buckshot loads indicate that a buckshot load's effective range is almost never over 30 yards–and with most shotguns, 25 yards is pushing it. For deliberate shooting, even below-average performance with a Foster slug triples this range, so the choice would be obvious.

Today, though, several options beat the heck out of a Foster slug. A number of years ago, the great German arms genius Wilhelm Brenneke designed his Brenneke slug, still offered by RWS. The Brenneke slug features an over-powder wad solidly affixed to the projectile itself. The wad helps seal the bore, creating a tighter fit and a significant improvement in accuracy. Similar, and perhaps even better, is the Vitt slug, which uses a plastic obturating cap attached to the slug. Most conventional shotguns will shoot a great deal better with either of these designs than they will with Fosters.

Newer and still better are the sabot slugs, now offered in various forms by Remington, Winchester, and Federal. As the name implies, this type of slug is actually a bullet encased in a sabot. The sabot seals the bore and prevents deformation of the slug itself. It separates from the slug shortly after leaving the muzzle, allowing the slug to fly onward and do its work.

It's impossible to say exactly what accuracy gains can be expected from the sabot. After all, some shotguns shoot very well with Fosters–and you're still talking about a smoothbore barrel not much different from what both sides used at Bunker Hill 220 years ago. But in most cases, the gains will be adequate to realize genuine 100-yard accuracy.

The projectiles themselves have changed. Federal loads a lead hollow-point slug in their sabot loads, while Winchester uses the Ballistic Research, Inc. (BRI) projectile. Remington's is unique; their Copper Solid sabot slug is a solid copper hollow-point projectile that expands much like the Barnes X-Bullet. It's devastating–but keep in mind that any one-ounce projectile at over 1,100 feet per second (the remaining velocity of a 12-gauge Foster slug at 100 yards) will be devastating on deer.

The trick is to *hit* the deer, and hit him in the right place, with that huge chunk of lead or copper. And here's where improvements in slug shotguns have made even greater strides than the slugs themselves.

Many years ago, when I was stationed in Virginia, I was obligated to use a shotgun for deer for the first time in my life. Like many neophyte deer hunters, I made do with what I had. What I had was a Model 12 skeet gun, and by carefully sighting down the rib I could do sort of okay out to 40 or 50 yards. Pretty dumb, really. Serious deer hunters have known for years that the first key to slug accuracy is good sights, and for decades all the major manufacturers have offered rifle-sighted slug guns or "buck specials." With decent sights, even the worst performance makes 50-yard shooting fairly simple, and under the best of circumstances 100 yards is practical.

The latest development is the fully rifled barrel or rifled choke tube. Custom makers and aftermarket barrel makers like Hastings started the trend, and now most major manufacturers offer some version of a rifled shotgun. At first, these arms were not legal in some states that specified "smoothbore," but those troubles are mostly over. The intention in requiring shotguns has always been to limit the hazards from stray projectiles, and rifling does not increase the maximum range a slug will fly–it only keeps the slug under the shooter's control for a greater distance!

Obviously, a fully rifled barrel is much more effective than a rifled choke tube at the end of the muzzle–but the rifled tubes do help. In combination with sabot slugs, rifled-barrel shotguns are awesome. Groups at 100 yards of three inches are fairly common, and smaller groups are quite possible. At some point, the arcing trajectory of a shotgun slug makes hitting very difficult. And of course the velocity and energy begin to fall off radically beyond 100 yards. However, with a rifled barrel and good slugs there's no reason why shots at 125 yards shouldn't be as routine as shots at 75 yards used to be–and that's a dramatic improvement.

If you're obligated to use slugs for deer, do yourself a favor. Experiment with everything available and find out what works best in *your* shotgun. Chances are you can extend your range by a significant margin–and even a few yards of extra effective range is well worth going after.

More than 99 percent of all slug shooting is done on white-tailed deer. However, the slug in any of its forms is an extremely deadly projectile. A shotgun would not be my arm of choice unless I was obligated by law to use it, but a slug is certainly effective against animals much larger and tougher than deer. The late gun writer Art Blatt and I were hunting pigs on a rainy day in northern California some years ago. Art was using a slug-loaded shotgun because of an article he was writing, and since it was raining cats and dogs we were having trouble finding a pig. We found one eventually, bedded in a cave on the far side of a deep, narrow ravine. Only his head was visible, so we decided to throw some rocks to get him to move.

The first couple of rocks had no effect, but when one landed close to him, the pig–a hefty boar–was up and moving in a flash. He came out of the cave and headed downhill toward the creek with a full head of steam. He'd made about five yards–most of it straight downhill–when Art's slug caught him on the shoulder. It didn't just knock him down. It *halted* his forward progress and set him back on his haunches. Then he slid down into the creek on his nose. This was one of the most dramatic effects of sheer impact I've ever seen, and it convinced me that a slug is awesome. Others agree.

An Alaskan guide I know typically carries a Drilling, the three-shot European gun, for backup on brown and grizzly bears. The rifle barrel is a 7x65R, the shotgun barrels 12 gauge. He carries Brenneke slugs in the shotgun, and has stopped two bears at very close range with them. I wouldn't personally choose a shotgun for such work because of the range limitations–but I wouldn't hesitate to tackle anything in North America with a shotgun slug at close range. They work!

Part II

North American Rifles

Chapter 19

North American Rifles: 1865–1940

The long and bitter American Civil War was a universal watershed for military tactics and weaponry. Among many other things, it saw an end to Napoleonic tactics, a beginning of aerial warfare in the form of balloons, and the first use of armored naval vessels. It also saw the first widespread use of metallic cartridges and repeating firearms. And since sporting arms have generally stemmed from military applications, the Civil War provides a sensible beginning for a historical perspective on American hunting arms.

Breechloaders of various types had been in widespread use long before the Civil War. The Ferguson screw-breech flintlock saw some use in the American revolution, and the Hall breechloading flintlock saw service in early Indian campaigns and the Mexican War. By 1861, there were quite a number of very fine percussion breechloaders, the most famous being the Sharps rifle employed by Berdan's Sharpshooters. The problem was that the paper cartridges of the era were perishable and only marginally effective. It was the self-contained metallic cartridge that was needed for breechloaders and–especially–repeaters to be truly viable propositions.

Metallic cartridges as we know them probably began with the French pinfire system around 1850. Aside from improvements like better primers and better brass, the self-contained centerfire cartridge as we know it today was invented by Englishman George Daws in 1861. The centerfire cartridge probably did not see service in the Civil War, and the fragile pinfire may have seen only limited use in the hands of individuals who armed themselves. Between these two developments came the rimfire, and it was rimfire repeaters that gave the world a whole new opinion of repeating firearms.

The repeaters of the Civil War were the Spencer and Henry. Both were lever-action tubular-magazine rifles, the former with the tube running from the buttplate up through the stock, the latter the more familiar form with the tube under the barrel. Both appeared in 1860, and both were extremely modest in both power and range, although the Spencer's .56-caliber bullet packed quite a punch. The Henry was expensive and seldom seen, generally carried only by a few Union officers who purchased it for their own use. Although its 15-shot magazine gave it awesome firepower, the unprotected tubular magazine dented easily and the rifle was generally considered too fragile for combat use. The Spencer, however, was rugged and reliable. This was "that damned Yankee rifle that you load on Sunday and shoot all week." It held seven cartridges, and although it was issued only in small quantities it proved decisive in several engagements.

Both rifles set the pace for several generations of the lever-action's dominance among repeating sporting rifles in America. The interesting thing, however, is that word *American*. The descendants of the Henry–Oliver F. Winchester's long succession of lever-action arms–were known and respected throughout the world. But only in America was the lever-action truly the most popular action.

Of course, it was some years after the Civil War before the lever-action really took over. The Model 1866 Winchester was really an improved Henry, retaining the .44 rimfire cartridge. It was both more reliable and more popular, but it was the greatly improved 1873 Winchester that made both Oliver Winchester's fortune and the lever-action's reputation. It was a handy, rugged repeater, and it was used on all manner of game throughout the continent. However, it had the same problem as the Henry and the 1866 Winchester: its brand-new .44-40 cartridge was extremely under-powered for serious big-game hunting.

For at least the first 20 years after the Civil War, the single-shot rifle remained the most popular sporting arm. The Sharps action was readily adapted to the new centerfire cartridges, and of course the trapdoor conversion was used to turn military muzzleloaders into breechloaders starting in 1866. Later, single-shot actions like the Remington Rolling Block and Winchester Hi-Wall followed. The single-shots were able to house powerful cartridges that early repeaters simply could not handle–and with heavy barrels and tightly sealing breeches they were generally far more accurate as well.

Westward expansion slowed somewhat during the Civil War, but began again in earnest with the close of hostilities. The 60 million buffalo that roamed the Great Plains in 1860–along with untold millions of elk, deer, and pronghorn–had been hunted sporadically for meat and hides since white men first started West. However, the small numbers of hunters armed with muzzleloaders had made little impact. After the war, the railroad made the shipping of hides and even meat eastward practical–and large fortunes could be made with the powerful new breechloading rifles.

Incredibly, this kind of buffalo hunting lasted less than 20 years. The great Kansas herds were nearly gone by 1870. The relentless buffalo hunters followed the herds first south into Oklahoma and the Texas Panhandle, then north into Wyoming and Montana. The last great hunt was probably the winter of 1884-1885, with Miles City, Montana, seeing the last big shipments. As the buffalo were eradicated, so were the pronghorn, deer, and elk. It's not a proud chapter in our history, but it happened.

The Sharps was the most famous of the buffalo rifles, and almost certainly was preferred by those who could afford one. It was, however, quite expensive. There were a great many Sharps cartridges, generally .40, .44, .45, or .50 in caliber, with a variety of case lengths, shapes, and charges of black powder. Bullets were heavy conicals, and velocities were low and trajectories like rainbows. The Sharps, of course, wasn't alone. There were Ballards, Bullards, Remingtons, and Peabodys—and each small company had its own proprietary cartridges. Most common, though, was almost certainly the trapdoor Springfield in .50-70 or the later .45-70.

As sportsmen, we must abhor the destruction the buffalo hunters wrought—but we must also be in awe of their marksmanship. These men knew their rifles and they knew how to estimate range. In the early years, "buffalo running" from horseback with the light-caliber repeating rifles and even revolvers was practiced. But serious buffalo hunters didn't like this technique. For one thing, it was extremely dangerous. For another, it spread the carcasses over several miles and made the skinning process too time-consuming. The serious and successful buffalo hunters sought to make a stand—to get within long range of a herd, 200 yards and more, and drop as many animals as possible in a small area before the herd took flight. They did not, as legend might have it, concentrate on head or neck shots. Instead their goal was to plunk the animals through the lungs. They found that the relatively placid bison would generally continue to feed, unbothered by the distant gunfire and unaware of what was happening. Often, several would be shot before the first stricken animal dropped or lay down. An animal shot too far forward—in the shoulder—or too far back, though, would generally stampede and panic the herd.

The Sharps cartridges and their kin were quite powerful for the day. The most common were probably the .45-100 and the .50-90. The former fired a 550-grain bullet at 1,360 feet per second, for a muzzle energy of 2,240 foot/pounds. The .50-90 is the cartridge referred to as the "Big Fifty" Sharps. It fired a 473-grain bullet at 1,350 feet per second for 1,920 foot/pounds. However, in spite of the slightly lower energy figure, the .50-caliber projectile was considered to deliver a heavier blow than any of the .44s or .45s.

These were the cartridges revered by hunters of the 1870s and 1880s. The repeaters were interesting toys, but were not considered serious hunting rifles by many. Winchester's Model 1873 rifle in .44-40 was a tremendous success, but the serious hunter needed a longer lever-action that could handle more powerful cartridges. He got it in the Winchester Model 1876, long one of Theodore Roosevelt's favorites. Its original cartridge was the .45-75 Winchester, a cartridge that approximated the performance of the .45-70 Government but used a shorter, fatter, bottleneck case. It fired a lighter 350-grain bullet at 1,383 feet per second, yielding 1,485 foot/pounds of energy. That isn't particularly impressive, but this was the cartridge Teddy Roosevelt swore by for grizzly, and it was certainly used during the last few years of buffalo hunting.

Among the majority of serious hunters, however, the single-shot held sway for at least another decade. But things were changing. The powerful

Model '76 Centennial Winchester was followed by the great Model 1886, the first collaboration between John Moses Browning and Winchester. The '86 was an even longer action than the '76. It chambered not only the .45-70 Government but larger rounds like the .45-90 and the .50-110.

Winchester followed the '86 with the '92 Winchester, another Browning design that remains one of the handiest, sweetest lever-actions ever made, despite its mild cartridges. And then, of course, the Model 1894 Winchester came along. Its initial chamberings were the black-powder .38-55 and .32-40, but in 1895 Winchester introduced the brand-new smokeless .30-30. The world has never been the same.

Of course, Winchester wasn't the only outfit in the lever-action game. There were great lever-actions from Marlin–the 1881, then the 1894, and the powerful 1895. And more–Ballards, Kennedys, and others. The trend continued with the Model 1895 Winchester, chambered for truly powerful general-purpose cartridges. And then Arthur Savage introduced his 1895 Savage and perfected it four years later in the Savage 99. By the turn of the century, America was lever-action country and the great single-shots were nearly forgotten.

Perhaps surprisingly, the rest of the world didn't go lever-action crazy. In sporting rifles, the British perfected the double-barreled rifle, a type that has never been popular with Americans. And then the bolt-actions came along. The British had American James Paris Lee's bolt-action before they had smokeless powder–first in the Lee-Metford with Metford rifling, and then the Lee-Enfield with Enfield rifling. The action itself changed very little from the 1880s until it was replaced after World War II.

On the Continent there were Austrian Mannlicher-Schoenauers, French Lebels, Norwegian Krag-Jorgensens. And in Germany, a prolific genius named Peter Paul Mauser. From the early 1870s until 1898, Mauser produced a new bolt-action almost every year–each a slight improvement over the one before. The final form, to be altered only in size and cosmetics, was the '98 Mauser–still considered by many to be the best bolt-action of all.

Englishmen who could afford them clung to their doubles, but the vast majority of English and Continental sportsmen were dedicated bolt-action fans by the turn of the century. Americans came around much more slowly. Prior to World War I, there were very few bolt-action sporters available–the Lee straight-pull, the Canadian Ross, a smattering of Mannlichers and Mausers, plenty of American '98 Krags, and relatively few Springfields.

The sporting press of the day held running arguments over which was the faster–the bolt-action or the lever-action. The superior accuracy of the bolt-action was known, but with less consistent ammunition and open sights the point was fairly moot. The .30-40 Krag was considered a fine choice for all-round North American hunting. But so was the .30-30. And, after all, the .30-40 cartridge was also available in the lever-action Winchester '95.

One of the real innovators of the day, perhaps surprisingly, was Arthur W. Savage. His arms company and his Savage 99 made the largest headlines in the sporting press of the day, first with the .22 Savage Hi-Power in 1912, a nifty little cartridge firing a long, heavy 70-grain bullet at fully 2,800 feet per second. It sparked one of the great smallbore fads of the day, and was used–and sworn by as well as sworn at–on game up to elk, moose, and big bears. The .22 Savage Hi-Power was developed by early gun crank Charles Newton, who also developed his own line of beltless magnums and bolt-action rifles. In 1915, Savage made even bigger headlines with another Newton development, the .250-3000. The initial factory loading pushed an 87-grain bullet to 3,000 feet per second. This was the first commercial cartridge to break the 3,000 fps barrier–and it's worthy of note that this was done in a lever-action, not a bolt-action.

But even then the worm was starting to turn. Newton himself, today best known for the .250 Savage, was one of the men who turned Americans toward bolt-actions. An early experimenter and wildcatter, he developed a line of superb unbelted cartridges whose ballistics are impressive even today. And he produced bolt-action rifles to handle them. From about 1913 until the early 1920s, through several failures and no great commercial successes, Newton made rifles for his .256, .30, and .35 Newton. He also made headlines, since he himself was a frequent contributor to sporting magazines of the day.

Newton stirred the pot, but it was really Kaiser Wilhelm who made it boil over. The First World War was a bolt-action war, and when America finally mobilized to join the fray, hundreds of thousands of city boys and country boys alike were introduced to the bolt-action for the first time. Our rifles, the 1903 Springfield and the 1917 Enfield, were clearly among the best rifles seen in that fray. Both lacked the firepower of Britain's 10-shot SMLE. It could perhaps be argued, too, that neither action was quite the equal of Germany's '98 Mauser–though both were Mauser derivatives. But our .30-06 cartridge was clearly superior to Britain's .303, and at least slightly superior to Germany's 8x57. When the doughboys came home, they had been converted for all time to the bolt-action.

With wartime tooling already in place, American factories began turning out bolt-action sporters on a large scale for the first time. Remington's Model 30 in its various forms was a barely civilianized version of the 1917 Enfield. Winchester's Model 54 was a Mauser-Springfield derivative. And genuine Mausers also found their way into the U.S. in large quantities.

For some years, it was almost exclusively a .30-06 world, but during the 1920s a few other cartridges began to creep in. The .270 Winchester came along in 1925, and a bespectacled English professor from Arizona named Jack O'Connor did much to spur its sales. By the time Winchester's great Model 70 appeared in 1937, the bolt-action was not only here to stay–it had passed the lever-action in popularity.

Of course, the bolt- and lever-actions weren't the only options. In shotguns, the slide-action was far and away the most popular, and it had its following in rifles as well. The Colt Lightning series of slide-action rifles–some of them chambered for very powerful cartridges–enjoyed some popularity in the late nineteenth century. As popular as slide-action shotguns remain, however, the slide-action rifle retains only limited appeal. Today, and for many years, only Remington has kept the action alive in centerfire calibers.

Remington also produced the first viable semiautomatic hunting rifles, starting with the Model 8 in 1906. An ungainly rifle with a long recoil spring around the barrel, it was nevertheless very reliable and was chambered for very effective cartridges like the .30 Remington (a rimless .30-30) and the good old .35 Remington. It was followed by the 81 Remington, and eventually gave way to the gas-operated forerunners of Remington's current Woodsmaster semiauto.

Winchester, too, had a run at early self-loaders. They actually beat Remington to the punch with their 1905 semiauto, but the .35 Winchester Self-Loading cartridge used in it was badly underpowered as a hunting round. Much better, though still no powerhouse, was the .351 Winchester for the much-improved Winchester Model 1907 semiauto. Three years later, they came out with the Model 1910 and the .401 Winchester cartridge. With a 200-grain bullet at 2,135 feet per second or a 250-grain bullet at 1,870 feet per second, it packed a tremendous wallop–but it was extremely short-ranged.

Over the years, semiautos improved tremendously, and they have remained on the scene. But they have never approached either the bolt-action or lever-action in popularity. Single-shots had virtually disappeared by 1940, and would not reappear until Bill Ruger made one of his more astute marketing moves.

World War II was, at least for Americans, a semiautomatic war. But in its wake, returning G.I.'s would not cling to the semiauto. Instead they returned to the bolt-action in the greatest numbers–and, to a slightly lesser degree, their beloved lever-actions. By 1940, the bolt-action was king–and so it would remain.

Chapter 20
Modern Single-Shots

It's been a quarter-century and more since William B. Ruger theorized that a certain group of hunters might appreciate the challenge and inherent sportsmanship of a single-shot rifle–especially if that rifle was well-made, affordable, and had the clean, simple lines that a single-shot action is so conducive to. A lot of people thought Ruger was nuts, but in a long career that has marked him as our century's greatest sporting-firearms genius, he's made few mistakes. This wasn't one of them.

The Ruger No. 1 single-shot caught on quickly and has remained popular throughout its history. So much so that it has almost no serious competition in the single-shot field. Quite a number of custom rifle makers like to work with single-shot actions–often the Ruger, but also custom-made actions. There are also a number of replicas of the great old single-shots on the market, including the Navy Arms Remington Rolling Block, and two Sharps reproductions from two different manufacturers. In conventional centerfires, though, there isn't much other than the Ruger No. 1.

Thompson/Center had a very fine break-open action for several years, featuring interchangeable barrels. It has recently been dropped, but T/C still offers a single-shot carbine based on the Contender action. New England Arms offers a dependable, inexpensive centerfire rifle on their break-open action. And then there's Browning's Model 1885. This is essentially a modernized version of the John Browning-designed Winchester Hi-Wall single-shot, a falling-block exposed-hammer single-shot. The 1885 is produced in much smaller numbers than the Ruger, but is almost certainly the second most popular single-shot in America. Relatively new is the Dakota Model 10, a semi-custom falling-block reminiscent of the Ruger action, but a bit more trim. The numbers will be limited, but the little Dakota action makes into one of the most beautiful rifles I've ever seen.

One of great strengths of the Ruger–and almost certainly one reason for its lasting popularity–is its availability in a wide range of calibers and configurations. Ruger No. 1 rifles are offered from .218 Bee and .22 Hornet on up to .404 Jeffery, .416 Rigby *and* Remington, and .458 Winchester Magnum. And most everything in between. The current list has 26 chamberings, suitable for everything from ground squirrels to elephants. It can be had as a varmint rifle; as a lightweight sporter in .257 Roberts or 7x57; as a long-range hunting rifle in .300 Winchester *or* Weatherby Magnum; or as a dangerous-game rifle. Or just about anything you have in mind. Configurations include the 1-V Special Varminter with heavy barrel;

the 1-A Light Sporter; the 1-RSI with Mannlicher-style stock; the "standard" 1-B sporter; and the 1-H Tropical in heavy calibers. If you want a single-shot, Ruger has one available.

While a semi-custom rifle like the Dakota can also be had in almost any caliber the customer desires, the caliber options are generally fairly limited with all other commercial rifles. The big-game chamberings for the Browning 1885 are just four: .270 Winchester, .30-06 Springfield, 7mm Remington Magnum, and .45-70. The New England Handi-Rifle drops the 7mm chambering but adds .30-30 and .243. T/C's Contender Carbine won't stand up to high-intensity cartridges, but it's chambered for cartridges such as 7-30 Waters, .30-30, .35 Remington, and .375 Winchester.

Although the selection is limited in rifles and (with the exception of the Ruger) chamberings, it seems there are easily enough single-shots to satisfy the market. The concept of the one-shot rifle and the one-shot kill has great appeal, and the single-shot rifle has great charisma. But only a certain number of sportsmen are going to accept both the challenge and the limitations.

As a design, the single-shot has both inherent strengths and inherent weaknesses. One of its strong points, literally, is the tremendous strength of the action, specifically the falling-block action type. The Ruger, particularly, is one of the strongest actions on the market. The single-shot is also rugged and simple, and no other rifle is as easy to load and unload–and to check to see if it's loaded or unloaded. From a manufacturer's standpoint, no other action is as simple to offer in a wide array of calibers. Little else is required beyond screwing in a barrel and making sure the ejector fits.

There are some weaknesses, however. Primary extraction is not nearly as strong as with bolt-action rifles. The famed Scottish Farquharson action, which was the basis for the Ruger No. 1, although marvelously strong, was always plagued by extraction problems. The Ruger doesn't normally have extraction difficulties, thanks to better modern brass and an improved extraction system, but it will not extract swollen cases with the same camming power as a bolt-action.

The single-shot is also generally not as accurate as the bolt-action. It can be; it has strong and consistent lockup, and it's easy to tailor ammunition for a single-shot in that bullets can be seated well out, with no worry about their being too long for the magazine. However, the two-piece stock of virtually every single-shot rifle makes bedding less stable and much more finicky than is common with bolt-action rifles. Make no mistake–many single-shots shoot exceptionally well. But others can be a real nightmare to get to shoot acceptably. Overall, accuracy is simply not as consistent as it is with run-of-the-mill bolt-actions.

In at least 99 percent of all hunting situations, however, there's a huge difference between theoretical accuracy and practical field accuracy. Even the most finicky single-shot is accurate enough for most hunting needs, and the most accurate of the breed are good enough for anything and everything. In chamberings, too, the single-shot is available in calibers that can handle any and all situations and any types of big game on this or any other continent. Sighting equipment is altogether up to the user. Scoping a Browning 1885 requires making sure there's clearance to properly and safely control the exposed hammer, but there are no real limitations on sighting equipment. Depending on weight of barrel and design of stock, single-shots can be heavy or light. And since there is really no action, just a breech, single-shots can have at least two extra inches of barrel over a repeater without increasing overall length.

If the cartridge is adequate and the bullet as well-chosen as it is well-placed, there should be no need for more than one shot. On the surface, it would seem that the single-shot rifle would be absolutely ideal for the full range of North American hunting.

Perhaps. While I have personal experience with few different varieties of one-shooters, I have a long and extremely happy association with the Ruger No. 1. I must have gotten my first one some time before 1970, a .243. I still have it. As I mentioned earlier, my idea for this rifle was just what the creators of the .243 envisioned–a combination varmint and deer/pronghorn rifle. It has served me well all this time, and only rarely can I recall needing more than its one shot.

That .243 was and is marvelously accurate, as was a heavy-barreled Ruger No. 1 .22-250 that I had. I also had a Ruger No. 1 Light Sporter in .270, a fabulously light and handy little rifle that I enjoyed immensely. Unfortunately, this was one of the finicky ones. After a great deal of experimentation, I got it to work "okay" with a couple of different loads. I shot a few deer with it–and certainly never missed anything because of the rifle. But I finally gave up on it as being too much trouble.

I also had a Ruger No. 1 Tropical in .375 H&H, and I shot quite a bit of African game with it. Again, I never felt handicapped by the one shot. It could happen, surely. However, given practice with the rifle, you learn to reload very quickly if a second shot is needed, and you learn to keep a second and perhaps third cartridge somewhere extremely handy–perhaps between the fingers of your supporting hand, perhaps in a Velcro wrist bandolier. Of course, one the great beauties of the single-shot rifle is that it makes you very, very careful with that first shot. Careful enough that you don't need a second or third shot quite as often as many of us–me included–do when we know they're available!

Enough hunters have used the Ruger No. 1 and similar modern single-shots on all types of game to prove it a perfectly adequate action type–just as it was in the 1870s. In fact, it's far better today since we have much better modern cartridges. Outdoor writer Jon Sundra really concentrated on the Ruger No. 1 for years, and quite literally shot them all over the world–as have many other experienced modern sportsmen. I've shot my very best pronghorn to date with a No. 1, some good whitetailed deer, mule deer, and a wide variety of African game. It works. However, its user must make a firm mental commitment before taking up the single-shot.

That one shot is all there is; there ain't no more. Maybe. With practice, especially a falling-block can be reloaded very quickly—and game doesn't always vanish after a first missed shot. Sometimes even the single-shot rifle is fast enough for a deliberate second opportunity. But not always, and it isn't something you can count on. The single-shot, therefore, is for the very deliberate shooter willing to gamble his hunt on that single cartridge in the chamber.

I don't think the single-shot rifle is necessarily well-suited to all types of North American hunting. It is available in cartridges more than adequate for the biggest bears, but certain one-shot kills are fairly unusual on grizzly and brown bears—especially extra-large ones. I wouldn't recommend a single-shot for a lone hunter. Even for guided hunters, it should be understood that choosing a single-shot may be asking for a guide's assist when it wouldn't have been necessary had a repeater of identical caliber been chosen. With dangerous animals, the ballgame simply must be ended as quickly as possible; if a big bear is headed for cover and the client's rifle is empty, only a fool would fault a guide for shooting! By the way, I feel very much the same about using a single-shot on Africa's dangerous game. It can be done, but it isn't the best or most sensible tool for the job.

An inherent inconvenience with the single-shot is the fact that it is either fully loaded or fully unloaded. I don't carry cartridges in the chamber when my rifle is slung, or when I'm negotiating rough country. The single-shot is totally out of action when its chamber is empty, while the magazine rifle requires just the working of a bolt or lever to put it into action. In the high mountains, this is generally not a problem; stalks tend to be well-planned and there is quite adequate time to load the single-shot and prepare for a careful shot.

In timber, whether for deer, elk, moose, or whatever, I see a real disadvantage to the single-shot. If it's cold and gloves must be worn, it's going to take altogether too much time to get an empty single-shot into action should an animal be encountered. The temptation to keep it loaded is even worse, for rifles simply should not have rounds in the chamber while hunters are climbing, negotiating deadfalls or other obstacles—or at any time when the rifle is not under the hunter's complete control. This difficulty also exists with horseback hunting.

Under no circumstances should a rifle have a cartridge in the chamber while on horseback, whether slung or carried in a saddle scabbard. That gives a repeater a decided advantage for any horseback hunt. If a fine bull elk is encountered on the trail, a hunter can drop off his horse, pull a repeater from the scabbard, and jack in a cartridge. With a single-shot, the hunter must first produce a cartridge from somewhere. The single-shot shooter will *always* have that cartridge readily available–but again, if heavy gloves are needed, fumbling is inevitable.

To my mind the single-shot, as good as it is, is best-suited to very deliberate hunting techniques where surprises are unlikely. This would include any form of stand-hunting, and most spot-and-stalk hunting. The last animal I shot with that Ruger No. 1 Light Sporter .270 was a classic example. It was a nice Coues buck that we'd spotted from about a mile away. We planned our route to come in on a ridge up above him, and although it took a bit of time and a whole lot of sweat, it worked perfectly. I crawled out on an outcropping, pushed my pack ahead of me for a rest, and *then* lowered the lever and put a round into the chamber. That it took more than one shot was altogether my fault; the single-shot was ideal and posed no handicap whatever. The same would be true for most sheep and goat hunting and a whole lot of deer hunting in the open West. It would, of course, also be true for stand-hunting for whitetails, hunting bear over bait, and even bugling for elk.

Where I feel the single-shot would be a handicap–perhaps even a serious one–would be for any form of still-hunting or tracking in thick cover and uneven terrain. If the hunting you're doing is such that you might encounter game at any time, but you can't predict when–and if the footing is uneven enough that you might need to sling the rifle or use one or both hands for support–then the single-shot is not a great idea. It needs to be used in situations where you either *know* you can keep both hands on the loaded rifle and have it absolutely ready, or you simply won't need it to be loaded until a time of *your*, not the game's, choosing.

Despite these limitations, the single-shot rifle is a wonderful concept, and we should all thank Bill Ruger for bringing it back. Whether it's ideal for every situation or not, every serious hunter should spend some time using a one-shooter. It's amazing what it will do for your first-round-hit capabilities.

Chapter 21

Lever-Actions Today

The lever-action is not as popular today as it was a century ago, and chances are it never will be again. Even though it isn't as universal as the bolt-action, however, the lever-action remains extremely popular in many parts of the U.S. Marlin has long been the largest American producer of rifles, and while a great many are rimfires, the sheer numbers of their Model 336 centerfire lever-action must not be ignored. Impressive, too, is the fact that the Model 1894 Winchester–a full century old at this writing–continues to sell and sell well.

The lever-action rifle started as an American peculiarity, and so it has remained. There have been very few other lever-action designs, and none of them have survived–in spite of their good qualities. A notable, and nearly forgotten, example is the Sako Finnwolf, a Finnish lever-action somewhat similar to the Winchester Model 88. It was a fine rifle, well-suited to high-performance cartridges like the .243 and .308. And it was a commercial disaster.

Failures, too, have been most American lever-actions since World War II. The wonderful Winchester Model 71, the last gasp of the classic Winchesters and the last incarnation of the memorable Model 1886, was introduced in 1936 with the .348 Winchester cartridge, a fine and powerful cartridge. The combination was arguably the best large-game lever-action rifle and cartridge ever made. The Model 71 made it into the Cold War era, but not by much. It was replaced in 1955 by the Model 88 lever-action and the .358 Winchester cartridge. The Model 88, too, was a wonderful rifle. It could handle spitzer bullets, which traditional tubular-magazine Winchesters could not, and it could handle flat-shooting cartridges like the .243, .308, and .284 Winchester. The Model 88 made it past Winchester's disastrous "pre-'64/post-'64" shift–but not by much.

Commercial failures like this would seem to indicate that the lever-action is dying. This is not so. While superb lever-actions like the Sako Finnwolf and the Winchester Model 88–and classics like the Model 71–died away, the lever-action in several archaic forms thrived. Today, "saddle guns" like the Winchester Model 94 and Marlin 336 continue to do just fine.

The darling of the pre-World War I era, the Savage 99, has had its problems. Its classic rotary-magazine form went out of production some years ago, leaving only the detachable-box-magazine version. That, too, went away for a few years. Savage Arms reorganized and is coming back strong at this writing, and with it comes the Savage 99–but I fear we will never again see the traditional rotary magazine. The only version resurrected so far has the detachable box.

Marlin has hung in just fine, not only with the 336, but also with the 444SS in .444 Marlin and the 1895SS in .45-70. Fairly recently, they reintroduced a series of 1894 Marlins in .218 Bee, .25-20, .32-20, .357 Magnum, .44 Magnum, and even .44-40 in their Centennial Model. For Marlin, the lever-action is alive and well.

In recent years, there have been reintroductions and reproductions of classic lever guns. One can buy current versions of the 1873 Winchester, the 1866, and even the Henry–not to mention the Model 92 Winchester from both Rossi and, for a time, Browning. Also from Browning, using the John Browning patents manufactured by Winchester, have come limited-edition Model 1886, Model 1895, and Model 71 Winchesters.

It would seem that the lever-action has a whole new lease on life, but this is misleading. With one exception only, all of our current lever-actions are turn-of-the-century (at best!) designs, kept alive by nostalgia and tradition. The single recent lever-action development still in production is Browning's BLR, now available in both short and long action, and thus the only lever-action chambered for high-intensity cartridges like the .270, .30-06, and 7mm Remington Magnum. It is a fine rifle, but in terms of numbers produced it does not compare with the Winchesters and Marlins.

In the 1990s, with the bolt-action in such universal use, how has the archaic lever-action hung on? And does it really have a viable position in North American hunting?

There is absolutely no question that the bolt-action is more versatile. It is chambered for more powerful cartridges, and can effectively handle any and all hunting situations on this or any other continent. The superior accuracy of the bolt-action also cannot be questioned. Its one-piece stock and sturdy lockup make it the odds-on choice for sheer accuracy. In case of problems, it also has extraction camming power–and protection against blowback–unsurpassed by other actions. And yet millions of American hunters still recognize that the bolt-action is not the only answer.

A great number choose the lever-action. Some do so because of nostalgia. After all, the lever-action and John Wayne won the West. Others do so because of tradition–after all, it was good enough for Grandpa. And still others–perhaps even the majority–do so because the lever-action does the job, as it has since the Civil War.

The lever-action today takes three basic forms, all of which overlap somewhat. There's the short-range carbine, typified by Marlin's 1894 and the reproductions of the Winchester 92 and other lever-actions chambered for what are essentially pistol cartridges. This group is truly useful only for small game and perhaps small deer at very close range.

Then there are the "brush rifles," chambered for cartridges of very adequate power but limited in range by arcing trajectories and rapidly diminishing velocities and energies. This group includes lever-actions chambered for the .30-30, .35 Remington, .375 Winchester, .444 Marlin, and .45-70.

Finally, there are the general-purpose lever-actions. This group includes the Savage 99 in .243 and .308, Browning's BLR in all its chamberings, and both Winchesters and Marlins in .307 and .356 Winchester. And, of course, the category also includes many discontinued lever-actions like Winchester's Model 88 in several calibers, generations of Savage 99s in calibers like .300 Savage and .358 Winchester, and "almost-modern" rifles like the Winchester 71.

There's little point in spending time on the first group. The .218, .25-20, .32-20, and even .357 carbines are wonderful fun to shoot. They're effective on varmints up to coyotes as far as their trajectories allow, and of course they will undoubtedly be used on deer by hunters who are either irresponsible or don't know any better. They are all just fine for game up to javelina, but none of them are deer rifles. Period.

The .44-40 really isn't, either, but at close range it will kill deer today just as well as it did in 1873. Lever-actions in .44 Remington Magnum are significantly better. The .44 is still a pistol cartridge, but with the velocity boost from rifle barrels it's a 100-yard deer cartridge. With selected bullets, the .44 Remington Magnum is certainly as capable of taking elk and black bear with a rifle as it is with a handgun, and more so–but it's still a 100-yard cartridge.

The second group is clearly the most prevalent. After a full century, the .30-30 Winchester cartridge remains one of America's most popular calibers–and so are the rifles that fire it. It is no powerhouse, far from it. It is, however, extremely effective on deer-sized game. The flat-nosed bullets it fires generally open well and tend to transfer energy quickly. As we've seen, although it isn't particularly impressive on the ballistics charts, it *is* adequate–as millions upon millions of hunters can attest.

Perhaps more important than the cartridge itself is the fact that the rifles that fire it are fast-handling, light, and a joy to carry. Generally they are not tack-drivers in the accuracy department, but they are neither intended for nor used at long range. Out to 100 yards, they're plenty accurate–and in careful hands will certainly stretch to 150 yards and more.

The .30-30, of course, is just the beginning of this "brush-rifle" category. Also included must be the .375 Winchester, the .35 Remington, the .444 Marlin, and the .45-70. None are particularly impressive in the downrange department, but all offer heavy bullets at moderate velocities, all deliver very heavy blows, and all are restricted to close-range use.

The .30-30 has almost certainly accounted for many multiples of every species of game on this continent. It will do the job on black bear and wild boar, given careful shot placement, but in spite of its successful use it's really not suited for larger game. The other cartridges listed certainly are. A century ago, such cartridges would have been considered more than

The .44 Magnum remains the most popular and most common of all hunting handguns. It's a short-range affair, but out to 75 yards or so the .44 Magnum is plenty of gun for deer-sized game, perhaps a bit larger with heavier bullets. This is the author's S&W Model 29, much loved for its astounding accuracy.

Here's a Contender fully set up as a big-game handgun: triple-ring mounts, sling-swivel studs, and Mag-Na-Ported barrel.

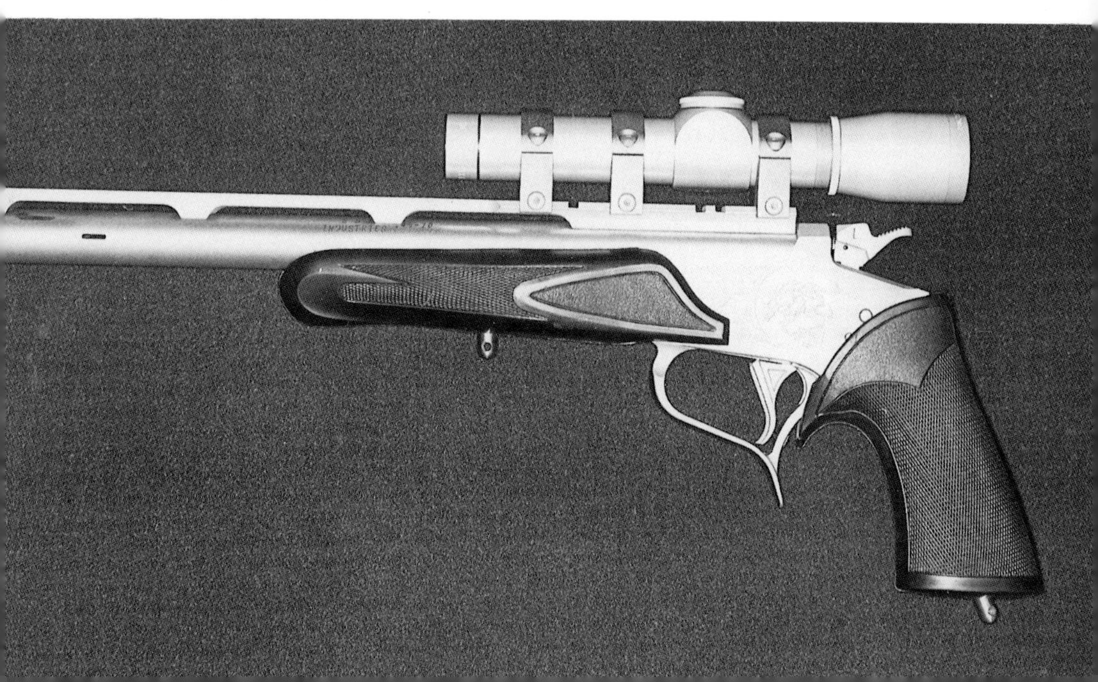

Left to right: .243 Winchester, .270 Winchester, 7mm Remington Magnum, .30-06. These are the most popular open-country deer cartridges today. The .243, though a fine cartridge, is over-rated in genuine long-range potential. The other three are just plain good choices, anywhere, anytime.

The good old .30-30 remains an extremely reliable deer-getter, but it's best-suited to country where shots over 100 yards are extremely unlikely. It did just fine on this South Texas whitetail–but there was lots of country out there that the rifle couldn't have reached!

Magnums aren't really needed for 99 percent of all deer hunting, but the 7mm Remington Magnum isn't out of place anywhere. Here, where it was a long shot or nothing on the author's best-ever whitetail, an accurate 7mm Magnum was extremely welcome!

The author grunted in this South Carolina whitetail to about 25 yards. A scoped .30-06 wasn't really necessary, but it handled this situation, and could handle just about anything else that might have arisen.

Even in the Eastern woods, where shots normally are fairly close, the bolt-action rifle has become the most common arm. Bill Bynum used a .280 Remington for this Georgia whitetail.

Prairie-dog shooting in the West is perhaps the most precise field shooting there is. It calls for accurate, flat-shooting rifles--and also demands that the shooter read the wind and pay attention to the basics of sight alignment and trigger squeeze.

There are actually several forms of varmint hunting. Predator calling doesn't really require a specialized rig, but can be done with any centerfire rifle. Calibers up to about .223 Remington, however, are best for minimizing pelt damage.

A heavy-barreled varminter like this .22-250 is a fine choice for the full gamut of off-season hunting, from predators to prairie dogs.

All of the Dakotas are very attractive, but they are offered in several configurations. This is the Safari Grade, chambered to versatile cartridges as well as big-bores.

The newest Dakota is the Model 10 single shot, a falling block rifle available in two action sizes and thus able to chamber darn near anything you can think of.

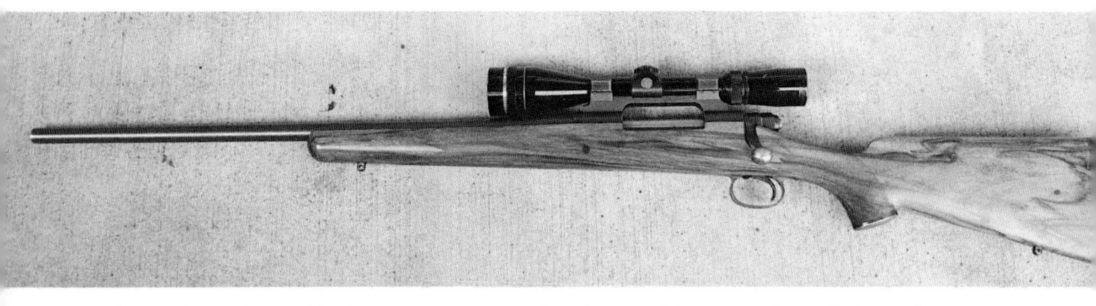

The author's David Miller custom 7mm Remington Magnum, loosely based on a Model 700 action extensively reworked, is one of the most accurate rifles the author has owned. Thanks to Miller's exclusive mount milled from bar stock, it has never changed zero.

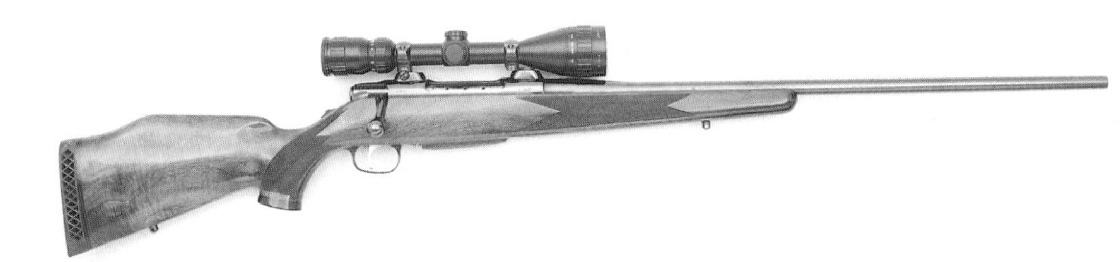

Increasingly popular today are scopes with large objective bells. Such scopes do gather a great deal of light, but make low scope mounting extremely difficult.

The author's .280 Remington with a fixed 6X scope has been a fine all-round rifle from the arctic to the tropics. It was used for this tropical whitetail in old Mexico.

Left to right: 7mm-08 Remington, .308 Winchester, .356 Winchester, .444 Marlin. Here's a quartet of fine deer cartridges, available in lever-action rifles. The two at left are superb all-round choices, while the two at right will really hammer deer-sized game at close-cover ranges.

Custom makers all across the country are doing a big business in "ultimate" slug guns. This is the Pennsylvania-made Tar-Hunt offering, which provides accuracy the equal of a great many out-of-the-box centerfire rifles.

The best rifle the author has ever owned is this David Miller custom 7mm, shown with long-range groups from various shooting positions. A custom rifle can give added confidence when the chips are down, but is no panacea for poor shooting habits.

This Oregon blacktail was taken with a Browning A-Bolt .30-06. For all-round deer hunting, it's pretty hard to beat the 90-year-old '06.

A traditional open-sighted or peep-sighted lever-action retains a great deal of appeal–and in very thick country such as is common in the Pacific Northwest, a lever-action rifle is a very sound choice to this day.

America's bolt-action custom gun builders are among the best, if not the best, in the world. This rifle was built by David Miller of Arizona for a fund raiser by Safari Club International. It features the finest in rifle making. Its engraving, checkering, wood inletting as well as accessories are as good as found on any continent.

Quite a number of scopes today are compact, with short tubes between the bells. On long-action rifles, such scopes can call for extension rings, workable but a poor compromise that can interfere with rapid reloading. The best course is to match the scope to the rifle.

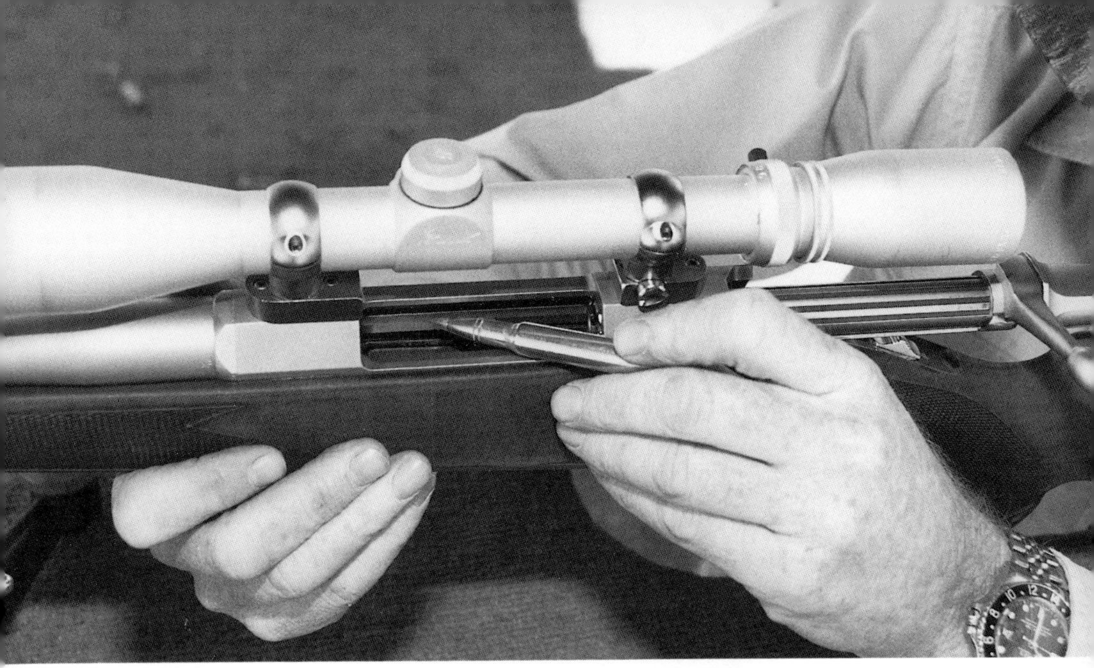

Midrange variables, from 2-7X to about 3.5-10X, are probably the best choice for most hunting purposes. A good rule is to leave the power setting on no more than 6X, turning it up only if you need to make a fairly long shot.

Detachable scope mounts have come back into vogue in recent years, and there are now several designs that work very well. This is the German-made EAW mount which works well for deer-sized calibers.

Long-eye-relief handgun scopes represent a new frontier and a new market for optics manufacturers. Handgun scopes have come a long, long way in recent years, with high-power variables now both durable and effective.

Here are just a few of the many reticles available. Far and away the most common–and, to the author, the most useful–is the plex-type, lower left.

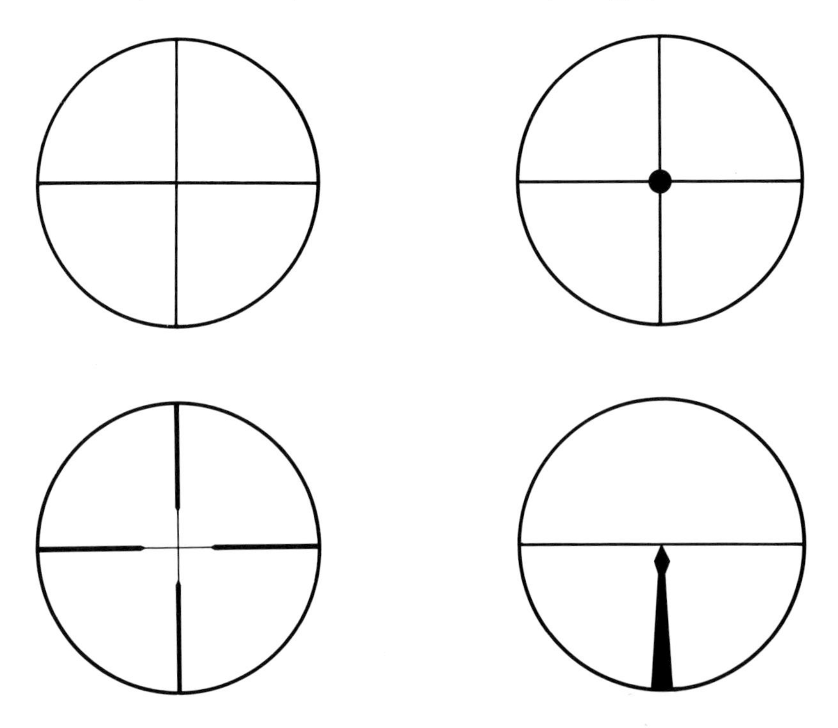

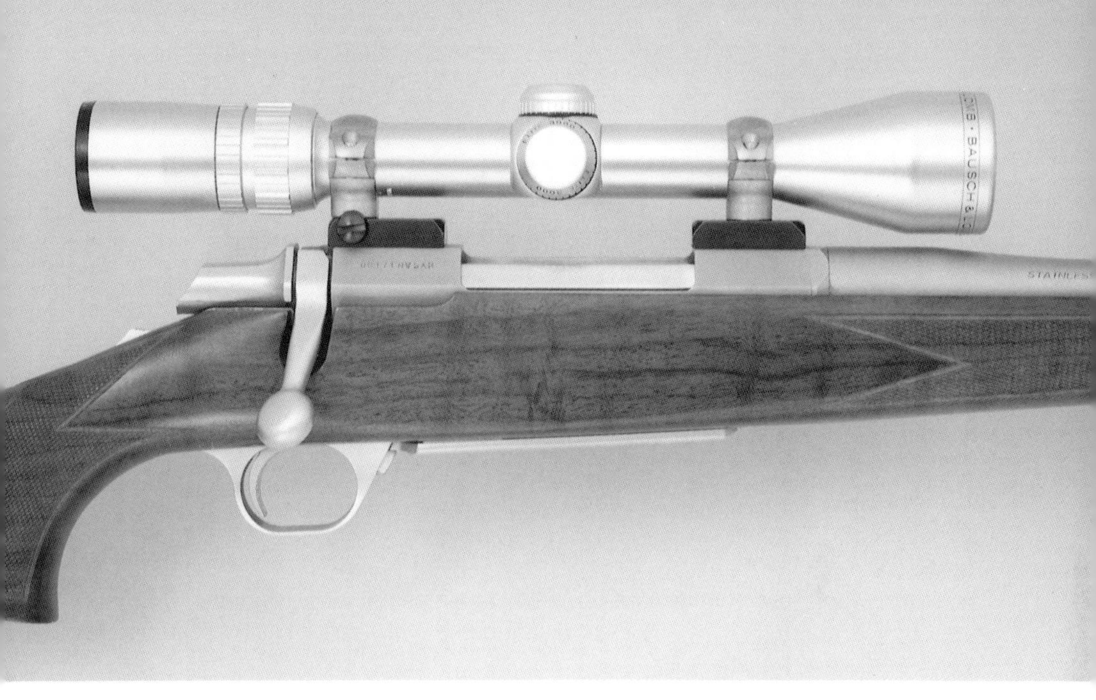

Matte silver finishes are increasingly available on both scopes and mounts today, to match up with stainless-steel rifles, but it can still take a bit of searching to get all components to match. This Bausch & Lomb mates well with a Stainless Browning A-Bolt, as do the rings–but blue bases were all that could be found.

Taurus is one of very few handgun manufacturers to offer porting on factory models. This is the Taurus Model 44, with an effective recoil-dampening brake created by four ports on each side of the sight ramp.

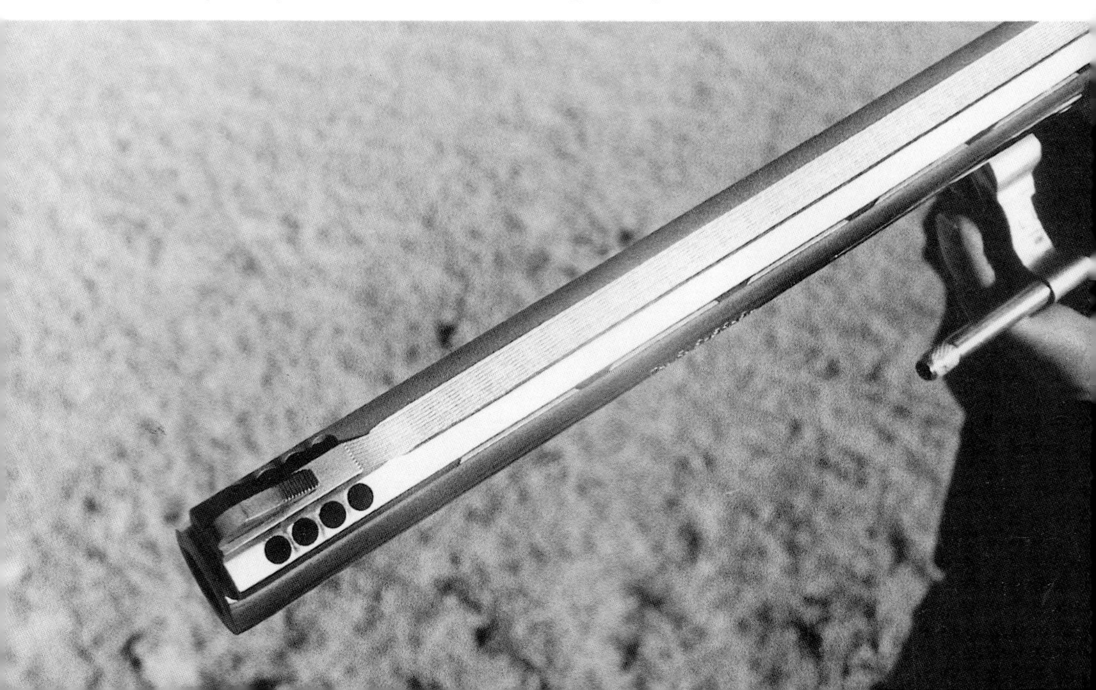

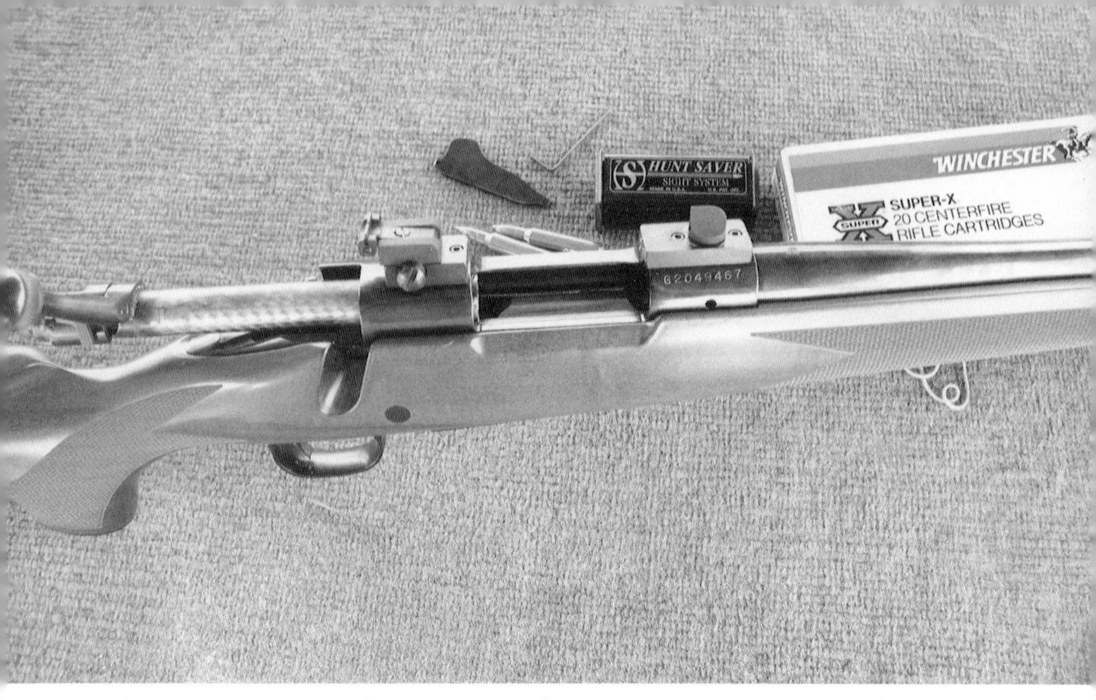

The HuntSaver is just what its name implies: an emergency iron sight that fits into a scope mount. It can be pre-zeroed, and in the absence of auxiliary iron sights could save the day.

The aperture, or "peep," sight is far superior to any open sight in both precision and speed, although not as rugged. The peep is actually an optical sight whereby the eye automatically centers the bead.

Most factory-supplied iron sights are more ornamental than functional today. The folding leaf on this aftermarket sight is unlikely to be used, but the standing leaf is as it should be: sturdy, rugged, and visible.

Leupold has joined the growing list of manufactures that offer quick-detachable scope mounts. It is as simple as can be, with only two parts that move. Simplicity of design is a important consideration for detachable mounts.

Shooting over a bench greatly enhances felt recoil because the body has nowhere to go. The best course is to use the bench as little as possible, concentrating practice in field positions where the body can give. On the bench, use as much padding as you need to keep comfortable.

The Harris bipod is one of the best-known shooting rests available–and one of the best. It adds weight to the rifle, but for hunting in wide-open country where rocks and logs are rare, it's a Godsend.

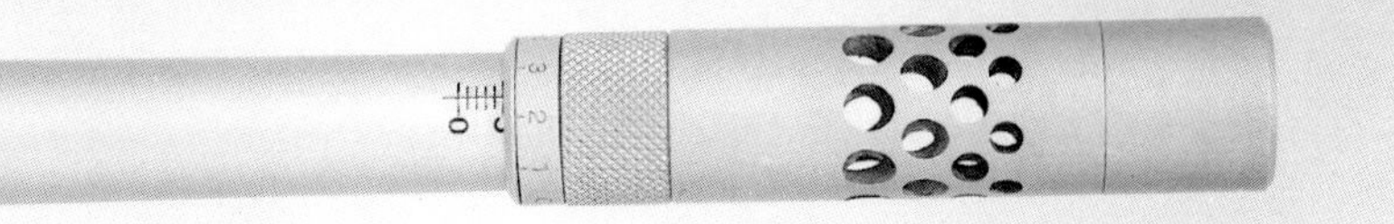

A close look at the Browning Ballistic Optimizing Shooting System–BOSS. It looks like, and is, a muzzle brake. But it's also an adjustable barrel weight that allows you to adjust your rifle to the desired load for improved accuracy.

Savage offers a unique muzzle brake that can be turned on and off by twisting the knurled ring and covering or uncovering the ports. This allows you to use the brake on the range with hearing protection, but turn it off for field use.

This Alaskan brown bear was shot with a .300 Winchester. The bullet was a 180-grain Nosler Partion, an excellent choice for any large bear. Author prefers 200- and 220-grain bullets in the .300 magnum caliber class for big bears. Whatever weight of bullet you do decide on, be sure your projectile is of the well-constructed premium variety. (SP Photo Library)

You never know when the weather might sour. This Coues deer was taken during several days of rain in northern Mexico. The author's synthetic-stocked .280 proved a fine choice.

This Alaskan black bear was taken in a driving rainstorm on a hunt that saw rain eight of ten days. The rifle is a walnut-stocked Model 700, but this is no place for a walnut-stocked rifle!

With practice, it's amazing how accurate good iron sights can be–but shooting with iron sights is almost a lost art.

Left to right: .358 Winchester Magnum, .300 H&H Magnum, .300 Weatherby Magnum, .338 Winchester Magnum, .375 H&H. Different approaches to moose cartridges: a .358 for close-in work, a .300 for all-round use, a .338 or .375 to really "numb" them. All will work, but only with good bullets well-placed.

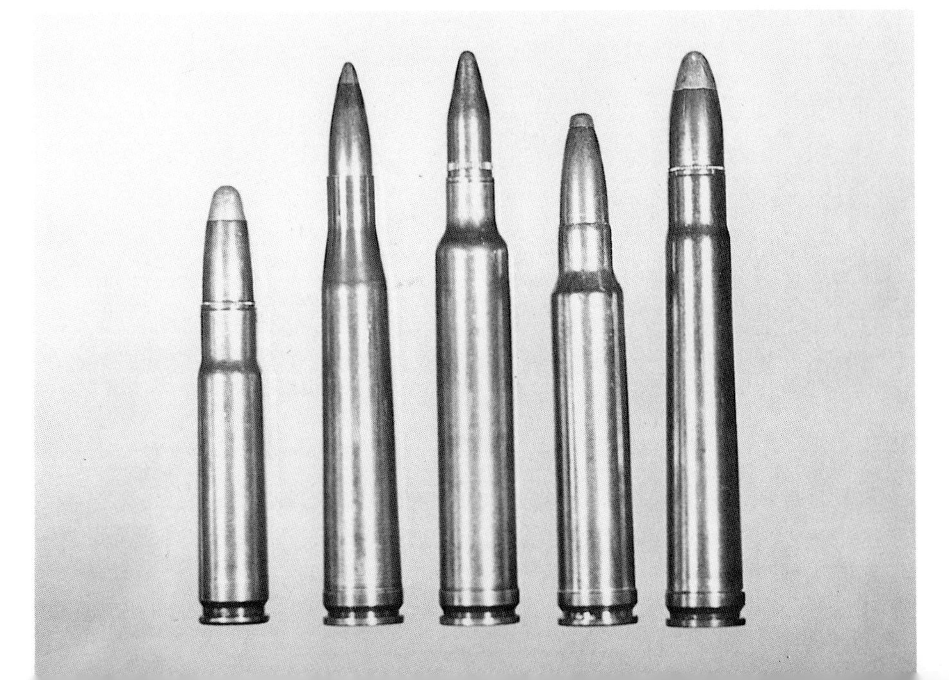

The Weatherby Mark V was one of the first American rifles to use a push-feed action rather than controlled-round feeding. The Mark V remains a classic hunting rifle.

Unlike most other action types, the bolt-action is the gun tinkerer's dream. It responds well to adjustments in bedding, can usually have its trigger sweetened, and is suitable for any caliber and any type of sighting device.

For most hunters today, it's a bolt-action world. While all the other action types are suited for most hunting applications, there is no big-game hunting on this continent that the bolt-action isn't a fine choice for.

Among the many strengths of the bolt-action are reliability and accuracy–both critical concerns in any hunting situation.

Most mountain ranges offer enough cover to make stalking fairly practical. The problem is that the opportunity to hunt sheep and goats is so limited today that you need a rifle and cartridge capable of taking advantage of any reasonable shot.

The Model 70 has been through many configurations and many alterations. This is a post-1964 Model 70, now called a "push-feed" action to differentiate it from the newly introduced controlled-round feeding very similar to the pre-1964 actions.

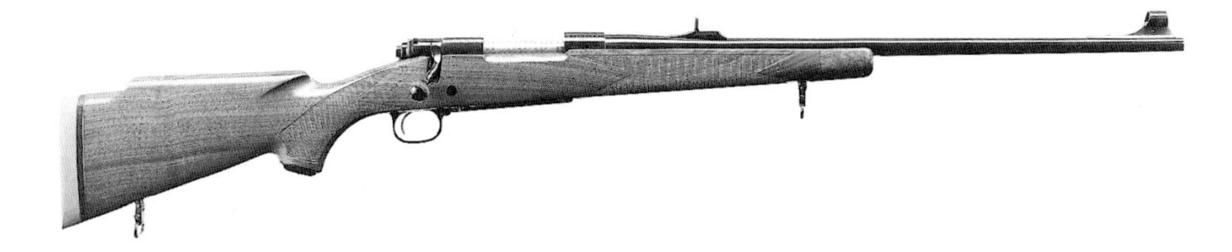

Remington's Model 11-87 Special Purpose Synthetic deer gun features all the bells and whistles: synthetic stock, cantilever scope mount, fully rifled barrel. Slug guns like this don't extend a slug's range but significantly extend the slug shooter's effective range.

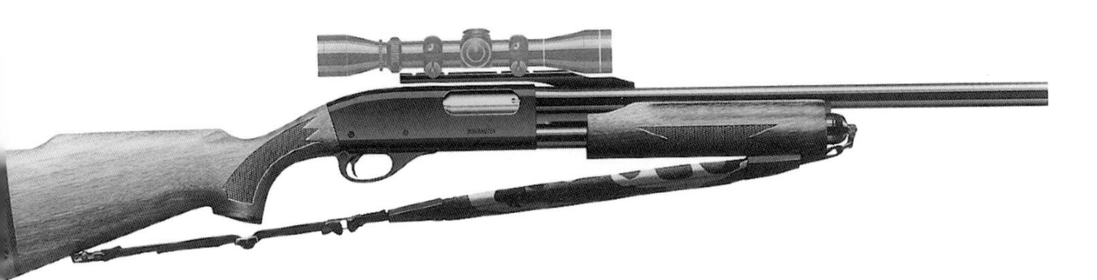

Only slightly scaled down is Remington's Model 870 deer gun with walnut stock. The real secret remains the rifled barrel, and on such a deer gun a low-powered scope makes all the sense in the world.

This New Mexico elk was taken with an 8mm Remington Magnum firing 220-grain Remington Core-Lokt factory loads. The 8mm Remington Magnum has never caught on and is unlikely to, but it remains a very fine elk cartridge.

By sheer poundage, the bison must compare with the largest game in the world, although by nature he is rarely dangerous. The author used a .348 Winchester on this bull–and he was badly undergunned. If he were ever to hunt bison again, the .375 would be a minimal choice.

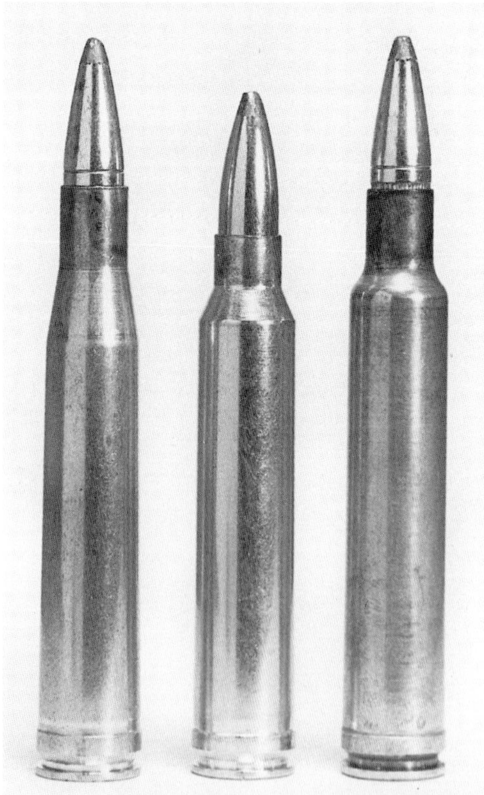

Left to right: .300 H&H Magnum, .300 Winchester Magnum, .300 Weatherby Magnum. The .308 Norma is almost a dead issue, so these are the three .300 magnums most worth considering today. The H&H is very limited in factory loads, while the other two are increasing in popularity.

Modern semiautos like this Heckler & Koch sporter are extremely reliable, and many are stunningly accurate. For hunting purposes, however, a significant drawback is that the bolt can't be "ridden" home–it must be slammed, and this is noisy.

The author took this Arizona Coues deer with a Ruger No. 1 Light Sporter in .270 Winchester. The No. 1 is a light, handy rifle with one of the strongest actions in the world—but the single-shot concept isn't for everyone, nor for every application.

What's the perfect all-round black-bear/boar rig? A simple .30-06 like this long-discontinued Harrington & Richardson firing a 180-grain bullet is a good answer.

Versatile rifles like the 7mm Remington Magnum with bullets of 160 grains or more are fine black-bear rigs--but will not offer as dramatic results at close range as the "brush cartridges."

Marlin lever-actions with side-ejection have always allowed for low, over-the-receiver scope mounting. Today's Winchester lever-actions have been modified so this is now possible with those rifles as well.

The rotary magazine, now replaced by a detachable box, was a particularly fine feature of the older Savage 99 rifles. It fed smoothly and precluded bullet deformation in the magazine.

The Model 71 in .348 Winchester is a long-time favorite of the author's. Mounted with a receiver (peep) sight, it makes a fine wild-hog and black-bear rifle out to 200 yards or so.

This Winchester photo, almost certainly from the 1930s, clearly shows the time when American hunters were in transition from lever-actions to bolt-actions. The hunter carries a Winchester bolt-action, apparently a new Model 70 in .375, while his guide has a Model 71 in .348.

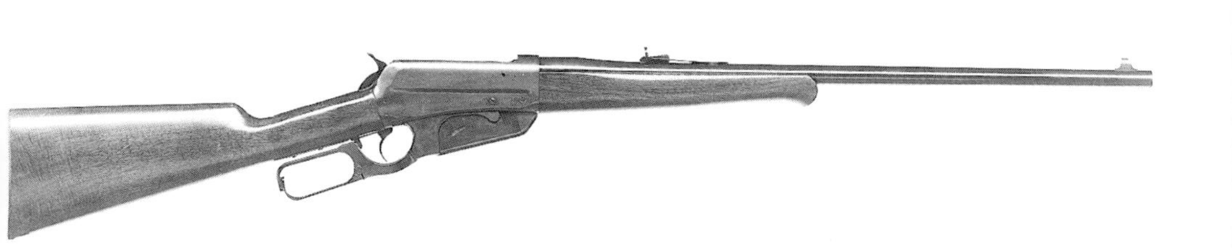

The Winchester Model 1895 was offered in a variety of powerful and versatile chamberings. Its most popular cartridge was the .30-40 Krag.

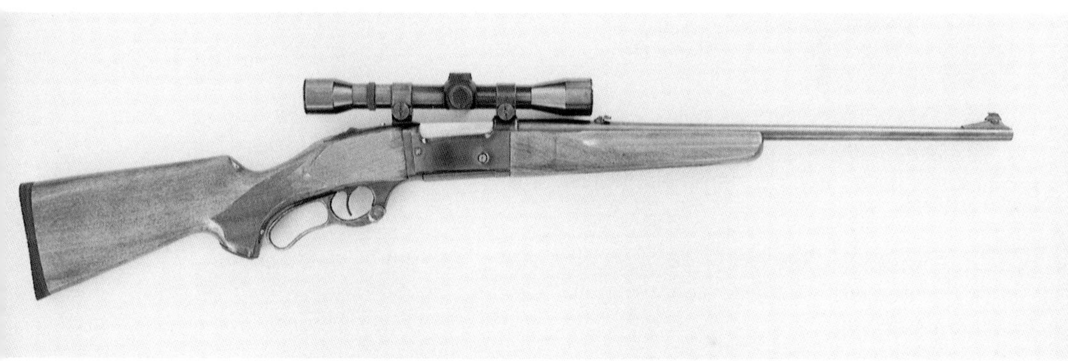

Savage's great Model 99, discontinued for a time, is now back in .243 and .308. Accurate and fast-handling, it remains a fine all-round lever-action.

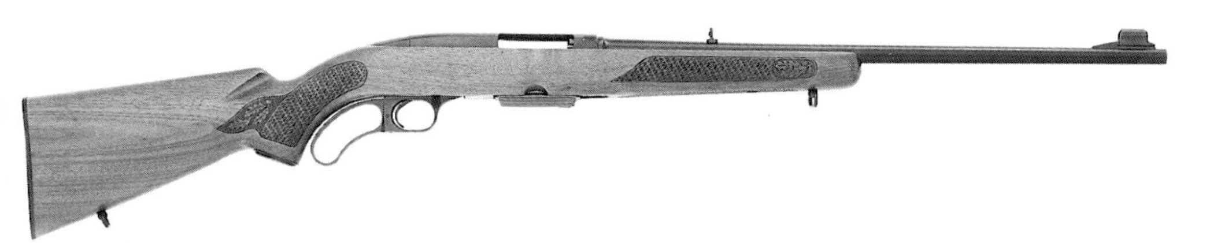

Winchester's Model 88, now discontinued, is a superb, ultra-modern lever-action chambered to versatile cartridges like the .243, .284, .308, and .358 Winchester.

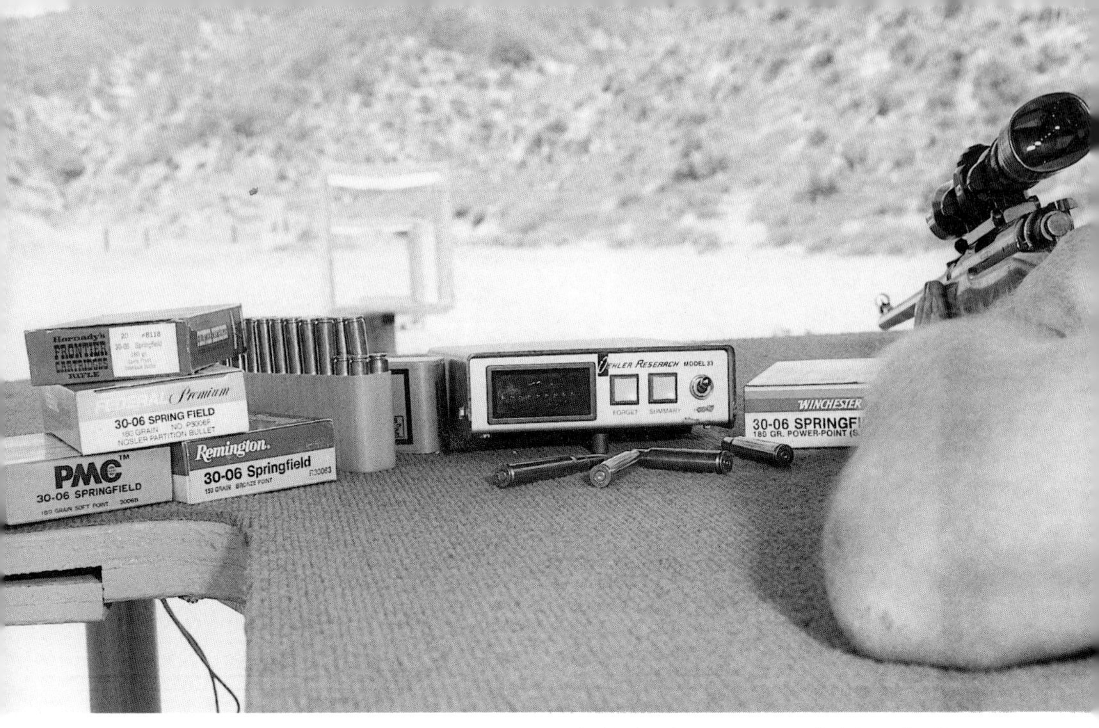

In years gone by, factory ballistics often included a fair amount of "blue sky." Today, a great many serious shooters have chronographs, and factory ballistic figures have become extremely honest.

The Nosler Partition was one of the first of the "premium" game bullets. It's still a great bullet, but today we have a much wider selection of truly outstanding hunting bullets.

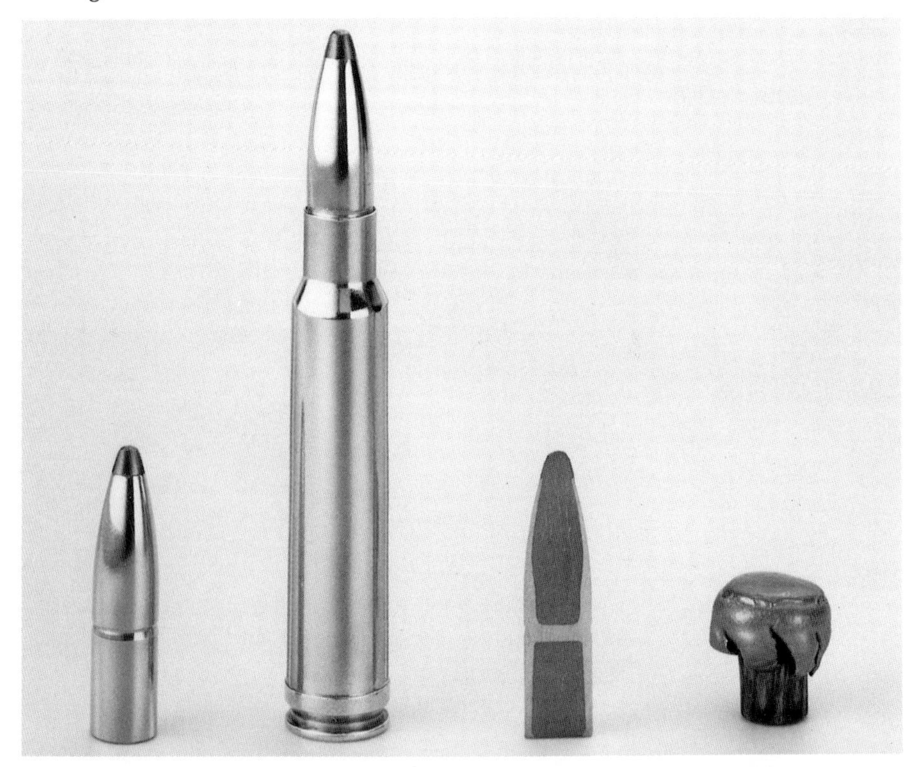

Although the author professes not to be a fan of the 7mm Remington Magnum, the record shows that he has used it a great deal! This backpack hunt, however, was one time he wished for a lighter, synthetic-stocked rifle, regardless of caliber.

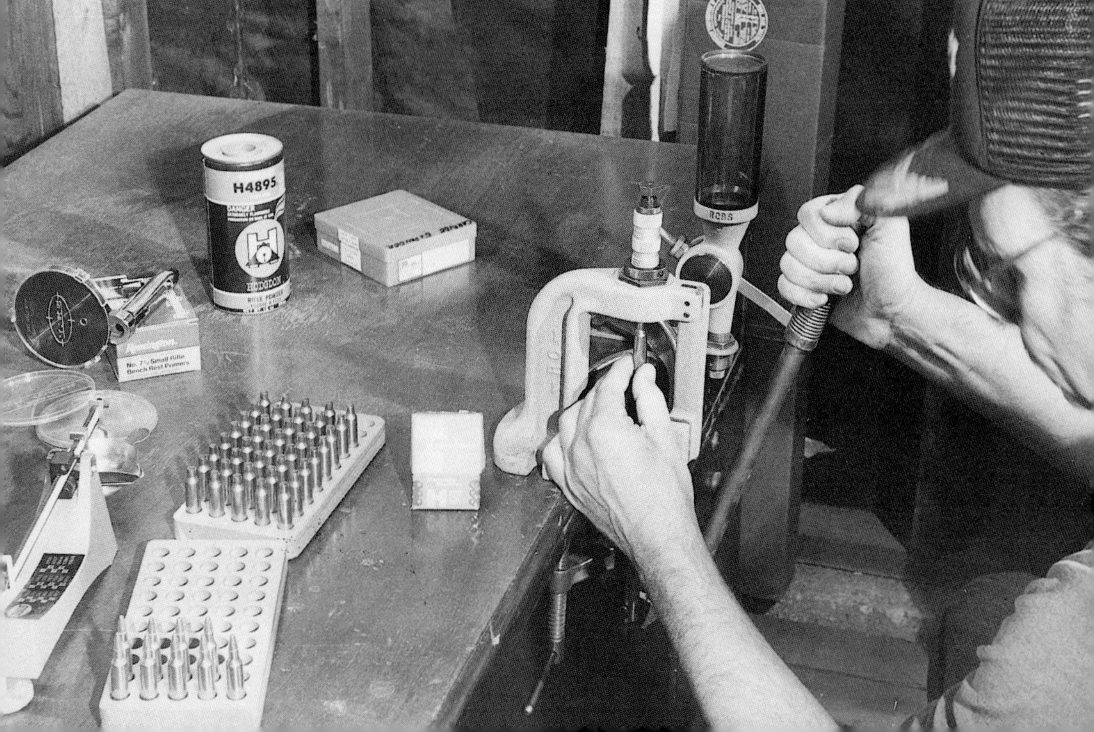

Factory ammo is so good today that handloaders are hard put to beat it. Handloaders, however, still have the opportunity to develop loads that are best-suited not only to the intended game, but also to their own rifle.

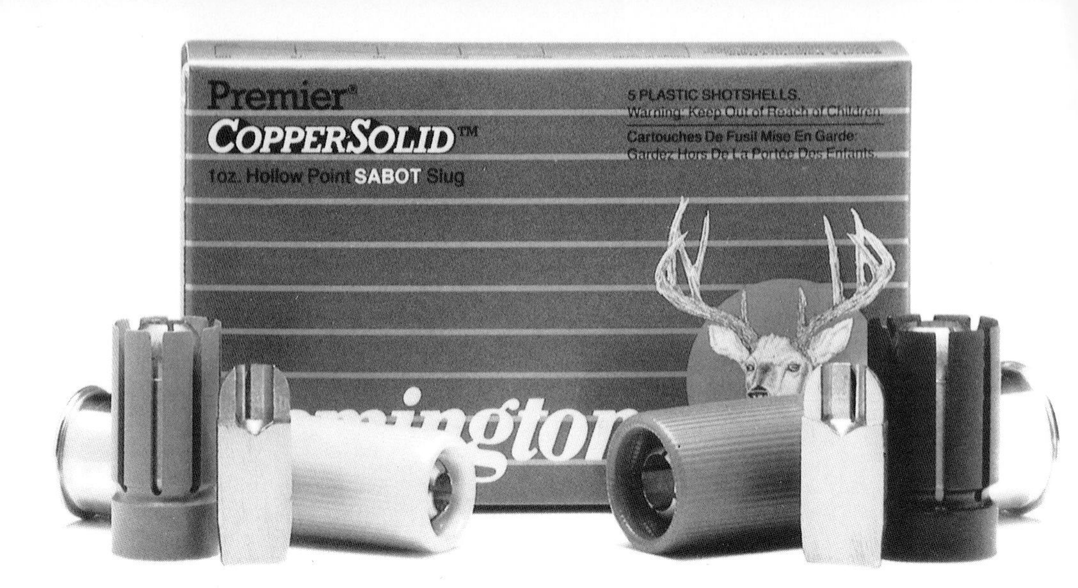

Shotgun slugs have come a long way, with a great many new designs that, in most guns, offer improved performance over the old Foster slugs. Remington's Copper Solid all-copper sabot slug is just one of several new designs.

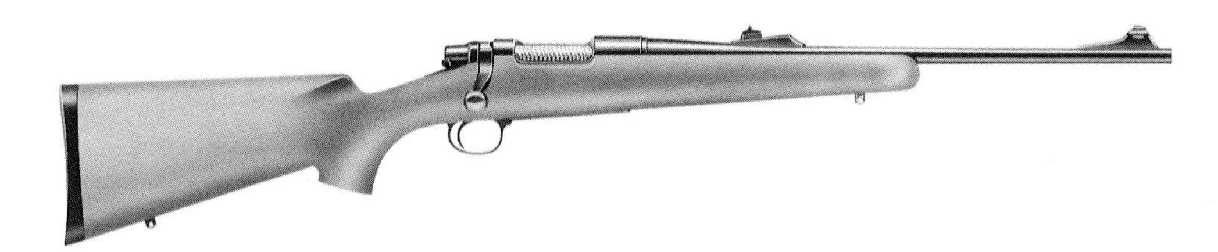

Remington's Model Seven is a scaled-down version of the Model 700, available in short-action calibers only. The Model Seven is one of the slickest little rifles on the market, and it's amazing it has not become more popular.

Remington's Model 700 is, arguably, the most popular bolt-action sporter in America today. It's available in a wide variety of configurations and options and an extensive list of calibers.

adequate even for grizzly, and clearly they will do the job. These days, however, with a more widespread appreciation for a clean kill–and the realization that a hunt for grizzly might culminate in just one opportunity–my thinking is that these cartridges and the rifles that fire them "top out" against elk and moose in very heavy cover.

Lever-actions for cartridges such as .45-70 are no longer the quick-handling lightweights that the .30-30 carbines are. They're full-sized rifles, and should be to handle the recoil. Given practice, the lever-action is inherently very fast for second and subsequent shots. But a shooter who really practices with his bolt-action is also very fast. I won't attempt to make a case for any action being faster than another–especially since it's the all-important first shot that counts. In fact, for inexperienced shooters, fire-power can be counterproductive!

Even so, the lever-action is fast and fast-handling, even though guns chambered for the larger calibers are much heavier than the .30-30 and its ilk. Now that Winchester has gone to an angle-eject, both Winchesters and Marlins can be scoped. A scope isn't really required for the short-range shooting this type of rifle is best for, but *everyone* can shoot better, aim faster, and shoot accurately in poorer light with a scope than with open sights. With the possible exception of black-bear hunting with hounds–or in country where rainy weather is the norm–even this type of rifle should wear a scope for serious hunting.

However, I must admit that there seems something aesthetically wrong about putting a scope on a classic "saddle gun." My own lever-actions in this class tend to wear aperture ("peep") sights rather than scopes. They're just as fast, almost as accurate, and at shorter ranges are markedly inferior to scopes only in very poor light.

With a low-powered scope or aperture sight in place, a lever-action brush gun is superb for almost any deer hunting in very heavy cover. Especially in the larger calibers, it's also an ideal choice for black bear over bait or with hounds. Such a rifle is one of my all-time favorite choices for wild-hog hunting by any method. There is, however, a *huge* difference between hitting a running pig with a .45-70 and making the same shot with a .30-06!

I know some very good hunters who regularly use this type of rifle to hunt elk and moose. However, the circumstances should be very specialized. Even more emphatically than in deer hunting, the hunter simply must *know* that he will not attempt a shot at much beyond 100 yards. He must simply not care that he has to pass up shots beyond that distance. Especially with rainbow cartridges like the .375 Winchester, .444 Marlin, and .45-70, not only does getting those big bullets in the vital areas start to get difficult, but energy figures begin to drop off a bit too quickly for comfort. Even so, there are numerous areas where these cartridges make lots of sense.

Hunting Roosevelt elk in the rain forests of the Pacific Northwest is one good example. Shots tend to be very close, and at bayonet range those big, slow-moving slugs are devastating. Likewise bugling for elk in oak-brush thickets or calling moose in the dense forests of central and eastern Canada. In circumstances like that, no problem–but you must be aware that you'll have a problem if you see your elk or moose on the far side of a clearing or pond.

For game bigger than deer and black bear, I think a better choice is one of the larger calibers in the "general-purpose lever-action" category. This group, of course, competes with bolt-actions, single-shots, semiautos, and slide-actions in chamberings for general-purpose use on big game. The .307 and .356 Winchester cartridges were designed to bring the Winchester Model 94–and later the Marlin 336–into this arena. They are, respectively, very similar to the .308 and .358 Winchester–until you get to 150 yards and beyond. Then they start to drop off, and quickly. Both cartridges are based on the .308 Winchester case with a rim added. Muzzle velocities are similar to the parent cartridge, retarded only by slightly reduced case capacity. The problem lies in the flat-pointed bullets required by the .307 and .356 because of the tubular-magazine rifles both cartridges were designed for. The .307 certainly has more reach than the .30-30, but is not nearly as versatile as the .308 with spitzer bullets. Thanks to its flat-nosed bullet, it drops below 1,000 foot/pounds of energy long before you get to 300 yards. Now, neither the .356 nor the .358 Winchester can be called a long-range cartridge–but the .356 runs out of steam a good deal earlier than spitzers or semi-spitzers from the .358.

To my thinking, the general-purpose lever-actions are those which can handle spitzer bullets and cartridges of fairly high intensity. The first of these was the 1895 Winchester. Over the years, a few more have come and gone, but today the only currently manufactured lever guns that fall into this category are the Savage 99 and the Browning BLR. The former is offered today only in .243 and .308, while the latter is offered in 11 chamberings, from .222 to .30-06 and 7mm Remington Magnum.

For general use in hunting North American big game, there are few drawbacks to a lever-action in, say, .308. As is the case with single-shots, the two-piece stock generally dictates that lever-actions are not quite as accurate as bolt-actions, although individual guns will sometimes surprise you with stunning accuracy. Even under the worst circumstances, however, field accuracy is certainly adequate for virtually all hunting needs.

The lever-action does not have the primary extraction power of the bolt (nor does anything else!), so handloaders generally have to use a bit of extra care in assembling loads. I had a Savage 99 "freeze up" with a stuck case on an African hunt one time. The cartridge was a handload, but I never knew for sure whether I'd trickled in a bit much powder, gotten a bad case, or simply let the cartridge sit in the African sun while riding around in the Land Cruiser. I do know that the rifle was totally out of action until I could get it back to the States and to a gunsmith!

Perhaps the most damning drawback to the lever-action is its trigger. Few things are as important to consistent, pinpoint shot placement as a good, crisp trigger pull–especially for deliberate shooting at long range. Bolt-action triggers these days are pretty horrible as they come from the factory, but most bolt-action triggers can be adjusted to at least a reasonable pull. And if they can't be adjusted, they can be replaced with a Timney, Can-Jar, or another aftermarket trigger. Most lever-action triggers are what they are, period. The mechanics of the action are such that very little can be done to alter a lever-action trigger without impairing its safe functioning. The Model 88, though a very accurate and very strong lever-action, was notorious for its mushy, creepy, heavy trigger pull. The Browning and Savage are a bit better, but their trigger pulls cannot approach the crispness of a bolt-action. For this reason alone, I would not recommend a lever-action if fairly long shots are the norm.

That said, the lever-action is appealing for a wide variety of hunting. It's fast-handling and a joy to carry. The slim profile and lack of a protruding bolt make both the Savage and Browning particularly outstanding for carrying in a saddle scabbard.

In chamberings like .308 and 7mm-08, these lever-actions are ideal for a full range of deer hunting. The Browning, regrettably, is the last lever-action chambered in .358. That's a shame, as this is a fine and underrated cartridge. In the Browning or an older lever gun, the .358 makes a perfect black-bear and wild-boar rifle, and is also a very fine choice for elk and moose in fairly close cover. Hitting with the .358 starts to get a bit tough at 250 yards or so–and energies start to drop as well. But it certainly has more reach than any of the tubular-magazine brush guns. (Even though it has a tubular magazine and shoots flat-point bullets, I also put the fast and powerful .348 Winchester into this general-purpose category. It can certainly reach beyond 200 yards with authority, and its real limitation is that its top-ejection receiver makes it very difficult to mount a scope.)

A lever-action Browning in .270, .30-06, or 7mm Remington Magnum would, of course, be suitable for anything these cartridges are suitable for–and that pretty much spans the full gamut of North American hunting. For serious long-range work, I'd personally prefer a bolt-action, but lever-action fans in search of a sheep or elk rifle now have one in the long-action Browning.

The only real limitation on lever-actions is their lack of truly powerful cartridges for hunting our biggest bears. Sure, you could do it at close range with a .45-70 or perhaps a .348 or .358. And you can do it with a .30-06 and very heavy bullets. But there are better tools available for our biggest bears. Other than that limitation, the lever-actions can do the job from coast to coast. Choice of action has much to do with simple personal preference; if you like levers, you need make no apology for your choice.

Chapter 22

Slide-Actions and Semiautos

The self-loading, or semiautomatic, rifle and uniquely American slide-action are both viable alternatives for North American hunting, and both actions have their following. In fact, both actions are quite popular in some areas–but neither offers serious competition to the bolt or lever among American hunters.

In both cases, the lack of widespread support is a bit surprising. The slide-action is uniquely American, with no following whatever elsewhere in the world. It remains extremely popular with American shotgunners. "Pump"-actions from Remington, Winchester, Mossberg, Browning, and Ithaca are dominant forces in the shotgun market. Rifles employing the same slide-action have been with us since the black-powder era, and in bygone days were chambered for extremely powerful cartridges. The Colt Lightning slide-action, for example, included Winchester's huge .50-110 cartridge among its chamberings.

For some reason, however, the slide-action rifle has never achieved the general acceptance of its smoothbore counterpart. In the black-powder era, it played second fiddle to the lever-action. Today it continues to lag far behind the lever-action–which has long since given ground to the bolt-action. The Colt Lightning is long gone, as are all the other turn-of-the-century slide-action rifles. For many years, Savage offered a very fine, economically priced slide-action in the Model 170, but it's now discontinued as well. Remington alone, with a long tradition of slide-action rifles, continues to keep this action type alive with the current Model 7600 slide-action rifle.

Both Remington and Winchester jumped on the semiautomatic bandwagon very early in the century. Rifles from both companies achieved some popularity, but it was the also-new bolt-action that became the darling of sportsmen the world over. After World War II, when millions of G.I.'s returned well-versed in–and well-impressed by–the semiautomatic rifle, some authorities predicted a huge upsurge in the semiauto's popularity. It never happened.

The 1903 Springfield, the American service rifle from 1903 until about 1942, could be made into a sporting rifle without parallel. Its successor, the semiautomatic M1 Garand, was equally accurate, equally rugged and reliable, and its identical .30-06 cartridge was equally powerful and flat-shooting. The Garand, however, was not particularly suitable for sporting use. (Now, Garand fans, don't get upset. If you like your Garand, use it–it's okay with me!) As a military rifle it was heavy, and its long underbarrel gas system didn't lend itself to the "sporterizing" so in vogue with military bolt-actions. It was very difficult to mount a scope on the Garand in a conventional manner because of the requirement to eject its eight-round clip after the final shot. And of course, the clip itself, though well-proven in combat, was a problem for sportsmen. The Garand could not be single-loaded, and in fact could only be loaded with its eight-round clip. It had virtually no chance as a sporting rifle, and I suspect that returning G.I.'s were delighted to resume using their lighter, simpler bolt- and lever-actions.

In the half-century since World War II, a great many semiautomatic sporters have come and gone. And of course, there are numerous military look-alikes available–many of which are imperiled by anti-gun hysteria and draconian gun-control laws.Like the slide-action, the semiauto has its fans. The market is similarly limited, however, and that statement is easily proven by the scarcity of semiautomatic hunting rifles today.

It is quite true that Springfield's M1A in .308, Heckler & Koch's SR-9, and similar semiautos have the range, power, and accuracy to be viable big-game rifles. But in the spectrum of rifles designed strictly as sporters, the only semiautomatic options today are Remington's Model 7400 and Browning's BAR Mark II. To this list probably could and should be added Ruger's Mini-Thirty and perhaps some other semiautomatc 7.62x39 rifles, with the caveat that this little cartridge is extremely limited in both range and power.

The semiautomatic is a viable action, and its ability to offer second and subsequent shots with no movement of the hands and no disturbance of the aim is appealing–especially if the rifle's accuracy is on a par with other action types, as it truly is with modern semiautos. The attenuation of recoil–even though slight–that the operation of a gas-operated auto achieves is also a plus. But in spite of these attributes, the semiautomatic has never risen to the top. It is probably, nationwide, somewhat more popular than the slide-action. But not by a great deal.

The purpose of this book is certainly not to turn the tide in favor of one action or another, any more than for one caliber over another. Like most Americans, I happen to be a fan of neither the slide-action nor the semiauto rifle, so their lack of popularity, though inexplicable, falls in line with my own preferences. We do have an obligation, however, to try to analyze objectively where these action types fit in the North American hunting scene.

Slide-actions first. Remington's Model 7600 is currently chambered in .243, .270, .280, .30-06, .308, and .35 Whelen. That's a wonderful line-up of exceptionally capable cartridges. As we've seen, the .270, .280, and especially the .30-06 are among the very best all-round cartridges available. The .35 Whelen is adequate for anything that walks on this continent, although somewhat limited in range. These cartridges chambered in the slide-action Remington are suitable for anything and everything the same cartridges would be suitable for in any other action. Period. Although limited in both appeal and available models, there are no flies on the slide-action as a hunting rifle.

Its limitations are essentially the same as the lever-action's: accuracy somewhat limited by the two-piece stock; a trigger than cannot be tuned to the degree a bolt-action's can; and limited power of primary extraction.

As an action type, however, the slide-action does have hidden strengths. First, it's extremely fast. Any serious shotgunner knows that a good man with a slide-action can shoot faster than any semiautomatic ever made. Speed without accuracy is useless, of course, but if you must shoot quickly, the slide-action has an edge over any other action type. As you complete working the slide, your supporting arm is moving forward–and pointing toward the target. I believe this natural movement toward the target significantly speeds acquisition or reacquisition of the target and thus helps you aim and fire a split-second faster than with other actions. Of course, speed doesn't matter if the shots don't find their mark, and spraying the landscape with a slide-action doesn't do much good. But the shooter who really works with a slide-action will be amazed at the speed.

Since I rarely carry a cartridge in the chamber until I'm actually ready to shoot, I am always concerned about being able to load the chamber quickly and quietly if I unexpectedly encounter game. Single-shots are probably the best in this area, with bolt-actions a close second. Lever-actions tend to clatter a bit, and semiautos are the worst since you must let the bolt slam closed, not ride it home, to ensure that the bolt goes fully into battery. With practice, you can open a slide-action fairly quietly, and close it in the same manner. I'd rate the slide-action a bit noisier than a bolt-action in this regard, but a bit better than most lever-actions.

Slide-actions remain relatively popular among brush and timber whitetail hunters, with a particularly strong following in Pennsylvania, where semi-autos are not legal for deer hunting. They probably make the most sense for serious shotgunners who use slide-action shotguns, but they're certainly a viable choice, limited only by the small number of chamberings available.

The semiauto has the obvious advantage of rapid repeat shots without moving one's hands, and of course the gas-operated guns have a bit softer recoil than other actions in identical calibers. Drawbacks are essentially the same as for lever-actions and slide-actions. Accuracy, though adequate, is generally not as flashy as the average bolt-action will produce. Extraction is also not as positive. With the semiauto, you should go a bit farther on this. Today's semiautomatics are extremely reliable, and jams are very rare. *However*, semiautos by their nature are a bit more finicky about the ammo they digest. Greater care should be taken in handloading for a semiauto. Cases simply must be full-length sized, and often a "small-base" sizing die is required for trouble-free operation. Shooters who use factory loads needn't worry, though; provided the semiauto is kept clean and properly lubricated, it should function.

My only real complaint about the semiauto is that it's noisy to load and unload. To ride the bolt home slowly is to invite disaster; there's a very good chance the bolt won't go fully into battery and the rifle will fail to fire. You really need to snap the bolt home, and that's a noisy proposition. For this reason, I think the semiautomatic is best suited to stand hunting. You get on stand, load the rifle, and you're all set to go. When it's time to leave the stand, you unload. The amount of noise is fairly meaningless. I "rode the bolt" on a Heckler & Koch .30-06 sporter one time, and when a deer ambled by, the rifle failed to fire. I had no choice but to pull the bolt back and let it snap forward. Of course, the deer ran, and I was just lucky to get him as he bolted through a little clearing. You simply can't baby a semiauto, so it's poorly suited to hunting situations where you may encounter obstacles and need to load and unload your chamber repeatedly.

The Remington Model 7400 comes in six chamberings today: .243, .270, .280, .308, .30-06, and .35 Whelen. Browning's BAR offers a bit more choice, being chambered in .243, .270, .270 Weatherby Magnum, .280, .308, .30-06, 7mm Remington Magnum, .300 Winchester Magnum, and .338 Winchester Magnum. All calibers are offered with Browning's BOSS (Ballistic Optimizing Shooting System), a muzzle brake/adjustable barrel weight that allows you to match your barrel harmonics to your chosen load. The accuracy gains are dramatic, and with the BOSS *properly* adjusted you can certainly match average out-of-the-box bolt-action accuracy with the BAR.

I'm not personally crazy about semiautos as hunting rifles, but many thousands of hunters swear by them. With chamberings in flat-shooting cartridges like the .270, .280, and the Browning's belted magnums up to .338 in power, there is nothing on this continent that a semiauto isn't suitable for. I'd be a bit careful about taking one into subzero cold. In very cold weather, any action will freeze, and thus must be degreased. However, in the case of a semiauto you would have to shoot it dry or with just a bit of powdered graphite as lubricant, and jamming would be a bit more likely than with a manually operated action.

Inherently, both the semiauto and the slide-action are fine choices for just about any North American hunting. Their limitations are few and are not severe, and both action types have real advantages. Their overall lack of popularity has little to do with the strengths and weaknesses of either action type, but rather is based on the positive attributes of the bolt-action as a hunting arm. And that's where we'll turn next.

Chapter 23

The Bolt-Action: Winner and Still Champion

My father and grandfather were shotgunners. Had they been riflemen, starting their shooting careers in the 1890s and 1920s, chances are much better than even that they would have been lever-action fans. My father didn't own a centerfire rifle until the early 1960s, and even then it was a Winchester Model 1894 in .30-30–like so many millions of beginning riflemen to this day.

I'm of another generation, and although both my first and second .22s were lever-actions, my first centerfire was a bolt-action–as have been most of the rifles that have followed.

As we have seen, all of our action types have their place and their following. And in the right chamberings and configurations, all have very close to universal application in North American hunting. The lever-action, slide-action, and semiauto can claim their highest popularity in brush country and timber, where shots are likely to be close. But in fact, all three types are available in chamberings and models practical for darn near anything. The single-shot likewise has universal application, but actually appeals only to the relatively small group willing to accept the challenge of a single cartridge.

Regardless of the actual, practical versatility of all other action types, however, the bolt-action rifle has become America's most popular choice from coast to coast and top to bottom. This is no accident.

Since before the turn of the century, the bolt-action has possessed all the attributes hunters want and need in a sporting rifle–and very few drawbacks. It's a moot question whether the bolt-action is actually more reliable than the other action types. All can be depended upon, but no one can say that the bolt-action is not at least as, if not more, dependable than all other actions. Without question, the turnbolt's strong camming power for extraction does make it the most reliable in the event of a swollen case. It is also generally stronger than most actions, except for some single-shots. And also, with the same exception, it's the one that offers the most protection to the shooter in case of a catastrophic failure like a ruptured case.

This issue of strength rarely comes into play. Apart from shooter error of the greatest magnitude–such as charging a rifle case with pistol powder, failure to notice and clear a barrel obstruction, or loading the wrong size cartridge–there is really no reason for any rifle action to fail to contain the combustion of its cartridges. Strength, however, does enter the picture with the huge array of high-intensity cartridges the bolt-action is chambered to. Although we now have a lever-action in both

.30-06 and 7mm Remington Magnum and a semiauto in chamberings up to the .338 Winchester Magnum, only the bolt-action and the single-shot have been chambered for our cartridges that yield the greatest pressure and the utmost in performance. Examples would be the .300 and .340 Weatherby Magnums.

Mechanics enter the picture, too. Although Browning has been very successful with their long-action BLR lever-action, and likewise with their semiauto BAR in short magnum chamberings, cartridges of about .30-06 length or very slightly longer are at the limit of workable design for all except the bolt-action and single-shot. Other actions chambered for cartridges of .375 H&H length have been attempted experimentally, and they work—but the results are ungainly and inefficient. The single-shot, of course, has no real limits on size of cartridge, nor does the double rifle. But the bolt-action doesn't, either—it's just a question of building a long enough bolt with a big enough bolt face, witness the monstrous bolt-actions chambered to the .50 Browning machine-gun cartridge. It's the bolt-action and single-shot alone that can be had in cartridges from .17 Remington to .416 Rigby and beyond.

So far, only the single-shot can do everything the bolt-action can do. But the bolt-action can do it as a repeater, and for the majority of sportsmen the repeater won out over the single-shot a century ago. The single-shot also does not have the extraction power of the bolt. Perhaps most important of all, however, is that the bolt-action, with its stable one-piece stock, is, at least so far, the most accurate of all action types.

A one-piece stock is a gross oversimplification for explaining the bolt-action's accuracy. The stock itself is more stable, offering a firmer platform for bedding that keeps barrel vibrations uniform. The bolt-action also offers the most secure and consistent lockup and headspacing and allows the least flex during firing—except perhaps for the single-shot. The bolt-action is also and absolutely the least finicky about its ammunition. Heavier loads are generally more reliable in a bolt gun, and although I believe all hunting handloads should be full-length resized, only with a bolt-action can you get away with neck-sizing with reasonable consistency.

A strength of the bolt-action is not necessarily its simplicity. Most bolt-actions have fewer moving parts than most lever-actions, but some bolt-actions are quite complex. The Sauer bolt-action, for instance, with its beautifully engineered retracting locking lugs, is actually a great deal more complex and has more moving parts than most examples of all other action types! But in concept, the turnbolt is relatively simple, and with normal maintenance there are few things that can go wrong with one.

This is not to say the bolt-action is foolproof. Feeding problems are not particularly uncommon, especially on brand-new out-of-the-box rifles. Generally, these problems can be cured with a little work on the feed rails, or in extreme cases with a different follower spring or even a different follower itself. It can happen, and it isn't a big deal–provided you thoroughly wring out all the functions of your rifle long before you take it hunting. Similar problems aren't uncommon with other action types, by the way. An actual jam with a bolt-action, assuming sound functioning in the first place, is extremely rare.

It is possible, however, for the shooter to fail to bring the bolt all the way back to pick up a new cartridge. This is shooter error caused by lack of practice and/or lack of familiarity with the particular rifle the hunter is using. It's probably most likely with shooters who are new to a bolt-action, or who might have shifted from a short-action .308 to, say, a .300 Weatherby. The only cure is practice, and lack of same is not the rifle's fault!

Slowness of repeat shots is another claim often levied against the bolt-action. In the days when the bolt-action was relatively new, many authorities–including the likes of Colonel Townsend Whelen and Charles Newton–wrote articles in the sporting magazines with comparative speed tests between the lever-action and bolt-action. Even 80 years ago, the results were inconclusive; it depended on who was doing the shooting–and of course, speed of fire depends heavily upon recoil and recovery from same. It's clear that the single-shot is the slowest of all. It's also clear that the double rifle, virtually unheard of in North America, is certainly the fastest for a second shot, given equal recoil levels. As I've stated, I believe the slide-action to be the fastest of all, followed by the semiauto. Chances are the lever-action and bolt-action are just about equal–given proper operation and plenty of practice.

If the first shot hits properly, speed is a moot point. But sometimes it doesn't, regardless of who the shooter is. Whether you're stopping a charge or stopping the escape of a poorly hit animal, that second shot can be extremely important, no doubt about it. The secret is practice. If you must take your bolt-action either partially or fully down from your shoulder between shots while you work the action, you simply haven't practiced enough–or if you have, you're practicing bad habits.

The bolt-action is not slow, provided you learn to keep the rifle on your shoulder, cheek against the stock, and work the action with your shooting hand. Although there are many variations, the drill generally is to fire, then release the pistol grip with your shooting hand and open the bolt with your cupped hand moving upward, catching the bolt handle about where the fingers join the palm. You use your cupped hand to ride the bolt *all the way* to the rear, then roll your hand outward and around so that you can slam the bolt handle forward and down with the fleshy part of your palm just below where the thumb joins. This movement is very fast and very positive. With practice, it's every bit as fast as any lever-action, and with proper cheeking does not require any loss of sight picture.

I certainly don't advocate spraying the landscape with a rifle of any action type, but shooters who choose bolt-actions should know how to get a second and third shot off very quickly for those rare occasions when follow-up shots are needed. There's no substitute for live-fire practice on the range, but a close second is dry-firing–preferably with dummy cartridges made up with fired primers and no powder. If you pursue this practice, of course, make certain the rifle is always pointed in a safe direction, and carefully *mark* your dummy cartridges with lacquer or nailpolish so you can't possibly make a mistake!

Genuine drawbacks to the bolt-action are both its size and shape. Bolt-actions can be made extremely short, light, and trim, as Melvin Forbes has done for years with his Ultra-Light Arms. There are limits, though. You cannot make a bolt-action as light or as trim as you can a falling-block single-shot. The protruding bolt itself is a real pain as well. As much as I love bolt-actions, I hate the extra bulge the bolt makes in a saddle scabbard, and I hate even more the way a bolt constantly bangs and catches when slung alongside a packframe–and the way the bolt snares on brush, especially when you carry your rifle slung in thick cover. Under these circumstances, a slim-profiled Savage 99 or Browning BLR makes an extremely appealing package!

Even so, like the majority of hunters today, I generally prefer a bolt-action rifle. Exceptions might be stand-hunting for black bear, where I know the range will be short and a powerful lever-action makes equal sense, or virtually any wild-hog hunting, where the nature of the quarry is such that a close stalk is usually possible. Or simply because I feel like using a different rifle on a given day. But for serious hunting, whether it's a long-range backpack hunt for sheep, a pack trip after elk, or simply a deer hunt in country where there's some chance for a really fine buck, I will almost invariably choose a bolt-action. A good reason is familiarity. As we've seen, all the other action types are available in models and calibers suitable for any but the most specialized of endeavors. But unlike many hunters of earlier generations, I grew up with bolt-actions–and nothing has come along yet to make a permanent switch worthwhile!

The bolt-action is rugged and reliable. It's plenty fast enough for any hunting purposes. And since it's inherently our most accurate type of rifle, its ammunition can be specifically tailored to the job at hand with the greatest ease and the greatest benefit. I love to handload, selecting just the right bullet for what I have in mind and working up just the right load, with the optimum balance of needed accuracy and desired velocity. The bolt-action's accuracy and powerful extraction make it the handloader's odds-on choice.

Because of its basic design, it's also the gun tinkerer's dream. No other action type is so conducive to restocking, rebedding, fine-tuning the trigger, and mating with the most desirable sighting equipment. Lever-actions, slide-actions, and semiautos are fairly basic tools, leaving much less room for the tinkerer to tinker with. The single-shot shares many attributes with the bolt-action, but its two-piece stock is the Achilles' heel of the shooter who demands the utmost in accuracy. All of our action types and the rifles built around them have their place, but its easy to see why the bolt-action has risen to the top.

By 1900, there were quite a number of successful bolt-action designs on the market. These included the Norwegian (and our own) Krag-Jorgenson, the Austrian Steyr, the American-designed Lee action which had evolved into Britain's Lee-Enfield, and Germany's Mauser–which in dozens of variations was rapidly becoming the world's favorite rifle. Of these, it was the Mauser that possessed the greatest combination of the attributes we now take for granted in a bolt-action rifle. The Krag was butter-smooth, but its rear lockup was relatively weak and its side-magazine was unwieldy and a nightmare to inlet and bed. The Steyr was also rear-locking, thus not as strong, and although it was extremely reliable, it appeared to have a weak extraction system. The Lee-Enfield was not strong enough for cartridges of much greater intensity than the .303 British–and it used a two-piece stock. The Mauser action, little changed since 1893 but finally perfected in 1898, remains for many shooters the benchmark of action design.

It features strong lockup with massive, opposing forward locking lugs, the characteristic long Mauser extractor, a secure and positive safety, a backup system for redirecting escaping gases in the event of a ruptured case, a stationary manual ejector, and controlled-round feeding. In its military form, it needed (and needs) alterations of both bolt and safety to allow scope mounting, but in terms of accuracy, reliability, and "tinkerability," the 1898 Mauser remains a complete, modern, and fully suitable sporting bolt-action.

While other bolt-action types–those mentioned plus long-forgotten designs like the Newton, the straight-pull Lee and Ross, the French Lebel, and many others–had varying degrees of appeal, the Mauser and its knockoffs dominated the bolt-action scene for at least 50 years. Mauser clones, by the way, are not be sneezed at. They include our beloved 1903 Springfield; our 1917 Enfield and the nearly-identical Remington Model 30 series; literally dozens of Mauser-pattern military and sporting actions from manufacturers far too numerous to list; and, of course, the Winchester Model 54 and its much more famous heir, the pre-1964 Winchester Model 70.

Even to this day, a great many hunters feel the original Winchester Model 70 is the ultimate Mauser–and thus the ultimate bolt-action. It was a streamlined action but retained the Mauser extractor and fixed-blade ejector, and it offered controlled-round feeding. Little would be made of this feature until there were a number of actions without it!

Although the Mauser is still very much with us in many forms, in the postwar era the bolt-action gradually began to change. The Mauser action, including its long extractor, was and is fairly difficult to manufacture. It was also not quite as strong as an action could be made, since the controlled-round feeding required that the bottom of the bolt face be open so a cartridge could feed up out of the magazine and be trapped by the extractor. Or so goes the theory.

Ever so slowly, there started to be more and more actions that lacked the long Mauser extractor and used a spring-loaded plunger ejector in the bolt face rather than the Mauser/Springfield/Model 70's fixed blade. Rather than allow the cartridge to feed up between the bolt face and the extractor and be totally controlled, these actions tended to push the cartridge ahead of the bolt into the chamber, and then the extractor snapped over the rim. The trade-off was that, with this engineering, the bolt face could be a solid ring of steel and thus be significantly stronger (at least in theory) than the Mauser's partially open bolt face.

Remington's big, bulky Model 30 action, reworked but little from the World War I 1917 Enfield action, simply could not compete with Winchester's slick, slim Model 70. Remington was therefore one of the first American companies to bring out one of these new push-actions. Their Model 725/722/721 series evolved into the Model 700 much as we know it today. The Savage 110 was another. Still another was the Weatherby Mark V with its nine smallish locking lugs of the same diameter as the bolt sleeve, instead of the Mauser's two huge lugs. Others include the Sako, the Browning A-Bolt, and many more.

In 1964, Winchester made what should probably go down as the firearms marketing blunder of the century. They took the most revered–possibly the best-selling–bolt-action in the world and scrapped it due to increasing manufacturing costs. The "pre-'64" Model 70 went away, and in its place was the "post-'64" Model 70. The latter was–and is–a very fine action. It's a push-action with an extractor in the bolt-face rim and a plunger ejector on the bolt face. It works flawlessly–but it wasn't the same Model 70 that made the model's reputation, and in one fell swoop Winchester lost its lead in the bolt-action market.

The original Ruger Model 77 came along later. This rifle is a combination action. It does have a long Mauser extractor, but it's a push-action with an enclosed bolt face, and the extractor is designed to snap over the cartridge head upon chambering. Of course, there are other actions as well. For a time, Remington marketed their inexpensive rear-locking Model 788, an accuracy phenomenon that proved rear-locking actions can shoot straight. And then there are the Sauer rifles, for a time marketed in this country as Colt-Sauer, with retractable rear locking lugs–another sound design that just might be the smoothest bolt-action ever made. And the Steyr-Mannlicher, and perhaps a couple of dozen others. Sound designs all–but it seems that the shooting world lined up as pro-Mauser or pro-modern push-action.

For the record, I'm a left-handed shooter. I love pre-'64 Model 70s, I love Mausers, and I love Springfields. None of these actions, except some custom copies and a few conversions, have ever been made with a left-hand bolt. I grew up with right-handed rifles in all three actions, but about 15 years ago, after an all-inclusive burglary, I made a conscious decision to switch to left-hand actions. For the last 15 years, easily the most active years of my hunting career, I have done the great majority of my shooting and hunting with rifles available in left-hand actions. The selection is growing rapidly, but historically I was limited to Weatherby Mark Vs, Remington Model 700s, and Savage 110s. None of these push-actions has ever failed me in the field or on the range—nor have I seen one fail. In theory, the Mauser's long extractor is more positive, but while I've never had a Remington, Sako, Weatherby, or Savage extractor fail, I have had a Mauser extractor fail and separate from the bolt sleeve.

In theory, the fixed Mauser ejector is also more positive. I have never had a Savage, Remington, Sako, or Weatherby ejector fail—but I have had a blade-type Mauser ejector on a Westley Richards '98 Mauser fail. It was worn out, which can happen. It was also very easily replaced. But the facts are the facts.

I have never had a catastrophic failure like a ruptured case, so I can't tell you which system is better. In theory, the modern actions which surround the case head in an extra ring of steel are unquestionably better—but I do believe the Mauser system, which incorporates a gas shield "just in case"—is more than adequately strong and more than adequately proofed against human error.

Much has been made of controlled-round feeding lately, especially for use against the dangerous game in such short supply in North America. In theory (that phrase again), controlled-round feeding is more positive. On the range, I have had feeding problems with both Mauser-type and push-actions, and I've done the necessary work to correct same. Once smooth feeding was assured, I've never had feeding problems with either type.

As an aside, much is made of the fact that actions with controlled-round feeding can function upside down, sideways, and under water. This is clearly desirable in military bolt-actions, and military standards might well be applied to dangerous-game rifles used in life-threatening (and saving) situations. I have written previously that the Mauser-type actions will feed upside down while the push-actions will not. To my undying shame, it took an Army officer—and, worse, an attorney—to prove me wrong. A good friend of mine, a colonel in the Army Reserve, Houston attorney Lee Ware, suggested I should try a Model 700 upside down before I commented again on controlled-round feeding. He was right and I was wrong. Push-actions will indeed feed upside down. I still don't know if they'll feed under water, and don't much care.

The point here is that modern bolt-actions, whether of Mauser or later design, just plain *work*. Personal preference is probably the most significant factor in making a choice. However, in the last few years there has been a decided shift back toward the original Mauser concept.

I think it started with Mauser/pre-'64 Model 70 clones like the Kimber and the Dakota bolt-actions. It continued with Ruger's Model 77 Mark II. The long extractor was kept, but the bolt face was opened to include controlled-round feeding. In the current Model 77 Mark II, you actually have a very basic Mauser action in almost all ways. Then Winchester brought back a controlled-round-feeding almost-pre-'64 action, differing only in modern manufacturing techniques and some new wrinkles like an effective anti-bind raceway. Initially, the old/new action was available on high-grade guns only. In 1994, as these lines are being written, the "Classic" Model 70, as it's now called, is available in a bewildering array of models and chamberings at a very modest premium over the post-'64 push-action. The push-action is currently still available in an *equally* bewildering array of models and chamberings, but I suspect the push-action will be phased out in years to come.

To some degree, this reflects shooters' tastes coming full circle, back to the '98 Mauser. Certainly it's an amazing step for Winchester to admit–after 30 years–that they goofed in 1964. To some degree, too, it simply reflects that modern manufacturing techniques–primarily computer-controlled machining–have again made the Mauser-type actions commercially viable. The customer is always right, and I'm sure the Classic Model 70 is even now regaining some of the ground its post-1964 predecessor lost. From an aesthetic and historical standpoint, I love the new Winchester action. I only wish they made it in left-hand. Someday I suspect they will.

In the meantime, I love equally a beautiful Dakota .270 with a very similar controlled-round feed left-hand action. And a Belgian Dumoulin .416 Rigby on a left-hand magnum Mauser action. And a left-hand Ruger Model 77 Mark II .25-06. But I don't necessarily love any of them more than my eight Model 700 Remingtons (at the present moment!) or a prized Weatherby Mark V, or a brand-new Savage 110, or, for that matter, a badly beat-up pre-1964 Model 70 .375 *converted* to left-hand bolt! They all work just fine, and I have total and equal confidence in them all. Whether of century-old design or brand new, the bolt-action rifle just plain works–and in the right chambering and configuration it can work for any hunting on our continent. That's why it's so popular today!

Chapter 24

Stocks: Wood or Synthetic?

I grew up with beautiful wood. I've mentioned earlier on that Jack Pohl, owner of the gunstock firm of E.C. Bishop & Sons, was a good friend of Dad's. My early shooting career was spiced with visits to their operation in Warsaw, Missouri. "Gunstock Capital of the World," proclaimed the sign on the way in to town; it still does, and is a well-earned nickname, since Reinhart Fajen is located in the same little town! I can well remember wandering around Jack's office and prowling his showroom looking at all the beautifully stocked rifles and shotguns–and dreaming of owning them.

Though Dad had no rifles when I was little, he did have some beautiful gunstocks. His own pet shotgun, a Browning Auto-5, had been beautifully restocked in exquisite walnut, the result fitting him so well that to this day I've never seen a faster or more efficient shot than Dad was even when he was well into his fifties. He also had a 20-gauge Winchester Model 12, equally beautifully stocked, that Jack Pohl had done for me the year I was born. I didn't really need it for a while, and when I did it turned out that the right-handed cheekpiece was a bit superfluous for the lefty I turned into. But it was still my shotgun, and it wore beautiful wood.

Thanks to that connection, my first few centerfire rifles–and Dad's–all sported Bishop stocks in good American walnut. A couple were fairly plain, and a couple were truly exquisite. These days I can appreciate the nuances of French and Circassian walnut, but for sheer beauty I doubt I'll ever beat some of those stocks Jack did for us. There was a .264 with schnabel fore-end, fairly straight where strength was needed but with wild fiddleback on the butt. There was an absolutely perfect Mannlicher-style stock on a Mark X Mauser in .270, dark walnut with lots of figure. And there was another Mark X in .300 Winchester Magnum, the stock made from a blank Jack had been saving for years. This one was a trim, American classic style, sans cheekpiece, very fine checkering. All three, plus a few more, were stolen. I hope whoever wound up with them appreciates them!

With a boyhood filled with beautiful gunstocks, it's no surprise that I still admire good walnut above all. Because of that, I came pretty late to the synthetic stocks that are all the rage these days. In fact, I didn't come to synthetics voluntarily at all. I got there because the great bugaboo of wooden stocks, warpage, happened to me. The rifle was a Savage 110, a left-handed 7mm Remington Magnum that also claimed two other firsts–my first rifle in that caliber and my first left-hand bolt-action. Every time it got wet, the stock would swell and warp so quickly and so violently that the barrel channel received pressure and threw the bullets a minimum of 10 inches off at 100 yards.

The first time I noticed it was when I got back from an extremely soggy caribou hunt in the Northwest Territories. Since I'd gotten my caribou, I didn't think much about it. Maybe I got lucky, or maybe it happened after I got my bull. But that first time, I put it down to shifting zero during the trip home. The second time, I watched it happen. It was that rarity, a torrential fall rain in the California foothills. Durwood Hollis, Payton Miller, and I pulled into a little canyon system that we'd scouted a week or so earlier, arriving just ahead of dark with the air heavy with moisture. The rain held off long enough to cook supper, and then the first drops fell. That didn't mean much, nor did it mean much more that it poured all through the night. More significant was that it poured equally hard until the late morning. Of course, we hunted anyway, seeing nothing but getting ourselves and our equipment thoroughly soaked.

In the late morning, it began to clear and we started to see deer. Payton and I jumped a very fine buck. I missed him clean; then Payton dumped him with a lovely running shot. I felt good enough about my shot that I thought I'd best check zero, and indeed my rifle was already shooting fully a foot to the right! I re-zeroed against a convenient rock. All three of us got bucks on that memorable day, quite an event for do-it-yourself hunters within 60 miles of Los Angeles. But I knew I had to do something about that rifle.

One of those newfangled synthetic stocks seemed a good idea, so I gave it a try. I no longer have that Savage–wish I did–but I must have liked the result. I now have fully a half-dozen synthetic-stocked rifles, a fairly complete battery from .25-06 to .416. A colleague of mine once called his synthetic-stocked rifles his "usin'" guns, while his walnut-stocked rifles were his "lookin'" guns. I won't go that far. I still use both, including some beautifully stocked rifles. But I have increasing respect for synthetic stocks.

Although they're exceptionally functional, I *still* don't like the looks of a synthetic stock. I find them ugly as sin, even though they can and these days generally do offer beautiful, simple lines. Regardless of whether you like them, though, they make much sense. Synthetic stocks absolutely eliminate the warpage problem associated with wood. Now, proper glass bedding and finishing of wood stocks greatly reduces the potential problem. But if it rains hard enough long enough, the problem cannot be eliminated in a wood stock. It simply does not exist with synthetics.

Synthetics can also reduce weight. Note that I said "can." A misconception is that they all do. This depends on the material, the construction, and the styling. Synthetic stocks molded as a solid piece of material are generally only slightly lighter than walnut. In fact, a wooden stock built trim and clean can weigh less than the average synthetic. However, stocks constructed from foam-filled shells of fiberglass or like material, generally reinforced with Kevlar, are usually much lighter than any wood stock. Ounce for ounce, they are also stronger. The problem with wood is that you lose strength quickly when you start to lose weight, especially in the critical wrist area and around the action inletting. Beautifully trim wooden stocks are comparatively fragile, much more than equally trim synthetics.

While wood stocks can sport a non-glare finish, synthetic stocks are generally painted with a final finish. Not only can they be non-glare; they can be any color you want, or they can be camouflaged. The most common is a "krinkle" finish of very rough paint that gives a good nonslip surface, almost as good as checkering. (And, of course, synthetics can also have molded checkering that's pretty good these days.) For me, the rough finish is almost too much of a good thing. I generally have to take fine sandpaper to the buttstock where my cheek touches it, lest I lose skin during recoil.

The significant advantages of synthetics are very real: imperviousness to weather, reduction in weight, and lack of glare. To these I'll add another: peace of mind. North American hunting is often hard work, and some of the best of it is done in thoroughly horrible weather. With a synthetic stock, you needn't worry about the effects of that horrible weather. Even better, you really needn't worry about the rifle, either. I love my walnut-stocked rifles–so much that I have a bad habit of taking them on rough hunts and then bemoaning each new scratch on that beautiful wood. It's crazy, really, to take a fine piece of walnut up a sheep mountain, on a long horseback hunt, or into weather you know is going to be wet. Sure, you can sand out all but the deepest gouges. You can refinish, and you can even recut worn checkering. But after a single tough hunt in rough country, you'll never again bring a piece of walnut back the way it was. Synthetic stocks get dinged, too. If painted, their finishes are actually fairly fragile. They'll scratch and gouge, and the paint may peel in spots. Personally, since I find synthetic stocks ugly anyway, I don't much worry about it. But if you do worry about it, it's a simple matter to repaint a synthetic stock. Bingo, like new!

During the writing of this book I made a brown bear hunt in Alaska. It turned out to be unusually tough–lots of walking with a packframe in very rugged country, and we had hard rain seven of 10 days. I chose a Remington Model 700 BDL in .375 H&H. Walnut stock, straight out of the box. Literally. The rifle was brand new. "Was" is the operative word! Rubbing against the packframe wore off the checkering in several places. And after a few days of rain, the stock turned that sickly white. There was rust on the metal, too, though I tried to stay ahead of it. The rust came off, and the stock could be cleaned up. With the incredibly heavy barrel that Remington uses on their .375s, a shift in zero was unlikely, and it didn't happen. The rifle shot just fine on the trip and still does. But it sure ain't new anymore, and never will be again. If there was ever a trip that screamed for a synthetic stock and a rustproof finish, this was it!

Of course, I knew better. I've done it before and I'll do it again. But it's for hunts like this one that I own a full battery of synthetic-stocked rifles. I should have used one! The plan was to save the walnut-stocked rifles for hunts where the weather is fairly predictable, weight is not a factor, and conditions aren't all that rough–Africa, stand-hunting for white-taileds, pronghorn hunting, that sort of thing. I planned the synthetics mostly around late season, wet weather, horseback, and high altitude. I should probably stick to my plan!

Regardless of whether you choose synthetics or walnut, stock style and fit are extremely important. What works for me may not work for you, and it's important that your rifle fit *you* properly and be comfortable. If it isn't, two things will happen. First, you'll get the hell kicked out of you every time you squeeze the trigger. Second, you'll be slow and inefficient when you must take a quick shot.

The average rifle stock, with a length of pull from 13¾ to 14 inches, is built for the average man. At five feet nine inches (well, on a good day, anyway!), I'm the average man. Most out-of-the-box factory rifles with factory stocks fit me at least passably if not perfectly. If you happen to be a five-foot-two-inch woman or a six-foot-eight basketball player, chances are the average stock won't fit you. It's easy to shorten a stock–more difficult to lengthen, but it can be done. To check length of pull, first make sure the chamber is empty, then take a natural shooting grasp around the pistol grip and allow your finger to rest naturally on the trigger as if you were ready to fire. Now see if the buttstock fits comfortably into the crook of your elbow, making contact with your upper arm but not applying pressure. With most people, this means a more or less proper length of pull.

Of course, not all people are built alike. Some have shorter or longer arms; some have longer or shorter necks. The goal in stock fit is for the rifle to come up naturally, butt against shoulder, cheek against stock, sights aligned on target instantly with no adjustment necessary. Again checking to make sure the rifle is empty, pick a spot on a wall or on the back fence. Concentrate on it and throw your rifle up. The sights should align on the object. If they don't, you have a problem. It might be your shooting position, but it's probably stock fit.

Height of comb is important. Since a scope sight is significantly higher than iron sights above line of bore, stocks intended for use with scopes must have slightly higher combs than stocks intended for use with iron sights. *No* stock is equally ideal for both! Auxiliary iron sights are nice, especially for rifles to be used on long hunts in wilderness country. But you don't really want a compromise stock that requires you to lift your head up to use the scope and scrunch your face down a bit if irons are used. If the scope is the primary sight, you want a stock suited for scope use. And that means you'll have to press your face into the stock to properly see the iron sights. That's okay.

There are tremendous variations in buttstock design today, and personal preference plays a huge role in which you select. I started out with Monte Carlo combs, the idea being that the forward slant of the comb pulls the rifle away from your face under recoil. I have more recently come to much prefer the American classic stock style. This is a fairly high, very straight comb. It puts the recoil pad a bit higher on the shoulder, and while it may technically kick the face a bit harder than a Monte Carlo, I think it offers less muzzle jump and more straight-line recoil. Take your pick.

Cheekpieces come in all kinds of shapes and sizes, from roll-overs on down. Again, this is personal preference and the shooter's idea of esthetics. I used to like cheekpieces, but have come to prefer a stock with no cheekpiece at all. I find them nothing more than a few extra ounces of wood. But if it feels good to you, do it. I do prefer a gently rounded comb. Few things accentuate recoil more than a thin, sharp comb digging into your cheek every time you fire.

The butt itself, too, is important. The thin crescent butts of our grandfathers' day are an abomination–and the thin steel buttplates that look so good are almost as bad. I like a fairly wide, flat "shotgun-style" butt. Esthetics control how big a butt can be (no levity intended), but the wider and deeper the rifle butt, the larger the area recoil is spread over. Regardless of how the stock is configured, a rifle should have a rubber buttpad. Modern recoil pads like Pachmayr's Decelerator, made from shock-absorbing material, work exceptionally well. But not all rifles really need a recoil pad, *per se*. Lighter calibers will do just fine with a thin rubber pad. The reason for the rubber isn't so much recoil attenuation as stability. A rubber pad will keep the rifle from slipping on your shoulder, not only between shots, but for the first shot as well. Even a checkered wooden butt, a real classy touch, is much more likely to slip on your shoulder than a rubber pad.

Obviously, a walnut stock can be made in any configuration desired, from the thumbholes that I abhor all the way to a simple classic. It used to be that synthetics were pretty much vanilla ice cream, with few variations. Today you can also get synthetics in almost any imaginable configuration. Virtually all the major manufacturers now offer synthetic-stocked models, and a myriad aftermarket stocks in almost any configuration are available.

I still don't think they're for everyone, and they certainly aren't needed under all conditions. But these days I do believe a rifle intended for all seasons and all conditions should probably wear one. Ugly or not, it just doesn't make sense to stick with walnut knowing you're going to ruin it!

Chapter 25

Slings, Rests, and Recoil Reducers

I'm not much for hanging unnecessary things on hunting rifles. The options are quite endless, from bipods to ammunition carriers to compasses and the kitchen sink. Problem is that almost anything you put on the rifle can change its balance and, perhaps worse, create new obstructions to snag on things.

There are, however, a wide variety of accessories that have tremendous merit, at least in some situations if not all. The first we'll talk about is the rifle sling. A sling has two purposes, or at least it should. The first is to carry the rifle over shoulder or back, freeing the hands while negotiating obstacles or simply to conserve energy on a long hike. The second purpose is to aid in steady shooting.

Almost any sling will do for the first purpose, but not all are suitable for the second. Because of that, we'll deal with the second purpose first. When I speak of the sling as a shooting aid, I mean the use of either a tight sling in the way a competition shooter might use one, or a "hasty sling" looped around the forearm. Few hunters use a formal tight sling. Because of my military background, I do occasionally, and there's absolutely no substitute for a good tight sling, especially from the sitting or kneeling position. However, the tight sling takes significant time to get into–and a huge amount of practice.

The tight sling requires a military two-claw sling or the modified Whelen one-claw sling. It's really two pieces of leather joined by an open buckle, and to use the tight sling you must detach the rear swivel, put your supporting arm through the loop formed between a keeper and the front part of the sling, and tighten the loop down on your upper arm with the keeper. The bottom strap of the sling hangs free and is not used.

With the sling tightened against the upper arm, your forearm wraps around the sling and your hand is snugged up tight between the sling and the sling swivel. Try it–you won't believe the improvement in steadiness. The problem is the time required, not to mention the practice needed. And of course only the two-piece sling is suitable.

The hasty sling is much simpler. Both sling swivels are left in place, and the supporting arm is merely thrust through the sling and wrapped around once. When the rifle is brought up, the sling tightens and adds a significant measure of support. For me, the hasty sling is a great assist in shooting offhand, or standing, while the tight sling is of limited benefit in this position. The hasty sling helps tremendously in prone, sitting, and kneeling, but is not as good as the tight sling in these positions. There are no problems or drawbacks to the hasty sling; every shooter should practice it and employ it as a matter of course. However, it's extremely uncomfortable with the popular "cobra" type of riflesling that has a thick, padded forward section. Such slings are really just carrying straps. Best is a single strap of leather or canvas webbing. These last are wonderful. They don't slip on the shoulder the way leather can, and can be built wide enough to virtually eliminate shoulder chafing without getting heavy like a wide leather sling does. Problem is I don't know of anyone in this country who makes such a sling. I have bought several in South Africa, Spain, and Austria, so it seems this is a trick the rest of the world has figured out but we have not.

For most of us, the primary purpose of a sling is as a carrying strap. This is important, but it's also a trap. A rifle slung over the shoulder is not ready for action–and a rifle carried at port arms with a sling dangling is noisy. I do believe in slings; my arms get just as tired as anyone's. But I pay close attention to when I carry a rifle slung, trying to make sure that's *never* when I really feel I might get a shot. By the way, a rifle slung over the shoulder should *never* have a round in the chamber. A loaded chamber is for times when a shot might be imminent *and* you can maintain full control of the rifle and the direction of the muzzle with *both* hands. Period.

When I'm in very thick country–say, trying to still-hunt whitetails in country like northwest Montana's dense forest–I take the sling off and put it in my pocket. That does two things. First, it eliminates noise. Second, it avoids the temptation to sling the rifle when it really should be in your hands. As a drawback, removing the sling means you cannot use it as a shooting aid–but in close cover like that you shouldn't need it.

Because I do attach and detach the sling as circumstances dictate, I much prefer quick-detachable swivels. The best are the type that secure with a threaded detent, rather than the slightly less expensive spring-plunger type. Like all of us, I live with the screw-in post sling-swivel studs that are almost universal–but I hate 'em. Far better are the two-screw studs that will not turn, like the post studs all do, and cannot come unscrewed. I've even seen the screw-in studs on expensive custom rifles, and that strikes me as really dumb.

Fast use of a sling, whether hasty or a full-blown target tight sling, is an important shooting skill. Even so, use of a sling should be strictly a backup to a good, steady, *solid* rest. There is simply no substitute for a good rest. End of story. One of the really important field-shooting skills is learning how to find and use a natural rest *quickly.* The difficulty, of course, is that not all types of country offer rocks and stumps and fallen logs to use as rests. Sometimes, in fact, they aren't there when you need them the most.

The obvious answer is to carry your own rest. For years I thought this was somehow a bit sissy, but it isn't at all. After all, the goal is to drop your game with one well-placed shot–and anything that helps you do it isn't sissy at all. It's good sportsmanship and common sense combined. Pronghorn hunting is a classic situation where carrying along a rest may makes sense. There are few handy stumps in antelope country, and the grass is often too long to make shooting prone practical. The shots are usually on the long side, which makes things worse. A sling will help, but is no substitute for a steady rest if you can find one. Harris bipods have provided a good answer for many years. They attach to the front sling swivel, with the legs folding against the barrel. Several models are available with legs that telescope to different heights. The short-legged prone models are okay for varmint hunting, but for big game I like the model with legs long enough to use in a good, steady sitting position.

I have taken a Harris bipod along on enough pronghorn hunts to no longer feel sissy about it. In fact, I've taken a lot of shots that I probably couldn't have taken without it! The Harris does have drawbacks. It adds significant gun weight, and it adds an appendage that is pure murder in any brush at all. This is an open-country device–but in such country it's wonderful.

A new wrinkle is a gizmo called the Snipe-Stix, made in Montana. This is a two-piece unit. An adapter fits onto the sling swivel, but the bipod itself is stored in a belt pack until you need it. The adapter also allows you to cant the rifle for uneven slopes and uphill/downhill shooting. I like it very much, but since the unit must be reached for and attached prior to use, it's slower than the Harris.

There are many other commercial rests. Some attach to the rifle and some do not. Among them are various monopod arrangements. A monopod is not nearly as steady as a bipod, but it's a whole lot better than nothing. I don't happen to like them, but with practice they can be extremely effective. It's really more a matter of investing the practice time learning how to be most effective with an artificial rest than it is exactly which one you select.

A device that I do like very much is the Underwood Shooting Sticks. These are sections of aluminum tubing bungee-corded together and jointed at the middle to make shooting sticks like the buffalo hunters used. The unit is very light, can be carried comfortably on the belt, and is very fast. However, since this rest does not attach to the rifle, it takes time to learn the best hand placement.

The same can be said of the Tracker II. This is a nifty piece of gear. Also made of aluminum, it's a hiking staff that folds in the middle, forming a very sturdy bipod. One of my knees is a bit tricky, so a hiking staff is becoming a better idea all the time in steep country. A staff has its own uses, aside from something to lean on going up and downhill. With practice, you can use one to stabilize binoculars for glassing, and in a pinch there are several techniques for using one as a monopod for shooting. But this one can be adjusted to exactly the right height–and in just a couple of seconds you can undo a set screw, pull the two halves apart, and *presto*, you've got a great big bipod. I've carried mine all over a bunch of mountains, and although I've used the bipod just a few times (after all, there tend to be plenty of natural rests in mountains), it's another great idea.

There are also a very few companies offering built-in bipods. The best one I know of is made by Brent Clifton of Clifton Arms. Brent makes a really excellent custom synthetic stock, and his offers a couple of super innovations not found elsewhere. The bipod looks like a black pistol-grip cap with a couple of indentations. Squeeze the indentations and pull, and out comes a very functional bipod, its only drawback being that it's intended for prone use and isn't tall enough for sitting.

Clifton also offers a unique cartridge trap in the buttstock. A built-in cartridge trap is one of those wonderful custom features that I've always admired, but have never been able to afford. Clifton's is both affordable and extremely functional. The cartridges are held in place against the sliding door by individual springs. As you slide the door open, the cartridges are propelled into your hand one at a time; the intent is that, should you run your magazine dry, you can single-load from the trap one at a time without taking your eyes off the target. Pretty neat!

I've got a wonderfully accurate Clifton Arms 7mm Remington Magnum, and I've practiced a bit with the system. So far, I haven't run the magazine dry when hunting with it. I certainly have with other rifles, though, and the Clifton gadget saves a whole bunch of time.

Finally, let's turn to recoil reducers. I'm probably missing something, but I reckon there are three main forms: recoil pads; muzzle brakes and barrel venting systems; and mechanical or hydraulic systems. All three can work–and therefore can be extremely important in improving and maintaining accuracy. As he-men *macho* shooters, we hate to admit this, but it's a fact that recoil is unpleasant. At some point, it changes from unpleasant to painful, and that point is different for each of us. Every shooter has a different level of recoil tolerance; some of us have no problem with the 50 or so foot/pounds of a light .338 or heavy .375, while others start to have trouble with the 20-odd foot/pounds of a .30-06. The main point here is that if recoil is unpleasant, it can ultimately cause a flinch. Better to recognize your limit early on and do something about it.

A recoil pad is the simplest answer, and could well be enough. For a young shooter, even the very mild .30-30 can offer a pretty sharp whack, especially with the typical narrow butt of the average .30-30 carbine. A quick fix would be have a recoil pad installed. The thick rubber pads are good, but even better are pads made from shock-absorbing polymers. As I mentioned earlier, Pachmayr's Decelerator is a good example.

At the range, and perhaps even in the field, padding yourself may be required as well. The P.A.S.T. recoil shield, made from similar shock-absorbing materials, is a great gadget for attenuating recoil. On the bench, where recoil is greatly exaggerated by the body's lack of give, even a rolled up towel on your shoulder will make a big difference.

The next step up in recoil attenuation, at least these days, is some form of muzzle venting that reduces recoil through redirection of gases. Muzzle brakes are certainly not new. Weatherby offered barrel venting as standard on his .460 Weatherby almost from the caliber's beginning, and Larry Kelly's Mag-Na-Port system has been around for many years.

Kelly's system vents the muzzle itself, so it's not truly an add-on muzzle brake. There is some recoil attenuation, but what Mag-Na-Porting does mostly is reduce muzzle jump by directing escaping gas upward. This has two effects, both very positive. First, recoil is directed straight back, which is always where you want it. Second, since muzzle climb is reduced, recovery between shots is greatly reduced. My hunting partner, Joe Bishop, has a Mag-Na-Ported 7mm Remington Magnum. Personally, I wouldn't have thought to have so light a caliber ported, but Joe swears by it. His reasoning is that with a fairly light rifle so ported, muzzle jump is reduced so much that he can call his shots perfectly by actually watching bullet impact on the animal. I tried his rifle on a couple of African animals, and he's dead right–you can watch the bullet hit and know precisely what you've done or not done. Porting also helps tremendously on hard-kicking handguns like the .454 Casull. In fact, it's darn near essential to keep the muzzle down a bit.

Muzzle brakes, especially the ones we have today, attenuate recoil much more significantly than porting. The actual reduction can only be measured with fairly sophisticated lab equipment, and the degree depends a bit on cartridge velocity as well as its raw recoil foot/pounds. For instance, a very fast cartridge like the .340 Weatherby benefits more from a brake than does the relatively slow .458 Winchester Magnum. A reduction of about 40 percent can be expected in most cases, and that's a whole bunch.

The first really popular muzzle brake was, I think, the KDF Recoil Arrestor. Like most, the KDF threads onto the end of the barrel, and while the original version created an unsightly end-of-barrel bulge, the later slimline model was of the same diameter as the barrel. The muzzle brake functions quite simply by directing gases out and back through a series of holes in the brake. The main difference between the KDF and the several fine brakes that have followed it is the arrangement of the holes. The principle is the same, and they all work–some perhaps a bit better, some perhaps not quite as well.

A problem with all brakes, and to a slightly lesser degree porting, is that the escaping gases have to go somewhere. Since they go up, back, and/or outward, muzzle blast is increased significantly. The problem is usually not as severe for the shooter as it is for his hunting partner. On a hunt in Texas a couple of years ago, a colleague shot at a running nilgai, and because of our respective locations and the angle of the shot the rifle went off fairly close to my ear. It was a .416 Weatherby Magnum with a KDF Recoil Arrestor, and the muzzle blast absolutely flattened me–I was totally incapacitated for several seconds. No permanent damage (heck, like most longtime shooters I'm half-deaf anyway), but I think there could have been.

I wish I'd worn shooting protection as a youngster, but we didn't know much about that back then. I do now, but the barn door is open and the horse is long gone. Shooting protection should always be worn on the range, and I do recommend it in the field, especially for young shooters. If you or your partner uses a muzzle brake afield, wear hearing protection!

The KDF can be unscrewed and removed for hunting, with a thread protector screwed on in its place. I find that a really sound compromise, since you rarely feel recoil when shooting at game anyway. Some other brakes may also be installed as detachable.

Brakes that have followed the KDF are numerous. David Gentry's brake, which I have no personal experience with, is billed as the "quiet muzzle brake." Gentry is one of the best rifle mechanics I know, so if he says it works I suspect it does. Savage now has two types of muzzle brake available as standard on some of their rifles. One of them literally turns off and turns on by twisting the brake to cover or uncover the holes. Pretty good idea; you can have a brake on the range, but in the field you can turn it off and thus turn down the noise.

Most innovative is Browning's new BOSS, which stands for Ballistic Optimizing Shooting System. The BOSS looks like, and is, a conventional, functional muzzle brake. But it's also an adjustable barrel weight that allows the shooter to match his barrel harmonics to a given load–just the opposite of matching the ammo to the rifle, as handloaders have long done. Adjustment is done by loosening a lock ring and turning the weight in or out, using a small scale scribed on the upper surface. It takes a bit of range work to find what the Browning folks call the "sweet spot," but the results are both dramatic and significant. Using an out-of-the-box lightweight .22-250, after a bit of adjusting I was able to shoot 100-yard groups on the order of .332-inch–with factory ammo!

The idea of adjustable barrel weights isn't new. Olympic-competition smallbores have used them for years, and the French sniper rifle has an adjustable weight as well. But this is the first application to a hunting rifle, and it's extremely impressive. I've ordered an A-Bolt Mark II in .300 Winchester Magnum, thinking that a rifle in that caliber delivering half-inch groups should be a real confidence builder for long-range shooting. The BOSS is available only on A-Bolt Mark IIs and BARs, with no plans at this writing to offer it as an aftermarket accessory. In 1995 USRAC added the BOSS to the Model 70 Winchester.

If there's a drawback to the BOSS, it's that it's very sensitive. Few shooters, I suspect, will take the time to really work with it and realize the potential. It's also markedly affected by barrel fouling. But for the serious tinkerer and accuracy freak, BOSS is the latest word.

Finally, there are mechanical and hydraulic recoil dampeners, generally inletted into the buttstock. Some of these work very well, while others border on the Rube Goldberg. Best known is probably the Edwards reducer, popular among competitive trapshooters. Less known but extremely effective is Brownell's mercury-tube reducer. In a hunting rifle, I'm leery of anything that changes the weight and balance, so I would consider such devices a very distant third option.

However, it is absolutely essential that you not be afraid of your hunting rifle. Lots of sensible practice helps familiarize shooters with their rifles, but if your rifle approaches whatever your recoil threshold happens to be, practice is likely to just make things worse. The only options are to do something about it. A good recoil pad, perhaps a stock that fits a bit better and has a wider butt, and a muzzle brake are all good ways to go. If that doesn't do it, there's really little choice but to consider a lighter caliber. After all, shot placement is still the name of the game–better a .280 you can shoot than a .338 you can't!

Chapter 26

Iron Sights in America

I'm in my early forties at this writing. I started my hunting career in the 1960s, and I started hunting with a telescopic sight. Most hunters older than I probably began hunting with open sights–and most younger hunters, except perhaps a good number of thick-cover whitetail hunters, probably started with scopes. I suspect it remains almost universal for shooters to learn riflery with an open-sighted .22, as I did. But hunters of my generation and younger probably "graduated" to a scope-sighted rifle when they began actually hunting. And most older hunters, too, have long since graduated to scopes.

In fact, the telescopic sight is in such widespread use today that iron sights have become almost an anachronism; an unused, unwanted, and neglected appendage on rifles that still carry them. You could almost liken them to the human appendix–it's still there, but it doesn't do anything and nobody knows what its purpose used to be!

The situation today is that relatively few serious hunters actually know how to use iron sights–and the iron sights supplied on most factory rifles seem to be very much an afterthought.

In years gone by, when scope sights were relatively new and widely distrusted, the argument was generally made that iron sights were sturdier and more reliable than a scope. This has not been true for a very long time. Today's scopes and their mounting systems are both sturdy and reliable. Any mechanical device can fail, and there are certainly lots of things in a scope that can go wrong. Reticles can break, adjustments can get out of whack, the scope tube itself can bend or break if given enough impact, and of course the seals can give way, allowing the scope to fog. However, all of these potential failures are exceptionally rare–so rare that most hunters will never see them all in a lifetime of use, and very few will ever see more than one.

These days, iron sights are considerably more fragile than scopes! There are a couple of reasons for this. First, manufacturers know that most centerfire hunting rifles leaving their factories will be scoped. Why concentrate on something unlikely to be used? Iron sights as supplied by the factories tend to be fairly flimsy today, and may not be as securely attached as you think they are. Second, by their very nature iron sights are exposed and vulnerable. Front-sight blades and posts can bend. Rear sights, especially if barrel-mounted, are subjected to more severe vibration during recoil than receiver-mounted scopes.

Rear sights are generally adjustable, even if only drift-adjustable with a mallet. That means the adjustments are in the open and, if not secure enough, have the potential to move during recoil or simply as a result of the banging and bumping of a normal hunting day. A scope's adjustments are internal, and not nearly so exposed.

In my hunting experience, I have had very few problems with scopes. On the range I've broken a few mounts–and a couple of scopes–with extreme recoil. And I've had a couple of scopes simply wear out. I'm trying to remember, but I simply can't recall *ever* having a scope fail in the field. Fogging, for instance, seems to be a great (exaggerated) fear that hunters have. I did have a spotting scope fog up once, but I've never had a rifle scope fog. Never. I have had several serious problems with iron sights in the field–and keep in mind that I'm a scope shooter. My actual field use of iron sights has been limited, and many of my bolt-action rifles don't wear iron sights. Even so, I've had front sights bend, and I've had rear sights drift and come out of adjustment during normal field use. I've even had two or three rear sights simply fall off the rifle!

Although I started out with scopes and absolutely believe a scope is the way to go under almost all circumstances, in recent years I've been spending quite a lot of time with iron sights. Given practice, it's amazing what you really can do with them. But you simply must not take for granted that an iron sight is foolproof. If that's the sight you're going to rely on, whether for back-up or primary, you simply must make certain that both front and rear are securely attached to the rifle. Don't rely on the factory to have done this for you! Then, just as with a scope sight, you must carefully zero the sight for your intended load and make certain the sight is locked down tightly on those adjustments. A bit of Loc-Tite on any set screws is a good bit of insurance. Finally, in the field, you need to protect both front and rear sight as best you can, and make sure you inspect your sights frequently to avoid surprises.

As most of us do, I've been interchanging the terms "iron sight" and "open sight." They aren't necessarily the same thing. An open sight implies a front sight blade or bead and a rear sight that's a notch of some type–a V-notch, a U-notch, or perhaps a buckhorn. Such sights are iron sights, meaning no glass, but an aperture or peep sight is also an iron sight–though not technically an open sight. An aperture sight is actually an optical sight, and is far superior in most ways to an open sight.

The problem with open sights is that the eye must attempt to focus on three objects in three different planes: the rear sight, the front sight, and the target. No human eye can do this all that well, but younger eyes do it a great deal better than, say, *my* eyes can! With open sights, it's absolutely essential that the front sight be horizontally centered in the rear sight, and that the front sight be nestled in the notch the same way every time.

Everybody shoots open sights slightly differently. I tend to put the bead or the tip of the blade right down in the bottom of the V or U–what you might call a "fine" hold. Others center the bead a bit higher for what is called a "coarse" hold. I then tend to shoot center-of-mass, literally covering the spot I want to hit with the bead or the tip of the blade. It's considered more proper to use a six-o'clock hold so that you can actually see, rather than cover, the spot you want to hit. But there's no right or wrong, just an absolute necessity to personally zero your open sights for the way you want to shoot.

That done, you have the challenge of doing it the same way every time, and attempting to focus clearly on rear sight, front sight, and target. This last is impossible. You must see both rear and front sight in order to get a proper sight picture, so invariably and properly the target should appear somewhat out of focus. Younger eyes being more flexible, it's quite possible up to a certain age (different for each person) to really *see* both rear and front sight sharply and allow the target to fuzz out a bit. But at some point, even this becomes impossible for most shooters, so you must rely on experience and stock fit to center the front sight properly. Then you must focus *only* on the front sight and concentrate on putting it on the right spot on the target. Most shooters start having a lot of trouble with open sights somewhere in their forties.

Aperture, or peep, sights operate on a totally different principle. As I said, these are optical sights. The sights consist of a blade or bead front and an open circle varying in diameter as a rear sight. The eye *naturally* centers the bead or the tip of the blade in the middle of the open circle, so you never need to focus on, or even see, the rear sight. One plane is eliminated; all you have is the front sight and the target to worry about. This makes the aperture sight a great deal faster than an open sight. It's also much more suitable for older eyes, and significantly better in bad light.

Obviously, the scope sight is the simplest of all, at least in terms of focusing your eye. It really operates in just one plane; all the eye has to do is concentrate on the target and superimpose the reticle over the proper aiming point. For this reason, the scope is the fastest of all sights–even in close cover, even on moving targets. And certainly it's the best at longer ranges and in poor light. That said, it's amazing what *can* be done with both open and aperture sights.

We tend to regard iron sights as short-range affairs. For most of us, they are–but that's largely a matter of practice and familiarization, not so much genuine capability. In the pre-scope days, long-range shooting with open sights was the exclusive province of highly skilled and highly proficient marksmen–but it could be done. Hunting books written in the early days of smokeless powder are full of accounts of animals taken at ranges well exceeding 200 yards–ranges that, today, we would consider strictly for shooting with scopes. Today, 1,000-yard matches are still conducted with peep-sighted rifles. That kind of shooting is far beyond my own capabilities, but to this day every American Marine (me included) must qualify annually with his service rifle. Our course of fire includes slow fire at a six-inch bull at 300 meters, and rapid fire at a silhouette at 300 meters. The final string is slow fire, 10 shots, at a silhouette target at 500–all with the military aperture sight. That 300-yard slow fire is tough; the tip of the post sight fully obscures the bull. But it can be done. The rapid fire is easy; and provided the wind is at least reasonably steady, there's simply no problem with the 500-yard line.

Consistent shooting with open sights, however, requires a great deal more practice than is needed with a scope. I've been doing quite a lot of shooting with both apertures and open sights the last few years, and it's different. But with practice, it's amazing what you can do.

To some extent, your range is limited by the size and shape of the front sight. Even at fairly close range, a good-sized front bead will start to obscure large portions of the target. Up to a point, that's okay–your eye will work to center the sight, and it isn't really important that a great deal of the target is obscured. This is especially true if you shoot with both eyes open; subconsciously, your non-shooting eye will see the entire target or animal.

I had a Westley Richards .318 with the turn-of-the-century equivalent of precision long-range sights. The rear sight had folding leaves up to an extremely optimistic 500 yards, and the front sight was an extremely thin blade. I used that sight with no problems on game up to 300 yards. However, the trade-off was clear. That tiny blade didn't subtend much of an animal even past 200 yards, so long-range shooting was possible. But it was much slower to gain a proper sight picture than is the case with a fairly bold front bead.

Given that very few people today will plan to use an open sight much past 100 yards, I would opt for a highly visible gold or ivory bead–but not terribly large–as the best front sight for general use. Open rear sights are largely a matter of personal preference. The fastest is probably the traditional British express sight with a very shallow V. However, this is also one of the least precise, intended primarily for shooting very large game at very close range. I find our traditional buckhorn rear sights not all that bad, but I have trouble getting a consistent sight picture with the common U notch–I have a tendency to seat the front sight a bit high if I'm not careful. To my eye, the best open rear sight is a V with about a 90-degree angle, and I much prefer a platinum, silver, or gold centerline running from the bottom of the V. With a centerline scribed on the sight, it's much faster and easier to make sure the bead is properly centered.

Aperture sights usually come with screw-in apertures, providing different-sized holes. The tinier holes are intended for target work–the smaller the hole, the more precision is possible. Almost every work that mentions aperture sights suggests throwing away the screw-in aperture and just using the large opening that's left. For very fast work on dangerous game, I guess that's okay. But I don't like it. I much prefer to use a proper-sized aperture designed for hunting, with a fairly large hole–but not large as the opening left when the aperture is removed. Since I shoot with both eyes open, I never actually see the aperture or even the sight, but while a very small opening is murder in poor light, I don't like the huge opening that's left when you remove the aperture insert altogether.

I have Lyman receiver sights on my Model 71 Winchester .348 and my Model 94 .30-30, and I used one for years on a Savage 99 in .358. I'm very, very comfortable out to 150 yards or so with this kind of set-up, and I've shot several wild hogs out to 225 yards or so with the Model 71. At that range, the bead starts to subtend most of the front shoulder area, but as long as I did my part all of my shots at that range have been awfully close to where I wanted them.

While a scope is almost always intended to be the primary sight, these days iron sights may be intended as primary or as an alternate in case the scope goes bad. Obviously, great attention must be given to an iron sight that you *know* is going to be used. As I said, I'm pretty much a scope guy, and I can think of very few circumstances where an iron sight would actually be better. One is in a driving rain.

Even with the very best of scope covers, if you're hunting in wind-driven rain it doesn't take many drops of water on either lens to render a scope useless. Iron sights may be more limited in range, but they're much more all-weather than any scope. While aperture sights are much better in rain than any scope, here the nod must go to old-time open sights. Water droplets can collect in the aperture of a peep sight and render it just as useless as a water-spotted scope. Open sights don't have that problem. For this reason, a fair number of hunters in the Pacific Northwest's rainforests stick with open sights and accept their limitations.

Another situation where iron sights are possibly better than scopes is hunting black bear or cougar with hounds. The shot will be very short in any case, but think of the advantage if a bear or cat comes out of the tree and starts mixing with the dogs. The animal must be dispatched very quickly lest he maim prized hounds–but the greatest danger to the hounds at that point is from a misdirected bullet. With open sights, it's a bit easier to keep your peripheral vision on the dogs and find a clear spot to shoot, avoiding the tunnel vision that a scope promotes.

Honestly, I can think of no other situations where a scope isn't superior to open sights, including close-range work. In very close cover where shots are unlikely to exceed 50 yards, and 100 yards is a very long shot, there's no reason not to use iron sights–but even so, a low-powered scope is faster and will be much better at dusk and dawn.

I am somewhat divided in my opinion on iron sights as a backup. On backpack or horseback hunts in true wilderness country, where there's no way to get your hands on a spare rifle, *some* kind of auxiliary sighting equipment makes a whole lot of sense. On backpack sheep and goat hunts,

I've typically carried an extra scope–usually a very light 2½ or 3X compact, already set in rings–in my backpack. Since the chances of really *using* auxiliary sights are fairly remote, iron sights on the rifle probably make even more sense. However, most of my mountain or long-range rifles have plain barrels. Ken Elliott, longtime Publisher of *HUNTING* magazine, has much more definite feelings about this. He simply believes that any hunting rifle should wear iron sights, period–even though he hasn't used iron sights except on African thick-skinned game for at least 30 years!

If iron sights are planned as a backup, the same care should go into preparing them as you put into your scope and mounts. You should insure that they're securely attached, and they should be pre-zeroed, just in case. You must also make absolutely certain that you carry with you the means to take your scope off. That's easy if you have a detachable scope mount, but if you don't you should carry the proper screwdriver or Allen wrench. Your iron sights won't do you much good if you can't get at them.

A possible option, of course, is a "see-through" mount that allows you to use iron sights with the scope in place. In general, I abhor these mounts. They tend to put the scope so high that you must lift your head for a clear field of view, and that both enhances recoil and makes steady shooting much more difficult. However, I must admit that this kind of mount probably makes a lot of sense in very wet country. That way you can dry the scope lens if you have time–and if you don't, the iron sights are right there, ready to use.

Iron sights definitely have their uses, but these days fewer and fewer hunters are relying upon them. Let's turn now to the scopes and scope mounts that have become almost universal among American hunters.

Chapter 27

Scopes and Mounts

I've mentioned several times that the telescopic sight has become America's odds-on choice. I've also said why: Not only is the scope *at least* as reliable as an iron sight; it also enables us to see better, achieve sight alignment faster, and in any context except perhaps a driving rain, shoot better. Just the facts, ma'am, and them's the facts. I doubt if there's much argument out there; in my entire career I've run into just a couple of hunters who where against scope sights. Both were houndsmen. They rarely shot game beyond 10 yards, and their primary concern was safety of their dogs in close quarters. One of them, by the way, was a South African bushpig hunter. He levied three requirements: First, no scope. Second, solid bullets only. Third, I had to keep up. The third requirement proved the most difficult!

So, if the issue isn't whether to choose a scope, the obvious issue is which scope to choose. It's not all that easy a question, but it's not all that difficult, either. Competition is so stiff among scope manufacturers today that there are very few really bad scopes out there. At least, I haven't seen one for a long time. On the other hand–more with optics than any other type of hunting equipment I know of–you do get what you pay for.

In a hunting rifle, a few, or even quite a few, extra dollars may buy you a better finish and a bit better wood. But it might not buy you additional accuracy. This is not the case with optics. Generally speaking, extra dollars *will* buy you more clarity, greater resolution, and increased light-gathering capabilities. It's up to you to decide whether you need these assets.

However, let me give you one caution. Europeans shoot with a different style than Americans do. Typically, Europeans use scopes with very large objective lenses. (In most European countries, hunting is legal as long as you can see to shoot.) This means scopes must be mounted very high. Thus, European riflemen learn to shoot with their heads high–not necessarily in contact with the comb at all. Americans, in contrast, tend to shoot with their heads down and their cheeks mated to the comb. Go grab a rifle and try these two radically different techniques. You should not be able to look through your scope from both positions, but that's okay. Notice that the American head-down position angles the forehead and places it considerably closer to the scope.

Get my drift? Eye relief is more important to Americans than it is to most Europeans. And if you play around with a lot of European scopes you'll notice that eye relief is both critical and minimal. That's the way they're built. The extra dollars the very fine European scopes cost are well worth the money in terms of optics–resolution, clarity, and light-gathering abilities. *But* European scopes are notoriously lacking in eye relief.

This problem generally doesn't manifest itself until you get to rifles with heavy recoil–light .300s, .338s, .375s, etc. But take it from me, a guy with *multiple* scars from scope cuts: eye relief is extremely important to the American style of riflery, and I sure wish the great European scope manufacturers would hurry up and figure that out!

Let's dispense with brand names by saying simply that you get what you pay for. Cheap scopes may or may not be more subject to breakage, but they will not have particularly accurate nor consistent adjustments. Nor will their optics be quite as good. The better you see, the better you shoot. I'd rather have a good scope on an inexpensive rifle than vice versa. But, again, optics have progressed so far these days that there are really very few bad scopes on the market–just some that are better than others.

A much more basic decision is whether to go with a variable or fixed power scope–and in either variety, what power or power range to choose.

When I was a kid, with younger and somewhat better eyes–I would have said that nobody needed anything beyond a fixed 4X scope. There is still merit to this concept. A fixed-power scope is the most goof-proof of scopes, both mechanically and from the shooter-proof point of view. Mechanically, a fixed-power scope has far fewer parts–and fewer moving parts–than a variable. Therefore, there's less to go wrong. From a user standpoint, you can't slip up and leave a fixed-power scope on the wrong setting.

I started out with a John Unertl fixed 4X, a very fine scope. It had simple, medium-weight crosshairs, and it responded well and consistently to adjustments. You really can't ask for more than that! Eventually, like most of us, I moved on to variable scopes. I learned that on longer shots I was altogether more confident–if not necessarily more accurate–with a 2-7X or 3-9X turned up all the way. The danger here, of course, is having too much power when you really don't need it. Almost any guide you talk to can come up with horror stories about clients who missed short-range shots because their scopes were turned up all the way and they saw nothing but hair. This might happen to me someday, but it never has. The obvious answer, and the strength of a variable, is that you can leave it on 4X or 5X–whatever midrange setting you're comfortable with–and bring it up to higher magnification only if you really need the power.

Some years ago, I went through a phase where I got to thinking the variable scopes were an unnecessary crutch, that a good, simple fixed-power scope might really be the way to go. At this time I have three hunting rifles with fixed powers: A .338 with a fixed 4X, and a .280 and a 7mm Remington Magnum with fixed 6X's. I've done a great deal of hunting with all three rifles, including some fairly long shots with all three, and I can't say that I've ever really needed more power.

On the other hand, most of my hunting rifles do wear variables. My close-cover and dangerous-game rifles, if scoped, wear low-range variables like 1½-6X or 1¾-5X. In general, I leave these scopes set at 4X, and I could probably get by with a fixed 4X across the board. But on a .375 or .416–or, for that matter, my .35 Whelen that might be used on a black bear or wild boar in close cover–it's comforting to know I can turn the scope down to 2X or so for bayonet range.

Like most Americans, the majority of my variables on general-purpose hunting rifles are 3-9X or 3.5-10X. I do own one 2-7X, but it's not mounted on a rifle right now. I don't see that the 2-7X scope has any real advantage over a fixed 6X, unless you really feel you might want to turn the power down all the way in the kind of country you hunt. For long-range work, though, a power of 9X or 10X really builds confidence.

If a little is good, then a lot must be better, right? These days the current trend seems to be toward more and more power in hunting variables. The first time I ever saw one of these big variables was back in 1979 or thereabouts. A buddy of mine, Tim Jones, carried a .270 with, as I recall, a 6-18X scope on a Wyoming antelope hunt that year. A scope that big was a real oddity back then, but these days you see them with some frequency.

I must admit that until quite recently I have had absolutely no use for such a scope. I didn't think all that power was needed, and I actually thought there was something a bit sissy about all that magnification. So of course I had never tried hunting with a scope bigger than a 3.5-10X.

That I finally did was quite an accident. I hunted Sitka blacktails on Kodiak Island late in the season, when the cover was beaten down and the slopes were wide open. I had made a big mistake in choosing a .35 Whelen for the hunt. While it was no problem getting close enough to shoot some kind of buck, there were so many deer that it was often impossible to make a close approach on a big buck–just too many other deer in the way. (What a problem to have!)

My hunting partner, Jake Jacobsen, had a .300 Winchester Magnum that wore a 6-18X scope. The first time I borrowed it was on a very fine 3X4 buck bedded on the far side of a little valley, with other deer all around him at varying distances. Jake and I marked a little knoll from afar and crept up the back side. The buck hadn't moved, but he was a bit over 300 yards away and that was as close as we were going to get. Perhaps I could have done that with my .35, but I didn't like the odds. So I borrowed Jake's .300, made a rest with a packframe, and turned the scope up. Even in that cold air there was too much mirage at 18X–but at 14X that buck looked wonderfully huge and the shot went exactly where I'd called it.

A couple of days later, we jumped a truly huge buck (as Sitka bucks go). I missed him running with my .35 Whelen, and a couple of hours later we finally relocated him up on a ridge, with nothing but bare ground between him and us. I think the range was 375 yards, certainly not less, probably not more. He was with a doe, and while we were closing in to that 375-yard range he bedded down. For long, long minutes–probably a half-hour or more–all we could see was the tips of his antlers.

I was lying down on a little grassy ridge, very comfortable, with the rifle again resting over my pack. It was as steady as a benchrest, and again I had the rifle on 14X. When the buck stood up he was facing us, not much of a shot at that range. And yet, with that big scope it was ridiculously easy. I aimed at his throat patch, putting the crosshairs a bit to the right because of the stiff crosswind, and a bit high for the distance. The bullet hit in the center of his throat patch, and he went down so fast I had to ask Jake what had happened. I had no idea. I'm not a record-book nut, but that buck scored very high by Boone and Crockett standards, and is the only deer I've ever taken that makes the book. So, arguably, I guess you could say that's the best deer I've ever shot. The experience gave me a whole new outlook on these high-range variables.

For most hunting purposes, I don't think there's a real need for extremely high power. The risk is that it might entice you to make shots longer than you should, and in any case mirage will often render power much above 15X or so useless. Still, in very open country there's a place for a 6-18X scope. Perhaps better are the newer scopes with slightly less power. Some time back we started seeing 4-12X scopes, and that's a good range. Leupold has a new 4.5-14X scope that they tell me is selling like gangbusters, and I think that's probably ideal for a high-range hunting scope. I can't imagine really needing more than 14X, and this particular scope is a great deal less bulky than the 6-18X class. To tell you the truth, I have one. It's sitting in my bookcase right now, and I plan to mount it on that BOSS-equipped Browning .300 Winchester Magnum I have on order. It should make the ultimate long-range rig! I also have a Nikon 4-12X on a .25-06, my idea of the ultimate pronghorn rifle.

Another current fad is toward scopes that enhance light-gathering potential. Now, any scope beats the heck out of any iron sight in this department, but some scopes are better than others. There are really just two ways to increase light transmission through optics. The first–and to my mind the best–is through sheer quality: quality of optics and quality of lens coatings. The second is by increasing the size of the objective lens. Note, however, that increasing the objective lens won't do much for you if the optics and lens coatings are done on the cheap!

Europeans are big on large objectives. For instance, an 8X56mm scope–usually with the larger 30mm tube–is extremely popular in Europe. There's a very good reason for this, namely that European hunting generally doesn't recognize shooting hours as such. Artificial lights aren't used, but Europeans stay on stand and continue to hunt–legally–long after American hunters have pulled the plug and gone home. I've shot red stag, wild boar, and roebuck over there when it was really full dark, and every bit of light the scope could suck in made a big difference. In all cases I was using typical American-style scopes with normal objective bells, and all those shots were exceedingly difficult.

Americans, though, don't shoot at night. In most states we have a legal cutoff, such as 30 minutes after sunset, and a starting point, such as 30 minutes before sunrise. Under our circumstances, there's really little need for scopes truly designed as "night scopes." Further, I find that the big objectives have a real downside: they must be mounted extremely high so the objective lens can clear the barrel. Generally this means that either you must have an abnormally high comb on your rifle or you must lift your head off the stock to see through the scope. As I mentioned, many Europeans actually shoot this way–head high, cheek loosely mated to stock if at all. Americans tend to learn to shoot with their heads down, cheek firmly planted on the stock. Neither system is right or wrong, but if you really want–or think you need–a scope with a big objective, be prepared to learn a whole new way of shooting!

On the other hand, a lot of field shooting is done in the first and last hours of the day. There's certainly nothing wrong with selecting scopes that gather lots of light, and if you hunt in heavy cover where shadows come early, there's a lot to be said for choosing scopes on that basis.

A scope with a big objective can be the answer, but it isn't really necessary to go that far for most of our purposes. Until recently, it was almost impossible to get mounts for scopes with the larger 30mm European tubes. Nowadays almost every manufacturer offers 30mm mounts. Keep in mind that the larger 30mm tube transmits more light than our standard one-inch (about 25mm) tube. Also keep in mind that the compact 1¾-5X variables–scopes that I like very much–tend to have straight one-inch objective lenses. Although compact and handy, such scopes are actually fairly poor in light transmission. They will not be nearly as good as, say, a straight 4X with a "standard" 36mm objective. A good compromise for a low-range variable that still gathers plenty of light would be, for example, Leupold's 1.75-6X scope with 32mm objective.

A number of American scope lines now offer a 50mm objective. They're great for gathering light, but I still find them a bit too big–again, higher mounts must generally be used, and I feel the big bell ruins the lines of a nice sporting rifle. A better compromise would be the fairly common 40 to 44mm objectives. Given a good-quality scope, I feel that's big enough to gather all the light you need–and you can usually use, if not low, at least medium-height mounts.

I am often asked whether the significantly more expensive European scopes are really worth the extra freight. That's kind of up to you. German and Austrian scopes are very, very good. The optics tend to be superb, but the one area where I feel these scopes (Zeiss, Swarovski, Schmidt & Bender, etc.) really excel is in the precision of their adjustments. Very few American scopes can really be relied upon to deliver consistent adjustments, i.e., moving the strike of the bullet ¼-inch at 100 yards if that's what the scope is supposed to deliver. In general (though not always), European scopes are better at this. However, European scopes tend to offer much less eye relief than American scopes. This is significant on rifles with stout recoil, and many otherwise superb European scopes lack enough eye relief for use on powerful rifles.

Scopes have become much more expensive in recent years, with many domestic firms now offering top-of-line scopes that rival the best European imports in price. Worth it? Probably, depending on the kind of shooting you do, and how much shooting you do. The best course, given today's prices, is to spend some time at a shop that offers several different brands of scopes and actually make some comparisons. Under those circumstances, you may not be able to really *see* subtle differences in quality of optics, but you can at least see what you like, and you can compare eye reliefs.

For me, choice of reticle is an open-and-shut case. I *much* prefer the plex-type reticle (thick wires stepping down to thinner wires in the center) over any other. A dot reticle is very fast to use, especially on running game, and there's really nothing wrong with a standard medium-weight crosshair–but I find the plex-type very fast, easy to see in any type of light, and there's no confusion. The post-and-crosshair, for instance, confuses my eye terribly about exactly where to place the tip of the post.

I do not like rangefinders within scopes, be they extra stadia wires or whatever. I know some very skilled marksmen who make them work–but I truly abhor these devices. I find them just one more thing to worry about and take my mind off what I should be thinking about, namely proper placement of crosshairs on the target and trigger squeeze. But if you like them, be my guest. Just do this one thing: If you're going to use them, practice extensively so you know exactly how to use them.

The plex-type crosshair can itself be used as a rangefinder, of course. It's a simple matter of figuring out at what distance and what power a game animal, backline to belly line, will be bracketed between the thick portions of the vertical reticle. No, I don't do that, either. Probably should. But I use a number of different makes and powers of scopes on several different rifles, and that's another piece of confusion I don't need. I either judge distance by eye or carry a rangefinder, and all I really expect the scope to do is help me see the target better and place the shot accurately. Over the years, that system has worked well for me, but whatever system you choose, practice with it and use it consistently.

Scope mounts are another area that I feel holds little mystery. If there's a scope-mounting system out there that doesn't work, I'm simply not aware of it! On most of my rifles, I use some variation of the old Redfield system with a rotating post up front and two big screws in the rear. This type of mount is manufactured by Redfield, Leupold, Millett, and others, and it's been adequately strong for many years. I also like and use the Conetrol system–also very strong, and somewhat more streamlined. For sheer "stout," though ugly and bulky, you really can't beat the old Weaver system. Tasco's Australian-designed stud mount is also excellent. So long as you follow the directions in mounting and use a bit of Loc-Tite, none of the common mounting systems should give you any trouble–at least at normal recoil levels.

When you start talking very powerful cartridges, with recoil levels above 75 foot/pounds or so–or the specialty pistols chambered for rifle cartridges–you're into a whole different realm. Weatherby has long used and recommended Buehler mounts for extra toughness on their heavy-recoiling calibers; and for hand cannons like the .375 JDJ, the maker–SSK Industries–recommends their mount with *three* rings versus the customary two.

Detachable mounts were in vogue years ago when scopes were distrusted by the relatively few shooters who used them. By the time I started shooting, however, scopes had become both extremely reliable and relied upon, and detachable mounts were very expensive and very rare.

Now we've come full circle. While scopes can be, should be, and generally are, trusted completely, detachable mounts are "in" again, and there are a great many varieties on the market. While under no circumstances do I believe in willy-nilly taking scopes off and putting them back on, there are several scenarios that make detachable mounts attractive–especially as inexpensive and dependable as they are today.

One is on rifles that have iron sights intended as auxiliary equipment. A detachable mount that can be removed via levers or a coin-operated slot makes a whole lot more sense than having to carry Allen wrenches or screwdrivers! Another option with detachable mounts is to have two scopes set in rings, the extra one also pre-zeroed. Then if you have any trouble at all, it's a snap to take one scope off and pop the other one on.

Among the numerous systems, I've had good luck with Leupold's new detachable mount, and also with the Warne mount. On my "pet" .375, a badly beat-up pre-'64 Model 70 converted to left-hand bolt, I have Dave Talley's really superb detachable mount. On this rifle, which I often take to Africa as my one and only rifle, I have good iron sights properly zeroed. In place on the rifle I have a Leupold 1¾-5X scope in Talley rings. And as yet another backup I have an old Leupold 3X, also zeroed, also set in Talley rings.

A simple and very inexpensive solution is Pilkington's lever, which converts a Redfield-type base to detachable by replacing one of the rear windage screws with a lever. I have a Pilkington lever on several rifles up to .416 Rigby in caliber, and so far none has failed to be repeatable. However, you cannot take the Pilkington lever on and off at will, since eventually you'll cause wear and thereby play in the front pillar. It's a good backup system, but once in place should be left alone.

The best detachable mounts in the world are almost certainly the European claw mounts, but they're extremely expensive. Other European mounts, like the Bock and EAW, are also very good up to medium calibers. However, I've had extremely good luck with American systems. The thing to keep in mind is that *any* detachable mount, including a claw, will develop play if you attach and detach it often enough. The best course is to leave the mounts alone unless you really need to take the scope off. If you do that, you can expect any of the good systems to be fairly repeatable throughout your hunting career.

Chapter 28

Custom Rifles: Are They Worth It?

Today's factory rifles are extremely good. They generally function well, and they shoot straighter than factory rifles ever have. They're also available in a bewildering array of calibers and options. Upgraded wood? The factories have it. Synthetic stocks? No problem. Today's factory rifles are no longer just plain vanilla ice cream. In today's world of "niche marketing" and digitally controlled computerized machining that enables even the majors to profit from limited production runs, you can get darn near anything you want right over the counter. On the other hand, a full-out custom rifle may cost 10 to 20 times as much as a very comparable factory rifle. And you might wait a year or more to take delivery. Is all that cost and hassle really worth it?

That kinda depends on you. A custom rifle is, or should be, a personal statement. It will reflect its maker's tastes and prejudices–but it should also reflect yours. A custom rifle doesn't have to be fancy. It doesn't even have to be beautiful–but it should fit *you* and suit *your* tastes better than anything you can get over the counter. And by doing so, it should give you that added confidence that can really make a difference when the chips are down.

Let's examine what a custom rifle really is–and what it is not. And let me first say that, in the context of seeking out a gunmaker whose tastes match mine, then conferring and deciding on caliber, action, barrel, stock blank, configuration, sighting equipment, and so forth, I have *never* owned a custom rifle–although I own some that have been custom-made.

Over the years I have owned many rifles that have been restocked. I mentioned earlier that the owner of the Bishop gunstock company was a family friend, and they built six or eight stocks for me. Some of these were true custom stocks, even to the point where I selected the blank itself as well as the final appearance. More recently, I've gone in the other direction several times; rather than replacing a factory stock with better wood cut to fit me, I've replaced some pretty nice walnut stocks with synthetics.

The stock is a significant and important part of any custom rifle. It could be fine wood, or these days it could be synthetic, but getting a handle that fits you perfectly is a huge step in the right direction. However, I honestly don't consider a standard action that's simply been stocked or restocked as a true custom rifle. A rifle so restocked has a most functional and possibly valuable custom feature, but it ain't quite a custom rifle. In the same vein, you can acquire a Mauser 98 or Springfield action, modify the bolt handle and safety, throw a stock on it, and call it a custom rifle–but it really isn't.

It's just been made into a functional sporter, that's all. (And that may be quite enough, depending on your tastes and needs.)

Today there's a growing class of semi-production (or semi-custom) rifles coming from small manufacturers. A classic example of this is the Dakota rifle; another is the big, beefy magnums from A-Square. These rifles are made to a certain style, and you can't really alter the style. But you can have a bewildering array of options, from upgraded wood to different checkering patterns to sighting equipment to a choice of virtually any caliber you can imagine. Such rifles generally cost three to five times what a "normal" factory rifle might cost–but about half the cost of a true custom rifle.

I have a .270 from Dakota and a .375 Weatherby Magnum from A-Square. The two rifles couldn't possibly be more different in styling, but both are very fine rifles that do their intended work well. I like both of them, and while neither of them is a genuine custom rifle, both offered a great deal of gun for the money.

All the major manufacturers have custom shops, with Remington's being perhaps the most active. Upgraded wood, different finishes, non-standard calibers, and much more can be done by the factory custom shops–and it's generally very good work at a very fair price. But although they're called so, custom-shop rifles are not quite full-out custom jobs. A Remington Model 700 from the Custom Shop will be gorgeous, but it's still going to be a Model 700 with Model 700 styling. I have a truly wonderful .30-06 out of the Custom Shop, and I love it dearly–it's one of my very best rifles–but it's still not quite a custom rifle in the strictest sense.

To me, a true custom rifle has all of the things I've alluded to, and more. In the purest sense, a custom rifle is a rifle built for you and you alone. Now, that means shopping for a maker before you even consider actually commissioning the rifle. We're fortunate to have a very considerable community of topflight custom riflemakers in both the U.S. and Canada. In fact, American gunmakers are building some of the world's finest rifles right now.

These guys are artists, and they express their art in their own way. You, as a customer, must have some pretty good idea what you're looking for in a rifle or you wouldn't be considering the custom route. But in this particular business, the customer isn't always right. If your idea of a perfect custom rifle incorporates a good piece of French walnut, then regardless of how good he is, you don't want to go to a maker who specializes in super-accurate synthetic-stocked rigs. If you want a rifle built on a Mauser action, you don't want to go to a maker who prefers to use only Model 70 actions. So your shopping must take into consideration not only how good the maker is–and of course whether his price is in your budget–but also whether your taste somehow parallels his.

Then you can start the fun business of deciding on caliber; barrel length, and contour; action; stock material, style, and dimension; and whatever else your heart might desire. And of course, you'll need to be measured so the stock is absolutely perfect for you.

As I said, I've never done this. I do have a couple of custom rifles, but they were built for other people and I picked them up second-hand. Still very nice rifles, but not really custom-made to my tastes. One of them is a gorgeous David Miller 7mm Remington Magnum, one of the relatively few left-hand rifles built by Miller. The stock is a piece of French walnut to die for. The action started life as a Remington Model 700, but from there Miller takes over, and it bears little resemblance to a stock action. Metal finishing is perfect, and of course it has Miller's characteristic scope mount milled to fit both rifle and scope from a piece of solid bar stock.

It's really a perfect rifle, and I'm fortunate that it fits me extremely well. But it was clearly made for someone else, and whoever he was, he had some odd ideas. He asked Miller to build it light and trim, and it is. But in doing so, at the customer's direction, the receiver was made so trim that it has a two-shot magazine capacity. I don't like that. And the two-shot magazine is blind. I don't like that, either; I prefer floorplates. And although the 7mm Remington Magnum is a fine caliber, if it were done for me I'd have ordered a .280 or .30-06. So although it's a wonderful rifle, and it was undoubtedly perfect for its original owner, it isn't perfect for me. So, in my very narrow definition, even this obviously custom rifle really isn't my custom rifle.

Probably because of my upbringing around good walnut, I tend to think beautiful wood when I think custom rifle. These days, that ain't necessarily the way it is. Some of our top rifle craftsmen today specialize in synthetic stocks, and what they do certainly qualifies as custom. Kenny Jarrett and his "beanfield rifles" have become legendary for their accuracy, and well they should be. Another up-and-comer is Mark Bansner. I've got a wonderful synthetic-stocked 7x57 that he put together for me. Nothing fancy, but boy, does it shoot. Since Mark and I worked out the specifications together–and the result is exactly what I'd hoped–that Bansner rifle actually comes much closer to being a custom rifle–for me–than even my Miller gun!

But whether either my Miller or Bansner rifle quite qualifies as a custom job by my standards, they're both great rifles, and so are the rifles made by many other fine craftsmen: D'Arcy Echols, Jerry Fisher, Joe Balickie, Al and Roger Biesen, and certainly dozens of other great craftsmen. And, for that matter, the rifles turned out by USRAC's and Remington's custom shops are wonderful rifles, and so are the Dakotas, A-Squares, McMillans, Clifton Arms, and so many other custom and semi-custom rifles being made all across the country.

Deciding who is the best custom maker in America is impossible. It's very much a matter of taste, sort of like trying to figure out whether Da Vinci or Van Gogh was the better artist. Tucson-based David Miller, a hunting buddy of mine, is certainly one of the best and, though price doesn't necessarily reflect quality, commands the highest figure I'm aware of for his work. I called David out of the blue and asked him what, in his opinion, made a custom rifle special.

"The rifle is fitted to you," he said without hesitation. "Balance is everything. There are no great secrets, really. The length of pull has to be right. Too long is a sin, too short not quite as bad, but just right is the goal. And we try to get the scope as low as possible, which we can control because of the mount we make. The goal is to make the gun feel alive in your hands.

"You know, if you're a carpenter you might have half a dozen hammers and several screwdrivers, but you'll keep coming back to just one of them because it somehow feels better in your hand. That's the goal in building a rifle. We want our customer to use it because it feels special to him.

"Some of our customers think our rifles make them better shots. Of course we can't impart shooting skill through our rifles–but there's some truth in this. I think we can sometimes take a hunter beyond his abilities through confidence in his rifle. I have a .300 magnum that I built for myself, and last year I fired three shots at game, all three one-shot kills. All were very long shots; the average for the three was 500 yards. I'm not really that good, but that rifle seems to take on a life of its own, and with it in my hands I know I can do it. That's what we hope to do for our customers."

Is a custom rifle worth it? Yes, if it shoots well, feels good, and you really believe in it, it probably is. When it comes time to make a difficult shot–not a marginal "hail Mary" that shouldn't be taken, but a possible and legitimate shooting opportunity that happens to be very difficult–there's simply no measuring the value of that confidence factor.

My own David Miller rifle, though it wasn't made for me, does indeed fit me the way Miller himself would want it to. And it gives me that kind of confidence. I've made a lot of easy shots with it, and I've blown a shot or two as well with it. But I have definitely made some of the most difficult shots of my career with that rifle, both on running game and several very long shots.

The problem with that rifle is that, at least on my budget, it's really too nice and too pretty to take into rough country where I probably most need the confidence it gives me. I simply haven't solved that dilemma yet, but undoubtedly the answer lies in the synthetic-stocked custom rifles now being made. I know that I have promised myself I will never again take a beautiful piece of walnut into rough country, but I almost certainly lied to myself. Just three days ago I received in the mail a Montana sheep permit, a permit I've been trying to draw for 20 years now. A sheep hunt is no place for a rifle I can't afford to replace–but there's a darn good chance that Miller rifle will get some new scratches this September.

Mine is not an uncommon dilemma. Many of us have come to own "lookin'" rifles and "usin'" rifles, the former in walnut and the latter in synthetic. That's okay, but I'm not a collector. I'm a hunter, and I really don't wish to own rifles that I won't hunt with. And since my idea of a perfect rifle is a hunting rifle that shoots straight, is well-balanced, and handles fast and sure, such a rifle really should be used, not just looked at.

As Miller himself said, balance is everything, but regardless of my definition of a custom rifle, it's *your* definition that should be important to you. If all that's required to make your rifle perfect is a little stockwork or a replacement stock, you're fortunate. If one of the semi-custom rigs in either walnut or synthetic suits your taste and gives you extra confidence, that's great, too. Or you can take the plunge and have a full-out custom job built to your specifications. Chances are you'll like the results. But if you go to that kind of trouble, I hope you plan on using the rifle afield, not leaving it locked in your gunsafe. It's a shame to waste all the talent that went into building a hunting rifle that's perfect just for you.

Part III

Guns for Game

Chapter 29

Handguns for Big Game

Handgunning for big game is not yet a huge part of American hunting. The numbers of handgun hunters are growing rapidly, however, and one thing's for certain about dedicated handgun hunters: they're an extremely avid and serious bunch!

In North America, we do have one problem with handgun hunting that just won't go away. Actually, two problems: It's not legal to take handguns into Mexico or Canada, and residents there are faced with serious difficulties in just owning handguns, let alone hunting with them. So, with apologies, handgun hunting is pretty much restricted to the U.S. alone. The good news is that handgun hunting is legal almost across the United States within rifle season, and a very few areas even have special handgun seasons, such as Arizona's "HAM" (Handgun, Archery, Muzzleloader) permits for javelina.

As we discussed under cartridges for handgun hunting, there are really two forms of handgun hunting and two types of firearms. The first variety is hunting with traditional pistols and revolvers, mostly revolvers, chambered for "handgun cartridges." Both semiautomatic pistols and revolvers may be scoped, albeit sometimes with difficulty, but the nature of the cartridges themselves makes this a short-range sport. The other venue involves the so-called "specialty pistols"–generally single-shot, though these days there are bolt action repeaters–chambered for powerful, high-intensity cartridges that give these handguns both power and reach.

Let's deal with the more traditional handguns first. Although there are a great many very fine semiautomatics and revolvers–in fact, virtually any handgun capable of reasonable accuracy–that provide good sport on small game and varmints, there are really very few handguns in either action type suitable for big game.

By law in most states, the .357 Magnum is the minimum handgun cartridge allowed for deer hunting. It can do the job, given short range and a very cool marksman, but it really isn't sufficient. For my money, the minimum serious hunting caliber is .41 Magnum. Better is the .44 Magnum, and better still is the .454 Casull. There are no other common choices, but there are some uncommon choices like the .475 Wildey Magnum in the Wildey; the .50 AE in the Desert Eagle and LAR Grizzly semiauto; and the .445 Supermag in the Wesson double-action.

There are just a handful of large-caliber double-action revolvers to choose from. They include the Colt Anaconda; the large-frame Smith & Wessons in several configurations, blued or stainless; the Llama Super

Comanche; Ruger's Redhawk; the interchangeable-barrel Wesson; and the long-awaited Taurus Model 44. I've shot most of these over the years, and all are good handguns. All can be scoped, if desired, but I've personally never been too excited about scopes on revolvers. For the hunting I do with a revolver, I much prefer to rely on open sights and get in close–it just seems to add to the game.

Over the years, my own favorite big revolver has been the Smith & Wesson Model 29. Quite a while back, I had an 8⅜-inch version. That's really too long a barrel for a guy my size, but it grouped like a target pistol. I made some really spectacular shots with it, including a paced 90-yard *offhand* shot on a javelina. My current Model 29 is the Classic Hunter six-inch model with underbarrel lug. It shoots even better, and I expect we're going to be friends for a long time.

While the 29 is my favorite, I have passing experience with all of the big double-actions. I took one of the very first Llama Super Comanche .44s to Rhodesia in the late '70s and shot quite a lot of game with it. In those days in that country, you carried a firearm everywhere you went, and the Rhodesians were extremely impressed by that huge revolver!

The selection of single-actions is a bit smaller. Ruger offers both .41 and .44 Magnums, and has the Super Blackhawk Hunter complete with scope rings and integral mounts. Then there's the wonderful Freedom Arms Casull. Made like a Swiss watch, this superb revolver is able to handle the pressures of the .454 Casull primarily because it's so well made.

Now, for me, there's nothing I really want to shoot with a revolver that I can't handle with a .44 Magnum. Deer, black bear, wild hogs, javelina–so long as you keep the range short and the shots careful, you've got no problem. But, as we saw in Chapter 16, the .454 Casull is a whole lot more gun–and the Casull revolvers are extremely accurate and dependable. If you're serious about hunting elk-sized game with a revolver, the Casull is one of the better options.

Or, if you really like punishment, consider the Century Model 100 for cartridges like .45-70, .50-70, .30-30, or .444 Marlin! I shot one of these in .45-70 years ago, and they're truly awesome–but too much of a handful for me! This is obviously a semi-custom, special-order sort of a thing, but it is the world's ultimate revolver.

In semiauto pistols, the choice narrows even more. There are the Desert Eagle, the LAR Grizzly, and the on-again, off-again Wildey–and that's about it. All three are real handfuls, but they do make extremely efficient and adequately powerful hunting handguns. Unlike the revolvers, semiautos are fairly difficult to scope, except perhaps the side-ejection Wildey.

The approach in hunting handguns is the special-purpose pistols. Most of these are single-shots, although both the McMillan and XP-100 are now available in bolt-action repeater versions.

Remington really started this ball rolling with their initial .221 Fireball XP-100. The Fireball itself is no longer offered and is just about obsolete, but the XP-100 has become a classic hunting handgun in a variety of much more powerful chamberings. Other bolt-action pistols include the McMillan Signature Jr., Ultra Light Arms' Model 20 REB, and the Wichita. Bolt-action pistols like these can be had in varmint chamberings such as .223, long-range performers like 7mm Benchrest and 7mm-08, and ultra-powerful (for handguns) cartridges like .308 and .35 Remington.

The bolt-action pistols are as easy to scope as a rifle, and in fact they're really much more akin to short rifles than to revolvers. The disadvantages, from a hunter's standpoint, are that these big pistols are hard to hold steady and handgun scopes tend to have exceedingly critical eye relief. It is almost essential that they be shot from a dead-steady rest–and the more magnification in the scope, the more critical this is. For the same reason, shooting at moving animals becomes next to impossible.

The handgun hunter's best-kept secret, though, is that in spite of these limitations today's bolt-action pistols are incredibly accurate. There's something about that short, stiff barrel that delivers awesome accuracy–on average, better than you can expect from any normal rifle. It's this wonderful accuracy that so enthralled Bob Milek–and many others who have fallen under the spell of the XP and its kin.

Since the barrel is short (by law, less than 16 inches) significant velocity is lost, compared to what the same cartridges can do in a rifle. This limits range somewhat, but with a decent scope and plenty of practice it's absolutely practical to shoot game out to 250 yards with this type of pistol.

I have a wonderful XP-100 in .223 that Rod Herrett stocked for me, and it's rapidly becoming my favorite prairie-dog gun. I've also shot several javelina with an XP-100 in 6mm Benchrest, a very efficient little cartridge. I must admit that I have had relatively little personal interest in hunting big game with this type of firearm–it just isn't my thing. I did shoot a very nice pronghorn last year with an XP-100 in 7mm-08 Remington, but after a long stalk the shot came at about 40 yards, so I wouldn't call that much of a test of what scoped bolt-action pistols are capable of!

An odd quirk to the bolt-action is that, on a pistol, it works backwards. Think about the placement of a right-handed bolt. On the right side, of course. Now, when that right-handed bolt is on a handgun and you shoot using a two-handed hold, you may not release the pistol with your shooting hand to work the bolt. You must reach over with your left hand to work it. Since I'm left-handed, my right-hand action XP is just perfect. I hold the pistol in my left hand, and after firing, my *right* hand is free to work the bolt! Recognizing this, McMillan, Ultra Light, and Wichita all use left-hand actions for their right-handed bolt-action pistols.

Bolt-actions are not the entire spectrum of specialty pistols. In fact, they're not even the most popular. Those honors must go to the Thompson/Center

Contender, far and away the most popular and most versatile of all the specialty guns. The Contender system is a break-open action with interchangeable barrels. It is not quite as strong as the bolt-actions and will not harness a full-house .308 Winchester or similar cartridge. But it is offered in a huge array of excellent hunting calibers, and there are aftermarket barrels in wildcat calibers up to the .375 JDJ and beyond, all the way up to .45-70.

The T/C is generally not as accurate as the bolt-actions, but it's certainly accurate enough for any field shooting, except perhaps serious long-range work. And the interchangeable barrels make the T/C uniquely versatile.

Over the years, I've played with them in a wide variety of chamberings from .22 Long Rifle to .45-70. My favorite hunting caliber in the T/C–and I think Bob Milek's as well–is the .35 Remington. In a handgun it's a very fine mix of power and acceptable recoil, and while it doesn't have a great deal of reach, with handloaded spitzers it will certainly handle shots well beyond the 150-yard line.

T/C barrels can be had either plain or with iron sights, and there are plenty of good scope mounts, including T/C's own mount. Keep in mind that the sights are part of the barrel, so if you want multiple barrels with scopes on them, the only sensible answer is to have a scope mounted on each barrel. The Thompson/Center sort of bridges the gap between the bolt-action pistols, which are clearly long-range rigs, and revolvers and semiautos, which are clearly short-range rigs. The T/C is both. I've used them with iron sights for stalking wild hogs and hunting black bear and cougar behind hounds; and I've used them with scope sights for both varmint and big-game hunting. With aftermarket barrels, the Thompson/Center has been used to take the largest game in the world, up to and including elephant. I don't personally think any handgun is a suitable choice for such game, nor, for that matter, for grizzly or brown bear. But if I had to attempt it, I'd take a T/C in .375 JDJ over any revolver ever made.

Handgun hunting is growing quickly, and I seriously doubt that either our handguns or their loads have yet reached their potential. New powders will close the velocity gap, and there will be more and better bullets, even more wildcats to choose from–and quite possibly new actions and certainly even better scopes. It's going to be interesting to watch over the next few years!

Chapter 30
The Big-Game Shotgun

We talked about shotgun slugs in some detail in Chapter 18. Although a couple of months have passed since I wrote that, I have not yet had any great internal awakening with regard to the use of shotguns on big game: Given a choice, I'll take a centerfire rifle every single time.

It's a fact, however, that millions of deer hunters don't have a choice. At least, they don't have the option of choosing a centerfire rifle. Often they *can* choose between archery gear, black-powder rifles, or shotguns. There was a time, and it wasn't very long ago, that under such circumstances the black-powder hunter's deep, dark secret was that he was actually *better armed* than his shotgun-toting buddies. Yep, that's a fact.

Many standard shotguns, and even a fair number of open-bored, rifle-sighted "slug guns," when loaded with traditional Foster slugs that rattle down the barrel, are a lot more dangerous to nearby trees than they are to deer when the range is a solid 100 yards or more. Black-powder hunters armed with a good-quality muzzleloader, shooting good conical bullets and carefully weighed charges, should have absolutely no problem with 125-yard shots. And, with practice and good range estimation, significantly longer shots are not beyond practicality. With selected and worked-up loads, today's muzzleloaders will actually provide the groups needed for shooting at fairly long range. Shotguns loaded with Foster slugs generally will not. To some extent, this "window of opportunity" helped sell a whole lot of muzzleloaders to Eastern deer hunters!

Even today, I'm not prepared to say that there's a slug gun made that will shoot tighter groups–or shoot as flat–as a good modern muzzleloader. But my, how the gap has narrowed! And there are a couple of things a good slug gun can do that no muzzleloader can, namely offer rapid repeat shots if needed *and* function with complete reliability regardless how foul the weather.

As mentioned earlier, both slugs and slug guns have been improved marvelously in the last decade or so. The traditional "slug gun"–called by some manufacturers a "Buck Special" or "Deer Special"–was really just equipped with a short, open-choked barrel fitted with rifle sights. It was a whole lot better than trying to sight down a ribbed or plain barrel, but the potential accuracy with slugs was really not much better than your standard quail or pheasant gun could offer.

Today, numerous major manufacturers offer "slug specials" that are indeed special compared with yesteryear's offerings. I believe the honors should go to Mossberg for being the first major manufacturer to offer a slug gun with a fully rifled barrel, theirs on their slide-action Model 500 Trophy Slugster. This gun also offers integral scope mount and optional "dual comb" stock, which, by means of clever comb inserts, can raise the comb for scope use.

Remington has followed suit with both rifled barrels *and* rifled choke tubes, and they also have an integral cantilever scope mount for both their 870 pump and 11-87 semiauto slug guns. Marlin has also introduced a short-barreled, bolt-action, fully rifled slug gun that is really super.

I have one of Remington's Special Purpose Deer Guns of the latest generation: black synthetic stock, Parkerized finish, cantilever scope mount, and, on my gun, interchangeable chokes with a rifled choke tube. In all honesty, I was experimenting with buckshot, so I needed an unrifled barrel for that work. The rifled choke tube was just an added attraction. With the rifled choke tube in place, I am actually getting pretty acceptable 100-yard accuracy: groups of about four to five inches with sabot slugs.

That isn't bad, but a fully rifled barrel will do *much* better. Remington expects–and delivers–2½-inch groups at 100 yards from their fully rifled barrels using their own Copper Solid slugs. With good ammo matched to the barrel (just like you seek out the best loads for your centerfire rifle), that level of accuracy should be quite possible with almost any rifled barrel.

The major manufacturers should be applauded for giving us the kind of slug guns we now have. Indeed, they have taken the slug gun to a whole new level of efficiency, and have made it at least a viable 100-yard gun–if not 125 or a bit more.

However, as is often the case with American gunmaking, the majors are just parroting what enterprising custom makers have been doing for years. Rifled shotgun barrels from Hastings and E.R. Shaw led the way, and now, finally, major manufacturers have followed with inexpensive and truly effective slug guns.

A very few custom makers are still doing a pretty brisk business in super-accurate, top-of-line slug guns. Alaskan outfitter Jim Keeline, with whom I hunted this past spring, had one of Randy Fritz's brand-new Tar-Hunt RSG-12 slug guns in camp this year. This was a shotgun unlike anything I've ever seen, and very possibly represents the wave of the future for those demanding the ultimate in slug performance.

This Tar-Hunt 12-gauge rifle used a detachable magazine on a custom bolt-action. The bolt was a massive piece of steel locking with two opposing lugs. The stock was McMillan synthetic, the barrel E.R. Shaw with integral muzzle brake. There were no iron sights–this "shotgun" wore a Zeiss low-range variable scope. Its groups were just one big ragged hole at 100 yards, well under two inches center to center. I had a burning desire to shoot a black bear with it, but when we found the bear I wanted, we couldn't get to a range I was comfortable with. So I chickened out and used my .375. That shot was at about 225 yards–just too far for a slug gun under any circumstances. But if we could have closed to anything under 150 yards, I'd have tried it with absolute confidence.

The Tar-Hunt isn't the only custom slug gun around. Pennsylvania gunsmith Mark Bansner, he who made me a lovely 7x57 Mauser, offers a superb custom bolt-action shotgun on a Mauser action, also using a McMillan stock. Bansner uses Hastings 22-inch fully rifled barrels, and will install the same barrel on bolt-action shotguns from Mossberg and Marlin.

Mark guarantees two-inch groups at 100 yards, as does Randy Fritz with his Tar-Hunt rifles. This is actually a fairly safe bet. Given decent ammo, two-inch groups are not a real problem with modern fully rifled slug guns. Relatively few over-the-counter semiautomatic, lever-action, or slide-action sporters will beat that by much, so it should be absolutely clear that slug-gun accuracy problems are cured for any hunter willing to invest in a rifled barrel.

That does not mean the shotgun slug has become a long-range projectile. It starts out fairly slow–and it sheds velocity like a hurled rock. You need to sight in a bit more than two inches high at 50 yards with most slugs to be dead-on at 100 yards–and at just 125 yards you will be about four inches low. That's okay, but at 150 yards you'll be more than a foot low, and sharply downhill from there. Energy drops accordingly.

The beauty of a rifled, super-accurate slug gun isn't really to extend your effective range much past the 100-yard line, because that really can't be done no matter how much you wish it could. Rather, the wonderful thing about a super-accurate slug gun is that you're no longer flinging big chunks of lead at 100-yard deer in the hope that you'll get a hit somewhere near a vital spot. Now, for the first time since shotgun slugs have been required, you can actually place your shots with surgical precision at sensible slug ranges. And that's a huge step in the right direction.

Among the modern, fully rifled slug guns, you have just three actions to choose from at this writing: bolt-action, slide-action, or semiauto. As with rifles, the bolt-action will be the most accurate by some measurable amount. But although I clearly favor bolt-actions in rifles, I'm not sure there's a clearcut winner in rifled shotguns. Provided you can get your accuracy down to about three-inch groups at 100 yards–and all three action types will clearly do that–you've really got all you need for the ranges shotgun slugs are suitable for.

Now, bolt-action shotguns will cut three-inch groups in half, especially some of the custom jobs I've mentioned. If you're a neck-shooter, or if you worship accuracy above all else, you'd best have one of these guns. The confidence factor alone is worth a great deal to most of us. But do keep in mind, for whatever it might or might not be worth, that bolt-action shotguns are a good deal slower than pump or semiautomatic shotguns.

If you hunt from a stand, that's insignificant. In fact, you might be best-served by the most accurate shotgun you can get your hands on, so you can thread your slugs through holes in the brush that reveal vital spots like throat patches and shoulders. But a good deal of shotgun hunting does include still-hunting and driving. Give some thought to the way you hunt and be honest with yourself. If most of your deer are moving when you shoot at them, you might either want to rethink your hunting technique or recognize that a second or third shot within three inches of point of aim at 100 yards might be worth a good deal more to you than a single shot within an inch and a half of where you called it!

Whatever action type you choose, do scope your big-game shotgun. Whether your deer is stationary or running like crazy through heavy brush, you're going to be faster and much more effective with a scope. Period, end of story.

There are really only two circumstances where iron sights might well have a slight edge. The first is for the fast-vanishing sport of running deer with hounds. This most traditional form of deer hunting is alive and well only in shrinking parts of the Deep South, but those who follow it pursue it avidly. I have absolutely nothing against the technique. I've done it, and I've even taken some pretty good deer doing it. Problem is that the human population is growing, and running deer with hounds takes a lot of space. So, right or wrong, this technique is being legislated out of existence in lots of areas.

In very swampy areas, almost impossible to hunt by most other means, it does make some sense. This type of hunting is also one of the last bastions of buckshot. Most hound-hunting groups mandate buckshot only–and some of the larger deer drives in the East and South also require buckshot only. A buckshot pellet in the right place will kill a deer at quite a distance, but you can't aim buckshot pellets. You can only aim your pattern, and a pattern of buckshot is pretty much done at 25 to 30 yards–sometimes much less. So if buckshot is necessary, you might well be better off without a scope–perhaps without sights at all, shooting just as if you were shooting very large birds!

The other circumstance favoring a scopeless gun is if you're planning on a slug-loaded shotgun for self-defense against bears and such. A whole lot of fishermen in Canada and Alaska, for instance, pack slug-loaded shotguns when plying salmon streams. Slug guns are popular, too, with bowhunters in grizzly country. Makes a lot of sense. I've packed moose on the Alaskan Peninsula and deer on Kodiak Island–and I would not care to do either with just a bow and arrow in my hands! But for such purposes you want the lightest shotgun you can carry, and no sights are needed at all. Short-barreled shotguns with pistol-grip stocks are actually a good choice here. After all, if you need sights you really aren't defending yourself, are you? And make no mistake, at point-blank range a slug-loaded shotgun is a far better tool than any handgun ever made.

Other than where mandated by law, or as a last-ditch defense against bears, I can see no other reasons to use a shotgun for North American big game. But the shotgun slug must be given its due. Its a devastating projectile. These days, with modern slug guns, you can even put that projectile exactly where you want it at reasonable ranges. In close cover, the requirement to use slugs is simply no longer a handicap—and that's some of the best news to deer hunters in the last several decades!

Chapter 31

Rifles for Practice and Predators

I will never forget my first introduction to a prairie-dog town. It was in the mid-1960s in Wyoming. Dad and I, together with Jack Pohl, had filled our pronghorn tags on opening morning. It seemed that, after all the anticipation, the hunt was over. In fact, the best was yet to come. Our rancher friend, Lester Wright, mentioned that there was a dog town just over the next rise.

Dad and I didn't really know what that meant, but Jack did. We headed over the hill and fired every shell we had. Now, I'd been shooting a rifle for years at that time. Dad had set up a little range in the basement, and I'd fired many thousands of .22 Shorts. We'd been antelope hunting before, and I'd shot the odd woodchuck with centerfires and the odd tree squirrel with .22s. But the vast amount of my experience was punching holes in paper. I was pretty good at that, but I knew almost nothing about reading wind or shooting from field positions. Dad, being a shotgunner all his life, knew much less.

Dad has often stated that, on that day in that prairie-dog town, for the first time he gained real confidence in his ability to hit something with a rifle. For sure that prairie-dog town–and the many towns that followed after we learned to seek them out–gave me more field shooting experience than anything else I could have done.

The focus of this book is on rifles and cartridges for North American big game, but I would be remiss in ignoring a huge class of rifles that, while not generally suitable for big game, give us the shooting skills we must have to be effective in the field.

The first rifle in this group is actually chambered for the most popular cartridge in the world. Of course it's the .22 rimfire. When I came to work at Petersen Publishing Company many years ago, the Editor at *Guns & Ammo* was Howard French. He was a tough taskmaster, always difficult to work for–but few people alive, and almost no editors of American gun magazines, have ever possessed Howard French's breadth and depth of knowledge regarding anything that goes bang. During the time I worked for him, Howard had occasion to interview quite a few prospective junior staffers, and he had a fairly standard series of questions. One regarded the differences in appearance between white-tailed and mule deer. Surprisingly, not a lot of prospective gun editors could handle that one. But if they couldn't, Howard carefully explained the differences. Lack of that piece of information wasn't always a showstopper. He would also always ask what firearms the man owned. (Sorry, ladies; in those days, all the prospective applicants were male.) If it wasn't mentioned, he'd get specific: "What kind of .22 do you have?" If you didn't own a .22, you had *no* chance of being hired.

Just like Howard French, I can't imagine anyone who's serious about firearms not owning at least one .22. I have three right now: my first .22, an Ithaca lever-action single-shot; a lever-action Marlin takedown; and a very pretty bolt-action Kimber wearing a one-inch-tube 4X Leupold compact. These three guns probably represent, in some fashion, three different "levels" of .22 rimfires. The first, like most single-shots (excluding high-grade match rifles), was and is a fine "first gun" for a beginning shooter. The second is an accurate, dependable, utilitarian rifle for plinking and small game. The third is a very accurate, very attractive sporter, a .22 that simulates centerfire handling under field conditions.

All three of my guns, and all three types of .22s, are actually equally suited to all the uses appropriate for a .22. These are, of course, serious shooting practice, non-serious shooting practice (read "plinking"), and small-game hunting. I suspect an increasing number of shooters now own a "serious" .22 with big-gun feel, be it a Ruger 77/22, a Browning A-Bolt 22, an Anschutz sporter, or one of several others. Most undoubtedly, most of them own a slightly less serious (but equally accurate and useful) .22 repeater from Marlin, Winchester, Remington, Browning, you name it. And almost all of us started with a single-shot .22.

Regardless of age or experience, the .22 rimfire should not be ignored. At a fraction of the cost of centerfire ammo–and with no recoil and little noise–you can practice to your heart's content. And regardless of what kind of hunting you do and what kind of centerfire rifle you shoot, there's no substitute for shooting practice. In the field, whether on small game like squirrels and rabbits or on nonedible rodents like prairie dogs and gophers, a .22 both teaches and refreshes stalking skills and shot placement.

Although my Kimber wears a scope, neither of my other .22's ever has. If I were serious about fried squirrel for supper, I'd want a .22 with a good scope–a one-inch tube, not one of the little ¾-inch-tube ".22 scopes." But if I were serious about working on shooting and stalking skills, or if I were instructing a youngster with his or her first rifle, I'd insist on an open-sighted .22. As I said, I grew up in the scope era. Had Dad started me with a scoped .22, as well he might have, chances are I would never have learned how to shoot with iron sights until I went into the Marine Corps. This would have been a loss, for although anyone and everyone shoots better with a scope, the lessons to be learned from open sights regarding sight alignment and precision of aiming are invaluable.

This is a lesson I like to relearn every now and again. Just last week, I had a ball shooting prairie dogs with an aperture-sighted .22 target rifle. At 40 or 50 yards, without an artifical rest, that kind of shooting will sharpen *all* your field shooting skills.

A step up from the "standard" .22 rimfire is the .22 WMR, the .22 magnum. Although it's a bit louder and the ammo is far more expensive than .22 Long Rifle, the .22 WMR is a lot more gun. Its 40-grain load leaves the muzzle at over 1,900 feet per second, making it a most viable 100-yard small-game and varmint rifle. While the .22 WMR is a bit destructive for edible small game and a bit underpowered for coyotes, a rifle so chambered makes an ideal set-up for the stalking varminter who likes to work in close to woodchucks and such.

Next we get to the centerfire "varmint" cartridges, ranging in caliber from the .17 Remington to the .220 Swift and in power from the .22 Hornet also up to the Swift. In some states, all of these cartridges are legal for deer, but I think we exhausted that discussion in the first chapter. Instead, let's talk about what these cartridges and their rifles are really intended for: shooting nonedible pests and furbearers from medium to very long ranges.

What we call varmint hunting is a sport that's growing by leaps and bounds these days. Hunting preferences are often based on prevailing conditions. When I was a kid in Kansas, hunters were bird hunters. Later, as land uses changed, most of my quail- hunting buddies wound up with duck leases. Today they're all whitetail hunters–but 25 years ago, darn few of them even owned a centerfire rifle. When I was a youngster, poisoning of prairie dogs was widespread and good dog towns fairly uncommon. Now that poisoning (thank the Lord!) has been pretty much over for a decade or so, rodents like prairie dogs, woodchucks, rockchucks, and gophers have made a strong comeback. Shooting is darn near the only means of control, so ranchers tend to welcome varmint hunters with open arms these days.

There are literally hundreds of hunters from all over the country who make annual spring and summer varmint safaris to Montana, Wyoming, and the Dakotas–often in lieu of a fall big-game hunt. These guys would rather come out for a week or two and shoot hundreds of rounds, instead of spending the same time and more expense to shoot one cartridge at a deer or elk. I was up in Medicine Bow, Wyoming, shooting prairie dogs just last week. There was a group of guys from Pennsylvania there who come out every year for a *month*, bringing their reloading equipment with them.

Predator hunters, too, have a fabulous opportunity right now. Not only has cessation of poisoning increased numbers of both prey and predator alike, but since the crash of the fur market there are very few serious trappers these days. Furbearers such as foxes, bobcats, and coyotes have probably never been as plentiful as they are right now–and the coyote has spread from coast to coast, giving Eastern hunters a brand-new off-season opportunity.

With these conditions in effect, there are really three kinds of varmint hunting today. The first is what I call "roving" or "stalking" for the pest species. This is for the guy who likes to walk as much as he shoots. Out

West, he might rove the hills for rockchucks or prairie dogs, perhaps the occasional badger. He doesn't care so much about shooting a lot of ammo as he does about getting some exercise and some stalking and sharpening his field-shooting skills. Then there's the deliberate, long-range varminter. He might set up at the far end of a beanfield back East or on a hill overlooking a prairie-dog town out West, but his game is precision marksmanship. Finally, there's predator hunting–generally calling predators to close or moderate range, but sometimes long-range sniping as well. Although many varminters pursue all three venues at one time or another, the ideal rifles and cartridges vary considerably.

The roving varminter is concerned about gun weight, but not necessarily about the utmost in long-range precision or maximum number of shots without overheating. He wants a light-barreled sporter with a scope of medium power, perhaps a 4-12X or 4.5-14X. The cartridge chosen depends on the country and the shooter's inclinations. Something as mild as a .22 Hornet, effective to perhaps 150 or 175 yards, might be ideal. A .17 Remington might be a good choice as well. Or, if he wants just a bit more reach, perhaps a .222 or .223.

Remember that light barrels are potentially just as accurate as heavy barrels–but they're harder to bed and won't give as many accurate shots as heavy barrels before they heat up. The shooter who roams the hills or hedgerows after rockchucks or woodchucks doesn't care about sustained accuracy during long shooting sessions–but he does care about having a rifle light enough to carry. The action will almost certainly be bolt or single-shot, the only two actions that can be relied upon to deliver consistent "minute-of-gopher" accuracy. For this kind of shooting, a sensible and most enjoyable option is a handgun like an XP-100 in .223–light to carry, yet extremely accurate to 200 yards and beyond.

The long-range precision varminter has altogether different needs. He wants a rifle that can deliver the utmost in precision accuracy shot after shot. He will opt for a "pure" varmint rifle–heavy of barrel, large of scope, bulky of stock, and extremely accurate. As varminting becomes more popular, more and more manufacturers are producing rifles like this. Remington, Winchester, Savage, Browning–all have varminters with bull barrels and target-type stocks. Unscoped, some of these rifles weigh as much as 10 pounds, and most will top 12 pounds with a 6-18X or 8-24X scope in place. These aren't rifles for carrying all day, but they're ideal for laying across sandbags and shooting all day!

Choice of calibers varies a bit, depending on the country and the game. The .22-250 is far and away the most popular. With a 55-grain bullet at nearly 3,700 feet per second, it will really do about all anyone needs a varmint rifle to do. The .220 Swift is making a comeback, however, and it is indeed a bit hotter. Some prefer the milder .223. It doesn't have quite the reach, but its recoil is noticeably softer–enough so that you can readily see the strike of your bullets, which you generally cannot do with a .22-250 or .220 Swift.

Some go heavier yet. Just the other day I did some shooting with a super-accurate rig, a Sako action rebarreled to the wildcat 6mm-284 firing 70-grain bullets. It was possibly the most awesome varmint rifle I've ever used, and the 6mms do buck wind better than any of the .22s. For this reason, both the 6mm Remington and .243 Winchester have some following, and a few hardy souls even use the .25-06. But for most of us, that's just too much gun for all-day sessions in prairie-dog towns.

Requirements for predator hunting can be different yet. Since it's rare to fire more than a couple of shots at a sitting, heavy barrels are not needed–especially when you consider that reaching calling sites usually calls for a fair bit of walking. In open country, you might well need a bit of reach and a fair measure of accuracy, while in close cover a premium should be placed on fast-handling abilities.

Although there might be a need for them in the most open country, cartridges like the .22-250 and .220 Swift are a bit too destructive on hides. This can be mitigated by using full-metal-jacket bullets (which require perfect shot placement) or by using 60-grain "deer" bullets, but a better compromise for a predator rifle is probably a .222 or .223. The little .22 Hornet and .218 Bee will do the job up close, but a big dog coyote is extremely tough and is starting to stretch the capabilities of these little cartridges.

Of course, there's no reason why you can't use your normal everyday big-game rifle, but don't expect to bring home much in the way of pelts! Better, to me, is a lightweight .223 sporter wearing something along the lines of a 3-9X scope. I have a little Kimber in that chambering on their mini-Mauser action, and it's a dream. However, calling predators is not strictly a bolt-action game. And it probably isn't a game for single shot-rifles. If the first shot is blown, it isn't uncommon to get a second or third shot. Nor is it uncommon to call up two or three coyotes, sometimes more, all at once. My idea of the perfect rifle for calling predators might well be Browning's BLR lever-action in .222 or .223, both available chamberings. The accuracy is adequate, and the speed and fast-handling capabilities could well be useful. For that matter, a good case could be made for a scoped semiautomatic like the Ruger Mini-14.

It should be mentioned, too, that calling predators isn't strictly a game for rifles. Given the fast-breaking nature of predator calling, the steady positioning and deliberate shooting required by a scoped handgun would be a liability, but in fairly heavy cover open-sighted revolvers or semiautos are effective–and challenging enough to be interesting. In very close cover, or in some of the small woodlot situations back East where coyotes have recently intruded, lots of skilled varmint callers use shotguns. A 12-gauge three-inch magnum or, better, a 10-gauge magnum, stoked with a full load of BBs, will do a real job out to 30 or 35 yards, sometimes farther depending on pattern. And that can be plenty of reach in very thick cover.

All three types of varmint hunting are extremely valuable for developing field marksmanship skills. Roving or stalking varminting is good for stalking skills and for spotting game, and it's ideal for developing field-shooting positions and speed in finding and using a natural rest–all critical. Long-range varminting is without parallel for learning how to dope wind and control breathing and trigger squeeze. If you can hit a seven-inch-by-three-inch prairie dog at 300 yards in a 25-mile-per-hour Wyoming wind, you can hit anything! The only caution is that it tends to make very deliberate, painstaking shooters. That ain't all bad, but few big-game animals–especially trophy animals of any species–give you the kind of time a prairie dog gives you.

Predator calling doesn't do as much for precise marksmanship, but nothing is better for learning to get on target and shoot quickly–and that just might be the most valuable big-game shooting skill of all.

Varmint hunting is, of course, an enjoyable pastime on its own merits, as more and more hunters are discovering. For Bob Milek, spring varminting was the highlight of his hunting year. For me, it's good practice for big-game hunting and nothing more–but I sure am pleased with the wealth of opportunity we enjoy today.

Chapter 32

Deer Rifles, East and West

Lumping all varieties together, there may be as many as 30 million deer in North America. And there are at least 10 million sportsmen and women who consider themselves deer hunters first and foremost–easily more than pursue any other type of hunting. It follows naturally that the vast majority of North American hunting rifles are deer rifles, or at least are used primarily for deer hunting.

Depending on your perspective, deer are either small or, at most, medium-sized on the big-game scale. They are not particularly thick-skinned, and although they are hardy, they're not especially difficult to put down. The easy answer, from coast to coast, would be to use a reasonably accurate .270, .280, or .30-06 in any action type, wearing a fixed 4X or medium-range variable scope. That would be the easy answer (and not necessarily the wrong answer) and this chapter could end right there.

As gun writers I think we have a habit of making the very simple seem altogether too complex–else, perhaps, we wouldn't have anything to write about. I have a good, accurate, appropriately scoped bolt-action in each of the above calibers. Any one of the three would suffice quite handily for any and all deer hunting anywhere in North America. So would quite a variety of other rifles that I own, and an even greater number of rifle/cartridge combinations that I don't own. My purpose here, however, is to discuss *ideal* rifles and cartridges for the prevailing conditions. To do that, we must get past this initial simplification and recognize that not only do we have widely varying sizes and kinds of deer across our huge continent, but we also hunt these various deer under wildly differing conditions. Let's do that, and then let's see, at day's end, how our .270s .280s, and .30-06s stack up. To do this, although it's another oversimplification, we'll look at what our record books now classify as the five North American deer: white-tailed, Coues white-tailed, mule, black-tailed, and Sitka black-tailed deer.

White-tailed Deer

Our most numerous and most widespread deer, by a huge margin, is the whitetail. Most deer hunters, and therefore most hunters, are whitetail hunters. There are, however, a great many more than just one race of white-tailed deer. Fully 38 recognized subspecies of whitetail exist from the Amazon Basin in South America to the treeline in northern Canada. In what we call North America, arguably from the Panama Canal northward, there are some 30 subspecies. Our goal here certainly isn't to try to differentiate all of them, but simply to recognize that there are white-tailed deer and then there are white-tailed deer.

The smallest of our subspecies are the protected Florida Keys whitetails, the Carmen Mountains whitetails of west Texas and adjacent northern Mexico, the Coues whitetails of the Southwest, and several little-known tropical subspecies in southern Mexico and Central America. The smallest of these, the Carmen Mountains, Florida Keys, and probably the tropical deer, may weigh as little as 60 pounds for a fully mature buck dressed out. The largest of them, the Coues deer, will rarely dress out over 90 pounds. Of all of our whitetail subspecies, only the Coues whitetail has been singled out for separate record-keeping, so we'll deal with him separately.

Whitetails provide a clear example of Bergmann's Law of subspecies development. This principle states that the farther north or south one gets from the Equator, the larger individual animals become within a species. In warmer climates, bodies are smaller and ears and tails proportionately larger to aid in heat dissipation. Farther north (or, in the Southern Hemisphere, farther south) animals develop larger bodies for heat retention and fat storage. Our northernmost whitetail subspecies–the North Woods whitetail of Maine and the Maritime Provinces and the Northwestern whitetail of Idaho, Montana, and western Canada–are giants compared to our southernmost subspecies. Bucks weighing 300 pounds in pre-rut fat are common, and deer weighing well in excess 400 pounds are weighed in every year.

In between the smallest and largest, depending on feed conditions and subspecies, we have tremendous local variation in the size of our whitetails. The corn-fed deer of the Midwest are of a large subspecies to begin with, and with ideal feed conditions they do get big. The Texas Hill Country whitetails–overpopulated and with marginal feed conditions– are very small, but farther south in Texas Brush Country, where densities are lower and the diet better, deer of the same *texanus* subspecies are a third larger. Clearly, to say that a whitetail is a whitetail is a whitetail is absurd, and it's equally absurd to say that the ideal caliber for a 100-pound deer is just as ideal for a 400-pound deer.

Conditions vary immensely as well. Whitetails are hunted in jungles, swamps, deserts, mountains, forests, and open plains (what did I miss?). Some shooting is typically (or possibly) very long, while some is short. Hunting techniques vary, too. Stand-hunting usually means a very deliberate shot. Still-hunting–and driving even more–usually means a very quick shot, often at a moving target. So how do we sort out whitetail rifles for all of these conditions and parameters?

Throughout the East and Southeast, deer are of modest size. big bucks are always possible, but any buck weighing in excess of 200 pounds is very, very big. The typical cover is brush, swamp, timber, or relatively small fields. Stand-hunters may occasionally have a 200-yard vista, but a maximum of 100 yards is more common. Since stand-hunting is at its best at dawn and dusk, the sensible choice is a scoped rifle. Action type is immaterial, since all of our action types are plenty adequate for this kind of shooting. A very sensible caliber minimum is .243, and virtually any cartridge from the .243 Winchester upward is quite suitable. Then there are some exceptions.

Hunters who are serious about hunting big bucks want to be well-prepared for 250-pound deer–and they want to be able to take any reasonable shot. Now we're back to my original .270-.280-.30-06 hypothesis! Equally good would be milder cartridges like the 6.5x55, 7x57, 7mm-08, and such. In fact, for stand-hunting in open or mixed timber, these cartridges probably represent the ideal.

There are also long-range specialists, hunters who choose to site their stands overlooking endless beanfields and grainfields. This kind of shooting is what custom maker Kenny Jarrett's "beanfield rifles" are all about. If you're serious about 400-yard shooting, then you need more than what I've just listed. Now you're talking about extremely accurate, large-scoped 7mm and .300 magnums–not for the power but for the reach.

Still-hunters in the same country could use the same rifles, but for all still-hunting, driving, horn-rattling–anything where the opportunity may be fleeting–you need a rifle that's fast and responsive. You also, perhaps, want a little more power, since the shot you're presented with may be less than ideal. I *still* believe a scoped rifle is the way to go, but in very thick country open sights may well be quite adequate. Under such conditions, a .30-30 is just as good a choice today as it was a century ago. But, again, a scoped .270-.280-.30-06 ain't bad!

I dearly love the good old .30-30, but let me tell you my best .30-30 story. Just last fall, I was sitting on a South Texas deer stand with my aperture-sighted Model 94 Trapper. That is *not* an ideal rifle for that area–I could see lots of country that was just plain out of reach. But I wanted to shoot a nice buck with my .30-30, so I chose it on purpose.

A buck walked out on a *sendero* at what I guessed to be just under 100 yards. Later I paced it at 90. I got the rifle up very slowly, got the hammer back, and waited until he turned broadside. Very carefully, with a dead-steady hold, I put the tip of the blade behind his shoulder, about a third down from the backline, and squeezed the trigger. Aside from the slight recoil and sound of the shot, three things happened in blinding sequence. First I saw dust kick just behind the deer, about right to indicate that the bullet had passed through. Then I heard the "whap" of the bullet striking what sounded like flesh. And then, in two great jumps but with no sign of a hit, the buck was off into the impenetrable black brush that country is known for. No problem. Wait 10 minutes, go find him.

There was no blood whatever–and on that hard-baked ground there were no tracks to follow. I was on John Wootters' Los Cuernos Ranch. Gary Sitton had shot a fine buck from another stand about a half-hour before I fired. He dropped his cleanly with a scoped .25-06, an ideal rifle for that country. In due time, Gary, John, and John's wife Jeannie descended on my stand to see my deer. They'd heard the shot–but I had nothing to show them, and I was grateful for the help.

Carefully we began to quarter through the brush my buck had headed into. No blood, no tracks clearly discernible as running or distressed. I was embarrassed, and I could well have passed the shot off as a clean miss. Except I know how that rifle shoots (very well indeed), and I'd heard the bullet strike flesh.

After a half-hour's search, we left to take pictures of Gary's buck, and then John and Gary took his buck to a cooler while Jeannie and I went back to continue our search. First we circled this patch of brush, about a quarter-mile square and bordered by a clearing, two *senderos*, and a sandy creek bed. No blood, nor any running tracks coming out anywhere. Then, with red flagging, we set out to search the entire quarter-section of brush in a grid pattern.

Our first pass, during which Jeannie and I were about 10 yards apart, took us parallel and about 40 yards into the brush from the *sendero* the deer had stood on. I was scouring the ground for any sign whatever when I spotted what looked like a fresh drag mark. I stopped and called to Jeannie, but before she reached me I found blood, just a couple of drops. On hands and knees we saw where the deer had left a couple of clear tracks, then a bit more blood. And then the blood stopped. We were searching for more, looking in both directions, when Jeannie said, "Here's your deer!"

The buck had piled up under a prickly pear, not five yards from where I found the blood–and not 50 yards from where he'd taken my bullet squarely behind the shoulder and through both lungs!

Does this mean the .30-30 is inadequate for deer? Good Lord, no! There are lessons here, but that isn't one of them. It isn't the least unusual for lung-shot deer to make the 50 yards this deer made, often a bit more. But I do know that a high-velocity expanding bullet from a .243, .25-06, .270, .280, .30-06, *et al*, might have dropped the deer in his tracks–and would have left a blood trail. That .30-30 bullet was a 170-grain slug from my 16-inch-barreled Trapper. At that low velocity, the heavy bullet at nearly 100 yards did not expand much if at all. If I had it to do over, I'd use the 150-grain bullet instead of the 170, perhaps getting a bit more velocity and therefore some expansion. I'd also shoot for the shoulder, not *behind*. If I'd hit some heavy bone, that would have made a big difference for sure. It's not a new lesson, of course, but how many deer, hit exactly that way, are lost each year?

Texas deer are also generally small. Even in the "big-buck zones" a 200-pound buck is almost unheard of, and the average for dressed weight is well under 130 pounds in the Hill Country and coastal regions. The shooting, however, is much different. The rolling oak ridges of the Hill

Country and Edwards Plateau can offer some fairly long shots–likewise the oak motte and coastal plains to the southeast. In the Brush Country, average visibility is nil, but there are those long *senderos* along which so much stand-hunting is done.

In areas where the deer tend to be fairly small and the shooting is rarely extreme, a scoped .243 or .257 Roberts would be a good choice. But for hunting Texas' largest deer in that *sendero* country, I think you need a bit more. The .25-06 is an extremely popular cartridge in that kind of country, and with good reason. The deer are not huge, but you need plenty of reach down those open rights-of-way–and distances are almost impossible to judge. I shot my biggest Texas deer with a 7mm Remington Magnum at something close to 400 yards, and I'm not the least ashamed for using such a big gun. An outfitter buddy of mine, Charley White, is perhaps the best whitetail hunter I've ever known. He uses a .300 Winchester Magnum, and he's not ashamed of his cannon, either. Of course, my .270-.280-.30-06 trio would all be excellent choices as well.

When you get up into the Corn Belt, the deer get much bigger. Now 300-pound deer are not uncommon, nor is it unusual to have to reach out across a field. Understand that, across the board, there's a difference between hunting for just any deer and hunting for a *big* deer. If you're looking for meat in the pot, you can pick and choose your deer and your shots. But if you're looking for a big buck, you won't get many chances and must be prepared to capitalize on any opportunities you might get.

When you get into the much larger deer of the Midwest, unless you're after just any deer, you're out of .243 country. I don't think the big magnums are called for necessarily, though they work. But I do think a .257 Roberts with hot loads or, better, a .25-06 is a sensible minimum. Depending on whether your hunting leans toward woodlot or open field, efficient little cartridges like the 7mm-08 and .308 Winchester would be outstanding. If your shots tend to be a bit longer, you're right back to my .270, .280, or .30-06.

In the forests of the Upper Midwest and the Northeast (including Canada's Maritimes), the game changes again. The deer are big and the cover is thick. In timber country, shots are fleeting and presentations rarely perfect. You want to hit your deer hard and fast, and you want to anchor him as quickly as possible. This last is for a variety of reasons. In forests that are nearly wilderness, the longer you must trail a deer, the harder it will be to pack him out. In country that's checkerboarded with private land, you don't want a wounded deer to cross into country where you haven't permission. And, although it's sad to say, in some of this region the seasons are short and the woods get a bit crowded. If you shoot a deer, you want him down right now so there's no argument over ownership.

Depending on how you hunt, the answer might be a powerful lever-action from .35 Remington up through .444 Marlin and .45-70. Or it might be a kind of compromise–a thumper with a bit more range like a .358 Winchester or .35 Whelen. Or it might be a garden variety .308 or .30-06. Action type is immaterial. Lever-actions, slide-actions, and semi-autos all have a following in this kind of country, but the bolt-action remains pretty universal. Whatever you choose, it must handle fast and speak with authority.

Finally, there are the giant whitetails of central and western Canada, and I'd include western Montana and Idaho in that as well. The country varies greatly. It might be unbroken timber, heavy brush, the edges of agriculture, or smallish woodlots. Deer densities are low and the hunting tends to be very, very difficult. But buck/doe ratios are good, and the bucks grow huge. These days, many veteran whitetail hunters are heading to Alberta, Saskatchewan, Manitoba, and western Montana in search of the bucks of their lifetimes. The monsters are there. The long-standing world record was broken in Saskatchewan in 1993, and I'm sure there are bigger bucks awaiting. In fact, I believe a Boone and Crockett minimum score of 170 (gross, not net) is a fairly *normal* rack for these big Northern deer at full maturity. But the hunting is tough, and your chances, or my chances, of getting one aren't that great. In a week's hunt in Alberta, Saskatchewan, or western Montana, you've done very well if you get one chance at a really big buck.

That chance may be in heavy brush, or it may be on the far side of a big grainfield. It may be stationary–but only if you're able to see, identify, evaluate, recognize, and *shoot* the buck you're looking at in less than five seconds. I think this is the most specialized of all whitetail hunting. It requires a rifle that is fast-handling, yet also has the reach in case it's a 400-yard shot or nothing. The Northern deer have a tough life; they're hardy as well as big, so the rifle must speak with authority as well. On both of my Alberta trips, I've carried my David Miller 7mm Remington Magnum because, for difficult shots, I trust it above all else. But I think it's extremely minimal in caliber! Although my .270-.280-.30-06 triumvirate would handle *most* shots, they won't handle *all*–so this is no place for them. A .300 magnum with 180-grain bullets is a fine choice.

Last year in Alberta, a young friend of mine from Virginia was in camp with a .340 Weatherby Magnum, a darned good choice. He had practiced endlessly with his cannon, and I believe he had mastered it. He had both good luck and horrible luck. On the first day, our outfitter, Don Tyschuk, said he expected everyone to see at least one good buck, but luck being as it is, he wouldn't be surprised if just one of us saw all the bucks. So it was. My Virginian friend saw, and shot at, three *different* Boone and Crockett bucks in six days. He missed them all, but it wasn't the rifle's fault and it really wasn't his. The first shot was the easiest, broadside at about 300 yards. The rest were much more difficult–crossing cutlines, moving, at longer distances.

This guy has shot more white-tailed deer than I will ever see, but he's probably never shot a deer beyond 150 yards in his life. The distances, all possible but very difficult shots, blew him away. The amazing thing to me–and I saw all three places he shot from, and where the deer were when he shot–is that he got his shots off at all. He had the right rifle and he could shoot it well, but even that wasn't enough.

Down in Montana, and to a lesser degree in Idaho, the biggest whitetails are now found in unbroken timber. This, to me, is even more difficult. My buddy up there, Ed Nixon, maintains that the .338 Winchester Magnum is the gun to use. Period. He reckons that most of his friends, and he as well, grew up with .270s–but most of the hunters in his valley have made the switch to .338s. For still-hunting whitetails in that thick timber, such a choice makes lots of sense to me. But remember that the .338 isn't the flattest-shooting gun around if you need to reach out across a clearcut or a field.

Coues Deer

As I mentioned, the Coues whitetail of the Southwest is just one of many whitetail subspecies. The fact that it's singled out for special attention really goes back to a taxonomic error, when early naturalists thought it was a different species. But hunting conditions are so different when seeking this little deer that I think the separate distinction is probably appropriate. The Coues is thinly distributed over huge country, and unlike most other whitetails, under most circumstances you can't hunt him from stands, you can't rattle him up, for sure you can't drive him, and you can't call him, either. You must hunt him primarily by glassing, as you would most mountain game.

Insofar as guns and loads go, I would lump the Coues whitetail together with our other small Southwestern whitetail, the Carmen Mountains whitetail of West Texas and adjacent Mexico. The desert mountains are much the same, the deer distribution is much the same, and these subspecies are more similar to each other than to "normal" whitetails.

These little desert whitetails are my favorite deer. I've hunted Coues whitetails extensively in both Arizona and Mexico, and I've hunted the Carmen Mountains deer in both Texas and Mexico. I love the desert mountains, but hunting them is a physical sport. Rifles simply must be fairly portable. And although I have taken some very nice rifles into Coues country, each time I knew it was a mistake. The footing is often steep and generally rotten granite, and every plant has thorns. This is a place for a rifle you don't have to worry about scratching up, and if I were smart I'd stick with synthetic stocks both for ruggedness and light weight.

This is also an accuracy game. The deer are small, and the country is so big that getting really close is a trick. Of many more than a dozen, the only desert whitetail I shot under 100 yards was a buck I shot in Sonora in an oak grove during a blinding rainstorm. That was unusual. I shot another Coues buck in Arizona at an honest God-awful distance. It couldn't be paced because of the up-and-down cross-canyon situation, but I believe it was an honest 500 yards plus change. That, too, was unusual. At least, it was unusual for me even to attempt such a shot. Gunmaker David Miller, one of the best (and certainly the most successful) of our modern Coues-deer fanatics, shot three Boone and Crockett bucks in three years. He reckons the closest shot was 400 yards. David uses a .300 Weatherby Magnum that he built for himself, and he practices regularly out to 500 yards.

I have also hunted Coues deer with a .300 Weatherby, but I don't believe you need that much gun. Outside of the very specialized quest for a monster buck, I also don't think you need to shoot that far. Most of my shots have been between 200 and 300 yards. Based on the size of the deer, a .243 would be ideal. But on the far edge of that 300-yard envelope, the .243 is getting dicey for deer-sized game. Although I have used a .300, my own Coues-deer hunting has mostly been done with a 7mm Remington Magnum, a .270, a .280, and a .30-06. (You knew I'd get to those three, didn't you?) I'll throw you a curve, though. I think the perfect Coues-deer rifles are bolt-actions chambered to something fast, flat, and, while not spectacularly powerful, easily capable of deer-anchoring energies well past 300 yards. The .300s will do that. So will the hotter 7mms. But to my mind, the ideal calibers center around the .25-06, .257 Weatherby Magnum, .264 Winchester Magnum, and both the .270 Winchester and .270 Weatherby Magnum.

For this kind of shooting, the scope is perhaps as important as the rifle. Some years ago, my Coues-deer mentor, Arizona guide Duwane Adams, and I were lying on a ridge looking at the next ridge where we knew a good Coues buck was bedded. Duwane had his 15x60 binoculars on the spot where the deer had disappeared. I had my .280 Remington with a fixed 6X scope. He could see the bedded buck. I couldn't.

"See that oak tree? Look underneath it. You'll see a little triangle of white. That's the buck's tail. He's facing away, angled slightly to the right."

It went on like that for a while. I simply didn't have enough optics to resolve the buck from the background. Of course, I went to my own binoculars, and I could see the buck. Finally I picked out the tiny white triangle through my scope, and eventually pinpointed what I thought was head and shoulders. I took the shot and I was right–the buck came tumbling down the ridge, very dead. But a bit more scope would have made life a lot simpler. My .25-06 wears a Nikon 4-12X for just such circumstances. I still don't think huge scopes are called for, especially given the heat waves and mirage in the desert mountains. But something along the lines of 4-12X, 3.5-10X, or 4.5-14X can make a huge difference over the fixed 6X I was using that day.

Mule Deer

Under most circumstances, hunting mule deer is just like hunting Coues deer–a difficult game of glassing and covering rough country. The major difference is that the deer are as much as four times bigger! For my money, serious mule-deer hunting isn't .243 country, nor (with apologies to the Milek clan) is it .25-caliber country. A case could surely be made for the .25-06 and .257 Weatherby, but when searching for the biggest mule deer around, I think most hunters are better served by something almost as flat-shooting–or better, flatter still–and with a bit more energy when the bullet arrives.

For this kind of hunting, there's absolutely nothing wrong with my trio of the .270, .280, and .30-06. I've taken very fine mule deer with all three calibers at a variety of ranges, including some fairly long stuff. But to that trio I really must add the .264 Winchester Magnum, the 7mm Remington and Weatherby Magnums, the .270 Weatherby Magnum, and all of the .300 magnums. Nothing on the North American continent is as hard to come by today as a really big mule deer, and any edge you can gain by your choice of rifle is worth having.

I shot my very best mule deer ever in his bed at 60 yards with a .280 Remington. I shot my second-best mule deer ever from one ridge to the next with a .300 Weatherby at something well over a quarter of a mile. Those are the parameters for taking big mule deer, and while I'm not suggesting magnums are really essential, you have to first understand the difficulty of finding big mule deer today, then choose your rifle accordingly.

Mule-deer rifles must also be very portable, especially for high-country hunts. A good scope is essential, but the larger powers are really not needed because the deer themselves are plenty big. A 3-9X or 3.5-10X variable is plenty of scope–but such a variable might serve most hunters better than a fixed 4X or 6X.

As much as I dislike doing so, I would probably have to vote for the 7mm Remington (or Weatherby) Magnum as the best mule-deer cartridge going. My own David Miller rifle (with which, honest, I have only shot one mule deer) in 7mm Remington Magnum, wearing a 3.5-10X Leupold and shooting 160-grain Noslers into three-fourths of an inch, is probably the most perfect mule-deer rifle I could ever imagine. But since it's too pretty to take into the high country, I have a Clifton Arms 7mm Remington Magnum that shoots as well and doesn't make me cry if I take a tumble!

While I think the 7mm magnums offer a bit of an energy edge over the .270 and .280–and a bit of a trajectory edge over the .30-06–there's nothing wrong with my "golden triangle" for mule deer. Nor, for that matter, is there anything wrong with choosing a .300 magnum. A few .243-toters might giggle at you–but not after they see your buck!

Most mule-deer hunting is in relatively open country, though fast, close-in shots are always possible. Surprisingly, the mule-deer hunting being done in Mexico today is just the opposite. The desert mule-deer there are hunted by tracking, and while a long-range shot is possible, most opportunities are close and fast. The desert there is quite brushy, so at the end of a tracking job a 75-yard shot is very far indeed. Often the deer are jumped from their beds and must be taken while running pell-mell through the cactus and paloverde. I don't think this situation changes the caliber requirements. The deer are not big-bodied, and anything between a .270 and a .300 is just fine. However, this kind of hunting places a premium on smooth, fast shooting, and too much scope is a very bad thing. Down there, a fixed 4X or 6X is just fine, and variables must be kept turned down while tracking.

Black-tailed Deer

Black-tailed deer are small mulies, and they're hunted in smaller country. Most of it, not all, is lower than classic mule-deer habitat, and is generally more brushy. In some of the rolling oak grasslands or Alpine meadows where blacktails occur, a long shot is possible–but in the rain forests of western Washington and Oregon, face-to-face encounters are much more likely. I have personally never had to make a particularly long shot on a black-tailed deer–and since I lived in California for 15 years, I've hunted them quite a lot. Based on this, I'd say the .243 and 6mm Remington are very acceptable and sensible minimums for blacktails. Optimum calibers are probably .257 Roberts, .25-06, 6.5x55, 7mm-08, and 7x57. Obviously, there's nothing wrong with my .270, .280, or .30-06.

Action type is not really important, but throughout most blacktail country bolt-actions are generally the most popular. An exception, however, might be in the very thick, very wet coastal forests of Washington and, to a slightly lesser degree, Oregon. Here the country is very wet and very thick, and opportunities for a long shot nonexistent. This is one of those rare instances where an aperture sight might well be superior to a scope because of the frequent rain. Any rifle used must be fast-handling and fairly light. Any of our action types can be both, but peep-sighted lever-actions in .30-30 or larger are both popular and effective for that kind of hunting.

Sitka Black-tailed Deer

The Sitka blacktail subspecies takes over from the Columbian blacktail somewhere in northern British Columbia and ranges north and west to coastal Alaska and many of the offshore islands. The hunting varies tremendously. B.C.'s Queen Charlotte Islands, for instance, are characterized by lots of small deer in genuine rain-forest. Don't worry about long shots, but worry plenty about keeping water off your scope lenses!

Much of southeast Alaska is the same, especially early in the season. Alaska, however, adds two more conditions to the equation. First, Alaska's Sitka blacktails, especially those on Kodiak and some of the other islands, are giants among blacktails. On Kodiak, deer weighing 250 pounds are not uncommon in the least. Alaska also throws her big brown bears into the deal. While it is not legal to kill a bear in defense of your deer, there is always the very real potential of a life-threatening encounter while packing deer out.

Alaska changes as the long season progresses. In August and September, the grass is long and the shooting generally fairly short. But in October the grass gets beaten down by wind and rain, and in November the slopes are wide open and bare, and the shooting is very long.

In spite of possible bear problems, the Alaskans I know tend to use cartridges like the .25-06 and .270 for their deer hunting. Personally, I would lean toward a .300 magnum. That gives all the reach you could ever want–and you could replace your 165-grain deer loads with a couple of 220-grain round-noses while packing your deer out.

Weather is a real problem–wind, rain, and snow. You do need a scope, so good lens caps are essential. Because of the frequent rain, especially early, this is a good place for a detachable scope and good iron sights. If the rain moves in during a stalk, you can simply remove the scope and continue, rather than having to worry about keeping rain off the lenses.

Well, in summary, I guess our .270-.280-.30-06 trio would be just fine for the vast majority of North American deer hunting. And while I singled out those three, you could add the 7mm magnums, 7x57, and .308 Winchester–and probably several others. We do have some special circumstances that require a little extra thought, but there should be no mystery to picking deer rifles. Cannons aren't needed but popguns aren't in order, either. Depending on the circumstances, you might or might not need a whole lot of reach. And while our middle-of-the-road big-game cartridges would do it all, part of the fun is always deciding what rifle and cartridge combination is exactly right.

Chapter 33

Rifles for Plains and Tundra

In the 1860s, the Great Plains held North America's greatest concentrations of wildlife–not only bison in the millions but elk, pronghorn, and deer beyond counting. But nowhere was game more accessible and vulnerable than on the wide-open plains. As farmers and ranchers advanced westward in unprecedented numbers, the abundance didn't last long. My home state of Kansas was a revealing microcosm of what happened. By 1874, bison were altogether gone from the Kansas prairies. Elk didn't last much longer, nor did the pronghorns. By 1920, even deer were considered extinct, and it wasn't until the World War II years that a few deer started drifting back in from bordering states.

Had the excesses of our pioneer era been halted more quickly, what we now consider plains or open-country game would differ radically from the current picture. Elk, for instance, were primarily plains animals until the survivors were driven into the mountains–where the bulk of the population remains to this day. Even grizzlies were probably more common on the plains of 150 years ago than they are now in western Canada's mountains. But never again will we consider grizzlies plains game.

Our genuine plains game today is limited to our uniquely American pronghorn antelope, really more like a goat-antelope cross than a true antelope, and a scattering of both mule deer and whitetails that share the pronghorn's rolling sagebrush habitat. Of course, our pronghorn habitat isn't this continent's only wide-open country. Far to the north, above Canada's treeline, lie the vast Arctic plains we call tundra.

The primary game there, of course, is caribou. Biologists and hunters differ on just how many varieties of caribou there are. Depending on which record-keeping system you follow, there might be a half-dozen different varieties, from the woodland caribou of Newfoundland and southeastern Canada on west to the barren-ground caribou of Alaska. For our discussion, however, the differences between one caribou and another are insignificant–all are hunted in wide-open, windy country. There are some regional differences in body size, but not enough to change caliber requirements. Although caribou grow the largest antlers in relation to body size of any antlered animal in the world, they are not really large animals. If you think of them as being a bit larger than big mule deer, you're probably thinking right. Body weights for bulls in the 350- to 400-pound class would be average–somewhat less among the most northern animals, and a bit more for the hefty woodland and mountain varieties.

Shooting conditions are actually somewhat similar for pronghorn and caribou, since in both cases you have wide-open country with no assurance that a close stalk will be possible, and windy conditions can be expected both on the Wyoming prairies and the Canadian tundra. There are obvious differences, too. With pronghorn, you're hunting a 100-pound animal that is fairly tough for his size. With caribou, you're hunting an animal about four times larger that is *not* particularly tough, pound for pound. Weather is another factor. When you're pronghorn hunting during the early fall seasons, you can generally expect glorious weather, with only the possible threat of an early snowfall. With caribou, you can expect the weather to be horrible–windy, rainy, snowy, and cold. The clear, sunny days I associate with pronghorn hunting just don't happen all that often up North, and are a treasure when they do!

We could complicate the equation by talking about the animals one might hunt in combination with either pronghorn or caribou. In the case of pronghorn, this is most likely to be deer, but could possibly be elk. If caribou is part of a multi-species hunt, the most likely combination is moose–but other Northern species, from muskox to sheep and goat and even grizzly, could possibly be on the menu.

With combinations in mind, rifle selection can get complex. The need for a flat-shooting, wind-bucking cartridge remains and must be answered, but the other game on the menu may well call for a good deal more power. The answer is obvious, of course. You must choose a cartridge that's adequate for the largest game you plan to hunt. If you're going to hunt Alaskan brown bear and caribou on, say, the Alaskan Peninsula, you'll probably be overgunned for the caribou, but you'll need to choose a cartridge that shoots flat enough for the one and hits hard enough for the other. You might, for example, choose a .338 Winchester Magnum or .340 Weatherby Magnum, neither of which is an optimum caribou cartridge but does fill the bill for your bear–plus the ability to reach out across the tundra for the caribou.

Our purpose here, though, isn't to discuss versatility but rather ideal rifles and cartridges for fairly specific purposes. Let's start with pronghorns.

Nothing in North America sees better than our pronghorn antelope. Uniquely, this creature relies very little on either his ears or his nose, but places his trust in that marvelous vision for keeping him out of trouble. His habitat appears wide-open and barren, and it would seem that all shooting at pronghorns would be very long indeed. Actually, things are usually not that grim. I do not condone the practice of chasing pronghorns with vehicles; not only is the animal cheated by such unsportsmanlike conduct, but so is the hunter. The real fun of pronghorn hunting is matching wits with this speedster on his own turf–staying out of sight by circling and crawling, anticipating his next move and placing yourself so those vast distances are whittled down to size.

Pronghorn country is usually neither as flat nor as barren as it first appears. There are generally hidden gullies and little dips, folds, and rises that provide cover for the careful hunter. Shooting at truly extreme ranges is very seldom required. On the other hand, shots at pronghorns almost certainly average a good deal longer than with most game animals. At some point, you usually run out of cover, and without cover you simply cannot approach a pronghorn. I have taken a couple of pronghorns at less than 40 yards–and the same number at more than 400. Most shots seem to fall between 200 and 300 yards. These are not extreme distances, hardly beyond the capability of any high-performance centerfire.

As with most big-game hunting, caliber selection depends a bit on your intentions. If you're a stalking hunter in search of a decent buck–but not necessarily a monster–you might be well-served by a light, handy .243 or 6mm Remington. As I mentioned, one of my favorite pronghorn rifles is a Ruger No. 1 in .243 wearing a 3-9X variable scope. I've used it a lot in eastern Wyoming, country that tends to have plenty of little gullies and breaks ideal for stalking. It's also country with plenty of pronghorns but very few really large bucks.

In more open country–or country known for producing extra-large pronghorns–I would not choose my .243. You get high winds, wide-open sagebrush flats, or a particularly large buck tending his harem–or, just as likely, some combination of these circumstances–and a .243 can get outclassed in a hurry. While the need for it is rare, with pronghorns more than most game you should be prepared for 400-yard shooting, especially if you're trophy hunting seriously.

For casual pronghorn hunting, the .243 and 6mm are fine, and so are mild, efficient little cartridges like the .250 Savage, 6.5x55, 7x57, 7mm-08, and so on. But a serious quest for a serious pronghorn calls for more specialized gear. Extremely powerful cartridges are not needed. Pound for pound, pronghorns are extremely hardy animals and should not be underrated; poorly hit, a pronghorn antelope will go forever and becomes so unapproachable that a lost animal is quite possible. However, we're talking about an animal that weighs little more than 100 pounds. All-round, versatile cartridges like the .280, 7mm Remington Magnum, and even the .30-06 and .300 magnums have the reach you need, and yes, I've shot pronghorns with all of these and probably will again. But these levels of power really aren't needed.

To my mind, the ideal pronghorn rig ranges from .25-06 to .270 (Winchester or Weatherby Magnum) and includes relatively few cartridges. The ones that come readily to mind, in addition to the .25-06 and .270s, are the .257 Weatherby Magnum, .264 Winchester Magnum, and perhaps the .240 Weatherby Magnum.

Shooting beyond 250 yards is always difficult, and anything beyond 300 yards is long range for almost all of us. Cartridges like these shoot flat enough to reduce somewhat the precision needed in judging range, and thus make long-range shooting as easy as it can be made–which still ain't very easy. Bullets should be as aerodynamic as possible, and should open fairly quickly. In the .25s, I'd use something around 115 or 117 grains; in the .264, I've had wonderful luck with Hornady's 129-grain spitzer, but the 140-grain factory loads are just fine; and in the .270s, I'd use 130-grain bullets or perhaps Remington's new 135-grain Extended Range load.

The ideal pronghorn rifle needs to be fairly portable. Barrel length is not an issue in such wide-open country, but gun weight is. Heavy rifles become burdensome very quickly when you're belly-crawling through cactus! Even so, I wouldn't scrimp on the scope. My .25-06 has a synthetic stock to keep the weight down, but I put some of that weight right back on with a 4-12X scope. A 3-9X should be the minimum choice, with 3.5-10X on up to the big 6-18X scopes a good range for this kind of work.

Although I pride myself on my ability to use a tight sling as a shooting aid, and also on being able to find and use a natural rest if there's one anywhere handy, pronghorn hunting is one of the best applications for an artificial rest. Sometimes you can find a handy clump of sagebrush to rest over–but not always, and usually there's nothing more substantial. For serious pronghorn hunting, I often clip a Harris bipod to the front sling swivel. The drawback here is that the Harris adds a bunch of gun weight and can be a real pain if you're doing serious crawling through cactus.

Other options are some of the fold-up rests carried in a belt pack. Underwood shooting sticks are excellent, and there's a new Snipe-Stix being made in Montana. Like the Harris, the Snipe-Stix is a bipod that attaches via the front sling swivel. But only the attachment receptacle is left in place, while the bipod itself folds up in a belt pack and attaches in seconds when you need it. Shooting aids like these help tremendously. Whatever you choose, make sure you practice getting it into play until it becomes second nature.

In many ways, caribou hunting is similar to hunting pronghorns. The country looks devoid of cover, but usually isn't. Caribou, by the way, are generally a whole lot easier to approach than pronghorns. But you have the same problem of a whole bunch of eyes, and once a caribou herd starts moving, they might not stop. As with pronghorns, sometimes you're going to get stuck a long way out and have no choice but to take your shot. The animals are a great deal bigger–more target area, but also more energy required to put one down. And it's worth repeating that the weather is more unpredictable at best, and often quite horrible.

Rifles on the order of .300 magnums are not necessary for caribou, but obviously they have the power, trajectory, and wind-bucking abilities you need. The .25-06 and .257 Weatherby Magnum represent sensible minimums, with the ideal being along the lines of the .270, .280, 7mm Remington Magnum, and .30-06. The perfect caribou rifle is probably a

.280 Remington or 7mm Remington or Weatherby Magnum. Caribou are not unduly hard to put down, but they are large enough to require good bullet construction. In the .270, I'd use either 140- or 150-grain bullets, and in both the .280 and 7mm magnums my choice has been 160- or 165-grain slugs. The 165-grain bullet is a good choice in the .30-calibers.

Synthetic stocks and rust-resistant metal finishes aren't essential for caribou hunting, but sure do make sense. It can rain for days on end up there, but aside from the sheer misery of it caribou can be hunted rain or shine. Gun weight is perhaps a more important factor than you might think. Walking over the tundra is difficult–a sloggy, boggy mess of tundra tussocks and uneven footing. If you happen to hit a caribou migration, you can sit by a crossing and take your pick of big bulls. But if you don't get that chance, you can be in for lots and lots of footwork. I hunted northern Quebec the year the George River herd changed its pattern. There were supposed to be caribou everywhere, but there weren't caribou anywhere. I finally got one, but I walked more than 50 miles the last three days to find a bull, and I'd have been delighted to drop a pound or two off of my wooden-stocked 7mm magnum!

Even at long range, caribou offer a big enough target that choice of scope isn't all that critical. A fixed 4X or 6X scope is just fine, as are 2-7X or 3-9X variables. Lens covers are essential; it would be most unusual to spend a week caribou hunting and stay dry the entire time.

To me, pronghorn rifles are either bolt-actions or single-shots because of the degree of accuracy required–especially as distance increases. With caribou, action type isn't an issue; even at long range, there's plenty of target to shoot at. Still, I'd reckon that a fairly light, synthetic-stocked bolt-action would be the best choice. I have shot the majority of my caribou with a 7mm Remington Magnum. There are no flies on that caliber for darn near anything on this continent.

Ideally, though, a .280 Remington might well be a more perfect choice because it offers plenty of performance and can be built a bit lighter. In fact, the ideal caribou rifle, as we'll now see, isn't far from being an excellent mountain rifle as well.

Chapter 34
The Mountain Rifle

On the North American continent, darn near any game can be mountain game at one time or another. Certainly a lot of deer hunting, most of our elk hunting, and almost all of our interior grizzly hunting is done in high country. When we talk about mountain rifles, however, the kinds of game that generally come to mind are our several wild sheep and our Rocky Mountain goat.

Even though actual hunting opportunities for our true mountain species are few and far between compared to hunting mule deer and elk, it's probably all right to think sheep and goats when you think mountain rifles. The size is about the same as for mule deer–200 to 300 pounds on average. Elk are so much larger that elk rifles are properly considered differently, whether for high country, forest, or foothill. Likewise are rifles for mountain grizzly considered differently. But a mountain rifle that's ideal for our sheep and goats will be just fine for deer, black bear, and whatever else might be encountered in the high country.

It's the very scarcity of hunting opportunity for our true mountain game that makes the mountain rifle such an object of campfire discussion. A big mule deer is harder to hunt and harder to come by than any sheep on any mountain–but hunters can pursue mule deer each and every fall if they so desire. Guides are required for sheep hunting throughout Canada and Alaska, and guided sheep hunts are very expensive. In the Lower 48, guides may not be required, but it can take a lifetime of effort to draw the required license. If and when drawn, it can be a once-in-a-lifetime chance. That, for instance, is the limit for desert sheep in Arizona–one per lifetime.

Given the serious financial commitment a guided sheep hunt requires–and/or the incredible luck required to draw a tag–it's no wonder so much thought is given to mountain rifles when the time comes to plan a hunt. I understand this better now than ever before, for just two weeks ago I got an envelope in the mail bearing a Montana bighorn-sheep license, the first sheep license I have drawn after more than 20 years of rejected applications in a half-dozen states. You bet I'm going to think long and hard about the rifle and cartridge I choose!

I have never considered myself a dyed-in-the-wool sheep nut, but over the years I have shot a dozen or so wild sheep plus several varieties of wild goats on four continents. Sometimes I have been wildly overgunned; my first wild sheep, a Stone ram taken in northern British Columbia's Cassiars, was shot with a .375 H&H. Likewise my first mountain goat. I can take some small comfort in being in good company while being so overgunned–the

Chadwick ram, arguably the finest North American trophy ever shot and the only North American ram exceeding 50 inches on both horns, was taken by L.S. Chadwick with a .404 Jeffery elephant rifle!

Nobody questions whether .404s and .375s will do the job on 200-pound sheep. Clearly they will. Actually, my old .375 wasn't all that outlandish a choice. Mountain sheep can generally be stalked to quite reasonable ranges, so while I had a whole lot more power than I needed, the .375's trajectory was unlikely to be a noticeable handicap. As things turned out, it wasn't. My Indian guide and I rode into a high saddle and spotted two rams way up above us. We left the horses right there and scrambled up a steep chute, coming out a bit above the rams.

If you must know the truth, I missed with my first shot, then rolled the largest of the two rams with a much more difficult running shot. I expect the results would have been exactly the same no matter what cartridge I was using.

Well, I'm certainly not going to build a case for the .375 as the ideal sheep rifle. It's about twice as powerful as you need, and rifles so chambered are much too heavy. But although you don't need a .375, you do need a rifle that speaks with some authority–perhaps a bit more than a 200-pound animal might generally call for. This is not because sheep are tough. They aren't (although, pound for pound, goats are *very* tough). Rather, it's because of the country these mountain dwellers inhabit. If you find a ram or billy in a spot where you can get to him, you want to anchor him right there. Goats live in worse country than sheep by far and are notorious for using their last bit of energy to launch themselves into precipitous places where recovery can be very dangerous–and sometimes impossible. Sheep will sometimes do the same. There's always the danger, too, of ruining cape, horns, and meat in a fall. Cannons aren't required, but plenty of power is–plus a bullet that will expand well and do plenty of damage.

Flat trajectory is also essential. The country dictates that long shooting is possible, so you must be ready for it just in case. Extremely long shots are fairly unusual since enough cover generally exists for a stalk to reasonable range. The longest shot I have ever made on a sheep or goat was in the Gredos Mountains of Spain, where I shot a very good Spanish ibex at about 250 yards. In contrast, I shot my most recent Dall sheep at about 60 yards, and an Alpine ibex in Switzerland at half that distance. Most of my own shooting for sheep and goats has fallen between 100 and 200 yards–closer to the former figure than the latter–and I think hunters with more experience than I've had would bear this out.

Even so, you can get caught in an open basin or reach a dead end during a stalk and need to make a cross-canyon shot. In purest terms, a .243 or 6mm is probably adequate, especially for the small-bodied desert sheep. But the occasional need for reach and the scarcity of the hunting opportunity dictates that most hunters are slightly overgunned.

The hotter .25s–both the .25-06 and .257 Weatherby Magnum–are good, sensible minimums. Cartridges that have both reach and power, yet can be built into short actions and thus save weight, like the .284 Winchester and 7mm-08 Remington, have much merit as well. But, for me, mountain rifles are built around full-length cartridges that offer both reach and power in good measure. These include the .270 Winchester, .280 Remington, and .30-06. The extra power offered by belted magnums in this caliber range–.264 Winchester, .270 Weatherby, and the various 7mm and .300 magnums–is really not needed. The other drawback to the magnums is that both the rifles and ammo are heavier. However, the magnums do offer flatter trajectories. Chances are you won't need it–but if you do have to make a long shot there will be a bit less guesswork in figuring the range.

If you need range you need accuracy as well, so action type should probably be either single-shot or bolt-action. I would favor the latter for two reasons. First, mountain hunting requires much climbing and constant negotiation of obstacles. You need both hands free, so I prefer to have a bolt-action rifle hanging on my packframe with the chamber clear but rounds in the magazine. If you choose a single-shot, the chamber will be empty most of the time, so you'll need to keep cartridges very handy in case a quick shot–rare but always possible–presents itself. Second, although the essence of mountain hunting is to plan and execute a stalk that culminates in one well-planned, deliberate shot, it doesn't always happen that way. That one shot may be placed perfectly, and yet you may still need to anchor your ram or billy so he doesn't dive off a cliff. You don't need rapid firepower, but you might well need a follow-up shot.

For my own mountain hunting, I've used a variety of rifles–a couple of .270s, a .280, a couple of 7mm Remington Magnums, a .270 Weatherby Magnum, a couple of .30-06s, and a couple of .300 magnums. Gun weight is important, but it depends a bit on the situation. If you're on a horseback hunt, for instance, gun weight is much less critical than on a backpack sheep or goat hunt.

On my last two backpack sheep hunts, one into Montana's unlimited-permit bighorn area and the other into the Northwest Territories' MacKenzie Mountains for Dall sheep, I carried a fiberglass-stocked .280 Remington with fixed 6X scope. On a hunt like that, you carry a rifle a whole lot more than you shoot it, and I was extremely happy with that choice both times–especially remembering a much poorer choice on another occasion!

This was another Dall sheep hunt in Alaska's Wrangell Mountains, and a little band of three rams had led us a merry chase over one ridge after another. By agreement, my guide wanted to shoot a ram after I had mine. So it was that we had two rams down in late afternoon, and we were very, very far from camp. We stumbled back to our tent 16 hours later–with two boned rams, two capes, two skulls with horns, and two very heavy rifles. Mine was a wooden-stocked 7mm Remington Magnum, accurate and dependable but at nine pounds scoped and loaded a whole lot too much rifle to be carrying. My guide's rifle was worse, a wooden-stocked custom .300 Weatherby weighing at least a pound more than my rifle! We shot our rams at about 100 yards, by the way, so we hardly needed the long-range machines we were carrying!

I well remembered that death march back to camp when I chose my little .280 for serious backpack hunting. On the other hand, when the time comes to choose a rifle to use to punch this long-dreamed-of bighorn tag I now hold, I don't think it will be the .280. It would probably do the job, but I think I want to be a bit overgunned just in case. I'm leaning toward a .300 Winchester Magnum, but if I go that route you can be assured it will be one that's built light. Such a choice, by the way, goes against some of my ingrained preferences in hunting rifles.

As a rifle nut, I feel that the most classic form of the mountain rifle is a bolt-action in .270 or .280, stocked in a nice piece of walnut that's been cut trim in an American classic style. Such a rifle need not weigh more than 7½ pounds or so all set to go, and that's really light enough to be pleasant to carry. I have at least two such rifles. One is a lovely Dakota Model 76 in .270; the other is my David Miller custom rifle in 7mm Remington Magnum. Either of these, optimally, is the kind of rifle I would like to hold while posing for the camera with my bighorn sheep.

Unfortunately, that begs the dilemma I discussed in the chapter on synthetic stocks. Mountain hunting is hard on hunters and hard on rifles, and it's especially hard on nice pieces of walnut. Mountain showers are likely on a daily basis, and early snowstorms are common. Rocks are going to scratch and gouge beautiful wood, and there's no way around that. For sheer practicality–ruggedness, stability, and light weight–mountain rifles should wear synthetic stocks. And although you don't really need magnum power, there's much to be said for a flat-shooting 7mm or .300 magnum, or, for that matter, a .264 Winchester or .270 Weatherby Magnum. The actual trajectory gains over a .270 or .280 are small, but they do exist. And when you're hunting unfamiliar game in unfamiliar country (and who today has enough experience with game such as bighorn sheep to be really familiar with their size in relation to their surroundings?) every bit of trajectory edge you can get lessens the need for precise range estimation if a long shot is required.

My hunting buddy Joe Bishop has a gun room full of some of the nicest sporting rifles ever built. His sheep rifle, however, is an over-the-counter synthetic-stocked Sako in 7mm Remington Magnum. With it he's taken nearly every huntable variety of sheep in the world, not only the North American grand slam, but most of the Asian sheep as well. Robert E. Petersen of Petersen Publishing Company also has a wonderful collection of superb hunting rifles. His current sheep rifle, however, is one of Kenny Jarrett's "beanfield rifles"–synthetic-stocked–in .300 Winchester Magnum.

Although such rifles are not exactly classic mountain rifles, they make huge amounts of sense when you're banking a once-in-a-lifetime tag on a single-shot at a big ram. With that in mind, I've ordered a Browning A-Bolt with the BOSS in .300 Winchester Magnum, and that might well be my choice when I head to the hills with that precious Montana sheep tag.

Scope selection is not really all that critical. The glass should be of high quality, of course, for both reliability and clarity of image. But a huge scope is not essential, and use of a moderate-size scope, no bigger than, say 3.5-10X, will save a bit of weight. A long shot may occur, but it probably won't be all that long, and even if it is, a ram or goat offers a fairly large target. Mounts, of course, must be solid and dependable–and I would not head up on a sheep hunt without a backup scope set in rings. I've never yet needed a backup scope, but if you take a hard tumble your rifle is going to suffer, and in mountain hunting more than any other place it's quite possible to take a fall and bend or break your riflescope.

Natural rests, whether handy boulders or logs, are fairly plentiful in the mountains. On foot hunts, I usually carry a packframe, and that makes a nice rest as well. On horseback hunts I'll have a daypack, and that laid across a boulder works well. In the mountains, I don't encumber myself with an artificial rest like a Harris bipod, as it's usually not needed.

I do always have a sturdy sling on the rifle, and I much prefer the detachable swivels that screw down and lock into place. A sling is a must so you can free up both hands while climbing, and is of equal value as a shooting aid–especially when your lungs are burning and you can't get your breath after a long stalk. I like a fairly broad strap of canvas webbing; such a sling provides a nonslip grip on my shoulder when carrying the rifle slung, yet is flexible enough to make a comfortable hasty sling.

As much as I admire the idea of a beautifully stocked lightweight mountain rifle in a "standard" chambering, I must lean toward the practicality of synthetics for this kind of hunting. And I must also accept the efficiency of flat-shooting magnums, tamed, if necessary, by muzzle brakes. It's possible, perhaps even likely, that this is what modern mountain rifles have evolved into, while the beautiful custom-stocked .270s and 7x57s Jack O'Connor wrote of so lovingly now belong to his era when sheep hunting was far more available and far less expensive than it is today. Of course, O'Connor's kind of rifle still makes a most sound and sensible choice. It depends on which type of rifle will give you the most pleasure to carry, and, far more importantly, the most confidence when the time comes for a shot!

As I said, when I wrote the first draft of this chapter I was in a dilemma regarding which rifle to choose for a long-dreamed-of bighorn sheep hunt. My choice narrowed down to a Browning A-Bolt, stainless steel, synthetic stock, BOSS-equipped, ultra-accurate, and the epitome of ultra-modern; or a Dakota .270–fairly light, beautifully stocked. In the end, tradition won out, and I shot Jack O'Connor's cartridge. As it happened, it was an easy shot, and the 140-grain Nosler Ballistic Tip did a fine job. I did have an earlier opportunity at the same ram. We were pinned down on the long side of 400 yards, and I simply wasn't going to try such a shot. Now, I think I could have done it. If I'd decided on the .300 instead, I *know* I could have done it. But as in most sheep hunting, it wasn't necessary to stretch the barrel like that. A couple of days later and we had the same ram dead to rights at 125 yards, the way it's supposed to be.

Chapter 35

Elk Rifles

I'm fortunate to have a tremendous amount of experience with African big game. And since I've written about that subject quite a lot over the years, I get a lot of questions regarding the myths surrounding African hunting. I'm often, for instance, asked about Cape buffalo charges. The answer is probably disappointing, because I've never seen a buffalo charge and don't expect to unless I make a huge mistake. Snakes are another hot subject, and I'm a disappointment there as well. Africa has some very bad snakes, it's true–but over the course of 30 safaris I've seen very few of them, and almost all were headed the other way when spotted. Perhaps the greatest myth of all is the legendary toughness of African game. Just like everywhere else, it depends on the animal. Impala are tough, sure. But so are white-tailed deer, and to call a 150-pound impala tough borders on ridiculous. Sable are fairly tough, pound for pound, while kudu are fairly soft. But it's the American elk or wapiti that really shoots holes in this myth.

Our elk are *tough*–by any standards, compared to any game in the world. The elk is big and strong to begin with, and pound for pound I rate him one of the toughest animals in the world. Poorly hit, an elk can go very far very fast, often without stopping.

Of course, it isn't really the animal's toughness that makes elk hunting as difficult as it is. There are many good calibers and hunting bullets that will penetrate into his vitals and do the job. He is no more bullet-proof than any other animal on this planet. The difficulty really lies in getting a shot in the first place.

Elk country is almost universally big and rugged. Sometimes it's very high, sometimes it's very steep, and often it's very brushy or heavily timbered. Occasionally, it's all of these things and more. There are plenty of elk in the American and Canadian West today, but each one requires a lot of acreage to survive. You can talk about state herds into the tens of thousands and local herds into the many thousands–but when you step off into elk country, you may cover a lot of real estate to find just one of them, let alone the thousands that are around somewhere. Add tough country and fairly thin distribution to the challenge of an animal with keen ears, superb eyesight, and a fabulous sense of smell. Then throw in those long, strong legs that can carry a herd to a whole new mountain range overnight, and you've got one of the most challenging hunts in the world.

It is not terribly difficult to pick out an elk rifle. There are plenty of good ones around, and a whole bunch more that will do in a pinch. But when you understand how much effort is required to maneuver yourself for that one ideal shot at an elk–especially a good bull–you then realize that both this grand animal and those who pursue him deserve and require the most effective rifles and cartridges available.

First let's look at how big elk really are, a subject of much discussion and more than a little exaggeration. I have seen weighed New Mexico bulls that field-dressed an honest 850 pounds–which should mean up to 1,100 pounds on the hoof. That's rare. Dressed weights for fully mature bulls run closer to 600 to 650 pounds. Spike bulls and cows run at least a third smaller on average. That's a very big animal, but certainly not a giant. Taking both size and toughness into account, a good rule of thumb is to deliver about twice the energy to the animal that you would want for deer-sized game. In other words, you want 2,000 foot/pounds of energy instead of the 1,000 foot/pounds considered minimal for deer. Clearly there are lots of cartridges that will do this.

If you accept that energy guideline, then the absolute bare-bones minimum elk caliber is the .25-06–and it drops below 2,000 foot-pounds at 100 yards. The .257 Weatherby hangs in just past 200 yards, but not much more. Likewise the .264 Winchester Magnum. Although the .25s and 6.5s will do the job, especially with well-constructed, heavy-for-caliber bullets, most North American hunters would agree that the sensible minimum elk caliber is the .270 Winchester. As we discussed earlier, much controversy surrounds the .270 as an elk cartridge. It would not be my choice, but it has the energy, it has good bullets available, and it will certainly do the job.

The surprise, though, is that if you subscribe to the 2,000 foot/pound rule (you don't have to, but it makes sense to me so I'm going to hold that thought for a while) you will note that the .270 Winchester also drops below 2,000 foot/pounds somewhere between 150 and 200 yards, depending on bullet weight and style! The .280 Remington with spitzer bullets over 160 grains will carry the freight to 200 yards with ease–but not much farther. In other words, we start to see that it takes a pretty powerful cartridge to carry 2000 foot/pounds of energy to significant ranges!

The .270 Weatherby Magnum is the smallest caliber that carries this energy to significant ranges, mainly by virtue of its very high initial velocity. The next one that does so is the 7mm Remington Magnum. The .30-06 with 180-grain spitzers will go to about 250 yards, but not much farther. Of course, the .300 magnums go the distance, as do the 8mm Remington Magnum and .338 Winchester and .340 Weatherby Magnums.

None of this is to say that you need an artillery piece to hunt elk. Good sensible minimums, to me, are the .270 Winchester and .280 Remington, and you could add the 7x57 into that mix as well. The point, however, is that if you choose fairly light cartridges like these, you have what you need but nothing to spare–and you do not have long-range capability.

Not all elk hunting requires long-range shooting. In fact, most of it does not. In the very heavy forests of the Pacific Northwest, where the large-bodied, stubby-antlered Roosevelt elk are hunted, most of the shooting is at very short range. In the few areas where rifle seasons for bugling elk are still open, ranges tend to be very short as well. Likewise in the thick timber and oak brush at medium elevations throughout the West. You have the greatest potential for long shooting when you get into the Alpine parks and basins at very high altitudes–usually, but not always, early in the season.

There are generally three different kinds of elk hunting best characterized by three different periods during which elk are hunted. The first is the early season, usually September into very early October. Elk are bugling during this time, and although bugling seasons during which firearms season is open are rare these days, that's probably the optimum time to hunt elk. Of course, if the rut hits a bit early or a bit late, you can wind up with the timber dry and noisy and the elk very high up. Next best–or, to many experienced elk hunters, the best of all–is late in the season. The rut is long since over and the elk are starting to herd up. Ideally, you have good tracking snow at lower elevations and enough snow up high to start the elk down toward winter range. The catch here is that, if winter doesn't start until after the season is over, this can be the most difficult period of all. The third time is everything in between. The rut is over and the elk are scattered, with the big bulls often by themselves licking their wounds. This is generally the most difficult time to hunt elk, although early snows can make it extremely favorable.

With regard to ideal rifles and cartridges, there are basically three different approaches: timber rifles for close-in hunting, long-range rigs for hunting the high open; and general-purpose rifles that can handle any situation. Which is the most sensible depends on the hunting conditions, but these three types of rifles don't necessarily follow the three distinct periods of elk hunting.

Let me explain. A rifle best-suited to close-cover work will be just fine throughout the season in the rain forests of the Pacific Northwest, and perhaps just as good on the oak-brush slopes of the southern Rockies. If an early-season hunt catches the rut just right, such a rifle would be perfect for a bugling hunt–but if the rut is slow and you need to reach across high Alpine meadows, you could be in trouble. Likewise, a large-scoped, flat-shooting rifle might be perfect for the middle and late seasons–unless lots of snow dumps early and the elk are down in the black timber. The tracking conditions will be great, but a long-barreled rifle with a big scope might become a real handicap. It's important, therefore, either to be in a position to accurately predict the hunting conditions, as most elk-country residents can, or to build some versatility into your choice. Let's look at these three types of rifles in greater detail.

Close-Cover Elk Rifles

This is a most specialized rig. Most of the suitable cartridges will not reach out across open meadows, but all will hit with authority and anchor an elk quickly, given a well-placed hit. More important than caliber, however, is that a close-cover elk rifle be responsive and fast-handling.

Everyone can pick their own minimum. Mine would be a .30-06 with 180-grain bullets, perhaps even heavier in very dense cover. Energy figures aside, there is no 7mm made that can equal the close-range punch of a good .30 caliber with heavy bullets. In that caliber, but in no other that I consider suitable, you can have your choice of all the action types–pump, auto, bolt, lever, single-shot. Any of the first four would be fine, but I would not choose a single-shot for close-cover work on elk. This was brought home to me in spades on a Colorado elk hunt two years ago.

The day before Colorado's first general season, we spotted a big herd of elk in a very high basin. Although it was too far in the gathering dusk to count points, there were a number of branch-antlered bulls. It seemed an ideal setup for the morning, although a fairly long shot seemed in the making. Next morning we crossed a 12,000-foot ridge in the dark, arriving above our elk basin just at dawn. We were already too late. The elk were there, but they were trooping down into the timber. We hustled to cut them off, and suddenly a long shot above treeline turned into a close encounter in black timber. We were lucky. Although a big six-point bull we'd spotted was with cows and wouldn't consider leaving, he was still bugling enough to answer us and pinpoint his location.

At about 40 yards, we could see tawny hide through a thick screen of stunted evergreen. I maneuvered a bit to the left, saw antlers and counted points, and found a bit of shoulder to shoot for between the trees. The only option was offhand, and my oxygen-starved body wouldn't steady the rifle. My first shot hit a tree. He was moving now, and I swung with him. The second shot also hit a tree. Now he was running, and I could just see his head and neck floating above the scrawny pines. In one of those brilliant (and very lucky) shots born of sheer desperation, I flattened him.

The cartridge happened to be a .30-06 firing 180-grain Nosler Partitions. For a neck shot at 60 yards, it could have been almost anything–but if it hadn't been a repeater, that first shot into an intervening pine would have been the end of the story. I shoot a bolt-action very well and, when I have to, very fast–and that rifle, out of Remington's Custom Shop, fits me very well. Regardless of action, that was another key–when there was no choice left, the rifle came up like a good shotgun and finally took over where I had failed and saved the day.

Above the .30-06 there are lots of other choices, although action type becomes quite limited. In a semiauto, there is only the Browning BAR in .300 and .338 Winchester Magnums. In slide-action, there's Remington's

Model 7600 in .35 Whelen. In lever-action there's the Browning BLR in .358 plus an assortment of more traditional Marlins and Winchesters in .356 Winchester, .375 Winchester, .444 Marlin, and .45-70. And of course, there's an even greater assortment of lever-actions on the used-gun rack: Savage 99s and Winchester 88s in .358; Winchester 71s (or Browning copies) in .348; even 86s in .33 Winchester and .45-70. Bolt-actions, of course, run on up the caliber scale from .30-06 and the magnum .30's past the 8mm and .33 magnums to .375 H&H and even the .416s.

The most limited of these rifles are the tubular-magazine lever-actions. The Marlins and Winchesters can both be scoped these days, but whether they're scoped or not, cartridges like the .375 Winchester, .444 Marlin, and .45-70 start to run out of energy and trajectory at 100 yards or so. The .356 and .348 Winchester give a bit more, but are still very shaky in the energy department at much past 150 yards.

However, if the country you hunt or the tactics you use sharply restrict shooting distances, there is absolutely nothing wrong with choosing a big Marlin or Winchester. The guns handle well, are very fast, and are a joy to carry. And provided shots are kept close, few things will thump an elk like a big flat-nosed bullet weighing from 250 to 400 grains.

In the same vein, there are no flies on a .358 Winchester, especially if you handload the 250-grain bullets no longer loaded in factory ammo. The .358, too, gives a bit more range if you need it. And, just like tubular-magazine lever-actions, a Browning BLR or Savage 99 is a real joy to carry. Lever-actions of both types are extremely popular in the Pacific Northwest, and for good reason.

The .35 Whelen, whether in Remington's slide-action or a bolt-action, is more versatile yet. With a 250-grain bullet, especially a round-nose, this is a devastating close-cover cartridge–and yet, with the same bullet weight in a spitzer design, it has a fair amount of reach as well. The Whelen offers a tremendous amount of punch at a surprisingly low cost in recoil and muzzle blast, and it can be built very light. My own .35 Whelen is a synthetic-stocked Remington Model 700, and it would be my personal choice for a close-cover elk rig.

Then there's the whole gamut of powerful centerfires chambered in bolt-actions. The wildcat .338-06 has quite a following for this kind of hunting, and it's a fine choice. So are wonderful elk cartridges like the .338 Winchester Magnum and .340 Weatherby Magnum. When it comes right down to it, I don't think you can hit an elk too hard, so if you happen to have a .416, there's no reason not to use it–especially if you tame it a bit with a lighter bullet in the 300 to 350-grain class. The only argument against it is that you don't need that much power, and you really don't want to carry heavier rifle than necessary in elk country. So I think the spectrum of really sensible close-cover elk rifles ends with the .375 H&H.

The .375 H&H is a wonderful elk cartridge, especially in close cover. Take a bull that's been bugled up and pumped full of adrenaline, and even the largest of calibers isn't likely to impress him right away. Thanks to excellent lightweight .375 bullets like Trophy Bonded's 240-grain Bear-claw, the .375 is actually a better elk cartridge than ever—but there will be a price to pay in gun weight.

For close-cover elk hunting, choice of scope isn't all that important, provided the scope isn't overly powerful. A simple, durable fixed 4X is plenty, and low-range variables in the 1¾-5X or 1½-6X range are just about perfect—if you choose to use a scope at all. Roosevelt-elk country is one of the last bastions of the aperture sight, and in that thick, wet country an aperture may well be a better choice than any scope.

Long-Range Elk Rigs

Rifles for open-country elk hunting are somewhat more versatile than close-cover rifles, although not by a huge margin. Now, by long range I don't mean desperation shots at 600 yards—the kind of shooting you might see or hear up in the hills but must not attempt and should not condone. An elk is a big animal, and he offers a big target—but most of it is nonvital, certainly not immediately so. I will not set an upper limit on how far a shot on elk should be attempted. That's where your skill and your conscience must reach an agreement. It depends on your ability to judge range as well as your shooting skill, and things like wind, shot presentation, steadiness of position, and so many other factors come into play. I will say that a serious long-range elk rifle should be able to deliver 2,000 foot/pounds of energy at 400 yards—and whatever point the energy falls below that figure is that cartridge's practical limit.

There are quite a few cartridges that reach that distance with 2,000 foot/pounds and more, but in almost all cases you must pick your bullets with care. For instance, the .270 Weatherby Magnum does it with a 150-grain spitzer. But even then it doesn't have much to spare. The 7mm Remington and Weatherby Magnums are much the same—with some bullet weights and styles (not all!), they can barely reach 400 yards with 2000 foot/pounds of energy. But that's about the limit. If you plan on sniping at elk at extreme range, I think you want all the downrange energy, bullet weight, and frontal area you can muster in a portable rifle that won't kick you into next week.

By those criteria, the available calibers are very limited, and action choice even more so. For this very deliberate kind of shooting, a single-shot would be fine, and Browning's BAR in .300 Winchester Magnum would also fill the bill. But in general, this is a bolt-action game, with very few potential calibers. The .300 Winchester and Weatherby Magnums, with aerodynamic bullets of 180, 190, or 200 grains will do it nicely. The .300 H&H

can, but only with hot handloads. Perhaps surprisingly, the 8mm Remington will not, at least not with factory loads, and the .338 Winchester Magnum also will not, or at best just barely with 225-grain bullets. The .375 H&H will just barely do it, and its trajectory is starting to arc severely.

To my mind, the best long-range elk cartridge we have is the .340 Weatherby Magnum. Yes, it kicks like a fiend. But with a 250-grain spitzer it hits the 400-yard mark with well over 2,500 foot/pounds of energy, and still has over 2,000 at *500* yards. Mind you, I have never fired at an elk in excess of 250 yards and I hope I never have to. But I do have a .340 Weatherby Magnum, and that would be my choice if I expected long shooting to be necessary. For those who like heavy calibers, a souped-up .375 like the .375 Weatherby isn't out of the question at all.

There are a number of hot wildcats that fill the bill, but the only other factory cartridge that's really in the running is the .378 Weatherby Magnum. With the right bullet, it can deliver 3,000 foot/pounds well past a quarter mile, but the price in recoil is simply too great for me. I'm very close to my limit with the .340, and it's all the gun any elk hunter could ever need.

Scopes for open country can be a bit bigger than close-cover scopes, but huge scopes are not needed and may well be bad news. An elk presents a huge target, and very high magnification can encourage shooting well beyond sensible ranges. I watched a friend of mine shoot at an elk up on a ridge using a .338 topped with a 4-12X scope. In that clear Alpine air, and with a silhouetted animal, I simply couldn't judge the range–I just knew it was very far. Through his scope, cranked up all the way, that big animal didn't look so far at all. He held just above the top of the shoulder–and his bullet hit a matter of *feet* below the bull. What he thought to be a very long but makeable shot was out in the stratosphere beyond 600 yards!

For elk, even for long-range work, there's simply no reason to go beyond 3.5-10X or 3-9X. Nor is there a reason to add gun weight with a big scope. Horseback hunting makes life a little easier, but sooner or later you do have to leave the horse. Open-country elk hunting is usually above 10,000 feet elevation, sometimes quite a bit more. You don't want to carry any more gun than you really need. An open-country elk rifle may need to be a bit heavier than a timber rifle. It may well sport a 26-inch barrel–both my .300 Weatherby Magnum and my .340 Weatherby Magnum do. But every ounce must be carried up and down the mountains, so reduce weight where you can. A good trade-off for a longer barrel may well be a synthetic stock. Elk hunting is tough and mountain showers are frequent, so the weatherproof feature of a synthetic can be as important as any weight saving.

Of course, any elk rifle should have a sling, just like any rifle for high-country hunting. But, as with mountain rifles, I generally dispense with artificial shooting rests as just another unneeded encumbrance. There are usually plenty of rocks or tree stumps to use as a rest—and if you don't have time to find one, you probably don't have the time you need for a deliberate long-range shot.

All-Round Elk Rifles

As you might expect, general-purpose elk rifles are a sort of mix between the other two extremes. You want plenty of power, but you want to be able to deliver it at some distance. On the other hand, you aren't seriously contemplating quarter-mile shots. These are the elk rifles most elk hunters choose for most elk hunting. There are choices available in all action types, and the list of potential calibers is quite long.

This is where cartridges like the .270, .280, .308, and 7x57 make sound and sensible minimums. You don't anticipate a bayonet-range encounter with an adrenalized bull in close cover, nor do you expect to reach out across a timberline meadow. Instead you expect your shot to come somewhere between, say, 50 and 250 yards. Except for a couple of bugling hunts, these are the ranges at which I have taken virtually all of my elk—and most elk hunters can say the same thing.

Better choices, to me, are the .30-06 with 180-grain bullets and the 7mm magnums with 175-grain bullets. There's more energy with the heavier bullets, pure and simple. Better still are the .30 magnums with bullets from 180 to 200 grains. And still better are what I consider to be "real" elk rifles: the 8mm Remington Magnum, the .35 Whelen, the .338-06, the .338 Winchester Magnum, the .340 Weatherby Magnum, perhaps the .358 Norma Magnum if you can find one, and certainly the .375 H&H.

Not all of these carry the freight at extreme range, but all work equally well from point-blank range to 250 yards. Several, as we've seen, will go well beyond that figure. In close cover, as I said, I'd go with the .35 Whelen. I love the light recoil and the way those 250-grain bullets perform. I've hunted elk with the 8mm Remington Magnum, and it's a fine cartridge. I've hunted elk a great deal with the .375 H&H, and it's a wonderful cartridge for almost anything in the world. And I have huge respect for the long-range capabilities of the .340 Weatherby Magnum. But for all-around elk hunting, I'll take the .338 Winchester Magnum any day of the week.

I'm not alone, either. Jack Atcheson—both Junior and Senior—went to the .338 for hunting their Montana elk years ago, and now use the cartridge almost exclusively for *everything*. It starts to fail a bit at very extreme ranges, but I've never had to shoot an elk at extreme range. From close in to fairly far, a 250-grain soft-point from a .338 can be relied upon to hit hard and penetrate deep. It hits with plenty of energy, and the frontal-area increase over any .30 caliber or smaller is noticeable in effect on game.

As with close-cover rifles, choice of scope is not critical. For the record, my own .338–a Brown Precision rig on a Remington Model 700 left-hand action–wears a fixed 4X Swarovski scope. I've used it not only on elk but on moose, caribou, bears, and a whole bunch of other stuff, and I can't honestly say I've ever wished for more power. If you feel better with a 2-7X, 2½-8X, or 3-9X variable, be my guest. More power than that is certainly not needed.

One word of caution with elk rifles. No matter what caliber you use, don't expect to bowl an elk over. If it happens, that's nice, but don't expect it, and don't dismiss your cartridge as too light if you make a good hit and nothing seems to happen right away. I've seen elk take fatal hits with such cartridges as the .338, .35 Whelen, 8mm Remington Magnum, and even the .375 and go right about their business for surprising periods of time. The animals are just plain tough, and the rationale for using fairly stout calibers isn't to flatten them instantly. That's asking too much. Rather, the idea is to make absolutely certain that you've driven your bullet into the vitals and done serious and irreparable damage.

With good, strong expanding bullets from fairly powerful cartridges, you will do that–and it's okay if it takes the elk a few seconds to succumb. Under many circumstances, a .338 will not put an elk down faster than a .270. But with a .338 you can be absolutely certain of reaching the vitals from any reasonable angle–and you'll do a great deal more damage when you get there.

Chapter 36
Moose Medicine

The moose is the largest antlered animal in the world. Next to the bison, he's North America's consistently largest game animal, although some Alaskan brown bears and polar bears occasionally outweigh the smaller varieties of moose. A big Alaskan moose can easily top three-quarters of a ton. Any animal that big demands respect when choosing rifles and cartridges. There's simply a great deal of moose to get through to reach things that are important.

However, moose are not tough like elk are tough. The animals seem to have fairly slow nervous systems, and it's very unusual to see a moose go down right away, regardless of what you hit him with. But while an elk may go a great distance with even a fairly good hit, moose are much more likely to stand for a second shot or simply fade off into the willows a few yards and lie down. It is uncommon to lose a moose that has been reasonably well-hit–whereas there's a real risk of losing any elk that has not been hit almost perfectly.

This is not to say that lighter calibers are okay for moose. They are not okay at all, simply because of the animal's sheer size. But cartridges that are acceptable for elk are generally very fine moose cartridges, even though moose are as much as twice the size of elk.

Common sense, I think, rules out the .25s and anything smaller. Nordic hunters, however, rely extensively on the 6.5x55 Swedish for the Scandinavian moose, which is generally about the same size as our Shiras and Eastern moose. I'm not about to tell them they're wrong, so let's just say I would prefer a bit more gun myself. If the 6.5x55 is a marginal but acceptable minimum for moose, then the .264 Winchester Magnum, the .270s, and the 7mms should be well on the right side of the margin.

Personally, I can't see it. I know the .270 with good bullets will handle moose, but I've never been inclined to err on the light side. Since I travel a long way to hunt moose, am generally looking for the best bull I can find, and may not have more than one chance, I want a strong comfort level in my rifle and cartridge. With most types of hunting, there's a difference between seeking a meat animal and seeking the best specimen available–and the difference between these approaches in selecting rifles and cartridges becomes more significant, the larger the animal in question is.

Hunters looking for just any moose–cow, calf, young bull–will do fine with cartridges on the order of .270, .280, .30-06, 7x57, .308, etc. The only caveat is that bullets should be fairly heavy for caliber and well-constructed. In .270, the 150-grain bullet is the minimal choice, and some of the heavier weights–160 and 170–though hard to find, are better yet. In the 7mms, the 175-grain bullet is the odds-on choice. In .30 caliber, 180-grain bullets are a good choice, but if ranges are expected to be short one might consider either 200- or 220-grainers.

Hunting bull moose is a bit different. Bulls are significantly larger in the body–and finding a good bull can take a whole lot of looking. You want to be able to take any reasonable shot offered, so you are probably best-served by heavier calibers–also firing good bullets. Remember, too, that if you're hunting during the rut you can encounter an animal that is not only very large, but also very full of adrenaline. Rutting moose routinely take on freight trains and large trucks and can be very hard to put down.

As far as I'm concerned, the .30-06 and .308 with heavy, well-constructed bullets are the absolute minimum that makes sense for moose. In either case, a good 180-grain bullet will be fine, but a 200- or even 220-grain bullet would be better still unless the country is such that a longer shot might have to be taken.

Ranges at which moose are shot varies widely by area. They are creatures of the Northern forest–more or less. What they really need is riverine or swampy country with willows and alders, and this ideal habitat may be surrounded by forest or it may be fairly open. In much of central and eastern Canada–and certainly in northern Maine and Minnesota–you'll hunt moose in typically heavy forest bordering the swamps and rivers. Shooting is likely to be very close, and the preferred hunting method is calling.

In the Rockies, where Shiras moose are hunted, the country surrounding the bogs and willow patches is more open. You will more likely glass for moose at the edges of meadows, and the shooting can be much longer. Hunting in Alaska and western Canada–British Columbia, the Yukon, the MacKenzies of Northwest Territories, and northern Alberta–is usually some mixture of the two extremes, with close shots coming occasionally but some reach also needed occasionally. Guns and loads should be matched to the country.

In habitat where shots are almost certain to be short, rifles ideal for close-cover elk hunting are also ideal for moose. Lever-actions in .444 Marlin, .45-70, and perhaps .375 Winchester will do just fine. But if the shooting gets out to 100 yards or more, these cartridges run out of steam very quickly. Marlin took several writers to northern British Columbia a few seasons ago, arming them with .444 Marlins as I recall, although some of the party may have used .45-70s. Most of the shooting was between 100 and 150 yards. No moose were lost and several were taken, so the hunt was certainly a success. However, multiple shots were required for each bull bagged, and Bob Milek reported to me that he desperately wished for a whole lot more gun when his opportunity came.

As with elk, cartridges like the .358 and .356 Winchester and the old .348 Winchester give a bit more reach and have plenty of power–especially

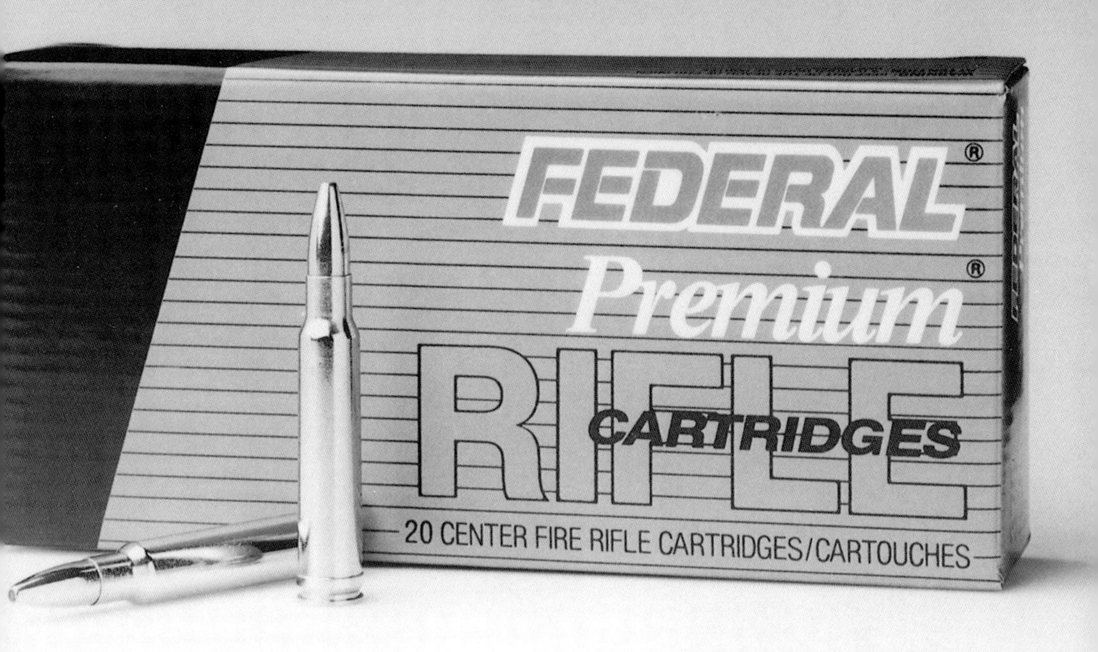

Commercial loading of "super-premium" bullets has given factory-ammo users new options. Federal now offers the outstanding Trophy Bonded Bearclaw bullet in a variety of factory loads, including a 225-grain .338 Winchester Magnum load.

One of the great strengths of the 7mm (.284 caliber) is the wealth of fine hunting bullets available. Ranging in weight from 175 grains (on the left) to 130 grains (on the right), this is just a small sampling of 7mm component bullets.

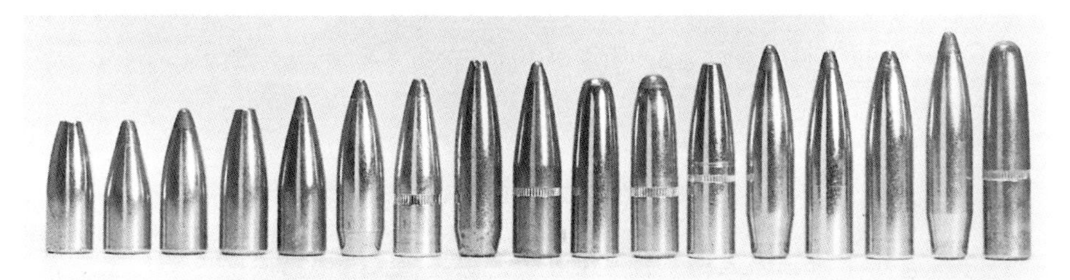

Thanks to the .30-caliber's lasting popularity, there's a tremendous variety of bullet weights and styles available in .308-inch diameter. The bullets shown range from 110 to 220 grains, and are just a fraction of the available .30-caliber component bullets.

The author's hunting partner, Randy Bello, took one of the very first sport-hunted caribou from the barrens of the Northwest Territories. The rifle isn't fancy, just a Model 70 in .30-06–doing the great job it has always done and will always do.

Though not huge, this MacKenzie Mountains ram was a welcome prize at the end of a two-week backpack hunt. A mountain rifle will generally be carried a whole lot more than shot, so weight and ruggedness are primary. The .280 Remington was quite adequate for the 60-yard shot on this ram.

Hunted under free-range conditions, the non-native aoudad can offer just as much challenge as our native sheep–and aoudad are much tougher. The author's David Miller 7mm Remington Magnum was a perfectly sound choice to hunt this aoudad in the rugged mountains of West Texas.

Although caribou hunting can mean a long shot, it often doesn't. Close stalking is usually possible–but bad weather and lots of walking are almost certain, so gun weight and imperviousness to weather are just as important as caliber.

For decades, the Savage Model 110 was a "plain Jane" basic rifle, but not anymore! Today it's offered in a wide array of calibers and configurations, including this fluted-barrel, synthetic-stocked stainless model with factory-installed muzzle brake.

The myth about having to shoot wild sheep at long range is mostly that--a myth. Relatively close stalks are usually possible, but you do want to be prepared for a long shot. Something on the order of a .270 or .280 is perfect.

Like so many worldwide hunters, Bruno Scherrer has hunted the mountains of the world with a .300 Weatherby. Did he need that power for this fabulous desert sheep? No, but he sure needed a rifle he had confidence in, and that was his .300.

The author with a fine mountain goat taken with his David Miller 7mm Remington Magnum. Mountain goats are as stalkable as sheep, but actually are a good deal tougher.

There's absolutely nothing wrong with choosing the .375 H&H as an elk rifle. The author took this New Mexico bull with a .375 firing 240-grain Trophy Bonded Bearclaws. Light, high-performance bullets like that extend the .375's versatility.

Here are two 180-grain .308-caliber bullets. Sectional densities are identical, but the spitzer boattail has a much higher ballistic coefficient and much better downrange ballistics. The round nose, on the other hand, will transfer energy more quickly and may be a better choice if you know the ranges will be short.

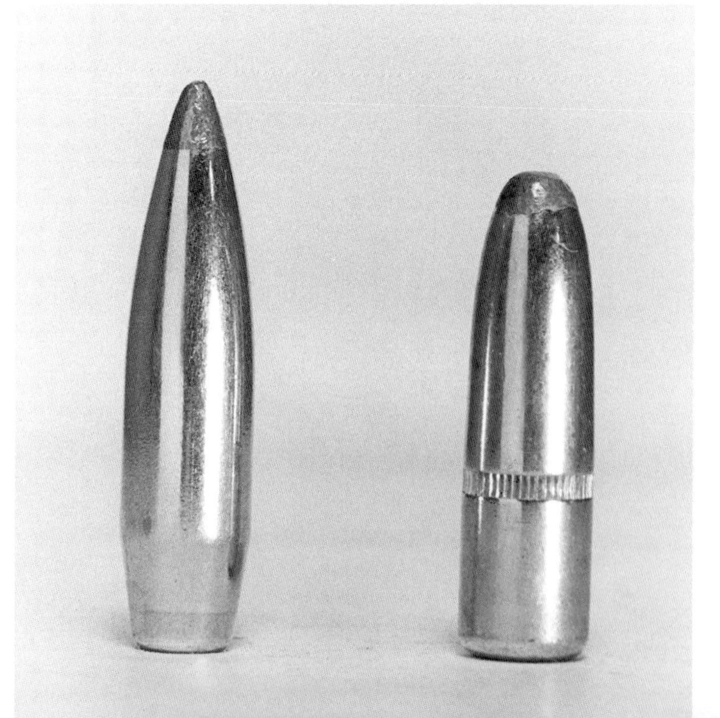

The new "Marksman" from Tucson gunmaker David Miller is a fine example of the new trend in long-range rifles: fluted barrel, laminated stock, and a 6.5-20X Leupold in Miller's milled scope harness.

This bull was bugled in and fell to a .35 Whelen with 250-grain Speer bullets. For anything except high alpine basins, the .35 Whelen is a superb elk cartridge.

Left to right, .357 Herrett, .35 Remington, .358 JDJ, .375 JDJ. All four of these cartridges are superb big-game cartridges for use in specialty pistols like the Thompson/Center Contender and the XP-100. All are wildcats except the .35 Remington.

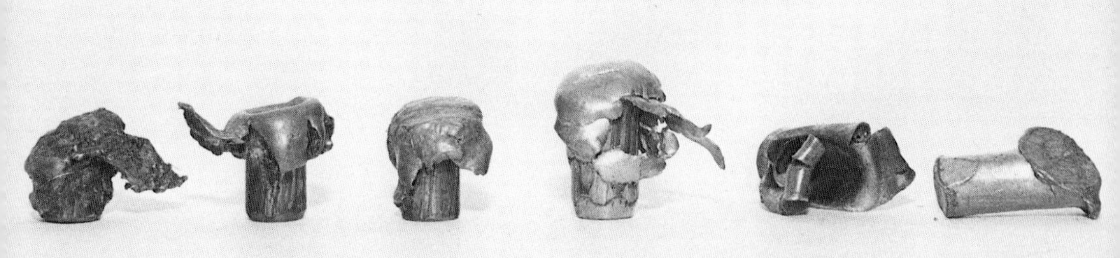

There is no way to exactly replicate bullet performance on game in testing media. These bullets were recovered from game, and while not all of them are pretty, all did their job just fine.

The Thompson/Center Contender has become one of the most popular hunting handguns of all time. Available in a wide variety of fine chamberings, this handgun is effective on small game as well as large game like wild hogs. It is also effective in long-range shooting with a scope.

One of the first animals taken with the factory version of the .35 Whelen was this fine Alaskan moose. A round-nosed 250-grain bullet literally bowled this bull over!

Most moose country is boggy, soggy stuff. The rifle must be capable, but you still have to carry it. Attention should be given to gun weight and weatherproofing.

A fine New Mexico mulie fell to a Clifton Arms 7mm Remington Magnum. In open country, the 7mm has a very slight edge over the .30-06.

This is a baffle board made up for testing bullet deflection. The bottom line is that no bullet can reliably get through any significant obstruction!

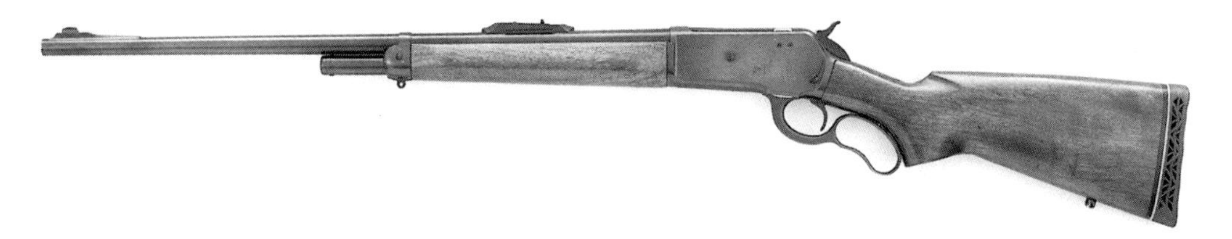

The Winchester Model 71 was the only rifle ever chambered for the .348 Winchester cartridge, and the Model 71 was offered only in that chambering.

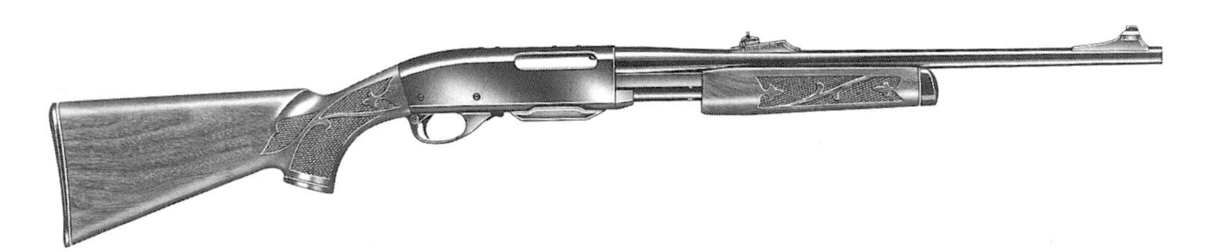

Remington's Model 7600 slide-action has the slide-action hunting-rifle market all to itself these days. The slide-action is very fast, and retains significant regional appeal.

The good old .348 Winchester remains one of the finest of all black-bear cartridges–but its utility is extremely limited by the near-impossibility of scoping its Model 71 Winchester rifle.

Lever-action fans can't go wrong by choosing a Browning BLR in .358 for close-range work on bears and boars. A 250-grain Speer absolutely flattened this Manitoba black bear.

Left to right: .22 Hornet, .222 Remington, .222 Remington Magnum, .223 Remington, .224 Weatherby Magnum, .225 Winchester, .22-250 Remington, .220 Swift. While most American hunters think of the .22 centerfires as varmint cartridges, they are legal for game up to deer in quite a few areas. The author doesn't recommend their use for deer, but admits that under ideal conditions they can be extremely effective.

Left to right: .300 H&H Magnum, .300 Winchester Magnum, .300 Weatherby Magnum, 8mm Remington Magnum, .338 Winchester Magnum, .340 Weatherby Magnum, .375 H&H Magnum. This group represents the large belted magnums that have genuine utility for North American hunting. All are quite versatile and very useful, but it's hard to build a case for a cartridge over .375 being really needed on this continent.

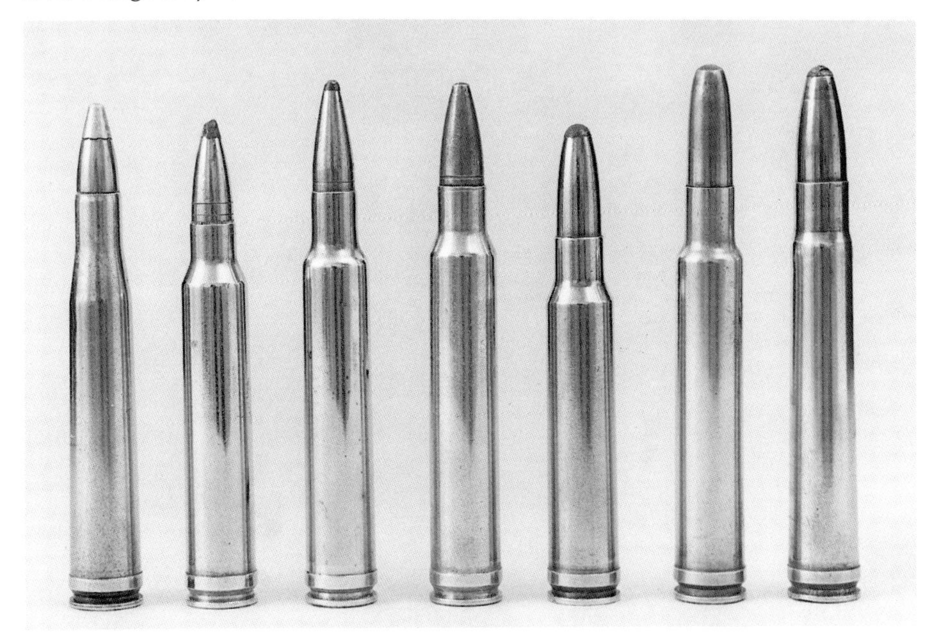

Like black bears, wild hogs are usually stalkable--but not always as close as you'd like. For general use, it's pretty hard to beat a scoped rifle with a bit of reach.

A Marlin .45-70 with 3X Leupold scope did a super job on this wild hog. This ancient cartridge is much more than a holdover--within its range limitations it's still great!

The Winchester Model 1886 was the premier "big bore" of the lever-action era. It was produced in a variety of chamberings up to .50-110, the last and most common being the .33 Winchester.

Remington's Model 700 line has long been available in a wide variety of synthetic-stock options. This is the "RS" version with Rynite stock.

The .375 H&H remains the most popular brown-bear cartridge, and with good reason. It has enough reach, and more importantly, it has the power to anchor even the largest of bears.

Left to right: .30-30 Winchester, .35 Remington, .375 Winchester, .45-70. These are classic "brush cartridges," and they are very effective for close-range use on game. They do not, however, "buck brush" any better—and perhaps not as well—as more versatile, higher-velocity rounds.

Left to right: .375 H&H, 8mm Remington Magnum, .338 Winchester Magnum, .340 Weatherby Magnum, .358 Norma Magnum, .378 Weatherby Magnum. These are the cartridges that make the most sense for use against our biggest bears. The only other serious contenders are the .416s and wildcat/proprietaries like the .330 Dakota and the .375 Weatherby Magnum.

The author on a muskox hunt in the High Arctic. Extreme cold is generally fairly dry, so firearms maintenance is not difficult--but all moving parts must be degreased.

Horseback hunting is extremely hard on rifles. A scabbard that has a hood over the butt offers much more protection, but the trade-off is that it takes ages to get a rifle out of such a scabbard.

This Dall sheep was killed with a .300 Weatherby in a custom Mauser action rifle. Although this caliber is not necessary for sheep, it was not too much gun for the grizzly, which was shot on the same hunt. (SP Photo Library)

The author used an A-Square .375 Weatherby on this muskox hunt. Few animals in North America really justify the use of such a powerful cartridge. The muskox probably isn't one of them, but it certainly worked!

The author with a management buck taken with a Steve Herrett-customized Remington XP-100. The accuracy of bolt-action pistols is absolutely phenomenal.

Texas outfitter Tommy Couch and Boddington with a desert mule deer taken with a .25-06 based on a Ruger M77 Mark II action. Built by Barnes Bullets' Randy Brooks, this is the author's idea of the perfect setup for smallish deer in big country.

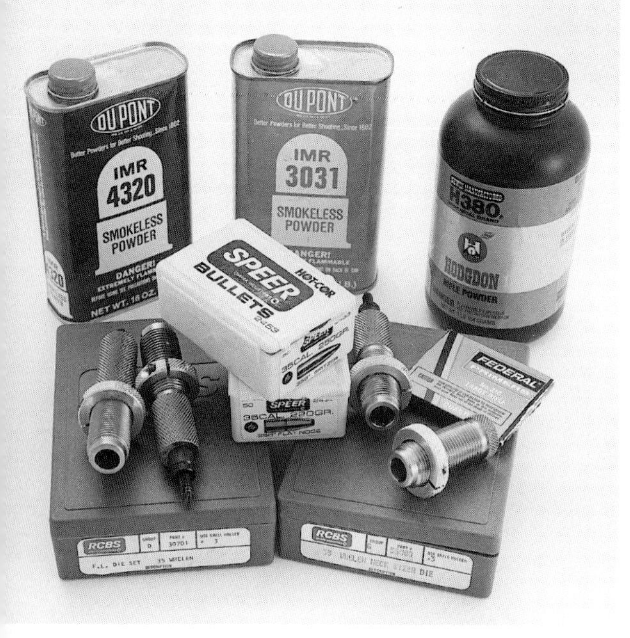

The 6mm Bench Rest in a custom XP-100 makes a fine long-range varmint rig, is ideal for javelina-sized game, and can be used on deer and pronghorn if the ranges are kept modest.

Thanks to the availability of dies and components, wildcatting has been pretty much an American pastime. Although now a "naturalized" factory round, the .35 Whelen existed for many years as a popular wildcat.

For the vast majority of elk hunting, it's hard to imagine anything that could beat a scoped bolt-action in a powerful chambering. This rifle is a Remington Model 700 in 8mm Remington Magnum, a fine and underrated elk cartridge.

This Chet Brown .338 Winchester Magnum is one of the author's favorite elk/moose rifles. A 250-grain Trophy Bonded Bearclaw, fired at fairly long range, made short work of this fine Shiras moose.

This South Texas whitetail was taken with Remington's then-new 140-grain loading for the .280. Although the author generally prefers heavier bullets, this was the most dramatic one-shot kill he has ever witnessed.

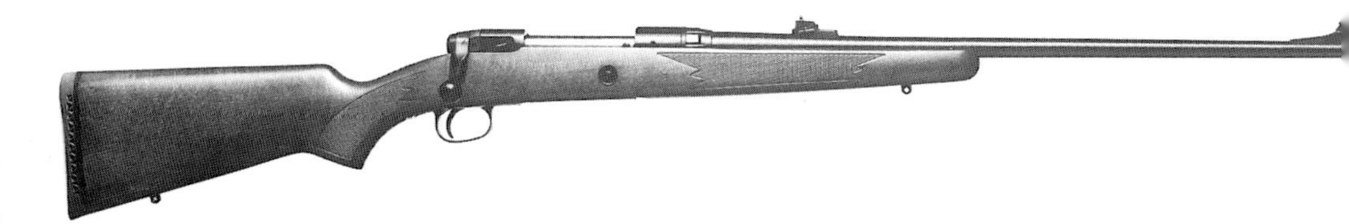

The Savage Model 110 is an exceptionally accurate rifle, and now a tremendous number of new variations are available. This is the 111GC with a classic-styled walnut stock.

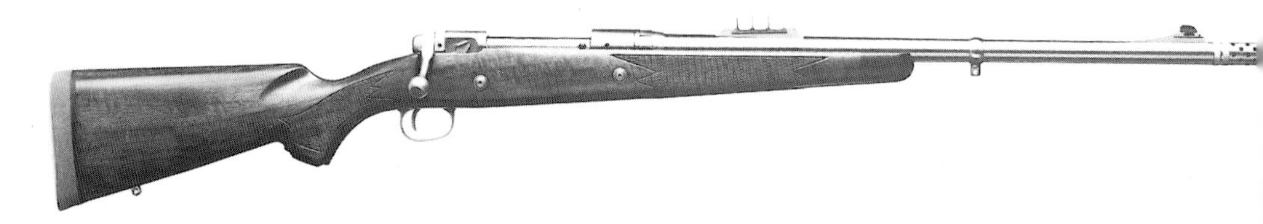

More traditional lines are also available on the 110 action. This is Savage's new Express rifle, available in .300 and .338 Winchester Magnum as well as African calibers.

The Winchester Model 70 is now available in a tremendous number of variations, including stainless steel for the first time ever.

The Burris Posi-Lock is a new innovation in scope stability. It's essentially an additional internal spring that locks the inner workings of the scope in place.

Winchester's Model 1300 Black Shadow Deer Gun has a non-glare finish, synthetic stock, and good sights. The rifled choke tube may not be quite as effective as a fully rifled barrel, but it still offers significant improvement in accuracy.

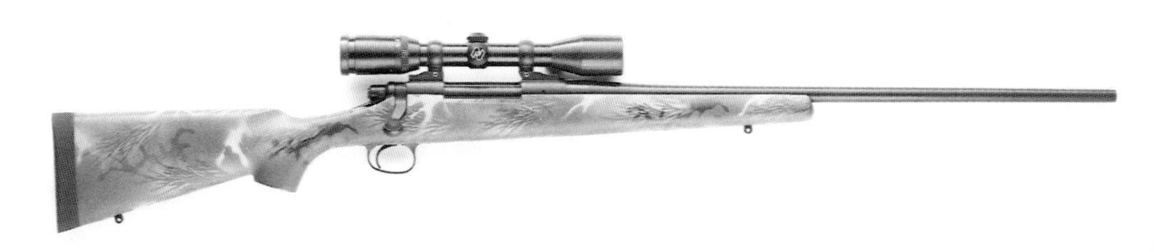

Brown Precision's High Country combines the ruggedness and accuracy of the Pro-Hunter with light weight for mountain hunting.

This Talley detachable mount can repeatably be detached and still will hold its zero.

A good .22 rimfire is an important part of almost any hunter's battery. It's the cartridge you start with, and also the cartridge you stay with for small game hunting and those all-important practice sessions. There's nothing like squirrel hunting to sharpen any hunter's stalking and shooting skills.

An early version of the "Rifleman's Rifle," a pre-1964 Super Grade in .300 H&H.

Brand new in 1995 is the Winchester Model 70 with the BOSS system introduced by Browning the previous year.

The author used a Weatherby Mark V in .300 Weatherby extensively for several seasons. The .300s aren't necessarily more effective on game than the .30-06, but they reach out a good deal farther and take a whole lot of the guesswork out of range estimation.

Outdoor writer Bob Robb often uses an extremely old pre-'64 Winchester Model 70 in .30-06. For decades this was the pre-eminent bolt-action sporter, well-deserving of its title, "The Rifleman's Rifle."

Ralf Schneider, from Germany, shot this South Dakota bison in the brain with a .300 Winchester. With a well-constructed bullet, this caliber is adequate for such shots, but marginal for body shots. (SP Photo Library)

The author's favorite elk rifle is a Brown Precision .338 on a left-hand Remington Model 700 action. This bull was taken with a 210-grain Nosler Partition, but in recent years the author has shifted to 250-grain bullets almost exclusively.

Marlin's new Slugmaster is an over-the-counter economical bolt-action 12-gauge with fully rifled barrel, offered complete with scope mount.

Texas-based Match Grade Arms is a new company combining light weight with benchrest technology to build ultra-accurate featherweights. The author's MGA .300, shown in full recoil, barely lifts off the bench and prints ½-inch groups!

Browning's A-Bolt II Medallion, in wooden stock and blue metal with the revolutionary BOSS stabilizing system.

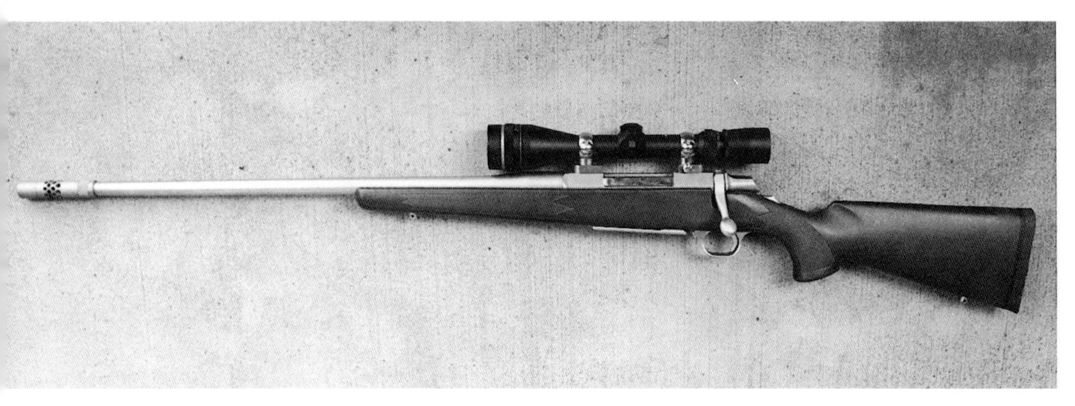

The author's ideal of an over-the-counter long-range rifle is realized by Browning's A-Bolt Stainless Stalker, in .300 Winchester Magnum, with BOSS, and mounted with the new Leupold 4.5-14X scope.

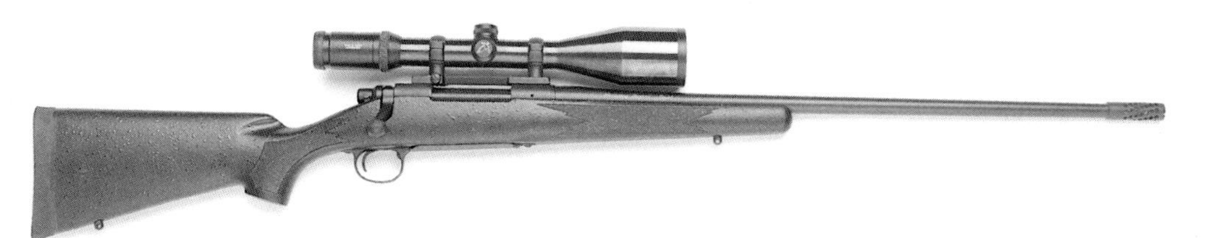

Here's the famed Beanfield Rifle made by Kenny Jarrett of Jackson, South Carolina. This is the accuracy legend for hunters who want to reach "way out and touch" their game.

In retrospect, the author doesn't see how anyone can look happy at 40 degrees below zero! In such cold, the bolt-action rifle is probably the most sensible choice. This bull was taken with an 8mm Remington Magnum firing 200-grain Nosler bullets.

Gunmaking legends Curt Crum, left, and David Miller with the new David Miller Marksman, a laminate-stock, fluted-barrel rifle designed exclusively for long-range shooting.

The Browning A-Bolt features a unique swing-away magazine with detachable box, a good compromise between detachable and fixed-box magazines.

An early JDJ barrel in .45-70 was used on this Arizona mountain lion. The .45-70 makes an extremely powerful short-range handgun cartridge, but the recoil is pretty fierce.

The Dakota Model 76 is an extremely attractive semi-custom rifle featuring excellent wood and a controlled-round-feeding action. Both right and left hand versions are available; this is a left-hand .270.

A fine desert mule deer from Sonora is just one of many animals the author has taken with his David Miller 7mm. The deer was in his bed, but the author was unable to see him until he jumped, instantly making an easy shot very difficult. That's when a rifle that fits well and promotes confidence is worth its weight in gold.

with the 250-grain bullets that have mostly been abandoned in factory loads. These are good "insurance" cartridges for country where the shooting should be short but might stretch out just a bit.

Unless the country is the kind where shooting is generally very close, however, most moose hunters–and certainly those who journey from afar–are best served by cartridges that offer a bit more versatility in the range department. These cartridges start with the .30-06, .308 Winchester, and 7mm magnums, but they sure don't end there. In fact, when you draw down on a really big bull moose, you aren't likely to get a lot of confidence from anything short of a cannon!

I've carried the .30-06 in moose country, likewise the 7mm Remington Magnum–and, for that matter, even a .270 on a couple of occasions. I've also used a .416. The first group of cartridges is too light for my taste, but an elephant gun isn't required, either. Moose are odd creatures in their reaction to receiving a bullet. I've shot them with both .416s and .375s, and neither cartridge seemed to impress them very much. No, they didn't go very far, but they didn't drop to the shot, either.

The only two moose I've ever seen really flattened were a bull I shot in Alaska with a .35 Whelen and a bull my Dad shot in northern British Columbia with a .308 Winchester. I have to regard instantaneous knockdowns like this as a bit of a fluke, since very similar shot placement with much more powerful cartridges has done nothing of the kind in much more numerous situations. But even though you generally can't count on knocking a moose tail-over-teakettle, you do want to absolutely ensure that you get a good bullet deep into the vitals. If you do, then your moose won't go very far. Especially if you're looking for a good bull, you also want to have a cartridge that will reliably do this at some distance if needed.

For my taste, the minimum moose calibers worth considering are the .300 magnums with 200-grain bullets. With the heavy bullets, the .300s will do it close as well as far, and have plenty of steam left at any reasonable range. Milder in the kick department but tremendously effective so long as the range isn't extreme (say, 250 yards as a sensible limit) are the wildcat .338-06 and the .35 Whelen. For general use, I'd put a good 225-grain bullet in the .338-06, and I'd use a 250-grain spitzer in the .35 Whelen. Remember, though, that a round-nose bullet imparts a great deal more initial shock than a spitzer, all things being equal. The one and only moose I've personally bowled over–flattened–was shot with a 250-grain round-nose from the .35 Whelen, at about 60 yards in thick timber. The results were incredible–but if I'd needed to make a 200-yard shot instead of one so close, I'd have been much better off with a spitzer bullet.

More powerful cartridges yet are even more suitable for the general run of moose hunting, provided of course that their users can stand up to their recoil and shoot them well. Near-perfect, to my way of thinking, are the

.338 Winchester Magnum and .340 Weatherby Magnum, both with the 250-grain spitzer bullets.

Several years ago, on a hunt in southern British Columbia, we were having a terrible time finding a moose. The rut was over and the bulls were in patches of house-high alders–and they weren't moving. Near the end of the hunt, we found a bull on a slightly raised little ridge right in the middle of such a patch. There was absolutely no way to get closer, and that bull was pushing 400 yards very, very hard. I was fortunate; I'd selected the .340 Weatherby for that hunt. I held just above the top of the shoulder and shot three times. Each time the bull walked just a few steps and stopped. Then he walked off the ridge and out of sight. He fell over within 20 yards of where he was seen last, never showing the slightest sign of a hit. All three shots were well-placed, fatal hits. His lack of reaction wasn't unusual, but the real point is that the .340 proved an ideal rifle and cartridge for that situation. The shot could have been made with a .300 or a .338, but with most anything else I might have chosen I wouldn't have considered making an attempt–and I probably would have gone mooseless that trip.

A more common situation was exemplified by a good bull I shot in the same area two years later. With the wind in our face, we walked into a little valley just at dawn, then climbed up on a rockslide to watch the alder thickets below. We saw several moose, but only one was worth a second look. This was a dandy, and he was picking his way through very thick cover right below us. The shot was about 225 yards or so, and I was using a .338 Winchester Magnum with handloaded 250-grain Trophy Bonded Bearclaws. Shooting down, I held high on his shoulder and fired when he stopped for a moment. He kicked into high gear, but there was no real reaction to the bullet. I fired again as he ran, but shot high and only clipped a big handful of hair from his withers. It didn't matter; the first shot was perfect, and we found him piled up just a few yards deeper into the brush.

The 8mm Remington Magnum would undoubtedly be an almost equally good moose gun, as would the .358 Norma Magnum. Neither of these cartridges, however, would be materially better than the .338 or .340, and in both cases the rifles and ammo are getting increasingly scarce. I seriously doubt that either cartridge will ever achieve significant popularity, and both may even be discontinued one of these days. So I wouldn't advise anyone to run out and buy one, although both are fine moose cartridges if you happen to own a rifle so chambered.

The good old .375 H&H is a superb moose rifle, one of the best. In several African countries, the .375 is the legal minimum caliber for eland, largest of the antelope. Eland and moose are very similar in size. I would not say that the .375 is the minimum needed for moose, not by any stretch–but if you have one and want to get some use out of it, you can't do much better. Extremely long shots such as I had to make with my .340 are somewhat rare on moose, and that's the only area where the .375 falls a bit short. It will handle fairly long shots, to be sure, but does not have quite the reach of faster, smaller-caliber magnums.

Although I've hunted moose with the .416 Remington Magnum, I don't honestly see a need for cartridges quite that powerful. It is not unheard of for a rut-crazed moose to charge, but to say that they're even remotely dangerous is a huge stretch. If you have a .416 and want to use it, there's no reason not to, but there's really no reason to accept the gun weight, recoil, and range limitations of the big bores for hunting our largest deer.

On the other hand, there's even more reason to treat this animal with plenty of respect. Moose are very large and very strong and respond almost not at all to bullet shock. It just makes sense to hunt them with powerful rifles and well-constructed, heavy-for-caliber bullets. No, cannons aren't needed, but perfectly adequate whitetail rifles aren't the right thing for animals eight to 10 times larger than deer.

Chapter 37

Guns and Loads for Black Bear and Wild Boar

The American black bear is, of course, a native animal that exists from coast to coast. While mostly a creature of the forests, he is found in southern swamps and southwestern desert mountains–a surprisingly adaptable beast. The wild boar is not native, but has established free-ranging populations in several parts of the U.S. Not only is the wild boar (or feral hog, wild hog, "Russian" boar, razorback, or whatever the local term happens to be) increasing in range and population nationwide; he is also increasing in importance as a game animal. As an example, wild hogs are well distributed in California and for many years now have been a more important game animal than deer in terms of hunter participation. It is outside the purpose of this book is to dwell on our non-native species–which can generally be hunted with equipment exactly the same as that for native game of similar size. However, I think it important to include the wild boar along with the black bear because of several traits the two share . . . besides both being predominantly black in color.

For one thing, they're hunted by similar methods: spot and stalk, trailing with hounds, baiting (more rare with hogs, but possible), and–although only locally popular with either–calling. For another thing, both are quite tough for their size, with strong bones and heavy muscle. Wild hogs are softer than bears in both departments, but make up for that with the thick gristle plate over shoulders and neck. Yet another similarity is the great disparity in size among individuals. A meat hog weighing 90 or 100 pounds is a whole different animal from a big boar weighing three times as much. And the average 200-pound black bear is not exactly the same as the 500-pound monster every hunter hopes to encounter!

Finally, both of these animals have the very real potential to turn the tables on their hunters. Black bears annually maul and even kill a great many more people than grizzly or brown bears. Undoubtedly this is due to their greater population and distribution–at least in part. But to ignore the fact that a black bear can be dangerous is very foolish. Likewise wild boars. Wounded or cornered, a boar is very fast and very deadly with his tusks. Injury to the hunter is very unlikely, but to ignore the possibility is just as foolish with hogs as it is with black bears.

The size differential between a really big hog and a really big black bear is substantial. There is no real limit on how big a black bear can get; there are legitimate recorded weights of as much as 800 pounds, though this is exceedingly rare. Bears get much heavier in the fall as they prepare for hibernation, and can weigh a third less–or even more than a third less–in the spring when they first come out. By any measure, though, a bear weighing 400 pounds is a big bear, and anything over that is a *very* big bear.

Hogs, too, put on weight very quickly when feeding conditions are good. Depending on forage, hogs vary regionally in size. In California's generally harsh, dry coastal mountains–where I have done most of my pig hunting–a boar weighing 200 pounds is a big pig. In good acorn years, I have shot boars weighing as much as 350 pounds, but that's a rare size on the West Coast. In parts of Texas and the Southeast, where water is available year-round and feeding conditions constant, weights up to 400 pounds and more are possible. But although I've heard of such things, I seriously doubt whether a hog living in the wild could actually reach 500 pounds. Domestic pigs, which are the exact same *Sus scrofa* species, do reach such weights, so I suppose it's possible. In any case, big black bears average bigger than big hogs–and the biggest black bear is much bigger than the biggest pig. Guns and loads for the two species are not exactly the same, but they're close. So we'll cover them together by hunting technique, which dictates–or at least strongly suggests–the proper choice of arm.

Baiting

This is probably the most common hunting technique for black bears. In Canada, it's practiced from Newfoundland west to Alberta. In the United States, it's legal in some areas, not in others, but remains strong in the forest country of the Upper Midwest. Baiting is practiced only rarely for wild hogs. Although not thought of as such, it's common in Texas where hogs often come to deer feeders and are taken as targets of opportunity. In other parts of the country, it's often kind of accidental–for instance, shooting hogs off of a cow carcass. With hogs, waiting by water holes or stock tanks is common and profitable–pigs must have water daily. While this is not exactly baiting, the conditions are much the same.

The significant factor in baiting, or similar stand-hunting situations, is that you know up front how far your shot will be. You want your stand far enough from the bait so the animal can approach undisturbed, yet close enough so that you have a clear, simple shot. In most baiting situations, 100 yards is a very long shot and somewhere around 75 yards is about right.

The other common factor in most baiting situations is that the animal is most likely to come in poor light. Bears, especially, are generally afternoon feeders, and the biggest bears usually move the latest. Most bait stations will be in thick forest so the bear can approach with confidence; dark will fall quickly and the shadow will be deep.

Since the shot will often come very late in the evening–and since heavy cover will almost certainly surround the bait–you want to hit the animal very hard and anchor him in his tracks or as close to that as possible.

Following up a wounded bear—or boar—in thick cover at last light isn't my idea of fun!

Since you already know the range, and it will be short, you don't need a flat-shooting cartridge. However, since the light is likely to be poor, you really do need a scope to ensure precise shot placement. And since you want to hit the animal very hard, I think you're best served by a fairly powerful rifle firing a bullet of heavy weight and large frontal area. I would lean toward round-nose or flat-point bullets over spitzers for rapid energy transfer.

In terms of caliber, anything from .270 upward is just fine for wild hogs. For bears, I'd start with the .308 or .30-06 and work upward from there. The best choices, however, lie in medium- to large-caliber "brush rifles." Cartridges like the .358 Winchester, .35 Whelen, .444 Marlin, and .45-70 are absolutely ideal. I would like to include the .348 Winchester, but rifles made in this caliber are almost impossible to scope, so they make poor choices for last-light shooting. Energy figures aside, the sheer "thumping power" of heavy bullets of .35 caliber and larger is much more devastating at these short ranges than bullets from typical "deer cartridges" in .270, 7mm, or .30 caliber—even though the latter may have more energy on paper.

As a case in point, on a hunt in Canada where two bears were allowed I took two rifles: a lever-action Browning .358 Winchester, and a 7mm Remington Magnum. My intention was to shoot one bear with each rifle, and I did. The first bear was broadside, and I shot him on the shoulder with a handloaded 250-grain semi-spitzer from the .358. He was knocked backwards about six feet and never moved. A couple of nights later, I shot a bear of similar size in the exact same place with a 160-grain Nosler Partition from the 7mm magnum. This bear ran off into the brush as if nothing had happened. He didn't go far—but I didn't know that until I followed up the blood trail.

Two bears prove nothing. But I've shot a lot more than two bears. Those I have shot with the .358, .35 Whelen, and .348 Winchester have gone nowhere—ever. Those shot with the .270, .30-06, 7mm magnum, and such have *always* either gone some distance or required multiple hits.

My experience with pigs is much the same, except that pigs are a bit smaller. The same .358, .35 Whelen, .444 Marlin, .45-70, etc., will be absolutely devastating. A .270, .30-06, or something on those lines will be only slightly less so. But with both animals, I simply don't believe in the 6mms, .25s, and 6.5s. The physiology of both animals is hard on bullets, and with both species you can get into big trouble with a wounded animal.

Oddly, although I've now shot something like 30 Cape buffalo, several lions, a couple of elephant, a couple of leopard, quite a few black bears, and four brown or grizzly bears, the two closest calls I've had were with wild hogs. One was shot a bit far back with a .30-06, not by me. The other was shot square on the shoulder with a 165-grain softpoint from a 7mm Remington Magnum as he quartered to me. In the first case, I stupidly got too close on the follow-up, armed with only a .38 Special revolver. The second instance was over bait and it was nearly dark. I rushed the follow-up because of failing light, and the boar came out of the gloom right at me. I jumped aside and pressed the muzzle against the pig as he passed, and that did the trick. I could be wrong, but in both cases I think a larger caliber—even though it might have carried less energy—would have prevented these near disasters.

While the brush calibers mentioned are just fine, there aren't any real upper limits here. A .338 Winchester Magnum is a perfectly acceptable rifle, especially for black bears. It really isn't needed for wild hogs. In the same vein, the .375 H&H is devastatingly effective. You don't need it, but with bears there's really no such thing as being overgunned.

Scopes are essential, but the exact scope chosen is not so critical for shooting at these ranges. A 4X scope is more than adequate, as are the low-range variables. Remember that the larger objective of a garden-variety 4X, given equal-quality optics, will gather more light than the straight tube of most variables in the 1½-5X class. Action type is not important, nor is gun weight. Gun *length* can be, as long-barreled rifles can be extremely unwieldy in the typical treestands built over bear baits. Depending on the circumstances, it can be wise, too, to remove the sling once you get into the stand. Even the slight creaking of a sling swivel, or, worse, a sling knocking against something as you bring the rifle up, can alert a keen-eared bear.

Hound Hunting

Use of bait has come under fire in several states, but the anti-hunter (and sometimes hunter) sentiment against hound hunting is much more widespread and vehement. We can do relatively little about what the anti-hunters think—certainly we can't expect them to understand our sport. But I hate to see hunters take a stand against legal hunting methods that they either don't understand or choose not to use. Our divisiveness—and eagerness to point fingers at others for somehow being lesser sportsmen because of the legal means they prefer—may eventually be the end of us. Regardless of whether you like to follow hounds or not, an extremely cogent argument for hound hunting is that it is one of the most selective hunting methods available. On good ground, you can check the track and make sure the animal is of the size you want before the hunt even starts. Failing that, you *always* have a shoot/don't shoot option at very close range. But that particular soapbox isn't the subject of this book, so back to business.

Hound hunting is shrinking in areas where it can be used, but it remains regionally popular for both black bear and wild boar. Again, the hunting of the two species by this technique is very similar, the only real difference being that bears sometimes tree (not always!), while pigs obviously never do. With both, the pursuit is fast and furious. The chase will lead over rough terrain and through the thickest brush and forest–and no pack of hounds can hold either a big boar or an angry bear forever. The hunters must get there quickly, else the animal will catch his breath and be off again.

Failure to catch up means that eventually the quarry will escape or, more likely, the chase will completely outdistance the hunters and it may take days to recover the hounds.

Selection of firearms should be very similar to the selection for bait hunting, with a few wrinkles. First, the shot will be very, very close. In theory, you could go with a lighter caliber, but that's not necessarily the right course since a wounded animal can wreak havoc on valuable dogs in short order. Still, point-blank range makes a difference. A lot of houndsmen stick with .30-30 carbines–light, easy to carry, and generally quite adequate with flat-nose 170-grain bullets. Powerful handguns, too, are adequate choices. The .44 Magnum, especially with heavier-than-normal bullets in the 300-grain range and heavier, will do just fine. The .454 Casull would be right at home. Better choices would be the same light carbines in .35 Remington or .356 Winchester. And all the other brush guns mentioned above would work marvelously as well.

Second, scope sights are not needed for this kind of work. In fact, they may be a huge handicap, depending on whether you shoot with both eyes open. If a bear makes his stand on the ground–and a boar always will–you must close in and pick your shot, being very conscious of where the dogs are and making sure they're out of the line of fire. Some houndsmen simply will not allow scope sights, since with open sights it's much easier to use peripheral vision and make sure the shot is clear.

Finally, gun weight is a big issue with this kind of hunting. You must cover ground quickly, and often it's very rough ground you must cover. A holstered handgun is a real blessing, but a short, light carbine is almost as good and certainly more effective in most hunters' hands.

Calling

In the case of bears, this is a regional technique employed by few people. In the case of pigs, this is brand new ground just now being broken. But calling works for both animals.

Ranges will be very short, so the kind of equipment used for either baiting or hound hunting will work just fine. One caution only: With bears, it's usually the larger ones that answer a call. And they come boldly, almost charging the call. Better to be overgunned than undergunned!

Spot and Stalk Hunting

This is my personal favorite technique for both species. It requires some flexibility in firearms, especially with bears, since you never know exactly how close the terrain or the animal will allow you to approach. A scoped rifle that shoots relatively flat and packs significant punch is probably the best choice.

With bears, a .30-06 is a good sensible minimum. With pigs, a .270, 7mm-08, or 7x57 will do just fine. With pigs, though, provided you keep the wind right, it is usually possible to work in fairly close. I've done quite a bit of spot-and-stalk pig hunting with a peep-sighted .348 and some amount with open-sighted .30-30s. I have not yet failed to get a pig because I was carrying an open-sighted rifle. The same is not true with bears.

On another two-bear hunt, I took both my .348 Winchester and a scope-sighted .338 Winchester Magnum. Early in the hunt, I stalked and shot a very nice black bear with the .348. Late in the hunt, I saw a beautiful cinnamon bear far down a forestry cutline. I can't remember why I had the .338 that day, but that was the rifle I had. The bear was picking dandelions as they do in late spring, but it was midafternoon and chances were slim he would stay on that cutline forever. I ran a half-mile or so, then slowed and really began stalking. I was still quite a way off when the bear crossed the cutline and started toward the forest on the other side. Perhaps he was just switching sides, but I was certain he was leaving and there was no time left to get closer. I lay down prone with a hasty sling and shot the bear–in about that much time. It wasn't all that far, no more than 250 yards at most. But I could not have made that shot with the .348, and I wouldn't have even tried.

For this kind of work, the .338 is not too much gun, especially if you encounter the kind of black bear you'd really like to meet. But for purists who hate to be overgunned, something on the order of the .338-06 or .35 Whelen is just perfect. My personal pick for this kind of hunting would be the .35 Whelen with a low-range variable or fixed 4X scope, but there are dozens of rifles and cartridges that will work just fine, provided the cartridge is adequate for the biggest bear–or boar–that you might encounter.

My two biggest black bears, by the way, were taken by spot-and-stalk hunting with a .375 H&H. On both occasions, grizzly bear was the intended quarry so I was a bit overgunned on purpose. But both of these bears–one in British Columbia in 1974, the other in southeast Alaska in 1994–squared well over seven feet. That's a lot of bear of any species, and with such a bear you are not overgunned with a .375. You might not be undergunned with a .30-06, but you don't have much margin for error. A .338 or similar cartridge would be a very fine tool for such bears, but both of those bears dropped to the .375 without a wiggle, so if you happen to have one I wouldn't rule it out as a darned effective black-bear gun. But I wouldn't get one just to hunt black bears. Rifles on the upper end of the deer-rifle scale are really just fine, provided you choose tough, heavy bullets and place those bullets where they belong.

Chapter 38

Loaded for Bear

Stopping runaway bison or moose can be like having to stop a train. Black bears are just unpredictable enough to be deadly if you get careless. Wild hogs, too, can be extremely dangerous and are without fear when cornered. Even the normally placid muskox can turn the tables on overconfident hunters. But North America's only consistently and unarguably dangerous game species are our big bears—and they rank alongside the most dangerous game animals in the world.

Whether you're hunting the polar bear in his icy domain, the brown bear of Alaskan alder thickets, or the mountain grizzly of Alpine basins, America's great bears are big, strong, indomitable of will, and thoroughly hazardous to hunt. Their corded muscles, strong bones, and that will to survive also make them exceedingly difficult to bring down. When selecting rifles and cartridges, no other animal in North America should command the respect of our great bears.

In size, the three don't vary all that much. Brown bears and polar bears are, at their best, by far the largest. A popular campfire argument centers around which is the larger, the polar or Alaskan brown bear. In truth, no one knows. Although zoo specimens of each have reached enormous weights and sizes, few bears of either species taken in the wild have been weighed. The outside skull dimensions of both bears are similar. Squared hides of the largest bears will also be similar; in both cases, a 10-foot bear is very large, and in both cases the occasional 11-foot-plus bear is heard of. Be aware, though, that few measurements in the hunting world are as consistently stretched (literally!) as the squared measurement of bear hides. Genuine 10-foot bears of both species exist but are exceedingly rare. A bear squaring a legitimate nine feet is a keeper in any area in any season, and there's nothing wrong with a fully mature 8½-foot bear.

Weights in the fall for such bears might range from 800 pounds to as much as 1,500 pounds, with polar bears being more streamlined in build and possibly not as heavy as the biggest brown bears. By any standard, however, a bear approaching a half-ton or more is a lot of bear.

Mountain grizzlies have a tougher time making a living. On average, they are much smaller than brown bears, with some of the more northern mountain ranges producing bears that average much closer to six feet than seven. Even so, interior grizzlies do occasionally reach eight or even nine feet. This, too, is a lot of bear—and even a smaller grizzly has the strength, stamina, corded muscle, and unpredictable disposition to make him (or her) an animal to be reckoned with.

With grizzlies, you might expect a smaller bear but you must be prepared for a real monster. With brown bears, you can expect a big bear–and you have a very good chance at a monster. With polar bears, the size parameters are about the same as for brown bears–and there's the added consideration that an ice bear may never have seen a human and regards all living things in his domain as prey. In all cases, powerful cartridges and the best bullets made are the only sensible choices. But hunting conditions for the three bears differ markedly, so we should examine separately the guns and loads best suited for each.

Interior Grizzlies

The Alaskan brown bear is the largest of the *Ursus arctos* clan, but to my mind a good grizzly bear from the interior mountains is the most magnificent creature on this continent. He ekes out a tough living in his remote mountains, yet he still grows large and powerful–and in a way that few creatures on earth can, he dominates his world.

The problem with grizzlies is that they're hard to find. To paraphrase Jack O'Connor, "even where there's lots of 'em there aren't many of 'em." The mountain grizzlies of interior Alaska, British Columbia, the Yukon, and the few other places where the great bears still exist in huntable number are thinly dispersed over some of the wildest, most remote country on this continent. I well remember, on a black-bear hunt in Alberta, looking far up and across the gorge of the Smoky River, seeing eagles circling. "Grizzly kill for sure," said outfitter Bob Morrison. Grizzly season was open, and it was a small matter to go to town and buy a license. But the river was in flood and uncrossable, and a journey of several days lay between us and that "sure-thing" grizzly.

So it is. In western Canada and interior Alaska, grizzlies remain fairly plentiful–but only because their habitat is still almost limitless. Regardless of the overall numbers, very few specific places hold more than the occasional grizzly. For one hunter to find one of these bears in a given place at a given time is very much like finding a needle in a haystack.

Even finding a grizzly is no guarantee the bear will be brought to bag. Earlier in this volume, I wrote about a British Columbia grizzly I shot with the .340 Weatherby Magnum. What I didn't mention before was that this bear was taken on the last day of a very long and very difficult hunt. It started as a full-mixed-bag hunt, and relatively early on we took a nice goat. But as the hunt progressed we–my outfitter buddy who had just bought the territory and I–learned that caribou were almost nonexistent, sheep were scarce and virtually inaccessible due to lack of trails, and we just didn't know where the moose were. So, with 10 days left and grizzly season opening, we moved into bear country.

Here there were grizzlies, lots of them. *Really* lots of them. Over the next 10 days, we had 32 sightings of what we believed were 17 *different* grizzly bears. Some were sows with cubs and some were so far away they might as well have been on the moon. But several we stalked–at least two of them more than once on different days. Each time something happened. The wind shifted, or the bear moved into the timber in the time it took to reach him. The bear we shot was a last-day bear, and the shot was born of desperation and frustration.

Grizzly hunting is often a game of endless glassing, day after day. Even in the best country, the great animals are so thinly dispersed that the majority of grizzly hunts are not successful. After a half-dozen blown stalks in 10 days, that hunt should have been unsuccessful, and it's a miracle that one last bear on the last day gave us a chance. Most grizzly hunts come down to one or two chances. If you close to a shot without the wind changing or the bear outdistancing or just plain eluding you, there must be no mistakes and no misses.

If you *knew* you could approach for a close shot, then a wide variety of rifles would do. Certainly any of our "close-cover elk rifles" would suffice. If you knew your bear would be the average 350-pound mountain grizzly, our "standard" deer rifle in .270, .280, or .30-06 would be just fine. If you knew you would run into a real mountain monarch, a king grizzly, and that you would close to 150 yards or so, you might well choose a powerful rifle like a .375 or .416. But you know none of these things.

When hunting interior grizzlies, you might get a shot at 100 yards, or it might be 250 yards or more and no chance to get closer. You might get a shot at a well-furred, very normal bear weighing 300 to 400 pounds, still a very fine trophy. Or you might get a shot at a monster bear weighing more than twice as much. The only thing you really know for sure is that you won't get many opportunities. You can hope for a close shot at a huge bear, but you may have a much longer shot that's a "take-it-or-leave-it" opportunity at a bear that may range from big enough to very big–but it's *your* grizzly if you can make the shot.

Clearly, this kind of a set-up calls for both power and versatility. A timber rifle may have the power, but very possibly not the ranging abilities you need. The average flat-shooting deer rifle may have the trajectory, but absolutely lacks the power if you encounter a very big bear. Very powerful cartridges like the .416s certainly have the kind of energy you want if you encounter the kind of bear any hunter hopes to–but most of the big bores lack the trajectory to make shots between, say, 200 and 300 yards as simple as they should be.

The great .375 H&H is an answer, but even the .375 gets a bit dicey at 250 yards–and its level of power isn't really required for even the largest of interior grizzlies. I shot my first grizzly with a .375, as described in the chapter on that caliber. But that was a long and difficult shot, and I was in my early twenties and full of confidence and ignorance. Today I'm fairly certain I wouldn't have attempted that shot–and if I had to, I know I wouldn't want a .375.

I'm certainly not advocating long shots on dangerous animals like grizzly bears. It would be nice if no one ever attempted a shot beyond 100 yards–and if that were the case, gun selection would be simple. I can't even tell you how far is too far. On a grizzly, 200 yards is a long shot and 300 yards perhaps beyond the outer limits. What shot you attempt is up to you and your skill level. But I am saying that there won't be many opportunities for a shot in grizzly country. If you have a rifle that gives you both the energy you need and the confidence required to make a well-placed shot somewhere between 200 and 300 yards, you're very far ahead of the game.

There are few such rifles for animals as tough and potentially dangerous as the grizzly bear. Minimal, to me, would be the .300 magnums with 200-grain bullets. Equally acceptable would be the 8mm Remington Magnum or its European counterpart, the 8x68S. Better would be the .338 Winchester Magnum and better still would be the .340 Weatherby Magnum, both with 250-grain spitzer bullets. Throw in the .358 Norma Magnum and top off with the .375 H&H, and to my mind you now have the entire world of truly suitable interior-grizzly cartridges.

It isn't the shot you *get* that's so important in this context. It's the shot you *might* get that you must be prepared for, realizing that with grizzlies you can't count on the kind of shot you'd really like. You need a rifle that can reach out with a great deal of authority–and also one that's accurate enough to guarantee precise shot placement. Clearly, that means a scoped rifle, and almost certainly a bolt-action. The only exceptions would be Browning's BAR in .338 or a single-shot if you were so inclined.

The exact scope isn't critical. A grizzly offers plenty of target area, and the longest shot you might take on a bear isn't really all that far. A fixed 4X would work just fine, or a low-range variable. Whether gun weight is critical depends a bit on whether you intend to hunt on horseback or afoot. If it will be the latter, keep in mind that grizzly bears now occupy few areas that aren't very high, very remote, and very rugged.

Alaskan Brown Bear

A good grizzly rifle in .338 Winchester Magnum or .340 Weatherby Magnum would make a good brown-bear rifle, no doubt about it. There are some slight differences, though. For one thing, brown bears are potentially much bigger. A huge bear I shot in Alaska in 1981 had a body as big as any Cape buffalo I've ever shot–and was as impossible to turn over.

It's said that brown bears can weigh three-quarters of a ton, and I believe that was such a bear. Whatever its weight, it was a whole lot more bear than a 500-pound grizzly, and more bear than any interior grizzly could ever become.

Another difference is that brown-bear hunting is often (not always) conducted in lower country with much thicker vegetation. A longish shot is still possible, but not nearly so likely. Yet another difference is that brown-bear populations tend to be much more concentrated. Statistics indicate that brown-bear hunting is far more successful than inland grizzly hunting–which means that, under ideal conditions, you can perhaps be a bit more selective about the shots you take or pass. If you choose to pass a 200-yard shot because it feels on the long side for so dangerous an animal, you have much better odds for another opportunity later in the hunt.

Finally, while shooting at longer distances is possible, close-range encounters in dense alder thickets, spruce forest, or high grass are even more likely. If you encounter a big brownie at 15 yards, you don't just want to cause him fatal injury. You want to flatten him if you can.

Rifles like the .30-06 with 220-grain bullets have accounted for a great many brown bears, and certainly the .300s with the heaviest bullets will work just fine. But with the largest of the world's predators, especially with the strong potential for close-range encounters, I think you want something a whole lot heavier.

A number of brown-bear guides use .458 Winchester Magnums, and a couple even use double-barreled rifles in .470 and .500 Nitro Express. The problem is that such rifles are almost useless if a 200-yard shot is called for. The .338 Winchester Magnum and .340 Weatherby Magnum, so ideal for interior grizzly, are good sound minimums for Alaskan brown bear. The .358 Norma Magnum would be a good choice as well.

Best of all, to my mind, remains the 1912-vintage .375 H&H. It has the reach if you need it–but, and this is more important, it has the knockdown power for close-range work. A 270-grain bullet would be all right, but I much prefer the greater penetration of the longer, more stable 300-grain bullets.

The .375 Weatherby Magnum, though rarely seen, would be worth considering. However, its primary advantage over the H&H version isn't more knockdown, but rather more range. You really don't need the range on brown bears, and a rifle in .375 Weatherby will usually be a whole lot heavier to help balance the significant increase in recoil.

A very strong case could also be made for one of the .416s. I would personally lean toward the .416 Remington Magnum. Its ballistics are identical to the .416 Rigby, but its much smaller case can be built into a significantly lighter rifle. The .416 Weatherby Magnum is fabulous, but again you're into gun weight, plus a whole lot of recoil and a two-shot bolt-action. The .416 Remington starts to get shaky long before you reach 300 yards, but it will reach to 200 and more with no problems, and I don't think you need to pay the extra price in recoil and gun weight for the extra ranging abilities of the .416 Weatherby.

The range limitations of larger calibers are just too great to make them sound choices. As backup guns for guides, okay–but not for the sport hunter.

I'm not sure it makes much difference whether you choose a .338, .340, .358 Norma, .375, or .416. All have the power and the range, and all can handle any bear you might encounter. Except for the .358 Norma, I have rifles in all these calibers and would be comfortable with any of them. I have shot brown bears only with the .340 and .375, and although the .340 worked just fine, I'm very comfortable with the .375 and chose it for my most recent (unsuccessful) brown-bear hunt. If I had it to do over again (and I will next spring), I would almost certainly stick with the .375–aside from one other possibility. That one other candidate is my synthetic-stocked .338, for the following reason.

Coastal brown-bear hunting is plagued by horrible weather. On my Southeast Alaska hunt this spring, it rained almost constantly seven of 10 days. The Peninsula, too, is wet and nasty more often than not. This kind of hunting screams for a synthetic stock; the walnut stock on my .375 was literally ruined in the course of a 10-day hunt. I happen to have a fiberglass-stocked .338, and I might well choose it rather than subject one of my wood-stocked .375s to that kind of abuse.

Although generally a low-elevation affair, brown-bear hunting is done in country that is either very steep or very boggy–usually both on the same day. Hip waders are worn constantly, and much walking is usually in order. Gun weight is a consideration, and of course that's a contradiction when you speak of powerful rifles. A .338 can be built lighter than a .375, and a .375 can be built lighter than a .416. I think I prefer the .375 as a caliber, but as a perfect brown-bear rifle I'd sure lean toward one built fairly light with a synthetic stock.

Again, choice of scope is not important so long as it's waterproof, rugged, and fairly low in magnification. A low-end variable remains a good choice. Due to the horribly wet weather that might be encountered, a strong case can be made for detachable mounts. Good scope covers are a must, but you still might need to complete a stalk in a rainstorm so strong that a scope would be rendered useless in seconds. It's a good piece of insurance to be able to remove the scope and continue. Rust-proof finishes also make a great deal of sense.

I must repeat as a caution that brown bears are very big and very powerful. I have shot only two, and may or may not ever shoot another. The first, that very large Alaskan bear, took five very good hits from a .375 to bring down. The second, on Russia's Kamchatka Peninsula, was taken with a single 250-grain Nosler from a .340 Weatherby. This does not mean the .340 is a better brown-bear gun. With the .375, that bear went down to every shot–but kept getting up. With the .340, there was no reaction whatever to the first and only shot, and the only thing that prevented more shots was intervening foliage. Brown bears are simply very hard to impress–and I suspect that the bigger they are, the harder they fall.

Cartridges in the .416 class and larger may have a better chance of really knocking a bear down, but it's still no sure thing. All you can do is place a well-constructed bullet from a powerful rifle as precisely as possible–then be prepared to do it again and again until the job is finished. Again, the Browning semiauto in .338, plus-bolt actions and single-shots, are really the only choices available.

I would lean toward a bolt-action repeater because of the noise in getting a round into the semiauto's chamber, and because clean one-shot kills are rare with this animal.

Polar Bear

The polar bear can grow as big as a brown bear and, if anything, is more dangerous. The country, however, is wide open. Close encounters around ice-pressure ridges are always possible, but not as likely as running into a brown bear in the alders. The use of dogsleds–and often dogs turned loose to bay the bear–means that long shooting is fairly rare, but point-blank shooting is more rare still. A .375 would be a good choice, but a .338 or .340 Weatherby might be better.

Conditions, although very icy and cold, are generally quite dry. There is no real advantage to synthetic stocks (but no disadvantage, either) nor is weight a factor since the rifle is generally carried on the dogsled. Scopes, perhaps surprisingly, are not really susceptible to cold-weather maladies, so a scope of good quality in good mounts should be fine.

More critical than anything else is the absolute necessity to totally degrease any moving parts and lubricate with dry graphite only. In this regard, a bolt-action is far and away the most suitable. Its bolt can be easily stripped and degreased, and dry graphite will provide more than adequate lubrication for the short haul. The bolt-action has the added advantage of being carried on the sled with rounds in the magazine, meaning no fumbling for cartridges in subzero cold.

Now that polar-bear trophies can again be imported into the U.S. after more than 20 years, this is a hunt that I'd like to begin planning. I don't yet know which rifle I will take, but I think I lean toward my battered old .338, fiberglass-stocked, with a fixed 4X scope. I could be wrong, but I don't think more is needed in either rifle or scope.

As we have seen, the differences between hunting our biggest bears are subtle. One rifle in a caliber between .338 and .375 would be just fine for all, but for none of our biggest bears would I go lighter–and only for brown bear would I go heavier. Regardless of the caliber chosen, and regardless of which bear, place much emphasis on bullet selection. Few animals in the world have as dense muscles or as heavy bones as our big bears, and this is no place for bullets with any tendency whatever to come apart. In fact, of all animals on this continent, the big bears are the ones that really make the super-premiums like Trophy Bonded Bearclaws, Swift A-Frames, and Barnes "X"-Bullets worth their weight in gold!

Chapter 39

Brush Busters–Fact or Fancy?

We have an entire class of rifles that we like to call "brush rifles." The typical specimen is probably a tubular-magazine lever-action, but there are bolts, pumps, and semiautos that fit the mold as well. These rifles tend to be light and stubby–short in the barrel, fast-handling, and, well, easy to employ in heavy brush.

The cartridges for which these rifles are most typically chambered are called brush or timber cartridges–and the general thinking is that this class of cartridge gives you the best chance of getting a bullet through intervening brush and twigs. I suppose this class of cartridge properly starts with the .30-30 Winchester and the nearly identical .32 Winchester Special, but generally we think about larger calibers when we talk about brush busters. The .35 Remington is a classic. So is the .348 Winchester. Other lever-action calibers in this class include the .356 and .375 Winchester, the .444 Marlin, and the ageless .45-70. Bolt-action brush calibers would include the .358 Winchester, .350 Remington Magnum, and .35 Whelen. The latter is available in a slide-action as well, and the .358 Winchester is best known for being chambered in "general-purpose" lever-actions like the Savage 99, Browning BLR, and Winchester Model 88.

Legend has it that the big, relatively slow projectiles from these cartridges will push through brushy obstructions, staying on course and finding their mark. It is true that bullets driven at extremely high velocity are likely to become very unstable if they hit even a very light screen of grass or thin brush. But it doesn't necessarily follow that slow, heavy bullets will push on through. In fact, *nothing* is foolproof at getting through brush.

I've written about it before, but the experience I'm about to describe was such an object lesson in bullet deflection that it's worth repeating. In Zimbabwe–then Rhodesia–some 15 years ago, I shot at a broadside buffalo at about 60 yards. The bullet was a 500-grain full-metal-jacket from a double-barreled .470 at about 2,130 feet per second. We don't need cartridges that large in North America, but if there's an ultimate brush buster, something like that must come close. The buffalo dropped to the shot, pole-axed. To drop a buffalo instantly like that is a bit unusual, but I shrugged and patted myself on the back . . . until I saw the entrance wound.

I had aimed at the shoulder, but the bullet entered squarely on the neck, nearly three feet from where I'd aimed. More interesting yet, the bullet clearly entered *sideways*, leaving an entrance wound that was an exact profile of that big bullet! I walked the ground from where I'd shot and found the offending branch about two-thirds of the way to the buffalo. It wasn't much of a branch–smaller than my little finger. But it was freshly and cleanly cut, and it was plenty big enough to divert even that big, slow-moving bullet.

The best course for shooting through brush is not to do it. Period. If you must try it, know that any bullet of any caliber can and probably will be knocked off course. The degree can vary significantly, but the chance of missing–or, worse, wounding–increases dramatically as the amount of obstruction increases. Where the obstruction is located in relation to the target is important, too. The worst case is a screen of brush some distance in front of the target. Chances of getting through are a bit better if the animal is standing right behind the obstruction. The best option is to try to find a hole through the brush–and if the animal's vital area isn't clear, just don't shoot.

While the classic brush rifle is often open-sighted, low-power scopes are actually a much better choice. With a scope you are much more likely to see intervening twigs and branches, and it's also much easier to see holes in the brush that will let you slip a bullet through. In the case of that buffalo, for instance, I never saw that bullet-eating twig over my express sights. With a scope, I probably would have.

It's well and good to advise not shooting through brush, but if the buck of a lifetime is standing just behind a brushy screen, his outline backlit and absolutely clear–and there is no clear spot ahead that he's likely to step into–most of us are likely to try the shot. If we must, are the classic brush busters going to give us the best chance for success?

Perhaps not. Some years ago, we made a dowel-rod baffle board, using offset dowel rods to represent a brushy obstruction. We placed targets behind the board at varying distances and attempted to shoot through the dowel rods with a wide variety of calibers and bullets. If the obstruction was right in front of the target, say a couple of feet, most bullets got through reasonably well. Oh, some keyholed and others were driven off course several inches, but most of them did get through and actually hit an 18-inch-square paper target. If the obstruction was farther from the target, 10 feet or more, the results quickly got quite hopeless.

Surprisingly, though, the legendary brush cartridges didn't fare so well. We tried, as I recall, the .30-30, .35 Remington, .444 Marlin, and .45-70 in this class. The .30-30 did the best, but none of these cartridges were particularly good. The great old .45-70 was particularly bad for keyholing and being driven wildly off course.

We also tried several "conventional" cartridges. The best of these in our informal round of testing was the 300-grain bullet from the .375 H&H. Now, that's a cartridge few North American hunters will use. But of the cartridges more likely to be seen afield, the real surprise was how well the 100-grain .243 Winchester load did. It beat the pants off of all the so-called brush busters. That seems to blow holes in the theory that high-velocity cartridges are less stable, but remember that the .243 isn't really all that fast–less than 3,000 feet per second–and its 100-grain bullets are fairly long, with good sectional density and relatively high ballistic coefficient.

The 7mm Remington Magnum also did well with both 160- and 175-grain bullets, and the good old .30-06 with 180-grain bullets did extremely well also. Overall, spitzer bullets seemed to do better than round-nose designs, and round-nose bullets did better than flat-points.

Caliber aside, it appears that long, relatively heavy-for-caliber bullets are going to be more stable in brush than short, fat bullets with low sectional density. This should come as no surprise, since longer bullets with higher sectional density absolutely give deeper and more straight-line penetration on game than short bullets with low sectional density. The theory is the same.

The problem with many of our brush cartridges is that they fire short, fat bullets that are relatively light for caliber. A 200-grain bullet is the heaviest factory load currently available for the .348 Winchester, .35 Remington, .358 Winchester, and .350 Remington Magnum. Although 200 grains is not a light bullet, it is fairly light for the .35 caliber, and will not be nearly as stable as the 250-grain loadings long since dropped by the factories. The .444 Marlin, though it's a fine cartridge, fires a very short and light-for-caliber 240-grain .44 Magnum pistol bullet. In the .45-70, bullets of 300 grains, though a good deal faster, are much less stable than the old 405-grain bullet with which the cartridge made its legend.

The .35 Whelen, of course, does offer a good, heavy 250-grain loading in both spitzer and round-nose design. My very limited and not particularly scientific testing indicates that the 250-grain spitzer from the .35 Whelen–or from any of the .35s–would be one of the better choices for getting a large-caliber "brush-busting" bullet through brush. However, there's another side of the coin worth examining.

One of the real strengths of the so-called brush busters may not be getting through brush but flattening game once and for all when the bullet arrives. A round-nose transfers energy more quickly than a spitzer, and a flat-point transfers energy more quickly than a round-nose. As mentioned earlier, I believe one of the reasons for the .30-30's solid reputation as a great deer cartridge, despite less than impressive paper ballistics, is the consistent performance of its flat-pointed bullets. Going up a step, the same is true–only more so–with the .348 Winchester, .444 Marlin, and .45-70. It's also true, although perhaps to a slightly lesser degree, with round-nosed slugs from the .35 Remington, .358 Winchester, .35 Whelen, and so.

It's true that these big slugs may tend to deviate from course in the brush–but so does everything else. It's just a matter of degree. The point is that if you can get those big, bluff-nosed slugs to the game, things happen quickly from there. I'm certainly not suggesting that it's okay to wing big bullets through brush in the hope that they'll hit the animal *somewhere*. It's not okay, because if you do attempt to shoot through brush you no longer have any control over exactly where the bullet might land. But I have to say that I'd much rather have a marginal hit with a great big bullet than with a little bitty one.

Light, small-caliber bullets at high velocity are just fine, but they work much better when placed in–or at least very near–the vitals. We don't really have a way to measure the effect of bullet diameter–frontal area–on game. Elmer Keith tried with his "pounds-feet" theory, and the late great elephant hunter John Taylor tried with his "knock-out" values. Both theories are somewhat subjective, while "foot/pounds" is a genuine means of expressing bullet energy. Unfortunately, the mathematics of figuring foot/pounds of energy requires that velocity be squared; thus, velocity has a greater impact in determining energy than bullet weight–and bullet diameter does not enter into the equation.

I'm not saying this is wrong. After all, foot/pounds of energy are real. But in *effect on game,* I believe bullet weight is important–especially bullet weight in relation to caliber–since sectional density has much to do with penetration. And I believe frontal area is also extremely important. As a theory, frontal area explains why the .45-70 is so effective even on very large game, despite its very low energy figures. Carrying that theory a bit farther, round-nosed bullets of, say, .35 caliber, may not have the foot/pounds of energy of a 7mm magnum–but more of the energy they do have is transferred more quickly over a more broad area. Moving from theory to reality, you can kill any big whitetail (or black bear or hog or, for that matter, moose) with a 160-grain spitzer from a 7mm Remington Magnum, but if you want to drop him in his tracks at relatively short range, the fact is you'll do it more consistently with the 1873-vintage technology of the .45-70.

So I do believe in the brush busters. Not for busting brush, but for dropping game *in* heavy brush. Experienced hunters all know that, except for brain or spinal-column hits, it's impossible to predict with any accuracy what a given animal's reaction will be upon receiving a bullet. A few will drop to a well-placed heart or lung shot, but most will run a short distance. A few will run a significant distance. One of the nuances of shooting game in heavy brush or timber is that the animal will almost certainly be out of sight in just a few bounds. A bullet of large diameter is generally more likely to leave a blood trail than a bullet of small diameter. However, the actions of bullets in game–and the actions of game upon receiving a bullet–are both so unpredictable that, except on good, clean snow, an easily followed trail can never be guaranteed.

There's really no excuse for losing a well-hit animal, but speedy recovery of game is always desirable. In the worst-case scenario, a slow tracking job with darkness coming on means spoiled meat–and *any* tracking job means unnecessary anxiety for the hunter. After all, if the game doesn't drop in sight, there's rarely 100 percent certainty of exactly where the bullet hit or where the animal might be. Though it's sad to say, in some of our hard-hunted whitetail and even elk country today a well-hit animal that doesn't drop within sight might well be tagged by someone else. Following up wounded–even fatally hit–game is a part of hunting we don't like to talk about, but it's going to happen.

I grew up with the understanding that "first blood" tags the game–but reader mail I've gotten indicates that there are quite a few folks in the woods who didn't get that kind of upbringing. Hunters in areas where they have to worry about following a blood trail to a drag mark tend to go fairly heavy in caliber. Depending on the country, they might use a .35 Remington, a .358 Winchester, a .444 Marlin, a .35 Whelen, or a .45-70. They aren't wrong. Given a reasonable hit, especially on deer-sized game, the big, slow-moving, large-diameter projectiles from cartridges like these do indeed have a better chance of both stopping and dropping game than faster, lighter projectiles that might have more energy on paper.

No, the brush busters won't necessarily bust through brush. Nothing will. Their strength lies in what happens when the bullet gets there. For the deer hunting I generally do, I don't have a need for such cartridges–but I don't hunt in the big timber of Maine, or northern Minnesota, or Michigan's Upper Peninsula, or a whole lot of other places I can think of. If I did, I might well unlimber a .358 or .35 Whelen–or perhaps a Marlin in .444 or .45-70. As you've seen, I do favor such cartridges for wild hogs and close-range hunting techniques for black bear. The reason is simple: If you place the bullet with reasonable care, you needn't worry about the outcome!

Chapter 40
From Horseback to High Arctic

As we have seen, North American hunting spans the full gamut of topographic and climatic conditions. We have–and hunt in–deserts, forests, swamps, mountains, tundra, and more. Unlike African hunting, where as many as 20 different species may be found and hunted in just one area, we generally go into these diverse conditions expecting–or hoping–to fire just one shot at one particular animal.

For instance, when we go elk hunting we're looking for an elk, period. Perhaps a mule deer will cross our path, but we're really hunting elk. Likewise when we go sheep hunting, bear hunting, or whitetail hunting. Sure, there are combination hunts, but they're becoming increasingly rare. This means that, rather than planning a high level of versatility into a hunting rifle, those of us who are rifle nuts tend to envision the "perfect" rifle and/or load for a given situation. That certainly doesn't mean we need 27 different calibers, one for each of our native game species.

One could hunt–and many have hunted–this entire continent with one of several versatile cartridges. Every hunter can establish his or her own minimum, based on the full range of game to be hunted, but obvious choices for a one-rifle American battery range from the .270 and .280 on up through the .30-06 and 7mm magnums to the .300 and .33 magnums. Such a rifle would almost certainly be a bolt-action. But even if one rifle were chosen for everything, chances are the bullet and load would vary with the conditions and game.

If, for instance, you desired to hunt everything in North America with a .30-06–as did the late Grancel Fitz–the load would certainly vary. An aerodynamic 150- or 165-grain bullet, pushed as fast as possible, would be the obvious choice for sheep, goat, and pronghorn. A good 180-grain spitzer would be best for elk, while a round-nose of the same weight would be closer to ideal for black bear. For grizzly and moose, you might choose a handloaded 200-grain spitzer, but for brown bear in the alders the only sensible choice would be a 220-grain bullet, or perhaps a handloaded Barnes 250-grainer.

Shooters who are first and foremost hunters, for whom the gun or even bow is just a basic tool, are likely to get by with just a couple of rifles. Sure, they'll usually vary the load a bit as circumstances dictate, but the rifle itself holds no great fascination, not much more than a shovel or an axe. Such hunters tend to do extremely well, by the way. They know their tools intimately and use them well. The old saying, "beware the one-gun man," is very, very true! This book probably is not for that kind of shooter.

On the other hand, there are hunters who are also serious shooters, for whom the rifle holds its own special fascination. It's much more than just a tool, and selecting the proper rifle and load for the job at hand is an important part of the hunting experience itself. I am clearly one of this group, and this book is undoubtedly of more interest to hunters and shooters like me.

For us, it's a great deal of fun to ponder exactly what makes the perfect rifle and load for pronghorn, sheep, deer, elk, bear, or whatever. When in doubt, one can always grab a .30-06, 7mm Remington Magnum, or .300 and go hunting–but it remains an enjoyable pastime and unending campfire debate to ponder just the right choice for a given situation.

In North America, this choice can be fairly specialized. With limited seasons and increasingly limited licenses, we tend to go after one or perhaps two specific animals in specific places. We know up front the basic size range of the game to be hunted, and we know generally (or at least we should!) the climate and terrain we face.

In this part of the book, I've been discussing the ideal rifles and cartridges for the various types of North American big game. Certainly there are no absolute answers, but I've examined some general parameters that make sense, at least to me. Sometimes, however, it isn't the game to be hunted that dictates the rifle and cartridge so much as the *conditions* under which that game will be hunted. Not everywhere in North America can you park your pickup truck alongside a road and go hunting. And not everywhere can you count on temperate climate and only a chance of light showers. Some of our hunting, especially for some of our most desirable game, requires penetrating deep into true wilderness, afoot or on horseback. And some of our hunting requires enduring some of the coldest and/or wettest conditions imaginable. To conclude our discussion of guns for game, let's examine ideal choices for some of these extreme situations.

Backpack Hunting: Backpack hunting, to me, doesn't mean leaving road's end with a daypack at dawn and returning at dusk. It means putting my camp on my back and heading into remote country for several days. This is a great way to see some of our continent's most magnificent country, and a great way to reach some of our finest game.

I personally think backpacking is the best way to hunt sheep and goats. Horses are nice, but eventually you must tie them up and walk–and then you'll have to come back to them. Good mule deer, some of our best blacktail hunting, and even a good deal of fine whitetail hunting is best accessed by backpacking.

Because of the extreme difficulty of packing out large game, I question the sanity of tackling elk and moose in this fashion, but it can be done. The rules of backpacking are simple: First, you must be in excellent condition–and know what you're capable of and what you're not. Second, you cannot hunt farther than you can carry your game out. In warmer weather, that means carrying it out, in however many loads are required, before spoilage sets in. Third, this type of hunting should not be attempted alone. You just never know what might happen, and a backpacking hunter alone could well die from a fairly minor mishap.

My good friend and colleague Bob Robb had a graphic demonstration of this rule just a week ago. An Alaskan resident now, he planned to hunt Dall sheep with a buddy. The buddy backed out, but Bob went anyway. He took a bad fall on a slick sheep mountain and could well have expired there. Fortunately, he had a radio and was able to crawl to a spot where he could get a signal out. Had a buddy been there, his extensive injuries would perhaps be just as severe–but he wouldn't have had the horrible experience of wondering whether he would make it out.

Since the backpack hunter must carry everything with him–and carry his game out–a premium must be placed on light weight. The same premium goes on reliability. It's a long way back to town to pick up a spare rifle! Finally, although the backpack hunter can get into super game country, his mobility is limited. Especially in tough terrain, movement is slow. The rifle and cartridge should be versatile enough to handle any reasonable shot that's presented, for a hunter on foot with a 60-pound pack will work damned hard for every shot he gets. Let's examine these three criteria separately.

Just a couple of decades ago, the garden-variety bolt-action hunting rifle weighed around 8½ pounds scoped, perhaps a bit more. Anything lighter than that was almost certainly a custom rig. These days, American hunters have become extremely weight-conscious, and there are a host of over-the-counter lightweights that shave a pound or even a pound and a half off that 8½-pound figure.

Then there are custom and semi-custom shops, probably the best-known being Mel Forbes' West Virginia-based Ultra Light Arms, which can shave as much as two additional pounds off that weight. Their short-action Model 20, for instance, weighs in at 4½ pounds unscoped and can be had in versatile calibers like 7x57, 7mm-08, .284 Winchester, and .308. Keep in mind that very light rifles are extremely hard to control when you're tired and breathing hard. This is not a real limitation in most mountain hunting, where you anticipate making a good stalk and having a steady rest when you make your shot, but it is worth remembering.

Lightweight offerings from the major factories include Remington's Mountain Rifle at 6¾ pounds, Ruger's Ultra Light at just six pounds; and Winchester's Featherweight at 6¾ pounds. A pound saved can make a big difference when you carry it for 10 days uphill and down. A couple of pounds saved makes even more difference.

Keep a couple of things in mind. First, synthetic stocks alone do not necessarily mean a saving in weight. A trim wooden stock will often weigh less than a more generous synthetic stock of homogenous material. The light synthetics are foam-filled shells reinforced with Kevlar and other materials at stress points. Next, you don't get significant weight savings from the stock alone. Shorter, thinner barrels and short, streamlined actions can actually shave more weight than the stock material. Finally, choice of scope and mount makes a big difference. And there are trade-offs.

Thin barrels are *not* less accurate than heavy barrels. They are harder to bed, and they do not have the sustained accuracy (without heating up) of heavier barrels, but thin barrels properly bedded will deliver all the hunting accuracy anyone needs. Short barrels, on the other hand, do restrict velocity. How much it's restricted is a great debate that can't be answered since it depends on the caliber and propellent powder. With belted cartridges, you'll lose a bit of velocity at 22 inches, and you really don't want to go below that. With unbelted, "standard" cartridges, you can go down to 20 inches without losing a huge amount.

Short actions are restricted to short cartridges. You can play with handloads all you want, but you will not get .280 performance out of a 7mm-08 or 7x57. For most hunting, you can certainly get by with short-action cartridges, but you are sacrificing some performance for the weight savings.

Finally, short, light scopes with small objectives save lots of weight–but you can't shoot as well or as far or in as low light as with a full-size scope. Ultimately you must decide, based largely on your physical condition, what you're comfortable carrying and what performance limitations you can accept.

The ultimate backpacker's gun, to me, would be a very light rifle in 7x57 or .284 Winchester. Topped with a compact 4X or 1¾-5X scope with light (but strong!) mounts like Conetrol, I think we could keep the whole thing–loaded with a light sling–under six pounds. But I don't have such a rifle, not yet.

A decade and more ago, in my twenties and early thirties, I'd go backpacking with a Weatherby Mark V .300 Magnum or a walnut-stocked 7mm Remington Magnum. Today, in my forties, I wouldn't dream of carrying a 9½-pound rifle on such a hunt. On my last two backpack sheep hunts, I carried a Remington M700 Custom KS, the version that has a Kevlar-reinforced fiberglass stock. The chambering is .280 Remington, and the scope a fixed 6X Swarovski in Tasco two-piece stud mounts. It's about 7½ pounds ready to go–not a true lightweight by today's standards, but a whole lot better than what I used to carry. The fixed 6X is a compromise between excellent light-gathering and the greater weight of a full-sized variable. In the future, as the mountains get increasingly steeper, I'll undoubtedly go lighter yet.

Reliability is without a doubt the most important consideration. The lightest rifle in the world won't do you any good if it doesn't function when the time comes. Now, the bolt-action holds no monopoly on reliability.

Especially for backpacking, a strong case could be made for a flat-sided Savage 99, Browning BLR, or Ruger No. 1, with no protruding bolt to bang against the packframe.

Personally, I would not choose a single-shot for such purposes, however. In backpack hunting you don't expect a hurried shot, and often your rifle is secured against the packframe in some way and darn near unavailable. But a hurry-up shot can happen. A repeater can be stowed on the pack with cartridges in the magazine and the chamber empty. A single-shot will require fumbling for cartridges. On a backpack hunt in the MacKenzie Mountains, while moving spike camp and traveling up a gravel streambed between two mountains, we ran head on into a band of rams. It was enough trouble just getting the rifle out of its pack scabbard without having to worry about fumbling for shells!

If a lever-action (or, for that matter, a pump or semiauto) is chosen, one must pay special attention to the ammo selected. The bolt-action alone has the camming power to extract a slightly sticky case, so factory loads or very conservative handloads should be used if other actions are chosen.

In any case, every aspect of the rifle should be checked for reliability and function before embarking on any backpack hunt. This includes running every cartridge to be taken on the hunt through the magazine and into the chamber.

Tape should be carried to tape the muzzle (no, tape over the muzzle has no effect on pressure or point of impact), and good scope covers are essential. A light cleaning kit should be carried, at a minimum some oil and a sectioned rod capable of clearing the bore should you take a spill and get mud into the muzzle.

Synthetic stocks should be a matter of course for backpack hunting. Good synthetics are stronger than wood, and many are a bit lighter. Most important, though, is the stability. On many backpack hunts rain can be expected, and you can't always get out of it. A week in the northern mountains will absolutely ruin a fine piece of walnut (I've done it!). Damage aside, there's never a guarantee that even the most carefully glassed and bedded walnut stock won't warp–and you simply can't be constantly checking your zero and expect to see game.

Finally, pay special attention to your sights. The mounts must be tight and strong and the scope absolutely reliable. Even then, some sort of backup sight system makes sense. Iron sights on the rifle are probably the best course–and you must have whatever tools are required to remove the scope. Even on backpack hunts–for instance, on that 14-day sheep hunt in the MacKenzies–I often carry a backup scope set in rings. The backup is a fixed 2½X scope, very compact and very light. I haven't needed it, but if I did, it would be a far better backup than any iron sight. There's also a new gadget called the HuntSaver, an iron sight that fits into the front and rear bases of scope mounts. It's a short-range affair, but precise enough for 100-

yard shooting, and it comes in a tiny box weighing just a couple of ounces. It's a pure backup, but will do exactly what the name implies.

Don't overlook performance. Whatever cartridge is chosen, it should be adequate to handle virtually any reasonable shot you expect to encounter. Of course, there are compromises. The .280 Remington I've carried lately is not nearly as versatile–nor as heavy–as the .300 Weatherby I used to carry. While I don't have an Ultra Light, I do have a very light 7x57 built by Mark Bansner. It's certainly a sheep-capable rifle of the right weight for backpacking, but I probably will not carry it for my Montana tag simply because I'm not comfortable with what I perceive to be its range limitations, especially on 300-pound sheep.

The best and most versatile backpacking rigs that offer full performance potential are probably built around the .270 and .280–with handloaded .284 Winchester ammo in a bolt-action hanging right in there. The most compact and lightest numbers could be built around a 7mm-08 or 7x57, and either can be quite flashy with handloaded 140-grain bullets. It depends on the size of game you're after and, perhaps most importantly, your comfort level with the cartridge. On a serious quest for an important game animal, I'm not yet willing to sacrifice the performance of a full-size cartridge for a half-pound or so in gun weight. Perhaps someday I'll have to.

Horseback Hunting: Depending on the type of game hunted and exactly how far afoot you expect to go after tying your horse, gun weight may or may not be a consideration. With most horseback elk and moose hunting, gun weight is not a factor. Such hunting is a good place for full-sized .300s, .338s, and .340 Weatherby Magnums. On the other hand, if you're sheep hunting on horseback, a little valley with good grass where you can hobble the horses may just be the jumping-off point! You should know exactly what you're getting yourself into before you saddle yourself with a 10-pound long-range rig.

Generally, though, weight isn't as big a consideration. Reliability certainly is, and the same conditions apply as in backpack hunting; it's still a long way to town! It's also worth noting that horseback hunting is potentially even harder on guns than backpack hunting. Saddle scabbards with a removable hood, though bulky and slow, offer some measure of protection. Even so, rifles take an incredible beating on a horseback trip–and lots of wooden stocks get broken. Never, ever walk away from your horse without taking your rifle with you. If you do, you may be assured that's the time the hayburner will decide to lie down and roll!

If your horse falls or rolls on your rifle, it will remain functional only through blind luck. I would tend to choose synthetic stocks or laminates as the optimum for horseback hunting. Synthetics are stronger than walnut, and laminates are probably the strongest of all, virtually indestructible.

The physical features of a horseback rifle really aren't that important. Barrels can be on the long side, and scopes can certainly be full-sized. But keep in mind that whatever rifle you choose will be in the scabbard under your leg. The bigger the rifle, the more uncomfortable it will be; and the longer the rifle, the harder it will be to pull from the scabbard when you need it.

Most of my own horseback hunting has been, and probably will continue to be, with bolt-actions. But there's a reason why the flat-sided lever-actions are called "saddle guns"–sheer convenience for carrying in a saddle scabbard. The chamberings available in Marlin and Winchester lever guns aren't optimum for quite a lot of the hunting done on horseback these days. Browning's BLR and the Savage 99, however, can be had in flat-shooting, versatile calibers. If you think the thicker profile of a bolt-action doesn't get uncomfortable after a long day in the saddle, you haven't done much horseback hunting! Because of caliber availability, I'd have to rate the flat-sided Browning BLR in long-action form as our top gun for horseback hunting today.

A word to the wise: Get your own saddle scabbard and make sure it fits whatever rifle you plan to take if you're going on an outfitted horseback hunt. Most outfitters have saddle scabbards, but they may or may not fit. One of the greatest shocks of my career was when British Columbia outfitter Lloyd Harvey produced a saddle scabbard for a *left-hand* bolt-action for me to use. I'd brought my own, but he insisted–that brand-new left-hand scabbard had been waiting for years for someone to need it!

Few outfitters go to the expense of procuring that kind of equipment. Likewise, despite what you read, very few outfitters have enough saddlebags to go around or oversized stirrups for cold-weather boots. If you're planning on multiple horseback hunts in your career, invest in those items, plus a good riding slicker. You'll be glad you did.

Extreme Weather Conditions: Here in the temperate climes of North America we rarely have to endure extreme heat while hunting. There are exceptions, of course. Sheep hunts in Mexico (for that matter, any hunt in Mexico) can get exceedingly warm. The relatively few early deer hunts we have (California and South Carolina both have rifle deer seasons in August) can be and usually are beastly hot. And any September hunt darn near anywhere can see temperatures well into the 90s. Firearms are relatively impervious to that kind of heat, and no special precautions are needed.

Hunters are not impervious, and neither is their ammunition. In warm weather, it's absolutely essential to carry plenty of water. I've done a great deal of hunting during California's August season, and in those baking-oven coastal hills, lack of water becomes life-threatening very quickly. Ammunition quite literally heats up if left in the sun. Handloads that are a touch warm in the first place can develop uncomfortably high pressures quickly if left, say, on the dashboard of a truck in hot weather. Air temperature doesn't get hot enough to make a big difference; it's direct sunlight heating the metal cases. Keep your ammunition covered, and don't leave it where it can soak up rays.

Wet weather is more of a problem, and cold weather worse yet. Rainy spells can happen almost anywhere in North America during a fall or spring hunt, but some areas are wetter than others. Hunters in the Pacific Northwest, from Oregon on up to southeast Alaska, contend with near-constant precipitation, and of course frequent showers are part of life in most mountain ranges. Synthetic stocks are the answer in wet weather, pure and simple. There is no guarantee that a wooden stock won't warp, but synthetics *can't* warp! They are unaffected. I've carried wooden-stocked rifles through a week or 10 days of rain, and I can promise you that even if, through some miracle, they don't warp, they'll turn gray and sickly and require complete refinishing.

Rust can appear literally overnight–and in a matter of hours in salt-air coastal climes. Stainless steel is the best answer. It will also rust, but it takes a whole lot more time. Always carry some oil, even on a backpack trip. You may not be able to dry your rifle, but you can hold rust at bay through daily light oiling. Keep your muzzle well-taped with waterproof electrician's tape, and replace the tape after you've fired a shot. No rifle actions are waterproof, but in extremely wet weather I must give the nod to bolt-actions. It's much simpler to strip a bolt-action and hold the rust at bay than is the case with other actions. I would even say that I prefer bolt-actions with floorplates rather than blind magazines, because the follower and the spring underneath it also need to be maintained in wet weather.

Keeping a scope clear enough to shoot is one of the biggest problems in a serious downpour. There are plenty of good commercial scope covers, but one of the best solutions I know of is to cut a big rubber band from a tire inner tube. It will fit watertight and can be snapped off just as you'd shoot a rubber band. While you're at it, also cut some little squares of rubber to use as fire-starters. You can light them with a match, and the rubber burns hot enough to ignite even wet tinder.

In a driving rain, your scope will stay clear enough to shoot for a only a very short time after you remove your scope covers. If you don't shoot, remember to wipe the lenses clear before you replace the covers. If it rains long enough, you'll run out of dry cloth to do this with. Then it's time to think about open auxiliary sights. The one advantage to iron sights that I know of is that they're waterproof. These days I don't worry that a scope of a good make will leak, but water-spotted lenses become useless in short order, with each water spot magnified until the scope is useless.

Internal fogging, though possible, is a remote problem solved only by auxiliary sights or an extra scope. External fogging, or condensation, is a real problem. This is usually caused by taking your rifle from the cold outside air into warm tent or cabin. The problem usually arises when you take it back outside. Keep your rifle as close to the outside air temperature as possible.

Extreme cold has one advantage: usually it's very dry when temperatures plunge below zero Fahrenheit. The external-fogging problem, of course, is magnified the colder it gets. The main problem in extreme cold, though, is action freeze-up. How cold it has to be depends on the lubricant used. Just last November, I neglected to "winterize" my bolt before an Alberta whitetail hunt. Temperatures plunged to minus 30 degrees, and although my striker would still fall, sort of, it was extremely sluggish. I *know* that rifle would not have fired had I seen the buck of a lifetime that first day. Fortunately, it was easy to fix.

A bolt-action is, to me, far and away the best choice for extreme cold. It's a simple matter to strip the bolt and degrease it with alcohol or a similar solvent. You can lubricate with just a bit of dry graphite. Besides simplicity of field-stripping, another advantage to a bolt-action is that, over the short haul, it will function better than other action types with a minimum or absence of lubricant. The bolt should be degreased any time you expect temperatures to drop below about 10 degrees or so, just for insurance. Below zero, you can count on slow striker fall, especially if you haven't stripped your bolt in some time and have a build-up of old lubricant and gunk. For game like muskox and polar bear, winterizing is an obvious step, but it should be done for any hunt in the Rockies or points north after the first of November, and probably for any late-season hunt north of the Mason-Dixon line.

As a final caution, remember the story about the little boy whose tongue stuck to the outside water faucet. In extreme cold, *do not* touch the metal parts of your rifle with a bare hand. A friend of mine jerked off his glove to work his bolt on a muskox hunt. Not only did he lose a whole bunch of skin getting his fingers off the bolt; his frostbite was so deep–in seconds–that it was some years before he regained full use of his hand. Always wear shooting gloves underneath mittens or whatever else you're wearing.

Chapter 41

The Professional's Choice in the Good Old Days

The years just following the Civil War probably saw the peak of hunting in the American West. The transcontinental railroad had been completed, giving unprecedented access to the Great Plains and also providing a means for rapidly transporting meat and hides to the Eastern markets. Buffalo hunting was at its height from the late 1860s into the early '80s, and along with bison came "incidentals" like elk, grizzly, pronghorn, and deer.

It didn't last long. The Kansas herds were gone by the early 1870s. The great Southern herds were depleted by the end of the decade, and in the early '80s, with the Sioux wars more or less over, the "buffalo runners" turned to the Montana herds for the final chapter. By 1885 it was all over; not only had the buffalo been nearly eradicated, but so had the plains grizzly. Surviving elk were pushed into the mountains, and even pronghorn and deer were badly depleted.

The bulk of this slaughter was performed with powerful single-shot rifles. Although repeaters had been perfected by then, the early repeating rifles were not strong actions and used very mild cartridges with little range and less energy. Even the great Spencer of Civil War fame, though of .56 caliber, propelled its 350-grain bullet at just 1,200 feet per second for 1,125 foot/pounds of energy. The .44 Henry was much worse–a 200-grain bullet at 1,150 feet per second, for just 594 foot/pounds. These cartridges were rimfires. Winchester's Model 1873, one of the most popular rifles of all time, made the quantum leap to the centerfire .44-40 cartridge, but it was hardly a powerhouse–its 200-grain bullet was just slightly faster than the Henry round, with little more energy.

Cartridges along these lines were much carried and much used; the repeaters that fired them were excellent for self-defense and would put meat in the pot. But the professionals stuck with their big single-shots.

Confederate veteran Colonel A.W. Pickett settled in western Wyoming in the 1870s. He used a .45-caliber Sharps single-shot with his own unique loads: 110 grains of black powder behind a 340-grain "Express" bullet, and the same charge behind a paper-patched 275-grain .44-caliber bullet. The Express bullet was an English concept–a hollow-cavity, light-for-caliber bullet to increase velocity. Patching sub-caliber bullets was not all that uncommon in those days, and is obviously a precursor to our sabot technology of today. Pickett's velocities were 1,830 feet per second for the 340-grain bullet, and a very high (for the day) velocity of 1,910 fps for the

275-grain load. He eventually concluded that the 275-grain bullet was too light for large game, but that the 340-grain slug was big enough for everything on the continent.

Although it appears as shameful excess today, the amount of experience some of these hunters had is mind-boggling. Pickett wrote that ". . . during the season of 1881, after I had become familiar with the habits of the grizzly bear, I killed, using an Express bullet with 110 grains of black powder, twenty-three of those bears, of which seventeen required only a single shot."

W.H. Wright, who hunted and guided out of Missoula, Montana, was almost exclusively a grizzly hunter. He also used a .45-caliber single-shot. His was a Winchester using the .45-100 case, but Wright much preferred a very heavy 600-grain solid lead projectile. His velocity was a normal (for the day) 1,300 feet per second, with a fairly high energy of 2,250 foot/pounds. On one occasion, he killed five grizzlies with five shots with this combination!

Relatively few of the buffalo hunters left any written record, probably because a great many of them couldn't read or write. Those who could tended to write about the Sharps more than any other rifle–but these were probably among the more affluent of the buffalo hunters, and the Sharps was one of the most expensive rifles of the day. It's quite likely that the single most common rifle on the plains was a trapdoor Springfield in .50-70 or, later, .45-70. Neither cartridge offers flashy ballistics, but the big, heavy bullets did their work well–well enough that the .45-70 remains fairly popular today.

One of the buffalo hunters who did write extensively about his exploits was Alfred Mayer: "The two best buffalo rifles, which were the choice of practically all the good runners were the Remington and the Sharps. I think the Sharps was the better of the two, but many preferred the Remington."

Mayer bought his first Sharps from Colonel Richard Irving Dodge, from whom Dodge City, Kansas takes its name. It was a .40-90-320 (90 grains of black powder and a 320-grain bullet). Later he acquired two more .40-caliber Sharps rifles, a .40-70-320 and a .40-90-420, and at the very end of the buffalo years he acquired a .45-120-550. This was probably the most powerful Sharps cartridge, introduced in the late 1870s. Other than reports like Mayer's, there is actually no remaining record of Sharps producing this caliber. The only thing that could have been more powerful is the .50-140, possibly introduced in 1880–or possibly a special-order cartridge, or equally possibly a "wildcat" made by rechambering .50-90 rifles. Sharps' records were destroyed in a fire, so firm knowledge of their later cartridges is sketchy. In any case, the buffalo were nearly gone by the time the .50-140 made it to the plains.

Mayer used telescopic sights on his Sharps rifles–serious scopes of 20 power. It's unknown how common or uncommon scopes were in that era, but they certainly did exist. By the way, Mayer also wrote that he paid $237.60 for his .45-120 with telescope–a vast sum in 1880.

Quite a few hunters hung onto their big single-shots until well after the turn of the century. Elmer Keith used Sharps rifles as a boy in Montana, acquiring a lifelong and well-documented preference for big bores as a result. But the real viability of the big single-shot died with the buffalo. The Sharps Rifle Company went under in 1881, and by then there were adequately powerful repeaters in the field.

One of the first, and certainly the best-known, of the repeaters more or less adequate for all big game on this continent was the Model 1876 Winchester. Its initial and most popular cartridge was the .45-75, firing a 350-grain bullet at 1,383 feet per second for 1,485 foot/pounds of energy. The goal was to produce a repeater that would duplicate the power of the longer .45-70 cartridge, and the .45-75 does that–except that the shorter, lighter bullet probably didn't hit quite as hard or penetrate as well as the .45-70's 405-grain slug.

G.O. Shields, editor of *Recreation* magazine, was an early fan of the .45-75 and did much to make it popular. Theodore Roosevelt, many years away from the White House, also used the '76 extensively and wrote about it quite a lot: "When I first came to the plains I had a heavy Sharps rifle, .45-120, shooting an ounce and a quarter of lead, and a .50-caliber double-barreled English express. . . . I threw them both aside; and have instead a .40-90 Sharps for very long-range work; a .50-115 6-shot Bullard express which has the velocity, shock, and low trajectory of the English gun; and better than either a .45-75 half-magazine Winchester."

By the latter years of the century, the switch to lever-action rifles was almost universal–at least in America. Winchester's Model 1886 and Marlin's 1881 (and later 1895) lever-actions were stronger than the '76 and could handle longer, more powerful cartridges. The Model 1886 in chamberings like .45-70, .45-90, .40-82, and .40-65 was a classic big-game rifle as smokeless powder came into play. The much lighter Model 94 and its faster cartridge, the smokeless-powder .30-30, found significant favor–but the switch to the faster, lighter smokeless-powder cartridges was neither rapid nor complete. (Witness the fact that the .45-70 remains popular to this day!)

A great many of the old-time hunters were still active when this shift occurred. Some of them made the transition smoothly, while others clung to their black-powder cartridges. Alfred Mayer lived and hunted well into this century. His last rifle was a .270 Winchester, quite a far cry from the Sharps single-shots of his youth.

The great grizzly hunter William Wright eventually gave up his .45-100 Winchester high-wall single-shot in favor of a Model 94 .30-30. But by then he had pretty much quit hunting and had shifted to photography of the grizzlies that remained his specialty. Had he still been hunting, one wonders if he would have gone with so light a cartridge.

William T. Hornaday, one of the great early naturalists (he who wrote *Campfires in the Canadian Rockies* among other works), did most of his early North American hunting with a .40-70 single-shot by Maynard. Later he switched to a .303 Savage, but deep down he was a big-bore fan. His favorite cartridge, after its introduction in 1904, was the .405 Winchester–of course in the Model 1895.

Theodore Roosevelt himself went through a very similar progression, from Sharps single-shot to heavy-caliber black-powder repeater, to the .30-30 Winchester, then to the .405 Winchester. As far as we know, however, Roosevelt did *not* use his beloved .405 Winchester "lion medicine" in North America. His lengthy 1909 safari endeared the .405 to him–but no more so than the .30-06 Springfield. It was the Springfield that Roosevelt used for virtually all of his hunting after 1910.

The popular author Stewart Edward White (*Land of Footprints* and many other titles) began his hunting career after the buffalo were gone; his early hunting was done with a .44-40, and he was not displeased with it. Later he graduated to a .30-30, then a .30-40, then a .405 Winchester, and finally the .30-06 Springfield.

Naturalist John Burnham hunted extensively throughout North America between 1887 and 1921, including Mexico, Alaska, and even Siberia in his travels. He started with a .40-82 Winchester, and was still using a .40-65 long after smokeless powder was in common use. But by 1905 he had made the switch to a .30-30, and by the end of his career was shooting the powerful .35 Newton in a bolt-action.

The exact period of time these turn-of-the-century hunters plied their trade determines the equipment they started with. Hunters who were active before about 1885 almost certainly began with big single-shots–but by 1890 were almost certainly shooting powerful lever-action repeaters. These same hunters were generally shooting smaller-caliber, smokeless-cartridge lever-actions by about 1905. Some preferred the .30-30 in Winchester or Marlin rifles; others preferred the Savage 99 in .303 Savage. Many chose the Model 1895 Winchester in .30-40. But among those who remained active into the late teens or early '20s, the shift to bolt-action rifles became almost unanimous.

A classic example is Major Ned Roberts, whose hunting career began in 1887 and ended in 1934. He started with the .40-60 Winchester, and in his middle years was a great fan of the .38-55 in a Marlin. He also went through the .30-40 Krag stage, but ended up being a staunch supporter of the 7mm Mauser. Today he is best known for creating the .257 Roberts cartridge.

Colonel Townsend Whelen was the dean of American gun writers for nearly half a century. His articles first appeared in American outdoor magazines in 1905, and he was still writing in the late 1950s. Like most Americans of his day, he was early on a fan of the .30-40 Krag. And, like the professional gun writer he was, he used and reported on just about anything you can think of during his long career. He used a wide variety of lever-actions, and had great admiration for the Savage 99. But he was one of the first who fully accepted the ascendancy of the bolt-action. In 1913, he wrote an article for *Outdoor Life* entitled "An All-Round Cartridge For American Big Game." His choice was the .30-06 Springfield in the Springfield rifle.

Charles Newton is yet another classic example. In 1911, he designed the .22 Savage Hi-Power, and in 1914 the .250 Savage. Also a prolific gun writer, he defended both of these cartridges and their lever-action rifles vehemently in the sporting press. This was in a more innocent age when nobody had chronographs and, American big game being at its lowest ebb, few readers had significant field experience. It was also long before our current proliferation of attorneys, and there weren't a lot of worries about libel lawsuits or product liability. Newton and the other writers of his era got downright nasty and personal in their attacks on each other. They also had a tendency to use liberal doses of blue sky when making their arguments. The .22 Savage Hi-Power and the .250 Savage, both designed for the Savage lever-action, are great cartridges–but today's writers would be strung up if they made some of the claims the early writers made when these two hot numbers appeared.

Though Newton designed these cartridges for lever-actions, he should best be remembered for his powerful cartridges intended for bolt-action rifles. His .256, .30, and .35 Newton were the most popular of his many bolt-action cartridges, and none of these could be harnessed in lever-action rifles. They were true unbelted magnums, with performance levels still impressive by today's standards. Through the teens and into the early '20s, his excellent rifles were manufactured in small numbers through several ventures that just didn't make it, and they are nearly forgotten today.

In 1913, the .30 Newton propelled a 180-grain bullet at 2,860 feet per second, outstanding velocity for the day and very close to .300 H&H velocities. Handloads with modern powders can bring the .30 Newton very close to .300 Winchester Magnum velocities. With the current trend drifting away from belted cartridges, this is an "unbelted magnum" that may be worth a second look after 80 years!

By the 1920s, the ascendancy of the bolt-action rifle was virtually complete, and the .30-06 ruled the roost. Of course, one has to be careful when speaking in absolutes. The lever-action retained its fans, as it does to this day. And many fine hunters preferred–and still prefer–slide-actions and semiautos. But by 1925, the "professional's choice" was a bolt-action–almost certainly in .30-06. For the next 30 years, the only cartridge that gave the .30-06 serious competition at all was the .270 Winchester, introduced in 1925 in Winchester's brand-new Model 54 bolt-action.

Jack O'Connor had much to do with the popularity of the .270. He latched onto it very early in his career, and it was his talisman for nearly 50 years. However, it's unfair to state that the .270 was the only cartridge he liked and used. He was a great fan of the .30-06, actually rating it more versatile than his beloved .270. He also admired the 7x57, .257 Roberts, and in later years acquired some experience with "new" cartridges like the .338 Winchester Magnum and 7mm Remington Magnum. For big bears, he chose the .375 H&H, which certainly removes him from the label of strictly a small-bore man. His wife, Eleanor, herself a great hunter, much preferred the 7x57 over Jack's .270–and since she had no obligation to write about lots of calibers, she used the 7x57 for literally everything.

Elmer Keith was not O'Connor's opposite number. In fact, had they been able to sit down and talk about it, they might have found significant elements of agreement. But their war of words was long enough and bitter enough that such a meeting was extremely unlikely. Elmer Keith had no use for the .270 and less for smaller calibers. Due to some bullet failures he witnessed as a young man, he didn't have much more faith in the .30-06. And yet he never advocated over-.40 calibers for American big game. He was a great fan of the .35 Whelen, as was Townsend Whelen himself, but eventually he settled on the .33 caliber with bullets over 250 grains as the ideal. His .333 and .334 OKH wildcats became the gospel he preached–and I think he'd be gratified to see how popular the .338 Winchester Magnum that he inspired has become today.

Although the title of this chapter may suggest a specific bygone period that I consider "the good old days" of American hunting, I actually harbor no such feeling. The 1870s probably saw the greatest abundance of game, but the great hunting country of western Canada was virtually unknown and unreachable then. Hunters in the early years of this century had tough sledding. There was almost no local deer hunting then, and so it remained (except in the most remote areas of the West) until after World War II. In truth, even the great Townsend Whelen, kept busy by an extremely active military career, had relatively little experience actually shooting big game. In many ways, the hunters of today have more opportunity than this continent has seen since the 1870s. White-tailed deer are at an all-time high, and most of our game is much more abundant now than it was in Whelen's, Roberts', and Newton's day.

However, no one in my profession will ever again acquire the extensive and varied experience of an Elmer Keith or a Jack O'Connor or a Warren Page. In fact, relatively few of our modern hunting/gun writers actually possess experience hunting a significant variety of game in significant numbers. Some who do include John Wootters, who, like all good gun writers (me included!) has written about a great many different cartridges. Given a choice, I *think* John would settle on the 7mm Remington Magnum for all-round use, with a .338 for game like moose and big bears. He would share his 7mm preference with the late Warren Page, who was indeed as experienced as O'Connor, and believed fervently in high-velocity 7mms.

Outdoor Life's Jim Carmichel–one of the most well-rounded of hunting writers–is another 7mm fan, but his preference for all-round use is the .280 Remington with good handloads. Like Wootters, though, he generally uses a .338 Winchester Magnum for larger game. Jon Sundra also goes the 7mm route, but he prefers his 7mm JRS wildcat, which uses a blown-out .280 case to achieve 7mm magnum performance in an unbelted cartridge. For heavier game, I *think* his choice would be his other JRS wildcat, the .375 JRS, one of several "improved" versions of the .375. Dave Petzal of *Field & Stream* has used a tremendous number of cartridges, and I have not been able to identify a strong preference among the lighter, "all-round" choices. But for elk and such, Petzal is a .33-caliber man, using both the .338 Winchester Magnum and .340 Weatherby.

Colonel Charles Askins, whose experience overseas is more extensive than on this continent, has made a lifelong mission out of promoting the 8mm bore diameter, usually in a hot wildcat. The 8mm has much to recommend it, but even the Colonel has had problems getting existing 8mm bullets to hold together at the velocities he pushes them to. His lifelong hunting partner, the late George Parker, was not a writer and, regrettably, wasn't as well-known and isn't as well-remembered as he deserves to be. Parker was a real American hero, a Border Patrolman, much-decorated World War II hero, rancher, and extremely prolific hunter.

He's perhaps best-known as the man who put more Coues deer in the record book than anyone else, but he also hunted extensively throughout North America and much of the rest of the world. Parker admitted to me one time that he didn't much care for recoil. For lighter game, he preferred the .257 Roberts, but for general use he almost never shot anything heavier than a .30-06. The only thing unusual about his choice was that, in later years, he used a .30-06 Improved (case blown out with sharper shoulder). The actual velocity increases with modern powders is fairly small with this particular Improved cartridge, but Parker used it all over the world, for game that included some of Africa's Big Five, and never wanted more.

Ernest Hemingway probably qualifies as a bit more than just another gun writer, but "Papa" wrote several hunting stories for *Field & Stream*. His favorite rifle, used for elk, deer, pronghorn, and bighorn, was a peep-sighted Griffin & Howe .30-06 Springfield. Hemingway fans will recall that, during the 1936 safari that yielded *The Green Hills of Africa*, Hemingway used his .30-06 with 220-grain bullets on buffalo, rhino, and lion–preferring it to his big double because he hated the heavy trigger pull on the big gun.

Grancel Fitz was an influential committeeman of the Boone and Crockett Club, and for the 1939 *North American Big Game* record book he wrote a chapter on "Rating of Trophies." Together with several other expert hunter/naturalists, he developed measurement charts and procedures that eventually (a decade after the project began!) resulted in far more accurate and equitable ranking of North American trophies. He himself collected a number of specimens for the American Museum of Natural History. It was Fitz, not Jack O'Connor as often attributed, who coined the phrase "grand slam" for taking one each of our four North American wild sheep. Fitz was one of the first of the trophy collectors as we know them today, hunters who have the time, resources, and desire to travel extensively in search of a great variety of big game. Grancel Fitz was the first, and still one of very, very few, who successfully hunted *all* varieties of North American big game. He did it with a .30-06 Springfield.

In more recent years, there has evolved a small group of traveling sportsmen following in Fitz's footsteps. The Weatherby Big Game Trophy, first awarded to Herb Klein, then to Jack O'Connor and Warren Page, has evolved into a lifetime-achievement award for these globe-trotting sportsmen. Recognition for hunting achievement brings egos into play and develops competition against other hunters in a sport where the only competition should be against oneself, the elements, and the game. A great many, perhaps most, American hunters have some qualms about this kind of trophy hunting, and I share their reservations. However, as a group there are no hunters with the *varied* experience to match the Weatherby Award winners.

These are guys who have hunted all the wild sheep of the world, not just the American varieties. And all the deer of the world, not just our American deer. And all the continents, under all conditions. Perhaps not surprisingly, most of these hunters are not rifle nuts in the way that I am, that gun writers must be, and in the way that many of you readers are. Heck, they're too busy running businesses and making enough money to support their hunting habit to tinker endlessly with rifles and loads! But they do know what works under any and all conditions. The vast consensus among this group (excluding rifles for thick-skinned dangerous game) favors the .300 Weatherby Magnum—and not just in deference to Roy Weatherby.

Most of this group, including such as Herb Klein, Elgin Gates, C.J. McElroy, Bob Speegle, Butch White, Jim Conklin, and so many more, have used the .300 Weatherby, nearly exclusively, to hunt all over this continent and the rest of the world. Their choice makes sense. Again, remember the saying, "Beware the one-gun man." Hunters like these know their one gun intimately, and they've chosen a cartridge that takes much of the work out of figuring the range—especially since much of their hunting is in unfamiliar country for hitherto-unfamiliar animals.

Now, among this group the .300 Weatherby isn't the only choice. One memorable Weatherby Award acceptance speech was begun with the statement that the recipient had never owned and never shot a Weatherby rifle. Roy, alongside the speaker at the head table, managed not to choke. Some have preferred 7mm magnums. In this group was Basil Bradbury, who registered more species in the Boone and Crockett record book than any other man before or since. Bert Klineburger, not a Weatherby Award winner because of his "professional" status, but one of the most experienced hunters in the world, is another 7mm magnum devotee.

Whether 7mm or .300, though, the common thread among these hunters is that they want one rifle that will do it all, one rifle that they know intimately and can rely upon under all conditions, at all ranges, and on any game short of the largest and most dangerous. The all-inclusive hunting they have done lends great credibility to their choices as true "all-round" rifles.

Most of us aren't concerned about hunting the entire world. And if we're rifle nuts, the last thing we'd care to do is to do it with just one rifle! The purpose of this book has not been to select one rifle and one cartridge for all of North America, but rather to discuss the best choices for, if not each of our game animals, at least for our various types of hunting.

It's of historical interest to study what our forebears used, and worthy of note to see what particularly wide-ranging and successful modern hunters have preferred. But for our purposes, it might be of equal or greater value to see what some true experts with in-depth experience in particular kinds of hunting have to say. Let's turn, then, to what real North American professional hunters–guides and outfitters–recommend for their type of hunting.

Chapter 42

The Professional's Choice Today

To obtain an in-depth picture of the rifles and cartridges modern expert hunters recommend for use on North American big game, I went to North American guides and outfitters. Now, you may or may not indulge in guided hunts–and you probably don't need to if you're hunting deer, elk, or whatever close to your home. You probably know what works in your area a whole lot better than anyone who lives half a continent away from you, me included.

If you're an Eastern whitetail hunter, you probably have a much better idea of what works on whitetails in the country you hunt than, say, a Colorado elk guide or an Alaskan bear guide. On the other hand, few elk hunters will shoot or see as many elk shot in a lifetime as a guide will see in a single season. Outfitters and guides, just like all hunters, run the gamut from dedicated students of hunting rifles to hunters for whom the rifle is just another tool, not much different from an axe or a shovel. Some of them have extremely specific ideas on what works best for their game in their area, while others make only very basic recommendations. However, these guys know what works for them, and they know what works–and doesn't work–for the general run of hunters they have in their camps. As with my own recommendations, you can add whatever liberal dose of salt you choose–but keep in mind that these men have serious, hands-on experience that very few hunters can match.

The Survey

Over 600 surveys were sent to guide/outfitter association mailing lists in several states and Canadian provinces. Not all states have such associations, nor are all such lists readily available. So I will make no claim to having attempted to contact every guide or outfitter in North America. Those who were missed and would have liked to respond have my apologies. The intent was to obtain a meaningful sampling of guides and outfitters who hunt North America's most prevalent and prominent species, and who hunt them under a wide variety of topographic and climatic conditions.

The survey was two pages, consisting of 11 questions, some of which had more than one part. The first question asked the number of years spent as a guide or outfitter, while the second and third asked about habitat conditions and primary hunting techniques. The first part of the survey also asked about the species the respondent hunts, and whether or not he carries a backup rifle when guiding.

Then we get to the real meat: first the guide/outfitter's personal choice for his own hunting, and then what he recommends that his clients bring. Although I didn't attempt to quantify differences here, most of the respondents recommended essentially the same type of rifle that they carried themselves. The only significant difference was that Alaskan guides tended to carry somewhat heavier calibers–for obvious reasons–than they always recommended to their clients.

The survey went on to ask about all-round likes and dislikes in hunting bullets, and recommendations for scopes and sights. I also invited any additional comments, and as we shall see, there are some very strong opinions out there.

The Respondents

Just over 100 responses were received, and I heartily thank all these busy men who took the time to answer. I think, and I'm sure you will agree, that this survey is the most valuable part of this book, and it wouldn't have been possible without their help. One outfitter alone chided me for not providing a stamped, self-addressed envelopes. I apologize, but it simply wasn't affordable. And, with many of those surveyed living in Canada, it wasn't practical, either. So my 100-plus respondents not only took the time, but also bought a stamp–and I do appreciate it.

The body of experience that these men offer is absolutely mind-boggling. The senior man was Idaho whitetail, mule deer, black-bear, and elk outfitter Jim Renshaw, with 42 years' experience. But he wasn't top dog by much! Harold Turner of Wyoming reported 40 years in the business, and nine others had more than 30 years under their belts. The junior respondent started guiding two years ago, and the average was a solid 20.6 years, for a total of more than 21 centuries in the field!

Throughout this survey, you will note that the responses do not match the number of respondents. Some questions required more than one response, such as habitat types and game hunted. In other cases, particularly caliber recommendations, more than one response was given by many guide/outfitters. And many respondents omitted some questions altogether. For instance, many didn't specify whether they prefer their clients to bring one or two rifles to their camps, and very few responded regarding auxiliary iron sights. That's okay; this survey was not designed to prove anything, to provide statistical validity for any of the questions. The intent is to obtain a reasonable cross-section of opinion from experts–and that we have.

The habitat types hunted span the gamut of North American geography. You will note that an inordinate number of respondents, however, ply their trade in mountainous regions. There are reasons for this. First, the large wilderness areas that lend themselves to viable outfitting operations are often in mountainous areas–and the hunting of mountain game is more likely to require an outfitter's assistance. Second, the majority of the available lists came from Western states and provinces, which undoubtedly skewed the response. Even so, plains and woodlands (meaning forested regions) are well represented, and the proportionately smaller numbers from desert, swamp, and tundra probably reflect with reasonable accuracy the percentage of American hunting done in these areas.

The great number of horseback outfitters who responded–54–certainly does not reflect the overall amount of horseback hunting in this country. However, as we've seen in earlier chapters, horseback and backpack hunting are the techniques most demanding of equipment, so I don't mind having these categories heavily represented. Obviously, many of the respondents use more than one hunting method, but it should also be mentioned that my category of hunting on "foot from vehicle" turned out to be a bit of a catch-all. Many Alaskan guides, for instance, checked this box with the notation that their hunting is done on foot after drop-off from an airplane–which, after all, is a vehicle.

I asked the respondents whether they carry a backup rifle when guiding. The tables show that 61 do and 42 do not. I didn't qualify the question, but many of respondents did. Often they said, "Sometimes," "Occasionally," "It depends on the game hunted," or, "Only for the client to use if his rifle fails." If they indicated *ever* carrying a backup rifle, they're included in the 61 positive responses. However, from the qualified responses it appears to me that a guide will have a backup rifle in much less than 50 percent of guided-hunt situations. That should suggest to readers interested in guided hunts that reliability of their own rifle is of primary concern–the guide is very likely not to have a backup if something goes wrong with your rifle.

While many respondents didn't answer the question regarding whether they recommend that clients bring one or two rifles, the response of 43 for bringing one rifle against 17 for bringing two indicates fairly strong feeling about bringing just one. The interesting thing here is that outfitters in remote country–Canada and Alaska especially–almost universally suggested that just one rifle be brought. Now, if a rifle goes awry it's a lot more difficult to beg, borrow, or buy a spare in the Brooks Range than it is in Gillette, Wyoming. But the outfitters in remote areas are obviously very concerned about baggage weight on horses or in light aircraft, so again you can read between the lines and put a premium on reliability.

In terms of species hunted, mule deer was the most common, followed by black bear and elk. This reflects to some extent a more regional response than I would have liked, but also reflects that these are the bread-and-butter species for the outfitting industry. I was glad to see that moose, sheep, pronghorn, and white-tailed deer were also extremely well represented. Overall, the species hunted by our respondents reflect an excellent cross-section of North American hunting.

The Professionals' Personal Choices

Deer: There were no real surprises here. Only 19 calibers were listed, and of these only three in significant numbers: The .270 and 7mm Remington Magnum tied at 24 mentions each; and the .30-06 followed with 16. It should be mentioned that a number of outfitters specified bullet weights; 130 grains was most common for the .270, 150 and 165 for the .30-06, and 140 and 160 for the 7mm magnum. Only two wildcats were mentioned, a 6mm Improved and a .280 Ackley Improved. Almost across the board, the rifles were bolt-actions. Two Browning BLRs were specified, one in 7mm-08 and one in .308, and one Ruger No. 1 was specified. It's obvious that the outfitters, on the whole, lean toward tried and true favorites for their deer hunting.

Elk/Moose: The lumping of these species together didn't really cause a problem, but it should be noted that the one vote for a .243 and the two votes for .25-06 came from elk hunters, not moose hunters, whereas the two votes for .375 came from Alaskan moose hunters. Otherwise, the results are pretty much random between primary elk hunters and primary moose hunters. I was very surprised to see the 7mm Remington Magnum come out on top with 22 mentions, while the .300 Winchester Magnum took a quantum leap upward to 19. The .30-06 tied with the .338 at 14 each, while the .270 took a nosedive from its popularity in the deer category, dropping down to 11. Those are all the double-digit mentions, with the rest receiving just a scattering of mentions. Again, all the cartridges mentioned, save one vote for the .33 G&A wildcat and one for the proprietary .330 Dakota, are garden-variety over-the-counter cartridges.

Bolt guns were specified again, except by a couple of outfitters who loved their slide-action .30-06s, the same two BLRs, and one Ruger No. 1. In this category, 175-grain bullets were often specified for the 7mm magnums, and bullets from 180 to 200 grains were specified for the .30 calibers.

Sheep/Goat: Only 12 cartridges were mentioned, and although the .270 came back strong with 17, the 7mm Remington Magnum really took over with 26 mentions. Here there were no wildcats, nor anything else even closely rivaling the .270 and 7mm magnum. The only real surprise to me was two mentions of the .243, but remember this is the personal rifle the outfitter/guide uses, not the rifle he recommends to clients for their use.

Bear: I caused myself a compilation problem here by not separating black bear from the big bears, and it proved an insurmountable problem to sort out because most of the grizzly/brown bear outfitters also hunt black bear.

In evaluating the data for yourself, the only caution I can offer is that all mentions of cartridges below the 7mm magnum in power came from outfitters who hunt only black bear, while the larger cartridges were primarily–but not exclusively–from outfitters who hunt grizzly and/or brown bear, and perhaps *also* black bear.

The clear winner here is the .338, with 16 entries, several of which came from black-bear outfitters. This preference for the .33 becomes even stronger if you add in two votes for the .340 Weatherby and one each for the .33 G&A and .330 Dakota. The .300 Winchester Magnum was also very strong at 14, and the .30-06 not bad at 13. With the .30 calibers, heavy bullets were usually specified, with several grizzly/brown bear outfitters suggesting 220-grain bullets. The .375 was also very strong at 12 mentions, most of these coming from Alaskan guides.

Recommendations To Clients

Deer: The surprise here, at least to me, was that the .270 was specifically recommended by far more outfitters than used it themselves–34 recommendations to clients against 24 who actually use it. The .30-06 also gained a bit, climbing to 19, while the 7mm Remington Magnum lost a couple of votes, down to 22. Fifteen cartridges were mentioned, but none of the others was even close, although I was surprised to see that the .243 had nine recommendations and shocked to see one for the .22-250!

Elk/Moose: Fourteen cartridges were mentioned, but only five had substantial support. The surprise (to me) winner was the 7mm Remington Magnum, with fully 33 mentions. The .300 Winchester Magnum and .30-06 were nearly tied, at 25 and 24 respectively; and the .338 and .270–altogether different solutions to the problem–were also almost tied at 18 and 16. Again, most of the .270 votes came from elk outfitters, while most of the over-.300 recommendations came from northern moose outfitters. You can make your own choice here, but the consensus is very clear for versatile cartridges somewhere between the .270 and .338.

Sheep/Goat: Only 12 cartridges were mentioned, and only two were serious contenders: the 7mm Remington Magnum with 23 and the .270 with 22. Nothing else even made a substantial showing, though the .30-06 and .300 were again neck and neck with nine each.

Bear: Here the 7mm magnums finally lost a bit of steam. The winner was the .338, with the .33 bore even stronger if you add in the .340, .330 Dakota, and .33 G&A. But it's only fair to point out that the .300 Winchester Magnum was very strong at 18, and the magnum .30 gets even stronger if you add in the five votes for the .300 Weatherby Magnum. Then throw in 16 votes for the .30-06, and America becomes a .30-caliber country again!

The fact that I threw all the bears together does cause a slight problem. The two votes for the .30-30 and one each for the 6mm, .25-06, and .308 are from outfitters who hunt black bear only, and those votes should not be construed as a recommendation for these cartridges for grizzly! Likewise, all 10 votes for the .375 came from Alaskan hunters of big bears.

All-Round Rifles

This was a "wish-list" question, specifically asking for the closest-to-ideal all-round North American rifle and cartridge, aside from what the respondent actually uses or recommends for his clients. With that in mind, the results were pretty interesting. Here the .300 Winchester Magnum was the clear winner with 21 votes; and if you add in another four for the .300 Weatherby, the case for the magnum .30 is stronger yet. The 7mm Remington Magnum and .30-06 were also very strong at 16 each, but for true all-round use the .270 slipped badly to just six votes, two behind the .338. Although 17 cartridges were mentioned, nothing else was in the running. All of the cartridges chosen are extremely versatile, with the obvious exception of the one vote for the .444 Marlin. I'd sure like to know exactly what train of thought, or what local hunting conditions, led to that choice for all-round North American use!

Relatively few respondents suggested makes and models, although quite a number simply said "bolt-action." Of those who did mention rifles, the Winchester Model 70 was tops with 11. However, several of these specified the pre-1964 Model 70, showing that the cult of the pre-'64 remains strong. A few others specified the new "Classic" action, and just one specifically recommended the push-feed Model 70.

Excluding the pre-'64 Model 70 Winchester, the Remington Model 700 was favored among currently available rifles, with the Ruger M77 a close second. No one differentiated between the older Ruger and the new Mark II action. Obviously, it's a bolt-action world among the outfitters, with two votes for the Browning BLR and the one for the .444 obviously meaning a Marlin lever-action.

Hunting Bullets

This part of the survey will clearly step on some toes. Nobody in the gun industry is as sensitive as bulletmakers–and in few areas do experienced hunters have such strong opinions as they do about bullets. Note, too, that opinion is sharply divided. Almost every bullet mentioned as being liked is also mentioned by someone else as being disliked. And the most-liked bullet, the Nosler Partition, is also the second most disliked bullet!

The interesting thing here is both the diversity of opinion and also the fact that the super-premium bullets are so well represented. Bullets like Trophy Bonded, Swift A-Frame, Winchester Fail-Safe, Barnes "X," and Jensen are well-represented here, but the opinions are so diversified that it's almost impossible to draw conclusions. The one common thread is that bullets designed for penetration–Nosler Partition, Speer Grand Slam, Trophy Bonded, etc.–showed up a bit stronger in the "liked" category than bullets designed for rapid expansion. But remember that, in aggregate, heavier game such as bear, elk, and moose was better represented in the survey than deer-sized game.

Scopes and Sights

The overwhelming support for Leupold products was a bit surprising, but Redfield, Zeiss, Swarovski, and Burris are also very well represented. In order to make anything of these numbers, one would have to know the market share of each make and thus have some idea of the frequency with which each brand might appear in a given hunting camp on a random basis.

More interesting by far were the recommendations for power of scopes. Versatile variables of 2-7X and larger were the runaway winners. They're also the best-selling scopes today, and clearly have the confidence and support of the outfitting industry. Most of the recommendations for 4X and low-range variables came from Alaska and Canada, with emphasis on bear-hunting specialists.

Relatively few respondents mentioned reticles, but among those who expressed an opinion, support for "plex"-type reticles was overwhelming. Likewise, few scope mounts were mentioned, but faith in the Redfield-type mount, whether from Redfield, Leupold, or Burris, remains very strong.

Strong, too, is the overall faith in telescopic sights. Only 12 respondents wanted their clients to have auxiliary iron sights. Twenty-two specifically didn't recommend them, and the rest–the vast majority–didn't care. That means, to me, that the outfitters and guides trust today's scope sights and aren't worried about failures in the field.

Outfitters' Comments

A great many outfitters took the time to provide additional notes, and while it would be impractical to quote them all, these from-the-shoulder tips offer a wealth of extremely valuable advice. In no particular order, the following are among the more interesting tidbits.

Yukon outfitter Terry Wilkinson personally carries a Browning BLR .308 as his Yukon backup gun. He says, "Most clients should bring a gun they trust. When testing guns, I prefer clients to rapid fire four or five shots, then see where the group is centered. This is very important for long shots where the guide is calling the shots."

Also from the Yukon, Dave Coleman came in with this comment: "The biggest problem we see in the Yukon and Alberta is clients bringing guns they're not used to and are afraid of."

This business of using rifles that you're used to and shoot well, and that don't kick too much was a common thread through several dozen surveys. James Richard Markin from Gillette, Wyoming, summed it up well: "The perfect rifle is the one that suits the person who owns it!" Pete Buist of Clearwater, Alaska, a 22-year veteran, added, "Bullet *placement* and *construction* are *far* more important than caliber. Caliber is no substitute for familiarity with your rifle."

A number of comments discussed suitability of particular rifles and actions, and there were some interesting ideas. Forest Stearns of Jackson, Wyoming, a horse outfitter, had this to say: "Rifles with semiautomatic actions are discouraged for our type of hunting because of the possibility of a round being chambered when the rifle is stuffed into a saddle scabbard." Hmmm. I never thought of that, but it's quite possible for the operating handle to catch and be pulled rearward when a semiauto is thrust into a tight saddle scabbard.

Others had praise for specific choices. From Alberta guide Everett Martin: "I think that any rifle bigger than .30-06 is not necessary for any North American big game." Alaskan legend Dick Gunlogson, a 30-year veteran, prefers his .338. "I bought a Winchester .338 in '59, the year of introduction. It was my personal backup gun for most of my guiding days. The original factory 300-grain bullet performed very well at short range. This gun has been as close to as many big bears as most any gun around. It never let me down and still shoots great."

Gunlogson also said that he doesn't allow his guides to use handloads for backup, and that he's having very good results with Remington factory ammo loaded with Swift A-Frame bullets. As to an all-round North American rifle, "There ain't no such beast!"

Russell L. Newton III, of Wildcat Outfitters, based in Michigan but hunting primarily in the Rockies, is that rarity among outfitters–a real rifle nut. It's he who uses the .330 Dakota, and he sent along a super information packet that he sends to all his clients, full of excellent advice on rifle and cartridge selection and sighting in. Although he has very specific ideas based on solid knowledge, he also states, "Choice of caliber is not as important as your proficiency with it."

Likewise Cliff Clark of Casper, Wyoming: "The most important thing is to be familiar with the rifle you use. I don't like to see people spend a lot of money and come out West bringing a gun they have never used. I have spoken to many visiting hunters who are using a borrowed rifle that is not sighted in for them. Adjust the sights properly and be familiar with the rifle!"

A regrettably unsigned survey states: "Promote the use of premium bullets with high sectional density of .250 plus. Encourage better shooting proficiency and proper use of a rifle sling for shooting. Discourage long-range shots and the 'kill at any cost' mentality!" Amen!

Feelings run very high regarding specific calibers. Colorado's Hollis Atwood stated: "The .30-06 is probably the most versatile rifle I have seen. The 150-grain bullet has proven good for most all big game we hunt." Not all comments are so favorable. Sy Gilliland, with 17 years' experience, says, "I do not like 7mm magnum rifles. If possible leave them at home."

Denny Simpson of Dubois, Wyoming, had this to say about the .270: "Since I guide primarily elk hunters, I'd like to take this opportunity to voice my opposition to the .270 as an elk cartridge. Although thousands of elk have been taken with a .270 (O'Connor swore by it), it also seems to wound more elk than any other caliber."

Denny's verdict wasn't unanimous, though. Bill Wallace of Collbran, Colorado, did recommend the .270 for elk, saying, "One thing lots of hunters do is try to shoot something they can't handle. I want them to shoot what they can shoot accurately. A well-placed bullet is what counts, not how big the caliber is."

This was a fairly common thread, indicating that, regardless of caliber capability, outfitters recognize that shooting ability is more important. Mike Schilling of Carbondale, Colorado, said this: "I know many hunters who can make a .270 outperform a .300 magnum on elk, even though the .300 is superior, because they are better men behind rifles they aren't afraid of."

Kurt Schultz, another Coloradan, prefers the 7mm Remington Magnum and states, "Most hunters cannot handle calibers over 7mm magnum effectively."

When you study the survey results, you'll note that one outfitter shoots a .243 on elk. That's Jim Brink of Jelm, Wyoming, and his rifle is a Winchester Model 88 lever-action. Interestingly, he says, "I was able to hunt with and guide with Elmer Keith some in the late '60s and early '70s. A good man, nice to be around." Elmer's preference for big bores obviously didn't rub off! Brink goes on to say, "I prefer my clients to bring a rifle they are comfortable with rather than bring something someone told them they needed. If they can shoot well, I'd prefer that to more firepower they aren't comfortable with."

Guides are opinionated just like the rest of us, and often the opinions run contrary to one another. One outfitter states that muzzle brakes help the 7mm Remington Magnum and .300 Winchester Magnum, but "nothing helps a Weatherby." Yet Buck Ward of Dolores, Colorado, recommends Weatherbys of various calibers right across the board, stating, "The best over-the-counter rifle for hunters new or old is the Weatherby." Phil Bates had a .270 Weatherby Magnum as his top all-round choice, stating that "you don't need a rifle that kills on both ends."

Dennis Bergstad, yet another Colorado outfitter, had this to say: "We do not hunt moose or brown bear so we feel many of our hunters are overgunned. We prefer something they can handle as opposed to something they are afraid of . . . If a client arrives with a .30-06 shooting a 165-grain bullet in a good bolt-action rifle he/she has shot a lot, we feel good about their chances."

Summary

I received a great many comments like these, and while I wish I could print them all, it's time for us to close our discussion of North American rifles and cartridges. We can argue caliber selection endlessly, and that's what campfires are made for. Some of us will lean toward the .270 school, and others will lean toward the .338 school. Most of us will probably be somewhere in the middle. There isn't any real right or wrong, although in some cases there might be choices between good, better, and best. Whatever calibers we choose, listen to the experts we've heard from above: *It's shot placement and shooting skill that matters most of all.* Yukon outfitter Rod Hardie said it best of all, so I'll close with his words: "I like clients who appear with a well-worn, scratched rifle in .30-06, .270, 7mm magnum, or even .300 magnum. It's *accuracy* that counts the most."

GUIDE/OUTFITTER SURVEY

GENERAL DATA

TOTAL RESPONDENTS:	103
AVERAGE YEARS GUIDING/OUTFITTING:	20.6
TOTAL YEARS:	2,121

TERRAIN AND TECHNIQUES

TERRAIN	NUMBER RESPONDENTS HUNTING	HUNTING METHOD	NUMBER RESPONDENTS EMPLOYING
Woodland	32	Horseback	54
Desert	14	Backpack	25
Mountains	73	4WD	21
Plains	26	Boat	9
Swamp	13	Stand	16
Tundra	17	Foot-From-Vehicle	39

Do you or your guide carry a backup rifle?
Yes: 61
No: 43

Do you recommend your hunters bring one or two rifles?
One: 43
Two: 17

GAME HUNTED

SPECIES	NUMBER RESPONDENTS HUNTING
WHITE-TAILED DEER	36
MULE DEER	66
COUES DEER	3
BLACK-TAILED DEER	6
CARIBOU	19
BLACK BEAR	61
GRIZZLY/BROWN/POLAR	22
MOOSE	40
PRONGHORN	38
SHEEP/GOAT	46
ELK	60
WILD BOAR	4
EXOTICS	3
COUGAR	4
BISON	2
WOLF	4

PROFESSIONAL HUNTERS' PERSONAL CHOICES

CALIBER	DEER	ELK/MOOSE	SHEEP/GOAT	BEAR
.22-250 Rem.	1			
.243	3	1	2	
6mm Rem.	1			1
6mm Improved	1			
.257 Roberts	3			
.25-06	7	2	3	1
.257 Wby. Mag.	2			
.264 Win. Mag.	2	1	3	
.270 Win.	24	11	17	3
.270 Wby. Mag.	1		1	
7mm-08 Rem.	1	1	1	1
7x57	1			
.280 Rem.	5	1	3	
.280 Ackley Imp.	1			
7mm Rem. Mag.	24	22	26	8
7mm Wby. Mag.		3		
.30-30 Win.	1		2	
.308 Win.	2	3		1
.30-06	16	14	8	13
.300 Win. Mag.	6	19	8	14

PROFESSIONAL HUNTERS' PERSONAL CHOICES (continued)

CALIBER	DEER	ELK/MOOSE	SHEEP/GOAT	BEAR
.300 Wby. Mag.	6		2	
8mm Rem. Mag.	1		1	
.338 Win. Mag.		14	1	16
.33 G&A		1		1
.330 Dakota		1		1
.340 Wby. Mag.		1		2
.375 H&H		2	2	12

PROFESSIONAL HUNTERS' RECOMMENDATIONS TO CLIENTS

CALIBER	DEER	ELK/MOOSE	SHEEP/GOAT	BEAR
.22-250 Rem.	1			
.243 Win.	9		1	
6mm Rem.	2		1	1
.257 Roberts	2			
.25-06 Rem.	4	1	4	1
.257 Wby. Mag.	1			
.264 Win. Mag.			2	
.270 Win.	34	16	22	9
.270 Wby. Mag.	1			1
.284 Win.	1			
.280 Rem.	6		1	
7mm Rem. Mag.	22	33	23	10
7mm Wby. Mag.		1		
.30-30 Win.				2
.308 Win.	2	2	1	1
.30-06	19	24	9	16
.300 Win. Mag.	7	25	9	17
.300 Wby. Mag.		3	3	5
8mm Rem. Mag.		1		
.338 Win. Mag.	1	18	2	20
.33 G&A		1		
.330 Dakota		1		1
.340 Wby. Mag.		2		3
.375 H&H		2		10

CHOICES FOR ALL-ROUND USE

CALIBER	RESPONDENTS CHOOSING
.300 Win. Mag.	21
7mm Rem. Mag.	16
.30-06	16
.338 Win. Mag.	8
.270 Win.	6
.300 Wby. Mag.	4
.264 Win. Mag.	2
.270 Wby. Mag.	2
.375 H&H	2
.243 Win.	1
25-06 Rem.	1
7mm Wby. Mag.	1
.308 Win.	1
.300 H&H	1
.330 Dakota	1
.340 Wby. Mag.	1
.444 Marlin	1

RIFLE	RESPONDENTS CHOOSING
Winchester M70	11
Remington M700	10
Ruger M77	8
Weatherby Mark V	5
Browning BLR	2
Browning A-Bolt	1
Colt-Sauer	1
Dakota M76	1
Marlin 444SS	1
Mauser	1
Sako	1

HUNTING BULLETS

LIKE

BULLET	RESPONDENTS CHOOSING
Nosler Part.	23
Trophy Bonded	7
Sierra	6
Hornady	5
Rem. Core-Lokt	5
Speer Grand Slam	4
Barnes "X"	3
Swift A-Frame	3
Win. Power Point	3
Win. Fail Safe	2
Win. Silvertip	2
Nosler Ball. Tip	2
Nosler Sol. Base	1
Sierra Boattail	1

DON'T LIKE

BULLET	RESPONDENTS CHOOSING
Win. Silvertip	9
Nosler Part.	6
Nosler Ball. Tip	4
Rem. Bronze Pt.	3
Sierra Boattail	3
Rem. Core-Lokt	2
CIL Sabre-Tip	1
Hornady Interlock	1
Nosler Sol. Base	1
Swift A-Frame	1
Win. Fail-Safe	1
Win. Power Point	1

SCOPES AND SIGHTS

BRANDS MENTIONED

BRAND	RESPONDENTS CHOOSING
Leupold	56
Redfield	14
Swarovski	11
Burris	11
Zeiss	8
Bushnell	3
Schmidt & Bender	2
Weaver	2
Bausch & Lomb	1
Nikon	1
Simmons	1
Tasco	1

POWER SETTINGS

POWER	RESPONDENTS CHOOSING
3-9X	48
2-7X	17
4X	16
"High-Range" Variables (above 3-9X)	4
"Low-Range" Variables (below 2-7X)	6

SPECIFIC SCOPE MOUNTS MENTIONED

BRAND	RESPONDENTS CHOOSING
Leupold	10
Redfield	9
Weaver	6
Conetrol	2
Burris	2
Ruger Integral	2
Buehler	1
European claw	1
"Tip-Off"	1

SPECIFIC RETICLES MENTIONED

RETICLE	RESPONDENTS CHOOSING
Plex-type	27
Crosshair	4
Post-and-crosshair	4
Dot	3
Tapered crosshair	1

Should the rifle wear auxiliary iron sights?

Yes: 12
No: 22
No Answer: 69

Part IV

Appendices

APPENDIX 1

FACTORY BALLISTICS

CURRENT AMERICAN CARTRIDGES

CARTRIDGE	BULLET		VELOCITY IN FPS (ENERGY IN FT/LBS)					TRAJECTORY (200-YD ZERO)		
	WEIGHT	TYPE	MUZZLE	100	200	300	400	100	300	400
.17 Rem.	25	S	4040	3284	2644	2086	1606	+0.9	−6.0	−20.2
			(906	599	388	242	143)			
.22 Hornet	45	S	2690	2042	1502	1128	948	+1.8	−19.4	−66.0
			(723	417	225	127	90)			
.222 Rem.	55	S	3020	2620	2254	1917	1612	+1.6	−8.5	−26.6
			(1115	839	620	449	317)			
223 Rem.	60	S	3150	2782	2442	2127	1837	+1.6	−7.5	−22.5
			(1322	1031	795	603	450)			
.22-250 Rem.	60	S	3600	3195	2826	2485	2169	+0.9	−7.4	−21.9
			(1727	1360	1064	823	627)			
.224 Wby.Mag.	55	S	3650	3192	2780	2403	2057	+1.0	−5.5	−17.0
			(1556	1244	943	705	516)			
.220 Swift	60	S	3600	3199	2824	2475	2156	+1.0	−5.4	−16.3
			(1727	1364	1063	816	619)			
.243 Win.	100	S	2690	2730	2510	2300	2100	+1.6	−7.1	−20.9
			(1945	1650	1395	1170	975)			
6mm Rem.	100	S	3100	2830	2570	2330	2100	+1.6	−6.7	−19.8
			(2135	1775	1470	1205	985)			
6mmBR Rem.	100	S	2550	2310	2083	1870	1671	+2.8	−10.9	−31.7
			(1444	1185	963	776	620)			

.240 Wby.Mag.	100	S	3406	3136	2881	2641	2413	+0.8	–5.0	–15.2
			(2577	2184	1843	1549	1293)			
.250 Savage	100	S	2820	2504	2210	1936	1684	+2.3	–9.5	–28.3
			(1765	1392	1084	832	630)			
.257 Roberts	100	S	3000	2736	2486	2251	2028	+1.6	–7.2	–21.3
			(1998	1662	1373	1124	913)			
.257 Roberts	120	S	2780	2560	2360	2160	1970	+1.9	–8.2	–24.0
			(2060	1750	1480	1240	1030)			
.25-06 Rem.	100	S	3230	2952	2690	2443	2210	+1.2	–6.1	–18.0
			(2316	1934	1607	1325	1064)			
.25-0 Rem.	120	S	2990	2730	2484	2252	2032	+1.9	–7.5	–22.0
			(2382	1985	1644	1351	1100)			
.257 Wby.Mag.	120	S	3305	3045	2800	2568	2348	+0.9	–5.2	–15.4
			(2884	2518	2193	1904	1646)			
6.5x55 Swed.	139	S	2850	2560	2338	2030	1790	+1.9	–8.7	–26.3
			(2515	2025	1615	1270	985)			
.264 Win.Mag.	140	S	3030	2782	2548	2346	2114	+1.8	–7.2	–20.8
			(2854	2406	2018	1682	1389)			
.270 Win.	130	S	3060	2800	2560	2330	2110	+1.8	–7.1	–20.6
			(2700	2265	1890	1585	1285			
.270 Win.	140	BTS	2960	2758	2554	2365	2183	+1.8	–7.2	–20.6
			(2724	2356	2029	1739	1482)			
.270 Win.	150	S	2850	2590	2340	2100	1880	+2.2	–8.6	–25.0
			(2705	2225	1815	1470	1175)			
.270 Wby.Mag.	150	S	3245	3029	2823	2627	2439	+1.1	–5.5	–16.0
			(3507	3055	2655	2298	1981)			
7x30 Waters	120	FP	2700	2300	1930	1600	1330	+2.6	–12.0	–37.6
			(1940	1405	990	685	470)			

7mmBR Rem.	140	S	2215	2012	1821	1643	1481	+1.8	−20.6	−50.0
			(1525	1259	1031	839	681)			
7x57 Mauser	140	S	2660	2450	2260	2070	1890	+2.1	−9.0	−26.1
			(2200	1865	1585	1330	1110)			
7x57 Mauser	175	RN	2440	2140	1860	1600	1380	+2.9	−13.1	−40.1
			(2315	1775	1340	1000	740)			
7mm-08 Rem.	140	S	2860	2625	2402	2189	1988	+2.1	−8.1	−23.5
			(2452	2142	1793	1490	1228)			
.284 Win.	150	S	2860	2595	2344	2180	1886	+2.1	−8.5	−24.8
			(2724	2243	1830	1480	1185)			
.280 Rem.	140	S	3000	2758	2528	2309	2102	+1.8	−7.3	−21.1
			(2797	2363	1986	1657	1378)			
.280 Rem.	160	BTS	2840	2637	2442	2256	2078	+2.1	−7.9	−22.6
			(2866	2471	2120	1809	1535)			
7mm Rem.Mag.	150	BTS	3110	2920	2750	2580	2410	+1.3	−5.9	−17.0
			(3220	2850	2510	2210	1930)			
7mm Rem.Mag.	165	BTS	2950	2800	2650	2510	2370	+1.5	−6.4	−18.4
			(3190	2865	2570	2300	2050)			
7mm Rem.Mag.	175	S	2860	2650	2440	2240	2060	+2.0	−7.9	−22.7
			(3180	2720	2310	1960	1640)			
7mm Wby.Mag.	160	S	3200	2991	2791	2600	2417	+0.9	−5.4	−16.0
			(3537	3177	2767	2401	2075)			
7mm Wby.Mag.	175	S	3070	2879	2696	2520	2351	+1.3	−6.1	−17.7
			(3662	3220	2824	2467	2147)			
7.62x39	125	S	2365	2062	1783	1533	1320	+3.1	−14.1	−43.3
			(1552	1180	882	652	483)			
.30-30 Win.	150	RN	2390	2018	1984	1398	1177	+3.6	−16.0	−49.9
			(1902	1356	944	651	461)			

.30-30 Win.	170	FP	2200	1900	1620	1380	1190	+ 4.1	– 17.4	– 52.4
			(1830	1355	990	720	535)			
.300 Savage	150	S	2630	2354	2095	1853	1631	+ 2.7	– 10.7	– 31.5
			(2302	1845	1462	1143	886)			
.300 Savage	180	RN	2350	2025	1728	1467	1252	+ 3.3	– 15.1	– 46.7
			(2207	1639	1193	860	626)			
.30-40 Krag	180	RN	2430	2099	1795	1525	1298	+ 3.2	– 14.2	– 43.4
			(2360	1761	1288	929	673)			
.307 Win.	150	FP	2510	2321	1924	1575	1289	+ 2.5	– 12.1	– 37.9
			(2538	1795	1233	826	554)			
.308 Win.	150	S	2820	2533	2263	2009	1774	+ 2.3	– 9.1	– 26.9
			(2684	2137	1705	1344	1048)			
.308 Win.	165	BTS	2700	2496	2301	2115	1937	+ 2.0	– 8.7	– 25.2
			(2672	2283	1940	1639	1375)			
.308 Win.	180	S	2620	2430	2240	2060	1890	+ 2.2	– 9.2	– 26.5
			(2745	2355	2005	1700	1430)			
.30-06	150	S	2910	2671	2444	2230	1298	+ 1.7	– 7.6	– 22.1
			(2820	2375	1989	1656	1373)			
.30-06	165	BTS	2800	2596	2399	2211	2031	+ 1.8	– 8.0	– 22.9
			(2873	2470	2110	1792	1572)			
.30-06	180	S	2700	2500	2320	2140	1970	+ 2.0	– 8.6	– 24.6
			(2910	2510	2150	1830	1550)			
.30-06	180	RN	2700	2348	2023	1727	1466	+ 2.7	– 11.3	– 34.4
			(2910	2203	1635	1192	859)			
.30-06	220	RN	2410	2130	1870	1632	1422	+ 2.9	– 12.9	– 39.1
			(2837	2216	1708	1801	988)			
.300 H&H Mag.	180	S	2880	2620	2380	2150	1930	+ 1.8	– 8.0	– 23.4
			(3315	2750	2260	1840	1480)			

.300 Win.Mag.	150	BTS	3275	2988	2718	2464	2224	+1.3	−6.5	−18.5
			(3573	3033	2603	2221	1887)			
.300 Win.Mag.	165	BTS	3100	2877	2665	2462	2269	+1.3	−6.5	−18.5
			(3522	3033	2603	2221	1887)			
.300 Win.Mag.	180	S	2960	2700	2450	2210	1990	+1.6	−7.5	−22.1
			(3500	2905	2395	1955	1585)			
.300 Win.Mag.	200	BTS	2830	2680	2530	2380	2240	+1.7	−7.1	−20.3
			(3560	3180	2830	2520	2230)			
.300 Win.Mag.	220	RN	2680	2448	2228	2020	1823	+2.5	−9.5	−27.5
			(3508	2927	2424	1993	1623)			
.300 Wby.Mag.	165	BTS	3450	3220	3003	2797	2599	+0.7	−4.5	−13.6
			(4360	3799	3303	3865	2475)			
.300 Wby.Mag.	180	S	3300	3085	2881	2686	2499	+1.1	−5.3	−15.4
			(4352	3804	3317	2882	2495)			
.300 Wby.Mag.	220	RN	2850	2541	2283	1984	1736	+2.3	−9.1	−27.2
			(4122	3047	2207	1560	1085)			
.303 Savage	190	RN	1890	1612	1372	1183	1055	+6.0	−24.6	−73.9
			(1507	1096	794	591	469)			
.303 British	180	S	2460	2233	2018	1816	1629	+2.5	−11.1	−32.8
			(2418	1993	1627	1318	1060)			
.32 Win. Spl.	170	FP	2250	1921	1626	1372	1175	+4.0	−17.3	−53.2
			(1911	1393	998	710	521)			
8x57 Mauser	170	RN	2360	1969	1622	1333	1123	+3.6	−17.1	−54.3
			(2102	1463	933	671	476)			
8mm Rem.Mag.	185	S	2830	2761	2464	2186	1927	+1.8	−8.5	−24.7
			(3896	3131	2494	1963	1525)			
8mm Rem.Mag.	220	S	2800	2501	2221	1959	1718	+2.0	−9.1	−27.4
			(3829	3055	2409	1875	1442)			

.338 Win.Mag.	200	S	2960	2658	2375	2110	1862	+2.0	−8.2	−24.3
			(3890	3137	2505	1977	1539)			
.338 Win.Mag.	225	S	2780	2572	2374	2184	2003	+2.7	−9.4	−25.0
			(3862	3306	2816	2384	2005)			
.338 Win.Mag.	250	S	2660	2400	2150	1910	1690	+2.3	−9.8	−29.1
			(3927	3185	2555	2055	1590)			
.340 Wby.Mag.	200	S	3260	3011	2775	2552	2339	+1.2	−5.7	−16.6
			(4719	4025	3420	2892	2429)			
.340 Wby.Mag.	250	S	2980	2780	2588	2404	2228	+1.3	−6.4	−18.9
			(4931	4290	3719	3209	2701)			
.348 Win.	200	FP	2520	2215	1931	1672	1443	+1.4	−17.7	−44.4
			(2820	2178	1656	1241	925)			
.35 Rem.	200	RN	2080	1698	1376	1140	1001	+5.4	−23.3	−70.0
			(1921	1280	841	577	445)			
.35 Whelen	200	S	2675	2378	2100	1842	1606	+2.3	−10.3	−30.9
			(3177	2510	1968	1506	1145)			
.35 Whelen	200	RN	2400	2066	1761	1492	1269	+3.4	−14.7	−45.2
			(3197	2369	1722	1235	893)			
.35 Whelen	200	S	2400	2196	2005	1823	1652	+2.9	−11.5	−33.6
			(3197	2680	2230	1844	1515)			
.350 Rem.Mag.	200	S	2710	2410	2130	1870	1631	+2.6	−10.3	−30.5
			(3261	2579	2014	1553	1181)			
.356 Win.	200	FP	2460	2114	1797	1517	1284	+3.2	−14.0	−42.9
			(2688	1985	1434	1022	732)			
.356 Win.	250	FP	2160	1911	1682	1476	1299	+4.0	−16.4	−48.4
			(2591	2028	1571	1210	937)			
.358 Win.	200	RN	2490	2171	1876	1610	1379	+2.9	−13.0	−39.4
			(2753	2093	1563	1151	844)			

.375 Win.	200	FP	2200	1841	1526	1268	1089	+ 5.2	– 24.6	– 74.0
			(2150	1506	1034	714	527)			
.375 H&H Mag.	270	RN	2690	2420	2166	1928	1707	+ 2.5	– 10.0	– 29.4
			(4337	3510	2812	2228	1747)			
.375 H&H Mag.	300	S	2530	2320	2120	1930	1750	+ 2.5	– 10.3	– 29.9
			(4263	3585	2995	2475	2040)			
.378 Wby.Mag.	270	S	3180	2976	2781	2595	2415	+ 1.2	– 5.7	– 16.6
			(6062	5308	4635	4034	3495)			
.416 Rem.Mag.	400	S	2400	2175	1962	1763	1579	+ 2.9	– 12.0	– 35.2
			(5115	4201	3419	2760	2214)			
.416 Rigby	410	RN	2370	2110	1870	1640	1440	+ 3.2	– 13.3	– 39.3
			(5115	4050	3165	2455	1895)			
.44 Rem.Mag.	240	FP	1760	1365	1098	955	863	+ 8.7	– 34.6	– 101.2
			(1651	993	643	486	397)			
.444 Marlin	240	FP	2350	1815	1376	1087	940	+ 4.6	– 23.4	– 76.0
			(2944	1756	1010	630	471)			
.45-70 Govt.	300	FP	1880	1650	1430	1240	1110	+ 7.1	– 29.6	– 89.4
			(2355	1815	1355	1015	810)			
.45-70 Govt.	405	FP	1330	1168	1055	977	918	+ 12.0	– 43.2	– 122.7
			(1590	1227	1001	858	758)			

APPENDIX 2

Traveling with Firearms

Some 15 years ago my Arizona hunting buddy, Duwane Adams, asked me to come over and share a spring bear hunt on the San Carlos Reservation, a place famed for huge bears that come to varmint calls. I could have driven over, but it was just as cheap to fly into Tucson. We threw my stuff into Duwane's truck and headed northeast, making camp well after dark. It was very late when I had a moment to gather my gear for the morning hunt, and after making up my pack, the last thing I did was open the gun case.

The stock of my .300 Weatherby wasn't just broken–it was shattered *lengthwise*. As a spare, I'd brought along a Browning BLR .358, and it was untouched.

Another time I wasn't quite so prepared. I went first to Remington's writers' seminar in southern Kansas, then flew on to Georgia for a whitetail hunt with RealTree's Bill Jordan. This time it was past midnight when we finally pitched up at Jordan's cabin. Yep, when I opened the gun case, the stock of my Remington .30-06 was broken off at the wrist. I didn't have a spare, and since Bill is primarily a bowhunter, he didn't have another rifle handy. We got back on the road and drove to a convenience store (Oh, thank heaven for 7-11!) where I purchased duct tape and Super Glue. With Bill holding and me gluing and taping, we put the rifle back together. Our makeshift repair held for three shots: one to see if the zero had shifted (it hadn't!), and one each for two whitetail bucks. I might not have been so fortunate.

These calamities happened in good, solid, hard gun cases. In neither situation was there external damage to the case, nor any indication of why this might have happened. It happens rarely, but it can happen. The point is to be better prepared than I was in either instance.

Remember the results from my outfitter survey in Chapter 42. While many outfitters prefer that their hunters bring just one rifle, a great many guides (sometimes as dictated by local law) do not carry backup rifles and may not have a spare available. I often travel to distant places to hunt with just one rifle, but these days I try not to unless I *know* that the folks I'm hunting with, whether they're guides or friends, will have some kind of a spare, "just in case." Most hunters who travel afar go with one or two friends. Three hunters don't need six rifles for the average North American hunt, but it's a real good idea to have one spare rifle in the party.

As we all know, it's amazing what can be done with duct tape and good glue, so always throw some in your duffel–don't count on a handy 7-11 store in the Brooks Range! We discussed elsewhere carrying a spare scope or at least having auxiliary iron sights, but make sure you have in your little repair kit the Allen wrenches and screwdrivers needed to tighten mounts, action screws, and such. And of course you should carry a small cleaning kit. Some solvent, oil, patching material, and cleaning rod are really all that's needed. However, for our purposes here take a genuine jointed cleaning rod, *not* a flexible, pull-through rod. If you take a fall barrel-first, or if you get debris in your saddle scabbard and it works into the barrel, you will probably need a real cleaning rod to clear the obstruction.

The hard case itself is not as critical as you might think. Both of the incidents mentioned above happened in a steel gun case. Theoretically, metal cases are the best, and certainly they last the longest. If you expect to travel quite a bit with firearms, a good metal case is well worth the investment. However, I've traveled quite a lot with very inexpensive hard plastic cases from Gun Guard and similar firms, and I have not had a problem. The requirements for a gun case are simple: It must be rigid, well-padded, allow adequate room for the gun or guns without any possibility of the guns shifting or rubbing together, and it must be lockable.

I generally remove the bolt on bolt-action rifles, wrapping it in a T-shirt or pair of heavy socks and putting it alongside the rifle. This facilitates inspection, which some airports or airlines may insist on, and also eliminates the projection of the bolt, which could cause damage if the case is dropped or someone runs over it with a forklift.

The do's and don't's of airline travel are simple. *Do* tell the folks at the check-in counter you have firearms. Always. It's the law. *Do not* put ammunition in your gun case. Carry it separately in your baggage. Airlines have different rules and enforce them differently. The best course is to call ahead and see if there are specific requirements, such as a wooden or metal box. Air Canada used to specify "original factory container" for ammo, and went nuts when I showed them my handloads in an MTM plastic case! The general rule for air travel is up to five kilograms (11 pounds) of ammo with no problems, and that's plenty for any North American big-game hunt. If you want to take, say, a case of shotgun shells, best call ahead.

At the ticket counter, you must sign a "firearms are unloaded" voucher. This used to go on the inside or outside, depending on how the ticket agent felt, but at this writing the new common rule is that the sticker–usually blaze orange–may be placed inside. I assume that's so the presence of firearms won't be advertised, but it seems to me that a hard gun case pretty much speaks for itself.

Traveling interstate, and across into Canada, by vehicle is actually a bit more complex. Rules change from state to state, and Canada's rules are changing even now. Especially in the East, it's a good idea to call ahead to the state police of states you'll be driving through and see if they have any special considerations for traveling with firearms. It should go without saying that firearms in vehicles should be unloaded and separated from their ammunition. If you have a trunk, locked in the trunk is generally quite sufficient. In trucks or sport/utility vehicles without trunks, it gets more difficult. Most states specify "inaccessible," so cased in the back end should be all right. However, the safest course is to lock the firearms in a hard gun case for transport. Then there should be no question and no problems.

This last especially applies in Canada these days. And while we're on the subject of Canada, *do not* leave the United States without obtaining the little customs form, Form 4457, for your firearms. It's a "Certificate of Registration For Personal Effects Taken Abroad." It takes two minutes to fill out, you have the only copy, and it guarantees no hassles when you return. I would assume that Canadians traveling into the U.S. have a similar situation.

Travel in Mexico is an altogether different story. There you must obtain gun permits, and this must be done in advance. The permit, by the way, is not a general Mexican permit but is valid only in the Mexican state where issued. Since all hunting in Mexico today must be done through a licensed outfitter, this simplifies things a bit; the outfitters or their U.S. agents will assist in the paperwork. It's tempting to drive down into Mexico for a hunt out of, say, Hermosillo. *Don't do it.* The sensible course, and the only sure course, is to fly in to your jumping-off point, where your outfitter can meet you and deal with customs officials, and vice versa.

Gun laws are changing so rapidly that it's always best to make a couple of phone calls and make sure there aren't any special local regulations you need to be aware of. In the main, however, common sense applies. There are more restrictions on handguns than on rifles, and the real "biggy" is that under no circumstances may you take handguns into Canada, at least at this writing.

Selected Bibliography

Barnes, Frank C. *Cartridges Of The World, 6th Edition.* Northbrook, Illinois: DBI Books, Inc., 1989.

Boddington, C. *America–The Men And Their Guns That Made Her Great.* Los Angeles, California: Petersen Publishing Company 1981.

—–. *Campfires and Game Trails–Hunting North American Big Game.* Long Beach: Safari Press Inc., 1989.

—–. *Shots at Big Game.* Long Beach: California, Safari Press Inc., 1993.

—–. *Safari Rifles.* Long Beach, California: Safari Press, 1990.

—–. *Deer Hunting Coast To Coast.* Long Beach, California: Safari Press, 1990.

Boone and Crockett Club. *Records Of North American Big Game 10th Edition.* Missoula, Montana: Boone and Crockett Club, 1993.

Carmichel, J. *Jim Carmichel's Book Of The Rifle.* New York: Outdoor Life Books, 1985.

De Haas, F. *Bolt Action Rifles.* Northfield, Illinois: DBI Books, Inc., 1984.

Donnelly, J.J. *The Handloader's Manual Of Cartridge Conversions.* South Hackensack, New Jersey: Stoeger Publishing Company, 1987.

Foral, J. *Gun Writers Of Yesteryear.* Prescott, Arizona: Wolfe Publishing Company, 1993.

Hornady Manufacturing Company. *Hornady Handbook Of Cartridge Reloading Fourth Edition.* Grand Island, Nebraska: Hornady Manufacturing Company, 1991.

Keith, E. *Big Game Rifles and Cartridges.* Onslow County, North Carolina: Small-Arms Technical Pub., 1936.

Keith, E. *Keith's Rifles for Large Game.* Huntington, West Virginia: Standard Publications Inc., 1946.

Keith, E. *Guns and Ammo for Hunting Big Game.* Petersen Hunting: Los Angeles, CA, 1965.

Lott, J. *Big Bore Rifles.* Los Angeles, California: Petersen Publishing Company, 1983.

Matunas, E.A. *Shooting.* New York: Outdoor Life Books, 1986.

Matthews, C.W. *Shoot Better II.* Lakewood, Colorado: Bill Matthews, Inc., 1989.

Nosler Bullets. *Nosler Reloading Manual Number Three.* Bend, Oregon: Nosler Bullets, Inc., 1989.

O'Connor, J. *The Big Game Rifle.* New York: Alfred Knopf, 1952.

—–. *The Rifle Book.* New York: Alfred Knopf, 1949.

—–. *Sheep and Sheep Hunting.* Long Beach, California: Safari Press, Inc., 1992.

—–. *The Last Book, Confessions of an Outdoor Writer.* Clinton, New Jersey: Amwell Press, 1984.

Page, W. *The Accurate Rifle.* New York: Winchester Press, 1973.

Roosevelt, T. *Hunting Trips of a Ranchman - Sketches of Sport on the Northern Plains.* New York: G.P. Putman's Sons, 1885.

Roosevelt, T. *Ranch Life and the Hunting-Trail.* New York: The Century Co., 1888.

Roosevelt, T. *The Wilderness Hunter - An account of the big game of the United States and its chase with horse, hound, and rifle.* New York: G.P. Putnam, 1893.

Roosevelt, T. *Outdoor Pastimes of an American Hunter.* New York: Charles Scribner's Sons, 1905.

Roosevelt, T. *Hunting Tales Of A Ranchman.* New York: G.P. Putman's Sons, 1885.

Sierra Bullets. *Sierra Bullets Reloading Manual Third Edition.* Santa Fe Springs, California: Sierra Bullets L.P., 1989.

Speer Omark Industires. *Reloading Manual Number Eleven.* Lewiston, Idaho: Omark Industries, .

Taylor, J. *African Rifles And Cartridges.* Harrisburg, Pennsylvania: The Stackpole Company, 1948.

Taylor, J. *Big Game and Big Game Rifles.* Long Beach, California: Safari Press, Inc., 1993.

Truesdell, S.R. *The Rifle–Its Development For Big Game Hunting.* Long Beach: California, Safari Press Inc., 1992.

Watrous, G. *The History Of Winchester Firearms 1866-1966.* North Haven, Connecticut: Olin Mathieson Chemical Corporation, 1966.

Wildlife Management Institute *Big Game Of North America.* Harrisburg, Pennsylvania: Stackpole Books, 1978.

Index

C

G

H

R